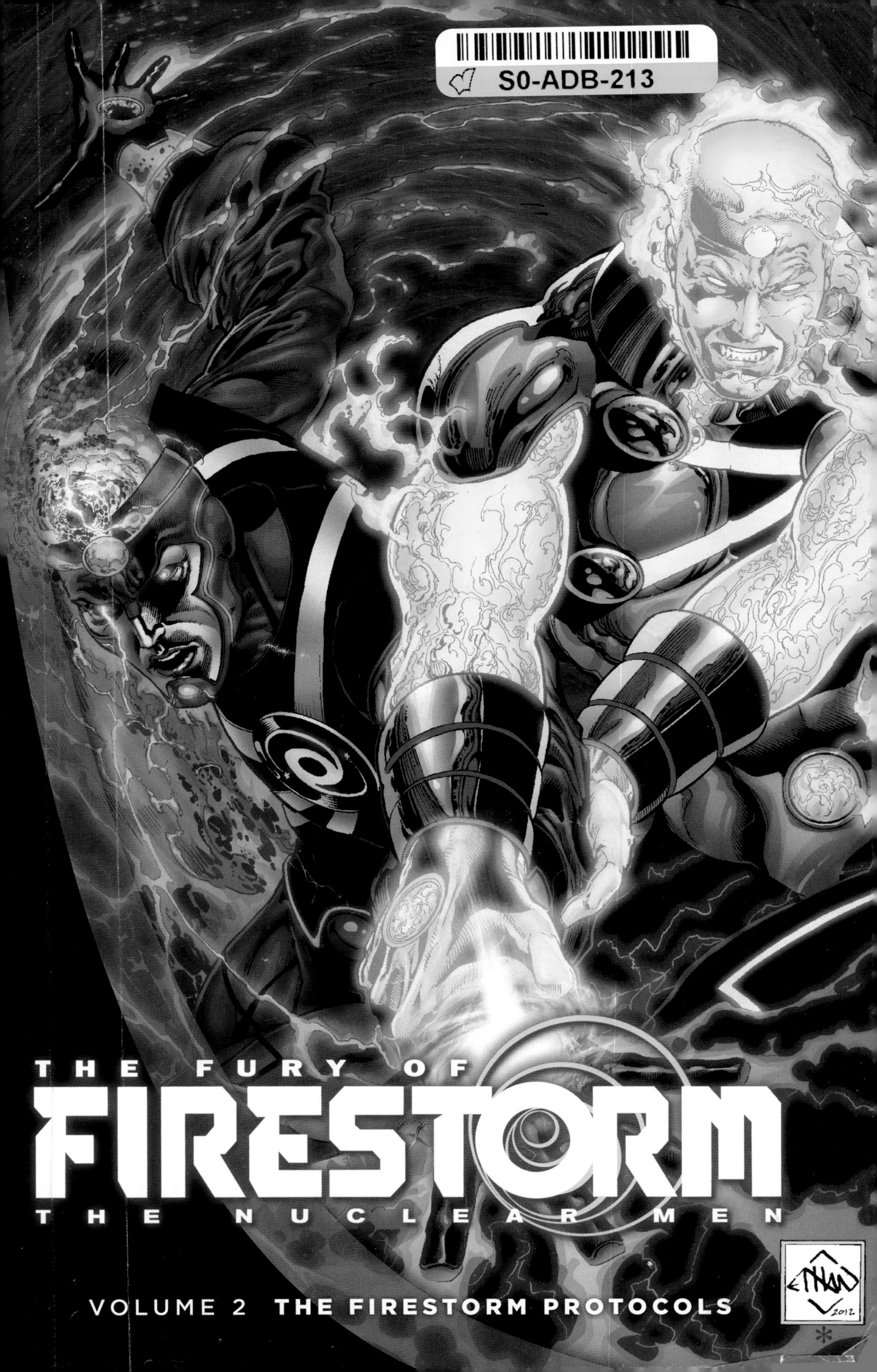
S0-ADB-213
THE FURY OF
FIRESTORM
THE NUCLEAR MEN
VOLUME 2 THE FIRESTORM PROTOCOLS

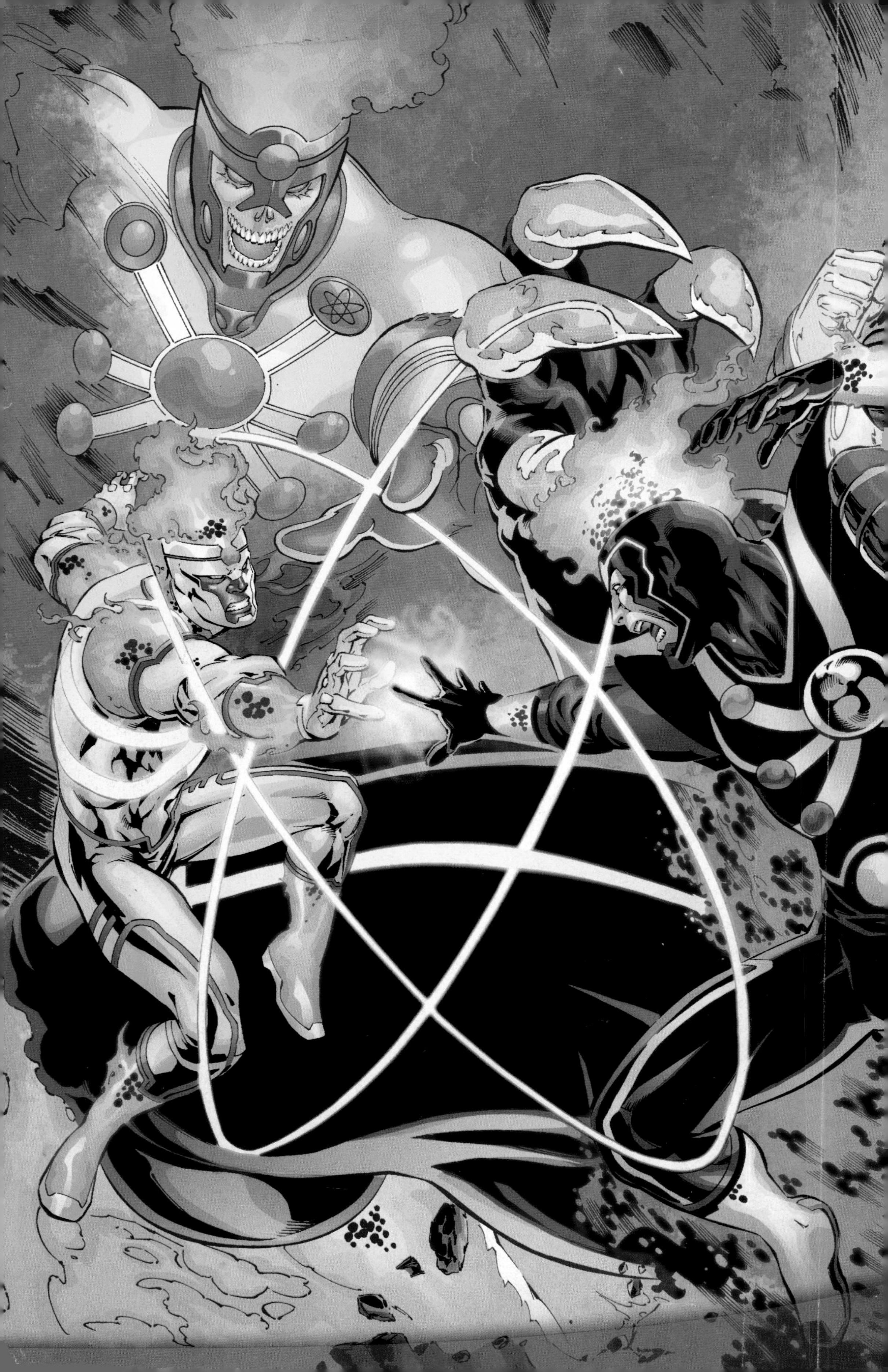

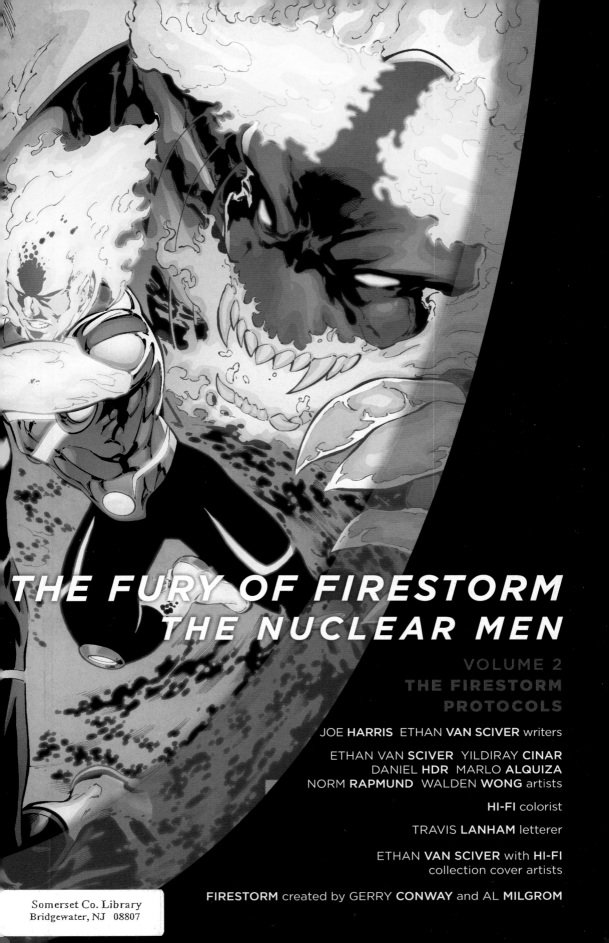

THE FURY OF FIRESTORM
THE NUCLEAR MEN

VOLUME 2
THE FIRESTORM PROTOCOLS

JOE **HARRIS** ETHAN **VAN SCIVER** writers

ETHAN VAN **SCIVER** YILDIRAY **CINAR**
DANIEL **HDR** MARLO **ALQUIZA**
NORM **RAPMUND** WALDEN **WONG** artists

HI-FI colorist

TRAVIS **LANHAM** letterer

ETHAN **VAN SCIVER** with **HI-FI**
collection cover artists

FIRESTORM created by GERRY **CONWAY** and AL **MILGROM**

RACHEL GLUCKSTERN Editor – Original Series RICKEY PURDIN Assistant Editor – Original Series
RACHEL PINNELAS Editor ROBBIN BROSTERMAN Design Director – Books
ROBBIE BIEDERMAN Publication Design

BOB HARRAS Senior VP – Editor-in-Chief, DC Comics

DIANE NELSON President DAN DIDIO and JIM LEE Co-Publishers
GEOFF JOHNS Chief Creative Officer
JOHN ROOD Executive VP – Sales, Marketing and Business Development
AMY GENKINS Senior VP – Business and Legal Affairs NAIRI GARDINER Senior VP – Finance
JEFF BOISON VP – Publishing Planning MARK CHIARELLO VP – Art Direction and Design
JOHN CUNNINGHAM VP – Marketing TERRI CUNNINGHAM VP – Editorial Administration
ALISON GILL Senior VP – Manufacturing and Operations HANK KANALZ Senior VP – Vertigo & Integrated Publishing
JAY KOGAN VP – Business and Legal Affairs, Publishing JACK MAHAN VP – Business Affairs, Talent
NICK NAPOLITANO VP – Manufacturing Administration SUE POHJA VP – Book Sales
COURTNEY SIMMONS Senior VP – Publicity BOB WAYNE Senior VP – Sales

THE FURY OF FIRESTORM: THE NUCLEAR MEN VOLUME 2: THE FIRESTORM PROTOCOLS

DC Comics, 1700 Broadway, New York, NY 10019
A Warner Bros. Entertainment Company.
Printed by RR Donnelley, Salem, VA, USA. 5/17/13. First Printing.

ISBN: 978-1-4012-4032-5

Library of Congress Cataloging-in-Publication Data

Harris, Joe, author.
The fury of Firestorm, The Nuclear Men. Volume 2, The firestorm protocols / Joe Harris, Yildiray Cinar, Ethan Van Sciver.
pages cm
"Originally published in single magazine form in The Fury of Firestorm: The Nuclear Men 7-12, 0."
ISBN 978-1-4012-4032-5
1. Graphic novels. I. Cinar, Yildiray, 1976- illustrator. II. Van Sciver, Ethan, illustrator. III. Title. IV. Title: Firestorm protocols.
PN6728.F4797H37 2013
741.5'973—dc23
2013003525

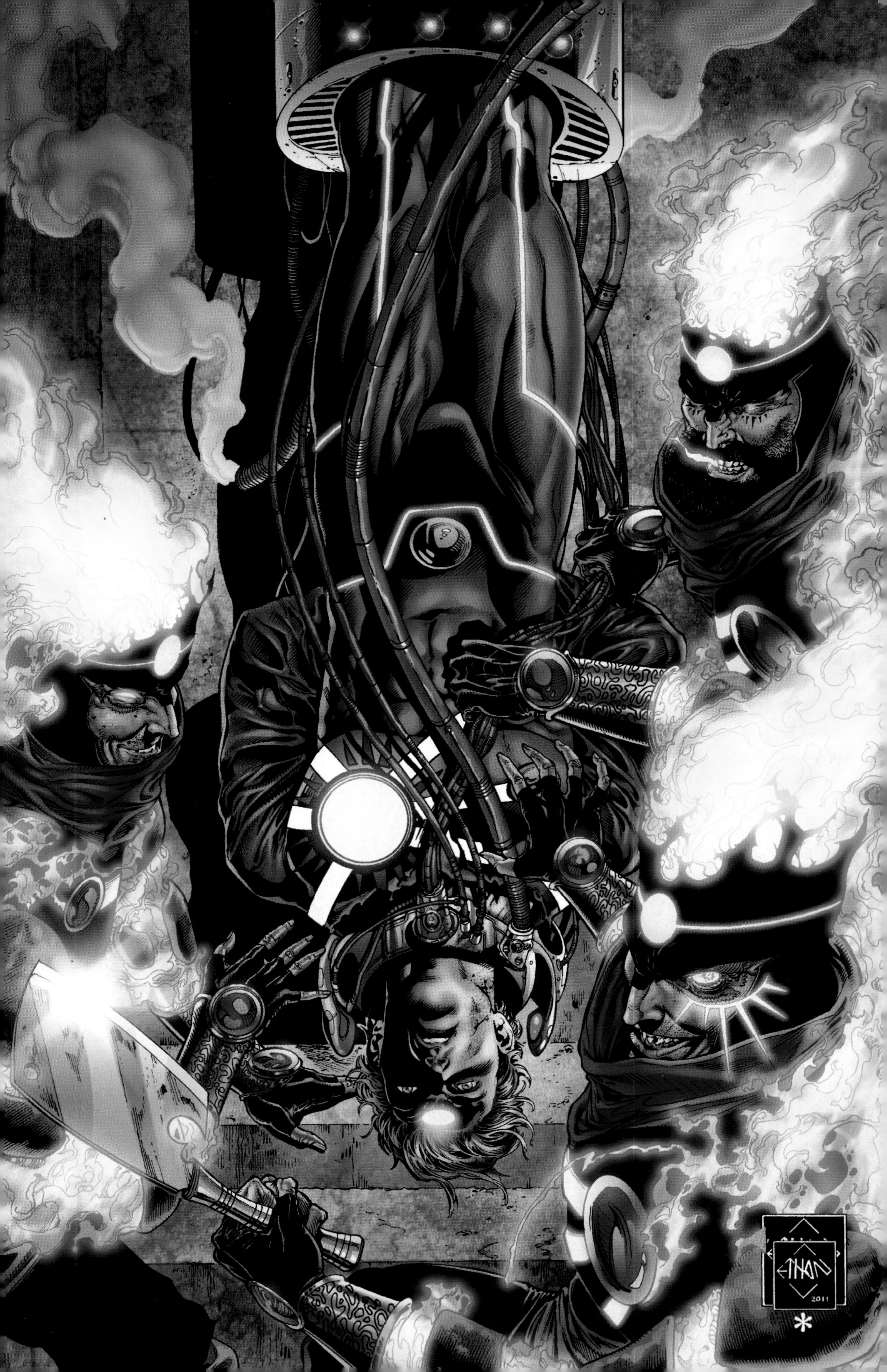

HEATSEEKER

ETHAN VAN SCIVER & JOE HARRIS plot JOE HARRIS script ETHAN VAN SCIVER artist

cover by ETHAN VAN SCIVER with HI-FI

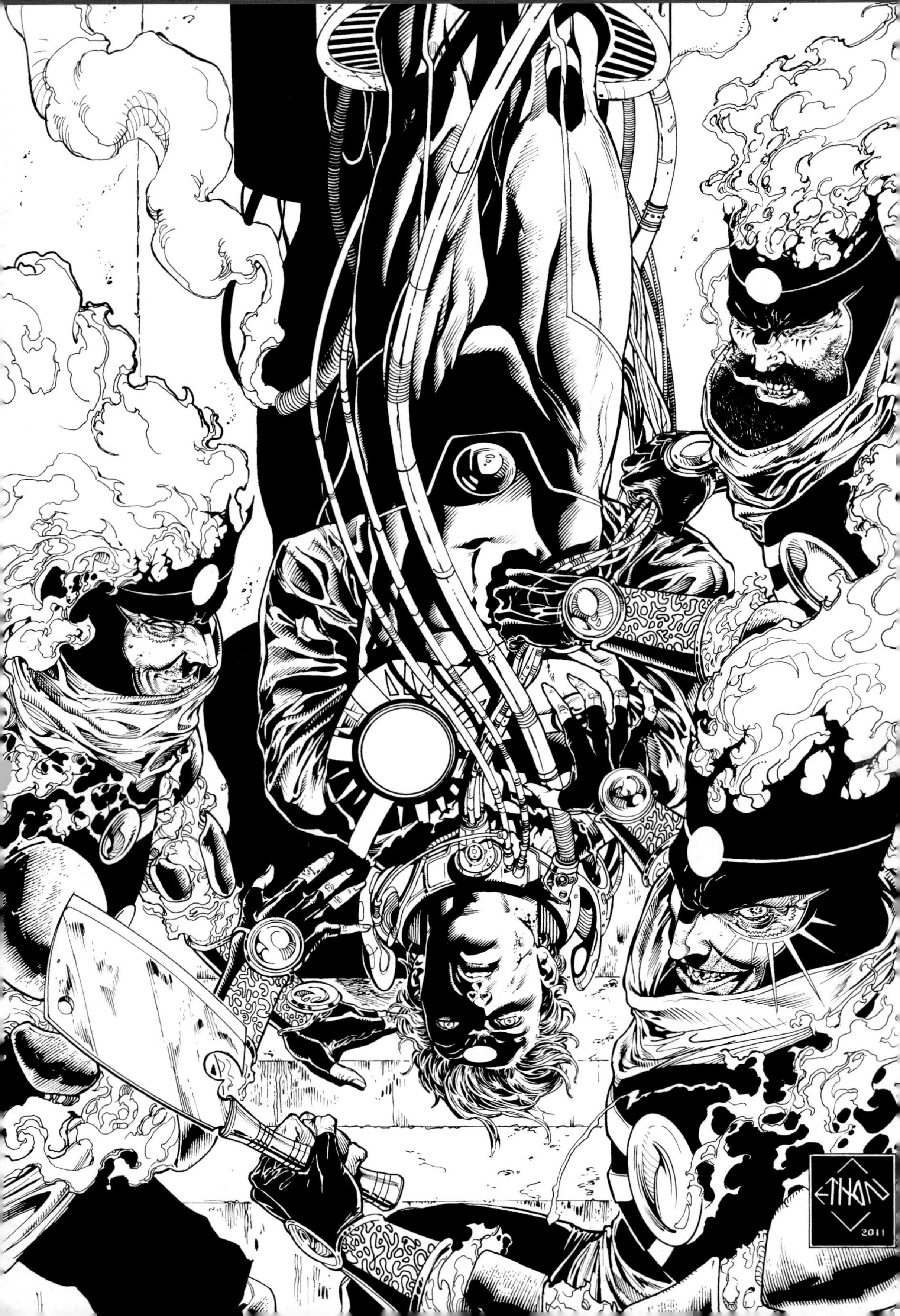
ETHAN
2011

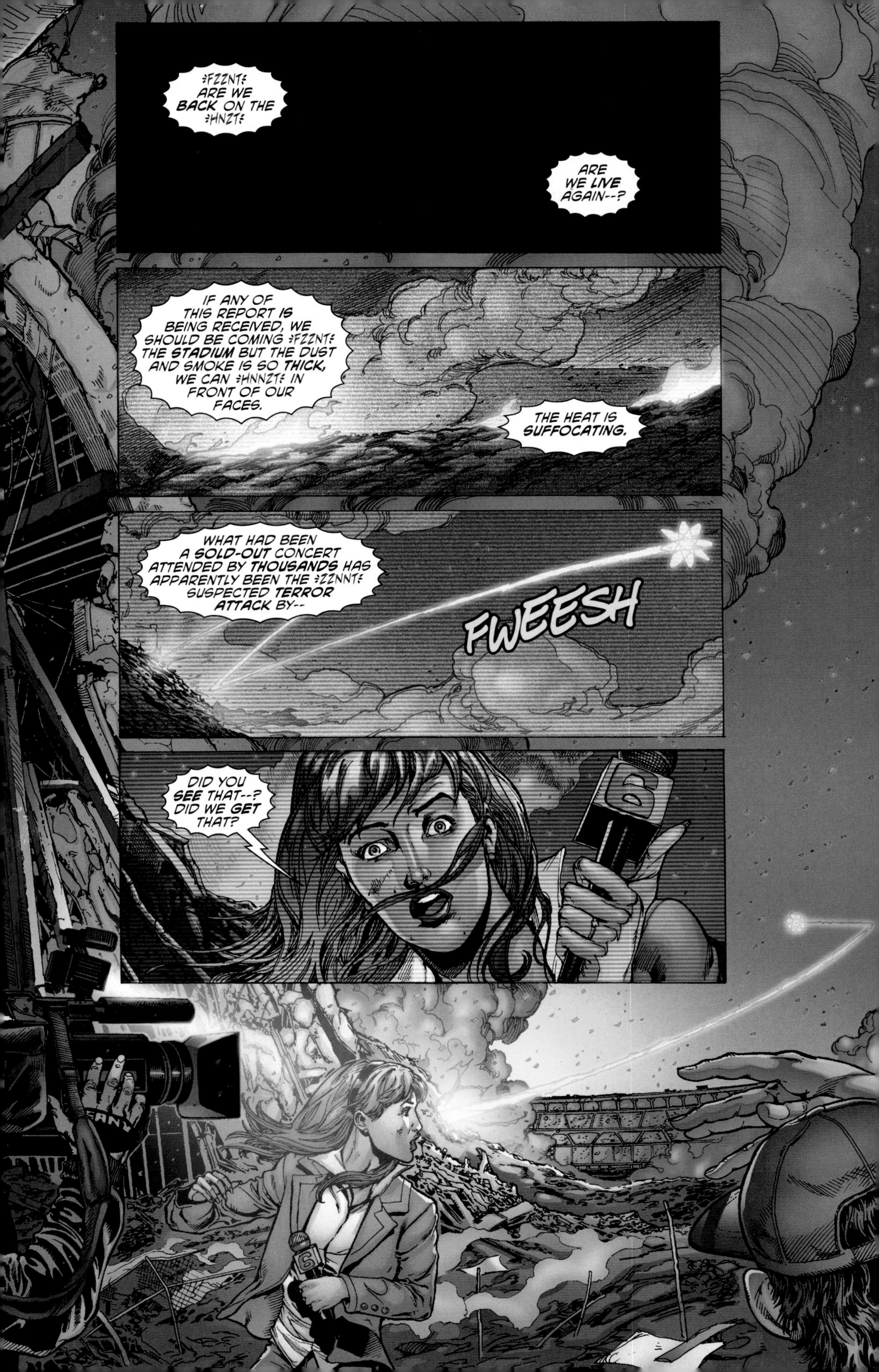

ꟷFZZNTꟷ ARE WE BACK ON THE ꟷHNZTꟷ
ARE WE LIVE AGAIN--?
IF ANY OF THIS REPORT IS BEING RECEIVED, WE SHOULD BE COMING ꟷFZZNTꟷ THE STADIUM BUT THE DUST AND SMOKE IS SO THICK, WE CAN ꟷHNNZTꟷ IN FRONT OF OUR FACES.
THE HEAT IS SUFFOCATING.
WHAT HAD BEEN A SOLD-OUT CONCERT ATTENDED BY THOUSANDS HAS APPARENTLY BEEN THE ꟷZZNNTꟷ SUSPECTED TERROR ATTACK BY--
FWEESH
DID YOU SEE THAT--? DID WE GET THAT?

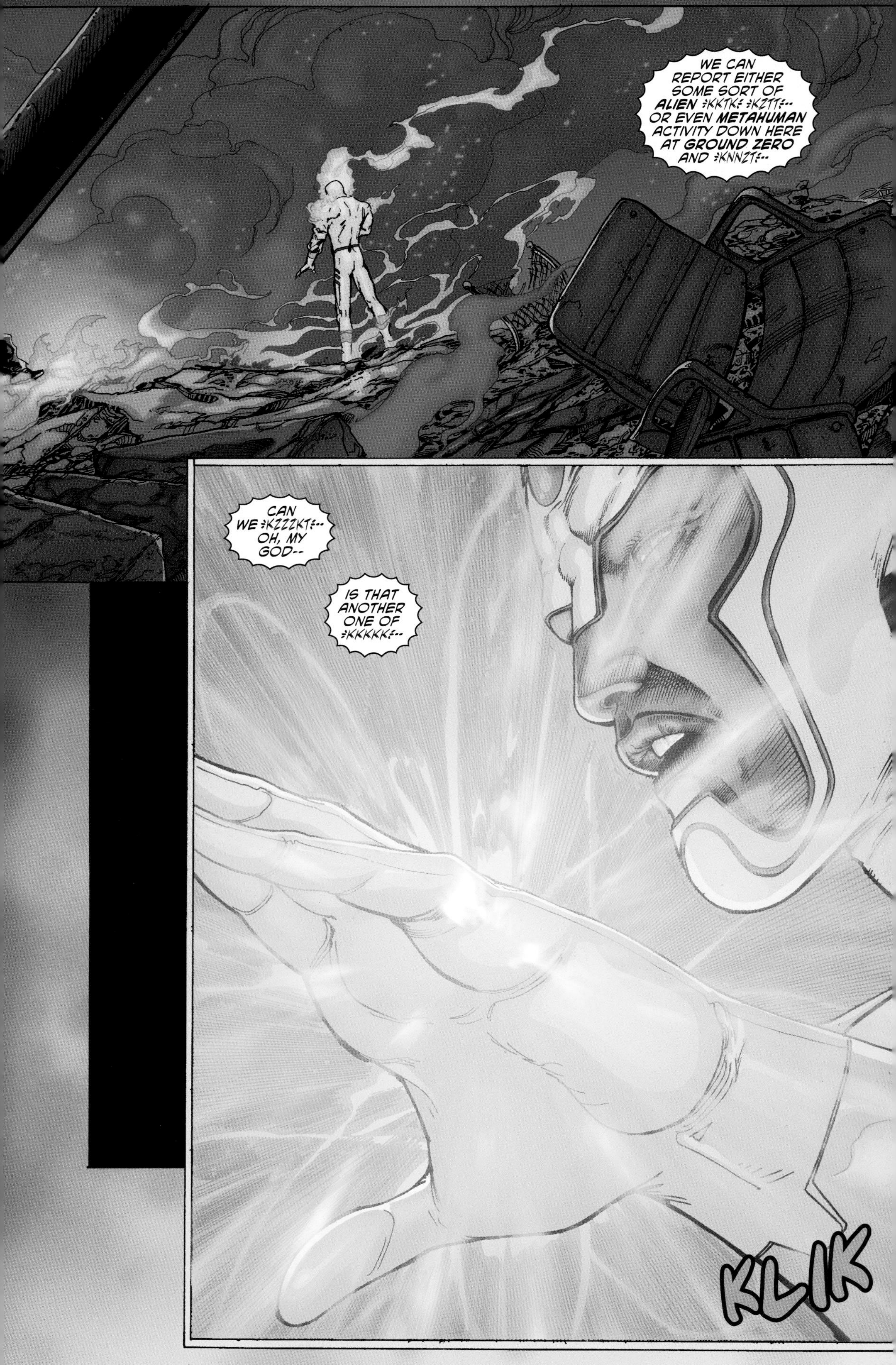
WE CAN REPORT EITHER SOME SORT OF ALIEN ≈KKTK≈ ≈KZTT≈-- OR EVEN METAHUMAN ACTIVITY DOWN HERE AT GROUND ZERO AND ≈KNNZT≈--
CAN WE ≈KZZZKT≈-- OH, MY GOD--
IS THAT ANOTHER ONE OF ≈KKKKK≈--
KLIK

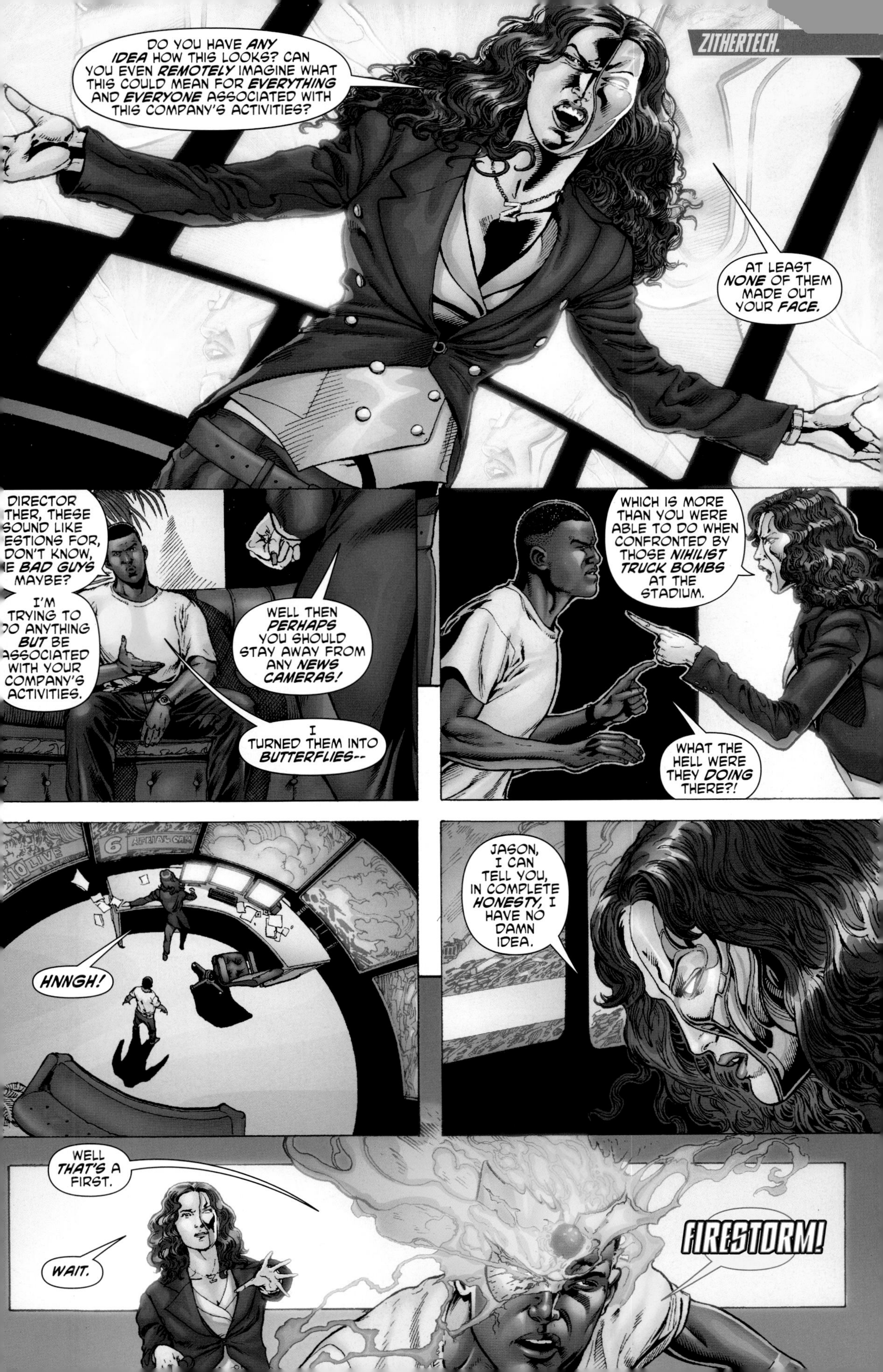
ZITHERTECH.
DO YOU HAVE ANY IDEA HOW THIS LOOKS? CAN YOU EVEN REMOTELY IMAGINE WHAT THIS COULD MEAN FOR EVERYTHING AND EVERYONE ASSOCIATED WITH THIS COMPANY'S ACTIVITIES?
AT LEAST NONE OF THEM MADE OUT YOUR FACE.
DIRECTOR THER, THESE SOUND LIKE ESTIONS FOR, DON'T KNOW, E BAD GUYS MAYBE?
I'M TRYING TO O ANYTHING BUT BE ASSOCIATED WITH YOUR COMPANY'S ACTIVITIES.
WELL THEN PERHAPS YOU SHOULD STAY AWAY FROM ANY NEWS CAMERAS!
I TURNED THEM INTO BUTTERFLIES--
WHICH IS MORE THAN YOU WERE ABLE TO DO WHEN CONFRONTED BY THOSE NIHILIST TRUCK BOMBS AT THE STADIUM.
WHAT THE HELL WERE THEY DOING THERE?!
HNNGH!
JASON, I CAN TELL YOU, IN COMPLETE HONESTY, I HAVE NO DAMN IDEA.
WELL THAT'S A FIRST.
WAIT.
FIRESTORM!

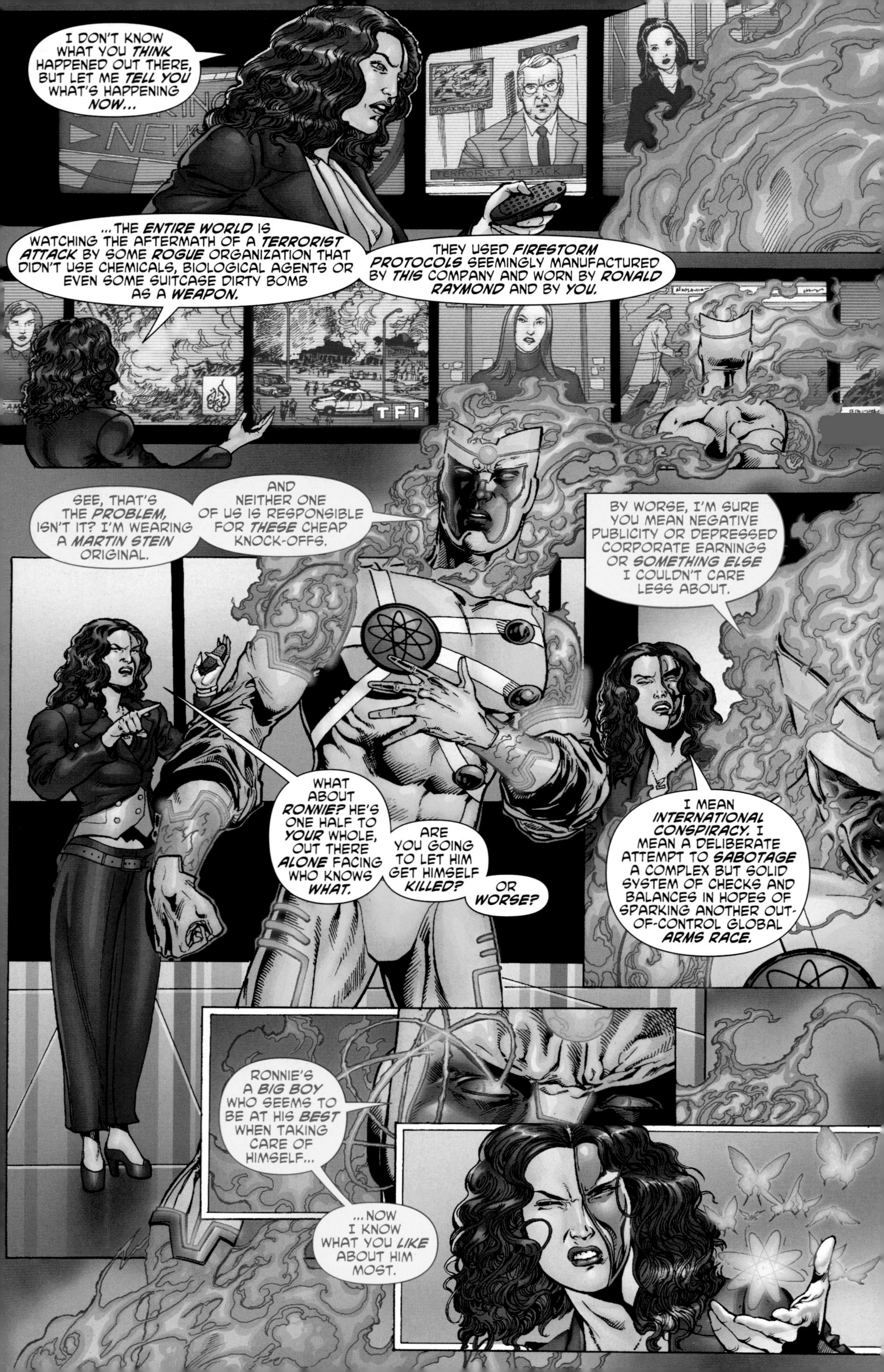

I DON'T KNOW WHAT YOU *THINK* HAPPENED OUT THERE, BUT LET ME *TELL YOU* WHAT'S HAPPENING *NOW*...
...THE *ENTIRE WORLD* IS WATCHING THE AFTERMATH OF A *TERRORIST ATTACK* BY SOME *ROGUE* ORGANIZATION THAT DIDN'T USE CHEMICALS, BIOLOGICAL AGENTS OR EVEN SOME SUITCASE DIRTY BOMB AS A *WEAPON.*
THEY USED *FIRESTORM PROTOCOLS* SEEMINGLY MANUFACTURED BY *THIS* COMPANY AND WORN BY *RONALD RAYMOND* AND BY *YOU.*
TERRORIST ATTACK
TF1
SEE, THAT'S THE *PROBLEM,* ISN'T IT? I'M WEARING A *MARTIN STEIN* ORIGINAL.
AND NEITHER ONE OF US IS RESPONSIBLE FOR *THESE* CHEAP KNOCK-OFFS.
WHAT ABOUT *RONNIE?* HE'S ONE HALF TO *YOUR* WHOLE, OUT THERE *ALONE* FACING WHO KNOWS *WHAT.*
ARE YOU GOING TO LET HIM GET HIMSELF *KILLED?*
OR *WORSE?*
BY WORSE, I'M SURE YOU MEAN NEGATIVE PUBLICITY OR DEPRESSED CORPORATE EARNINGS OR *SOMETHING ELSE* I COULDN'T CARE LESS ABOUT.
I MEAN *INTERNATIONAL CONSPIRACY.* I MEAN A DELIBERATE ATTEMPT TO *SABOTAGE* A COMPLEX BUT SOLID SYSTEM OF CHECKS AND BALANCES IN HOPES OF SPARKING ANOTHER OUT-OF-CONTROL GLOBAL *ARMS RACE.*
RONNIE'S A *BIG BOY* WHO SEEMS TO BE AT HIS *BEST* WHEN TAKING CARE OF HIMSELF...
...NOW I KNOW WHAT YOU *LIKE* ABOUT HIM MOST.

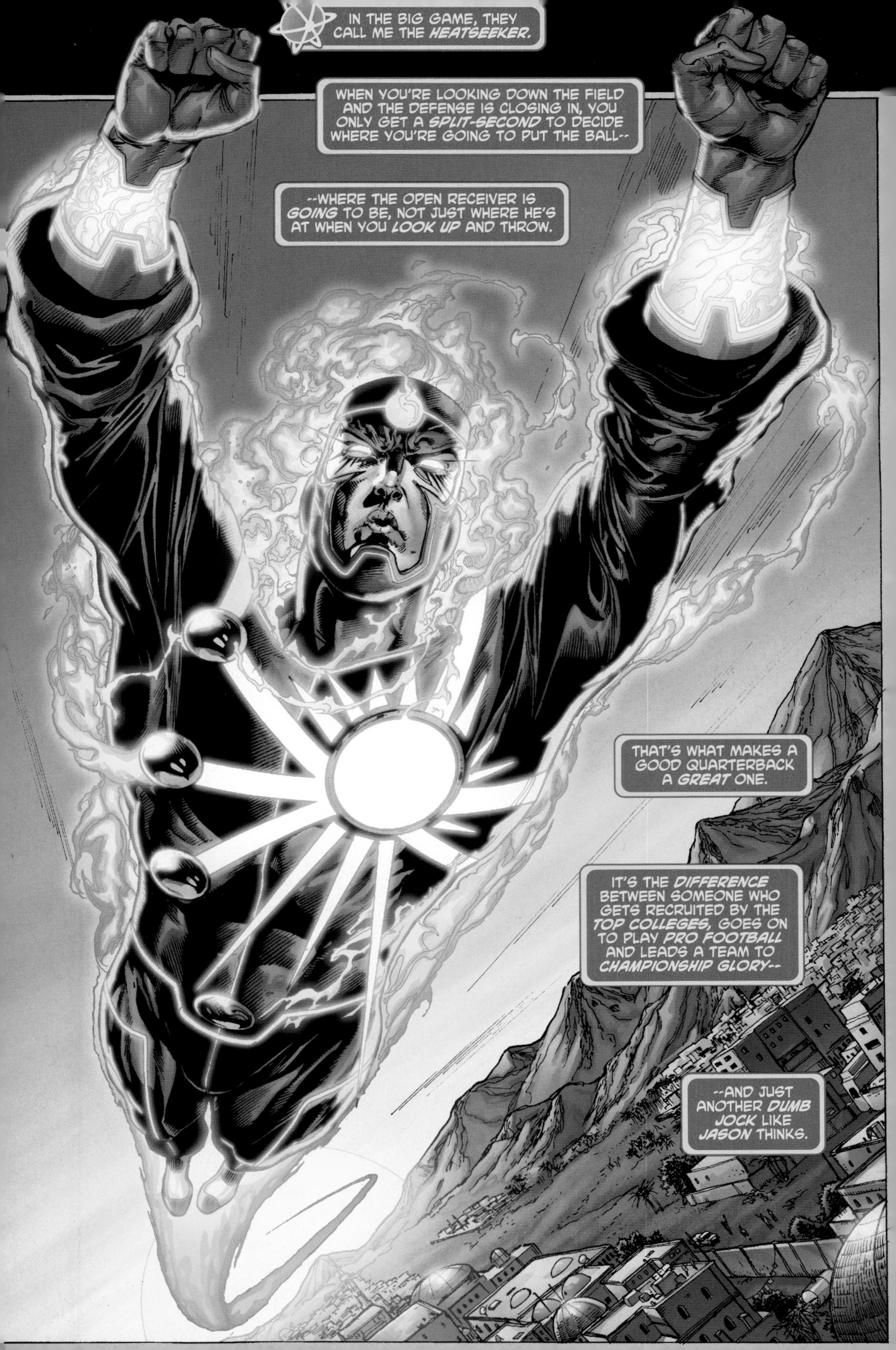
IN THE BIG GAME, THEY CALL ME THE HEATSEEKER.
WHEN YOU'RE LOOKING DOWN THE FIELD AND THE DEFENSE IS CLOSING IN, YOU ONLY GET A SPLIT-SECOND TO DECIDE WHERE YOU'RE GOING TO PUT THE BALL--
--WHERE THE OPEN RECEIVER IS GOING TO BE, NOT JUST WHERE HE'S AT WHEN YOU LOOK UP AND THROW.
THAT'S WHAT MAKES A GOOD QUARTERBACK A GREAT ONE.
IT'S THE DIFFERENCE BETWEEN SOMEONE WHO GETS RECRUITED BY THE TOP COLLEGES, GOES ON TO PLAY PRO FOOTBALL AND LEADS A TEAM TO CHAMPIONSHIP GLORY--
--AND JUST ANOTHER DUMB JOCK LIKE JASON THINKS.

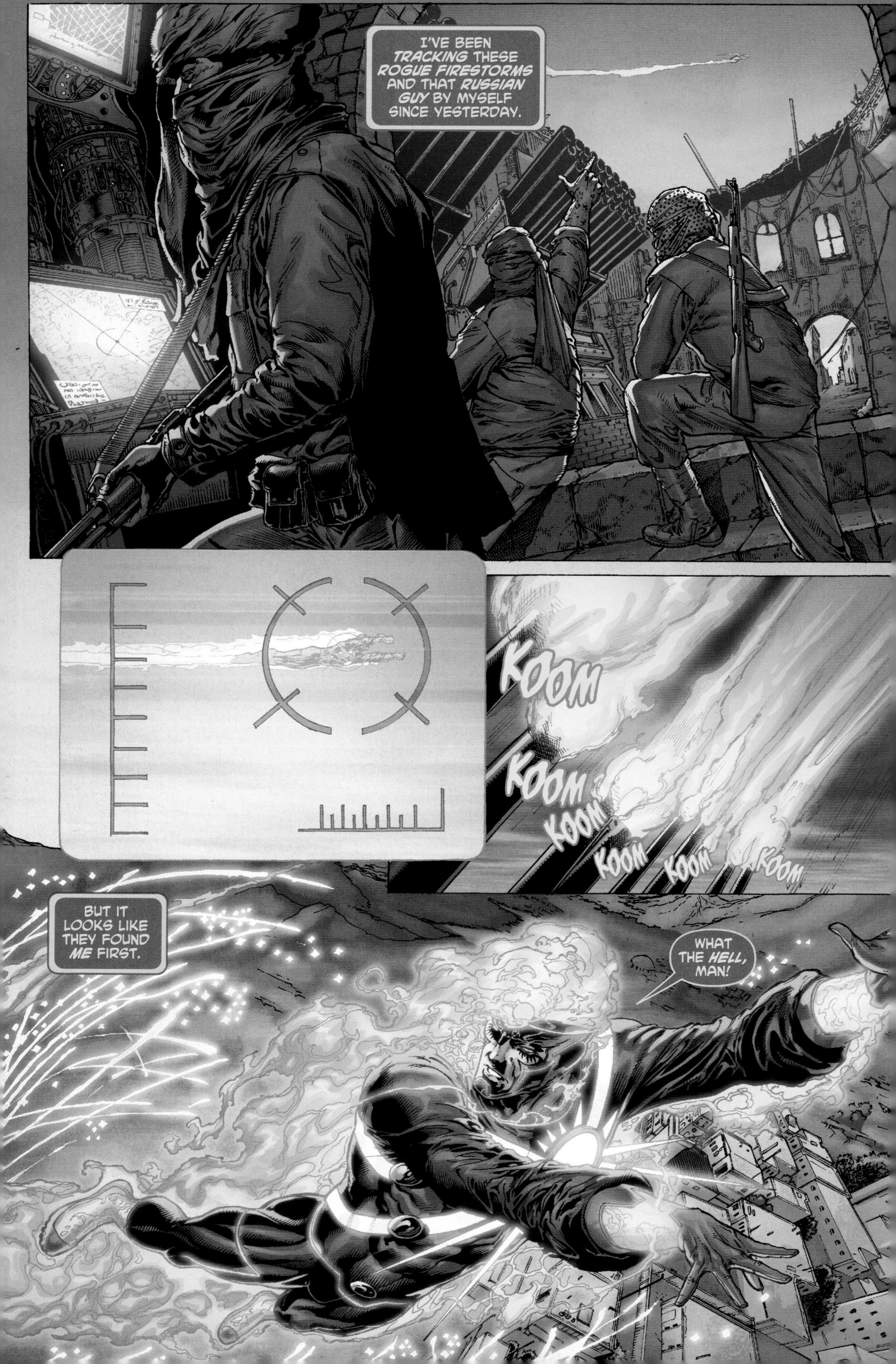
I'VE BEEN TRACKING THESE ROGUE FIRESTORMS AND THAT RUSSIAN GUY BY MYSELF SINCE YESTERDAY.
KOOM
KOOM
KOOM
KOOM
KOOM
KOOM
BUT IT LOOKS LIKE THEY FOUND ME FIRST.
WHAT THE HELL, MAN!

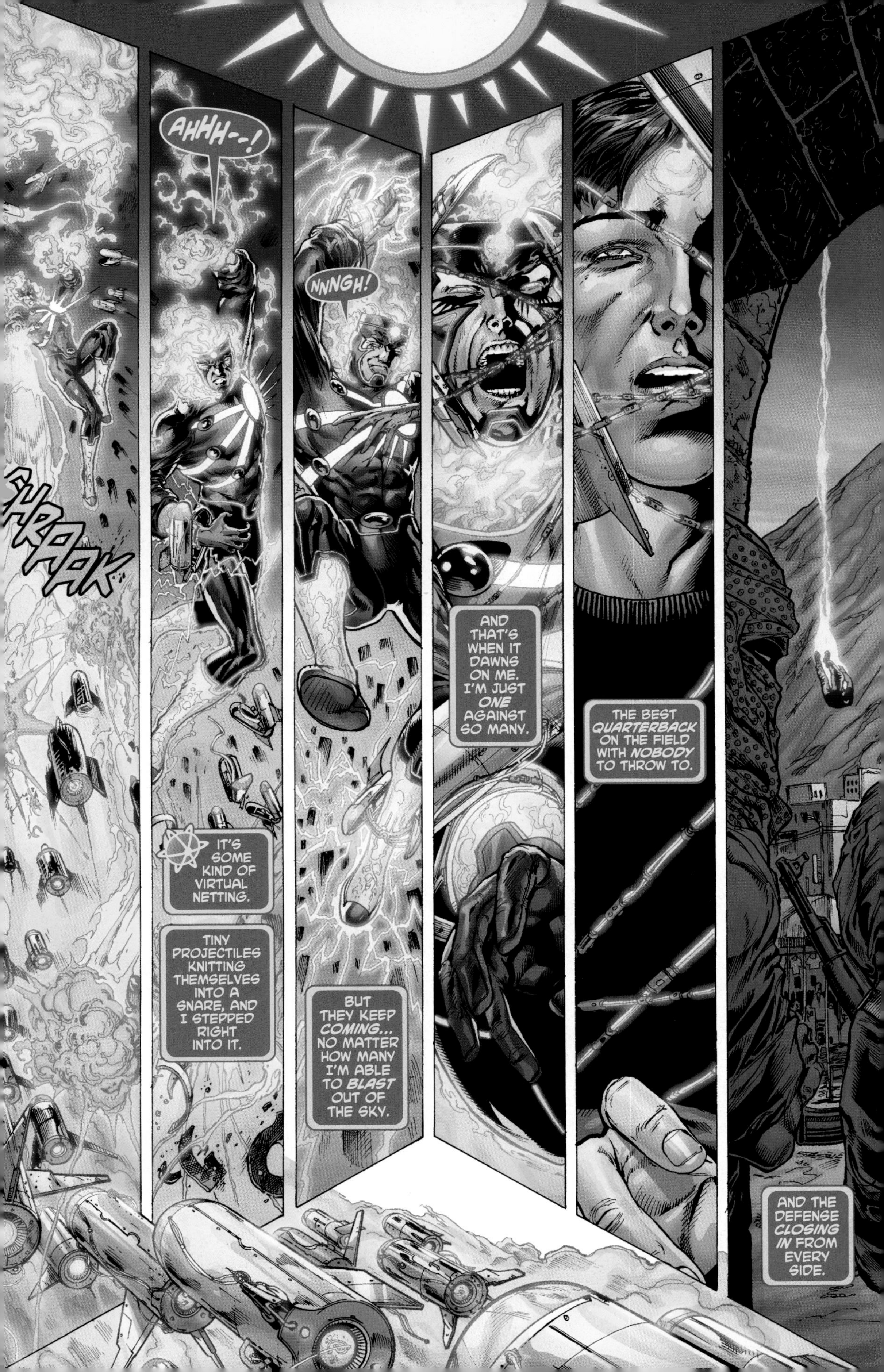

SHRAAK
AHHH--!
IT'S SOME KIND OF VIRTUAL NETTING.
TINY PROJECTILES KNITTING THEMSELVES INTO A SNARE, AND I STEPPED RIGHT INTO IT.
NNNGH!
BUT THEY KEEP COMING... NO MATTER HOW MANY I'M ABLE TO BLAST OUT OF THE SKY.
AND THAT'S WHEN IT DAWNS ON ME. I'M JUST ONE AGAINST SO MANY.
THE BEST QUARTERBACK ON THE FIELD WITH NOBODY TO THROW TO.
AND THE DEFENSE CLOSING IN FROM EVERY SIDE.

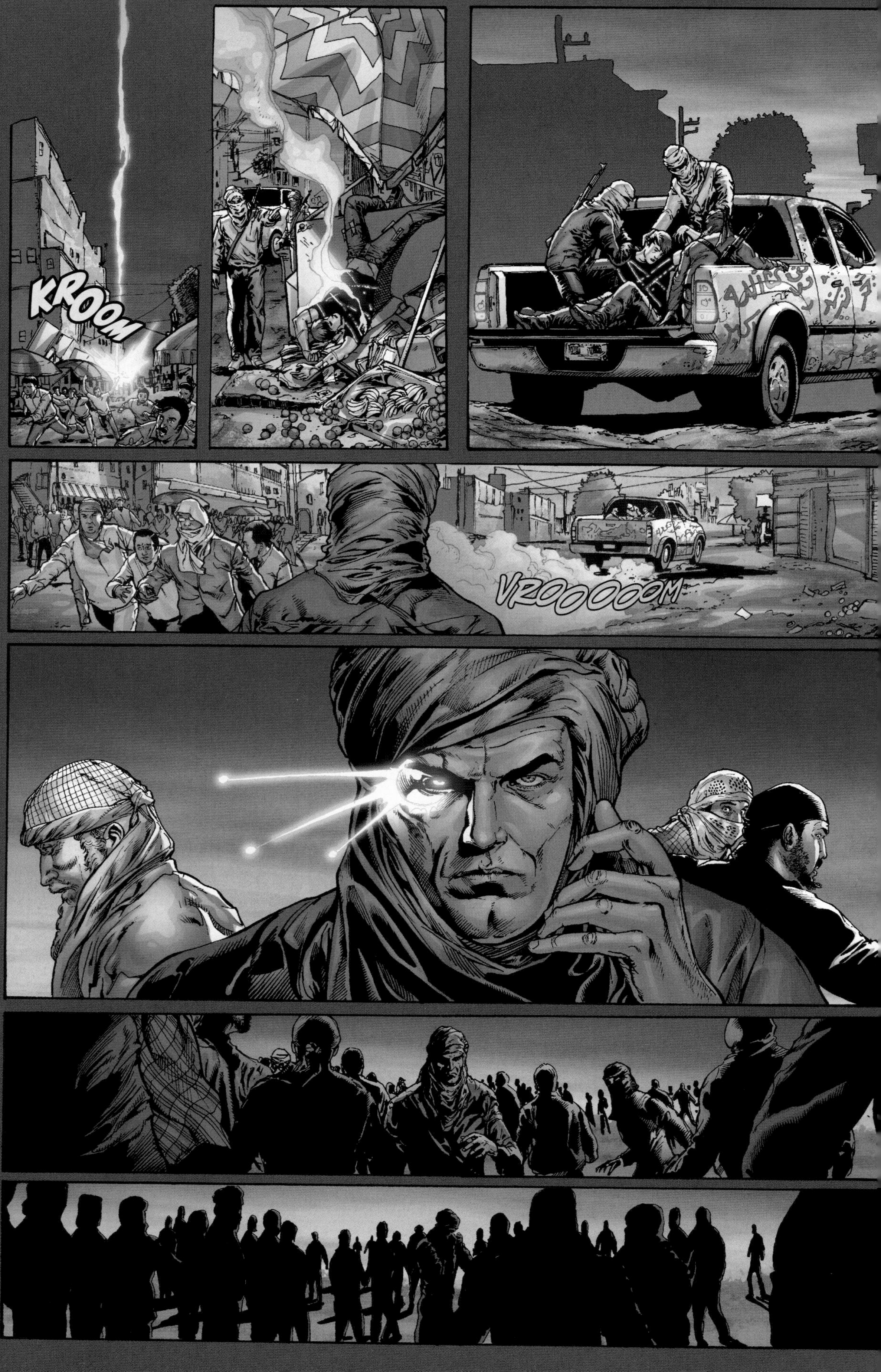
KROOM
VROOOOOOM

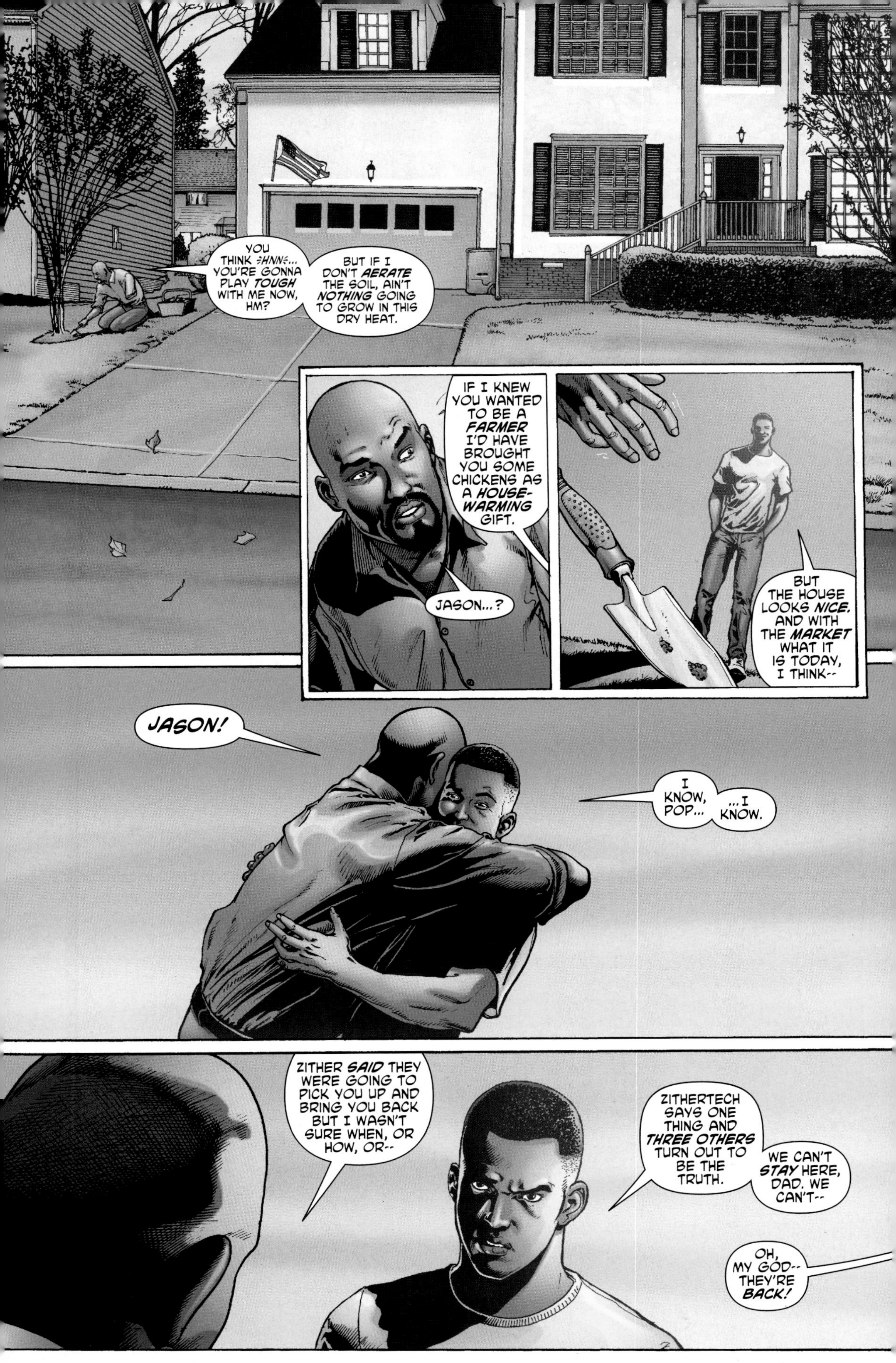
YOU THINK ≠HNN≠... YOU'RE GONNA PLAY TOUGH WITH ME NOW, HM?
BUT IF I DON'T AERATE THE SOIL, AIN'T NOTHING GOING TO GROW IN THIS DRY HEAT.
IF I KNEW YOU WANTED TO BE A FARMER I'D HAVE BROUGHT YOU SOME CHICKENS AS A HOUSE-WARMING GIFT.
BUT THE HOUSE LOOKS NICE, AND WITH THE MARKET WHAT IT IS TODAY, I THINK--
JASON...?
JASON!
I KNOW, POP...
...I KNOW.
ZITHER SAID THEY WERE GOING TO PICK YOU UP AND BRING YOU BACK BUT I WASN'T SURE WHEN, OR HOW, OR--
ZITHERTECH SAYS ONE THING AND THREE OTHERS TURN OUT TO BE THE TRUTH.
WE CAN'T STAY HERE, DAD. WE CAN'T--
OH, MY GOD-- THEY'RE BACK!

THE NEWS WAS JUST *CHAOTIC* AND THE REPORTS HAVE BEEN SO *CONFUSING...* BUT WHEN *ZITHER* TOLD US YOU WERE BOTH OKAY, I THOUGHT MAYBE SOMEONE WAS *WATCHING OVER* OUR BOYS AFTER ALL!

I TOLD YOU EVERYTHING WAS GOING TO *WORK OUT*, DIDN'T I?

BUT WHERE'S *RONNIE...?*

WHY DON'T WE LET JASON WASH UP. I'M SURE RONNIE WILL BE ALONG ONCE HE'S *DEBRIEFED* AND--

WHERE'S MY *SON?* WHY ISN'T HE *WITH* YOU?

THERE... WAS AN *INCIDENT,* MS. RAYMOND.

YOU *KNOW* WHAT HAPPENED AT THE STADIUM. IT WAS ATTACKED. WE WEREN'T ABLE TO *STOP* IT FROM HAPPENING.

BUT THERE'S *MORE* GOING ON THAN THEY'RE LETTING OUT. I'M NOT SURE HOW TO EVEN--

IS HE *DEAD...?*

DAMNIT, WHY WON'T ANYONE TELL ME THE *TRUTH?!*

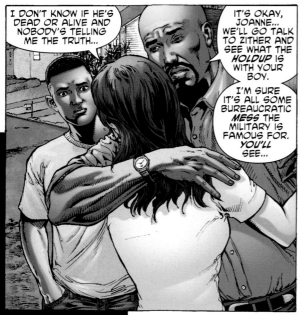

I DON'T KNOW IF HE'S DEAD OR ALIVE AND NOBODY'S TELLING ME THE TRUTH...

IT'S OKAY, JOANNE... WE'LL GO TALK TO ZITHER AND SEE WHAT THE *HOLDUP* IS WITH YOUR BOY.

I'M SURE IT'S ALL SOME BUREAUCRATIC *MESS* THE MILITARY IS FAMOUS FOR. *YOU'LL* SEE...

EVERYTHING'S GOING TO BE ALL RIGHT...

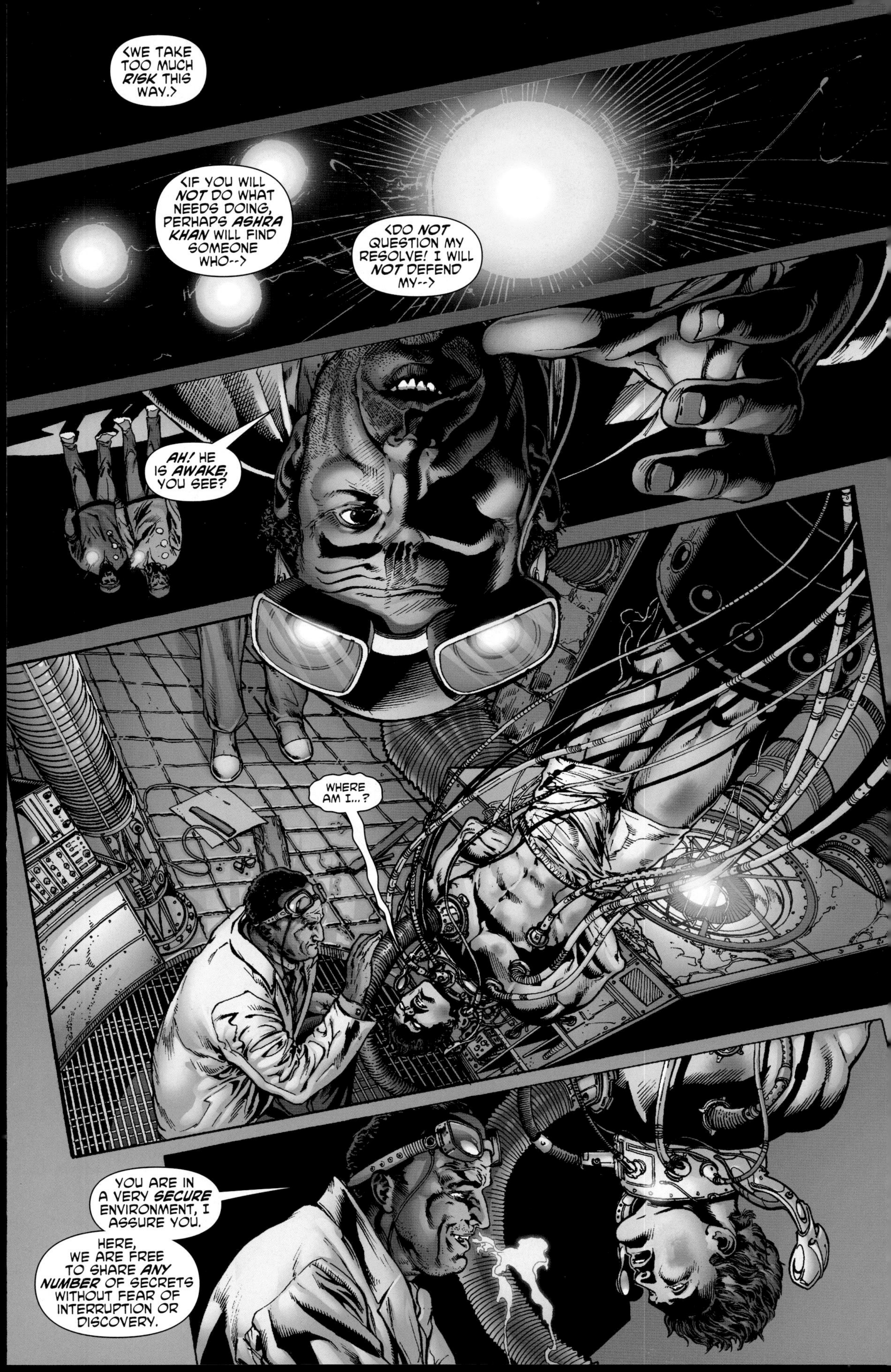

<WE TAKE TOO MUCH RISK THIS WAY.>
<IF YOU WILL NOT DO WHAT NEEDS DOING, PERHAPS ASHRA KHAN WILL FIND SOMEONE WHO-->
<DO NOT QUESTION MY RESOLVE! I WILL NOT DEFEND MY-->
AH! HE IS AWAKE, YOU SEE?
WHERE AM I...?
YOU ARE IN A VERY SECURE ENVIRONMENT, I ASSURE YOU.
HERE, WE ARE FREE TO SHARE ANY NUMBER OF SECRETS WITHOUT FEAR OF INTERRUPTION OR DISCOVERY.

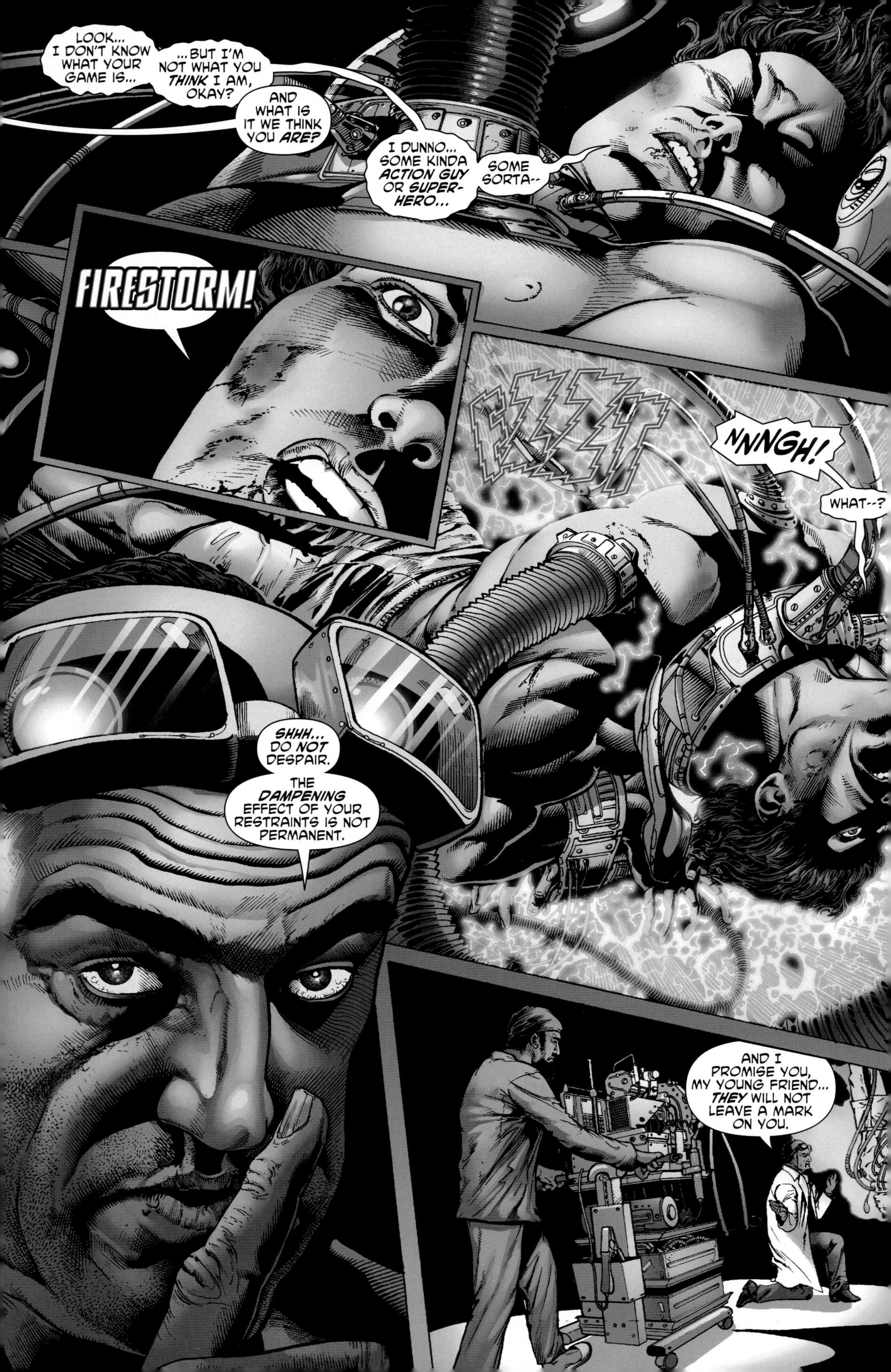
LOOK... I DON'T KNOW WHAT YOUR GAME IS...
...BUT I'M NOT WHAT YOU THINK I AM, OKAY?
AND WHAT IS IT WE THINK YOU ARE?
I DUNNO... SOME KINDA ACTION GUY OR SUPER-HERO...
SOME SORTA--
FIRESTORM!
NNNGH!
WHAT--?
SHHH... DO NOT DESPAIR.
THE DAMPENING EFFECT OF YOUR RESTRAINTS IS NOT PERMANENT.
AND I PROMISE YOU, MY YOUNG FRIEND... THEY WILL NOT LEAVE A MARK ON YOU.

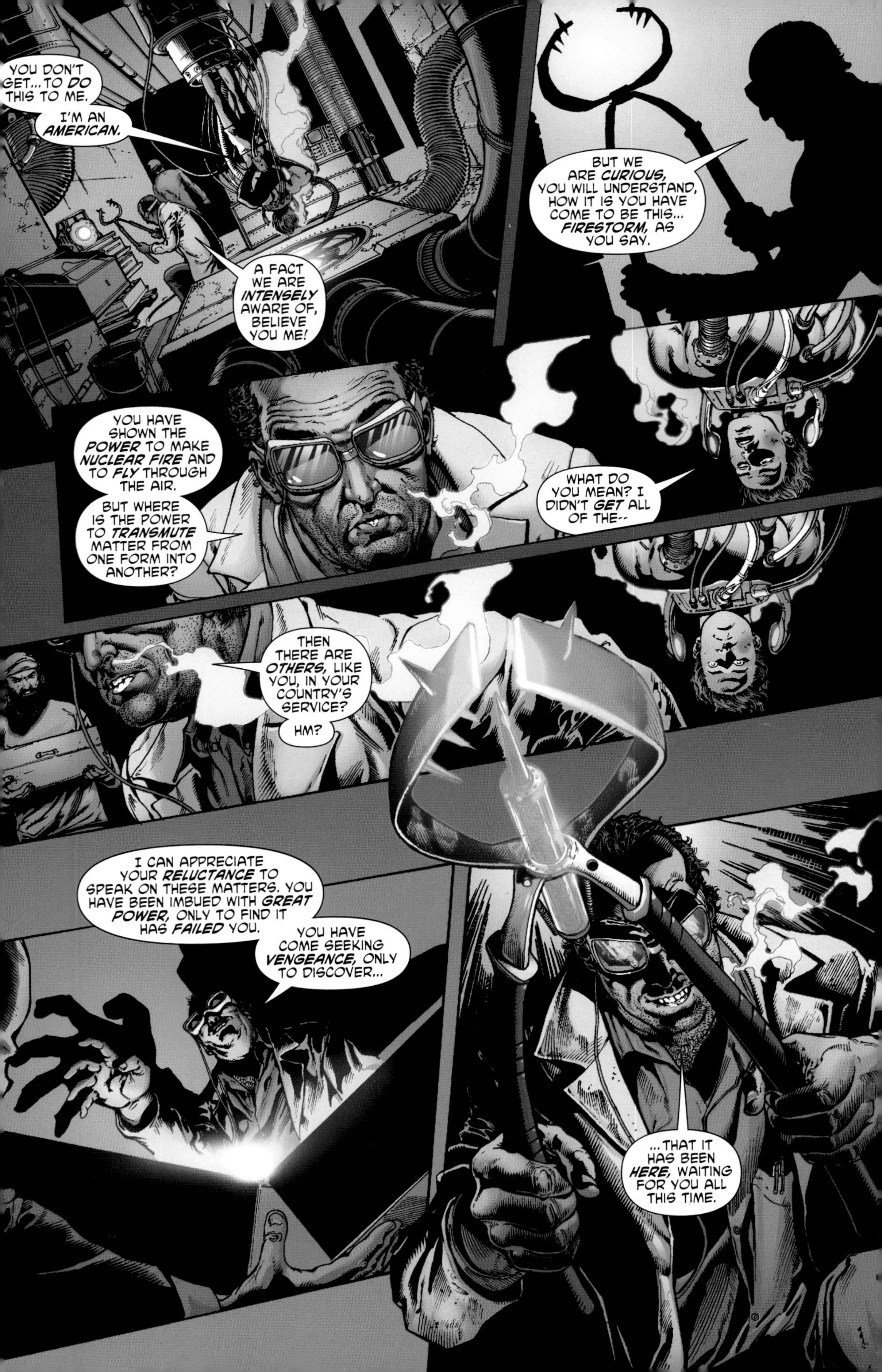
YOU DON'T GET...TO DO THIS TO ME.
I'M AN AMERICAN.
A FACT WE ARE INTENSELY AWARE OF, BELIEVE YOU ME!
BUT WE ARE CURIOUS, YOU WILL UNDERSTAND, HOW IT IS YOU HAVE COME TO BE THIS... FIRESTORM, AS YOU SAY.
YOU HAVE SHOWN THE POWER TO MAKE NUCLEAR FIRE AND TO FLY THROUGH THE AIR.
BUT WHERE IS THE POWER TO TRANSMUTE MATTER FROM ONE FORM INTO ANOTHER?
WHAT DO YOU MEAN? I DIDN'T GET ALL OF THE--
THEN THERE ARE OTHERS, LIKE YOU, IN YOUR COUNTRY'S SERVICE?
HM?
I CAN APPRECIATE YOUR RELUCTANCE TO SPEAK ON THESE MATTERS. YOU HAVE BEEN IMBUED WITH GREAT POWER, ONLY TO FIND IT HAS FAILED YOU.
YOU HAVE COME SEEKING VENGEANCE, ONLY TO DISCOVER...
...THAT IT HAS BEEN HERE, WAITING FOR YOU ALL THIS TIME.

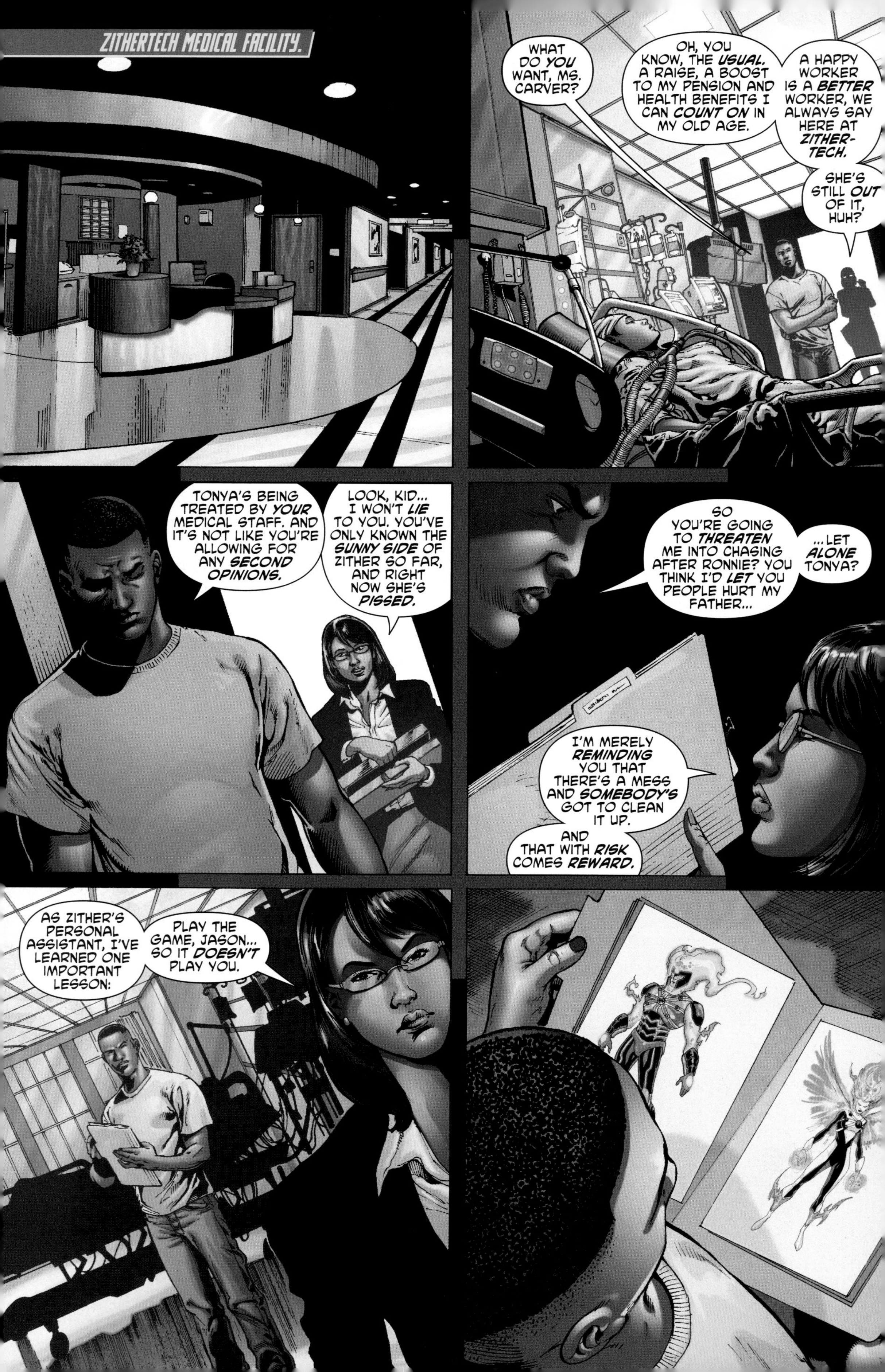
ZITHERTECH MEDICAL FACILITY.
WHAT DO YOU WANT, MS. CARVER?
OH, YOU KNOW, THE USUAL. A RAISE, A BOOST TO MY PENSION AND HEALTH BENEFITS I CAN COUNT ON IN MY OLD AGE.
A HAPPY WORKER IS A BETTER WORKER, WE ALWAYS SAY HERE AT ZITHER-TECH.
SHE'S STILL OUT OF IT, HUH?
TONYA'S BEING TREATED BY YOUR MEDICAL STAFF. AND IT'S NOT LIKE YOU'RE ALLOWING FOR ANY SECOND OPINIONS.
LOOK, KID... I WON'T LIE TO YOU. YOU'VE ONLY KNOWN THE SUNNY SIDE OF ZITHER SO FAR, AND RIGHT NOW SHE'S PISSED.
SO YOU'RE GOING TO THREATEN ME INTO CHASING AFTER RONNIE? YOU THINK I'D LET YOU PEOPLE HURT MY FATHER...
...LET ALONE TONYA?
I'M MERELY REMINDING YOU THAT THERE'S A MESS AND SOMEBODY'S GOT TO CLEAN IT UP.
AND THAT WITH RISK COMES REWARD.
AS ZITHER'S PERSONAL ASSISTANT, I'VE LEARNED ONE IMPORTANT LESSON:
PLAY THE GAME, JASON... SO IT DOESN'T PLAY YOU.

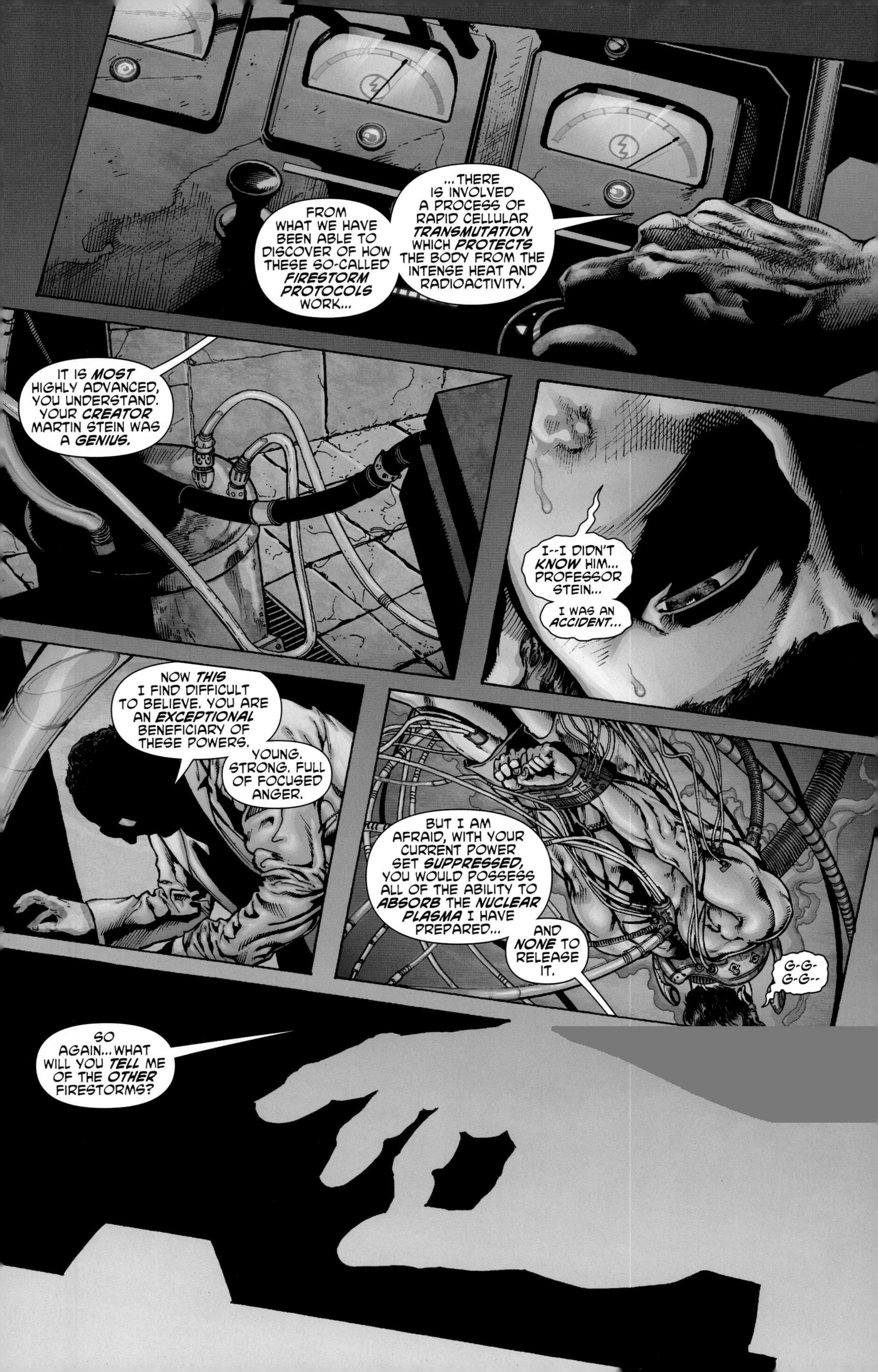
FROM WHAT WE HAVE BEEN ABLE TO DISCOVER OF HOW THESE SO-CALLED FIRESTORM PROTOCOLS WORK...
...THERE IS INVOLVED A PROCESS OF RAPID CELLULAR TRANSMUTATION WHICH PROTECTS THE BODY FROM THE INTENSE HEAT AND RADIOACTIVITY.
IT IS MOST HIGHLY ADVANCED, YOU UNDERSTAND. YOUR CREATOR MARTIN STEIN WAS A GENIUS.
I--I DIDN'T KNOW HIM... PROFESSOR STEIN...
I WAS AN ACCIDENT...
NOW THIS I FIND DIFFICULT TO BELIEVE. YOU ARE AN EXCEPTIONAL BENEFICIARY OF THESE POWERS.
YOUNG. STRONG. FULL OF FOCUSED ANGER.
BUT I AM AFRAID, WITH YOUR CURRENT POWER SET SUPPRESSED, YOU WOULD POSSESS ALL OF THE ABILITY TO ABSORB THE NUCLEAR PLASMA I HAVE PREPARED...
AND NONE TO RELEASE IT.
G-G-G-G--
SO AGAIN...WHAT WILL YOU TELL ME OF THE OTHER FIRESTORMS?

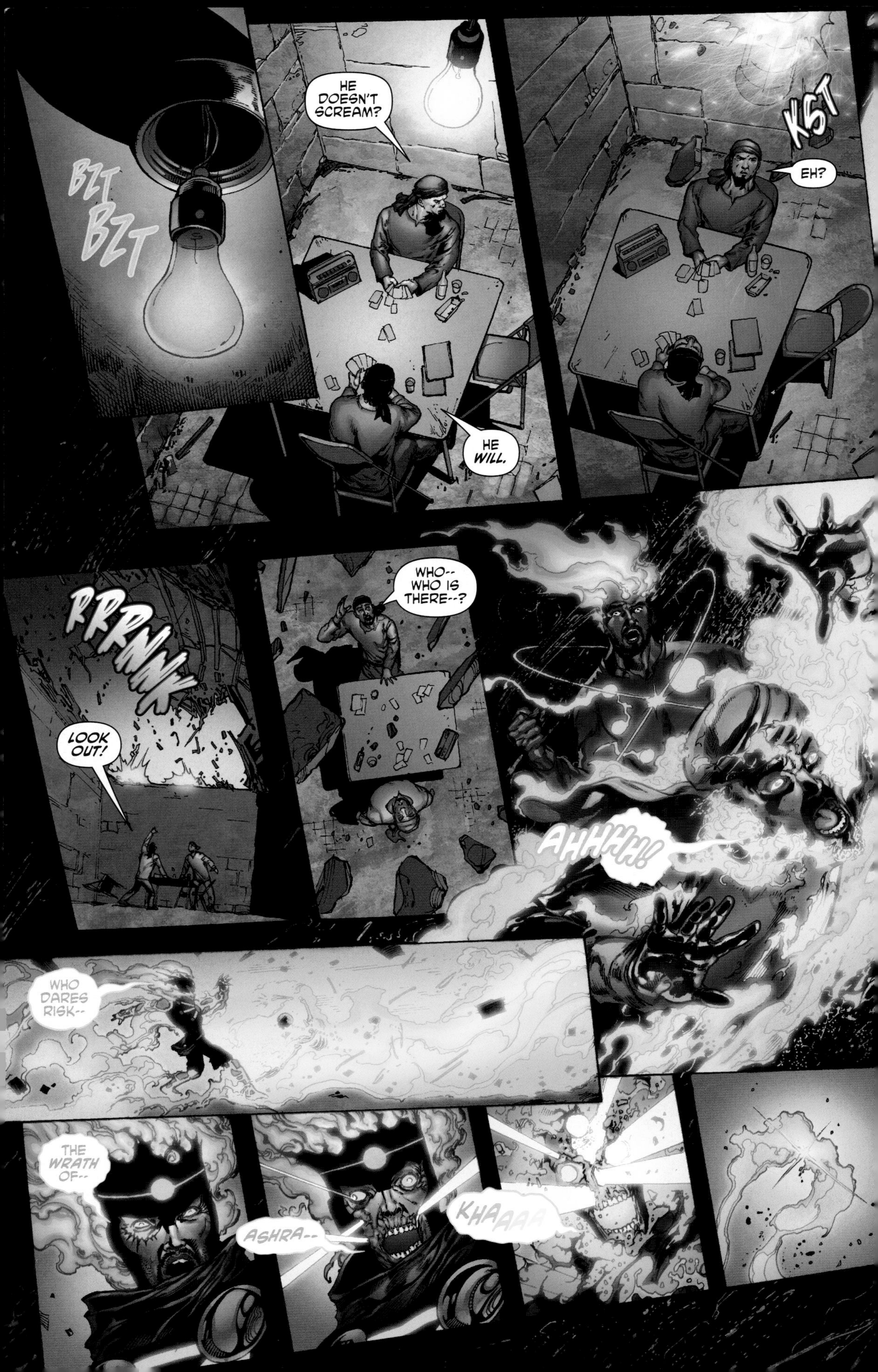
BZT BZT
HE DOESN'T SCREAM?
HE WILL.
KST
EH?
RRRNNNK
LOOK OUT!
WHO-- WHO IS THERE--?
AHHHHH!
WHO DARES RISK--
THE WRATH OF--
ASHRA--
KHAAAA

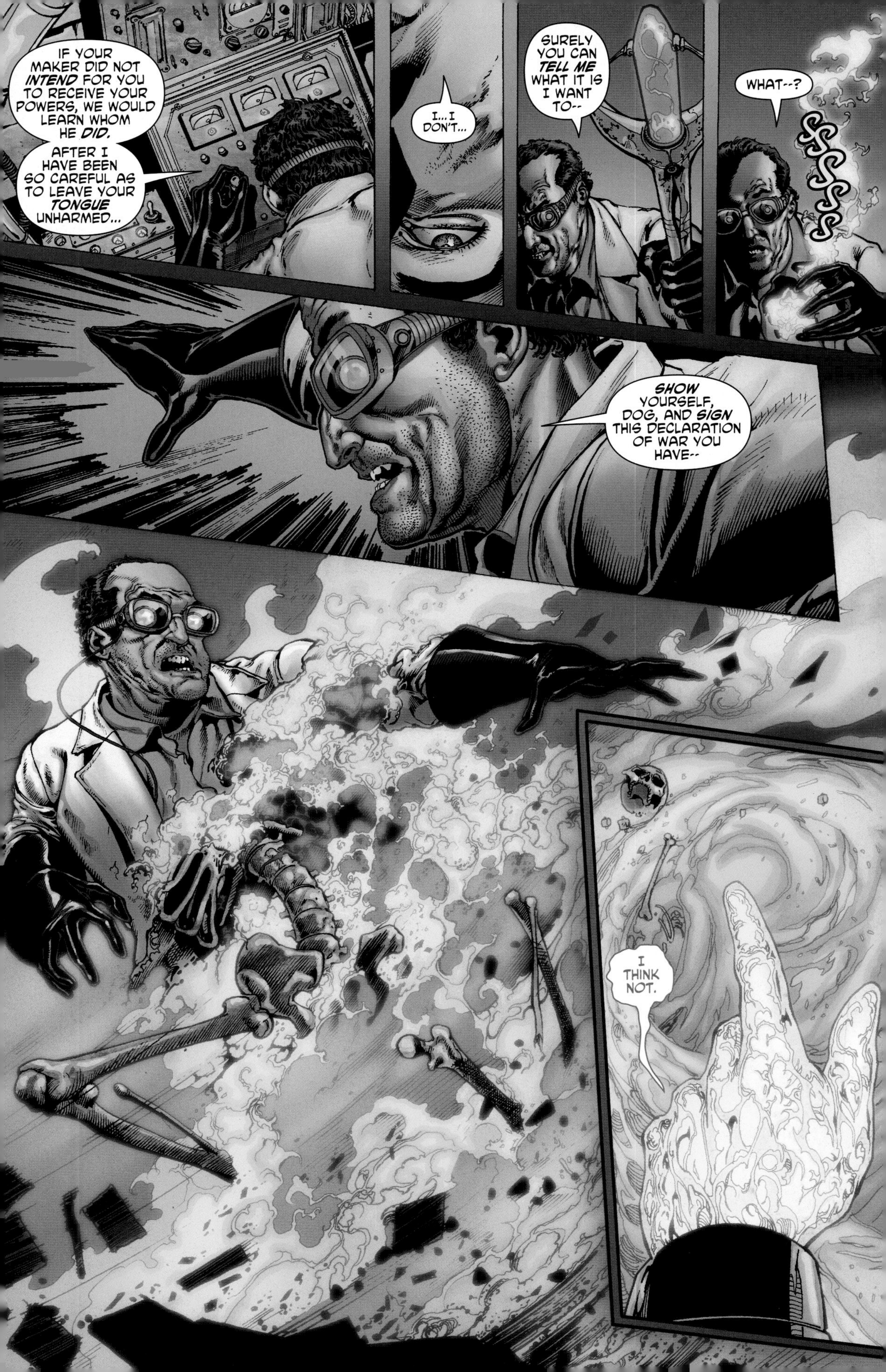
IF YOUR MAKER DID NOT INTEND FOR YOU TO RECEIVE YOUR POWERS, WE WOULD LEARN WHOM HE DID.
AFTER I HAVE BEEN SO CAREFUL AS TO LEAVE YOUR TONGUE UNHARMED...
I... I DON'T...
SURELY YOU CAN TELL ME WHAT IT IS I WANT TO--
WHAT--?
SSSS
SHOW YOURSELF, DOG, AND SIGN THIS DECLARATION OF WAR YOU HAVE--
I THINK NOT.

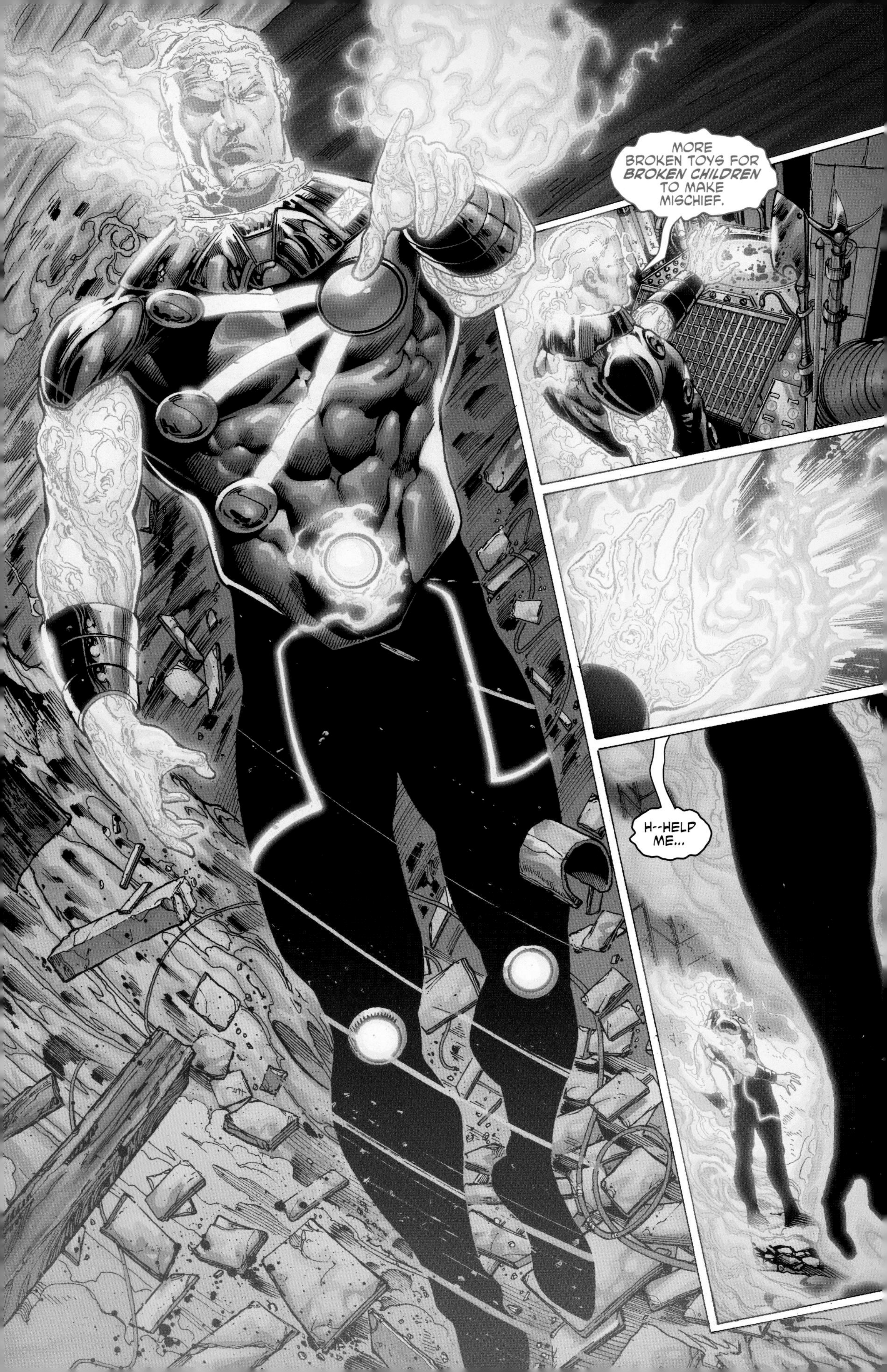
MORE BROKEN TOYS FOR BROKEN CHILDREN TO MAKE MISCHIEF.
H--HELP ME...

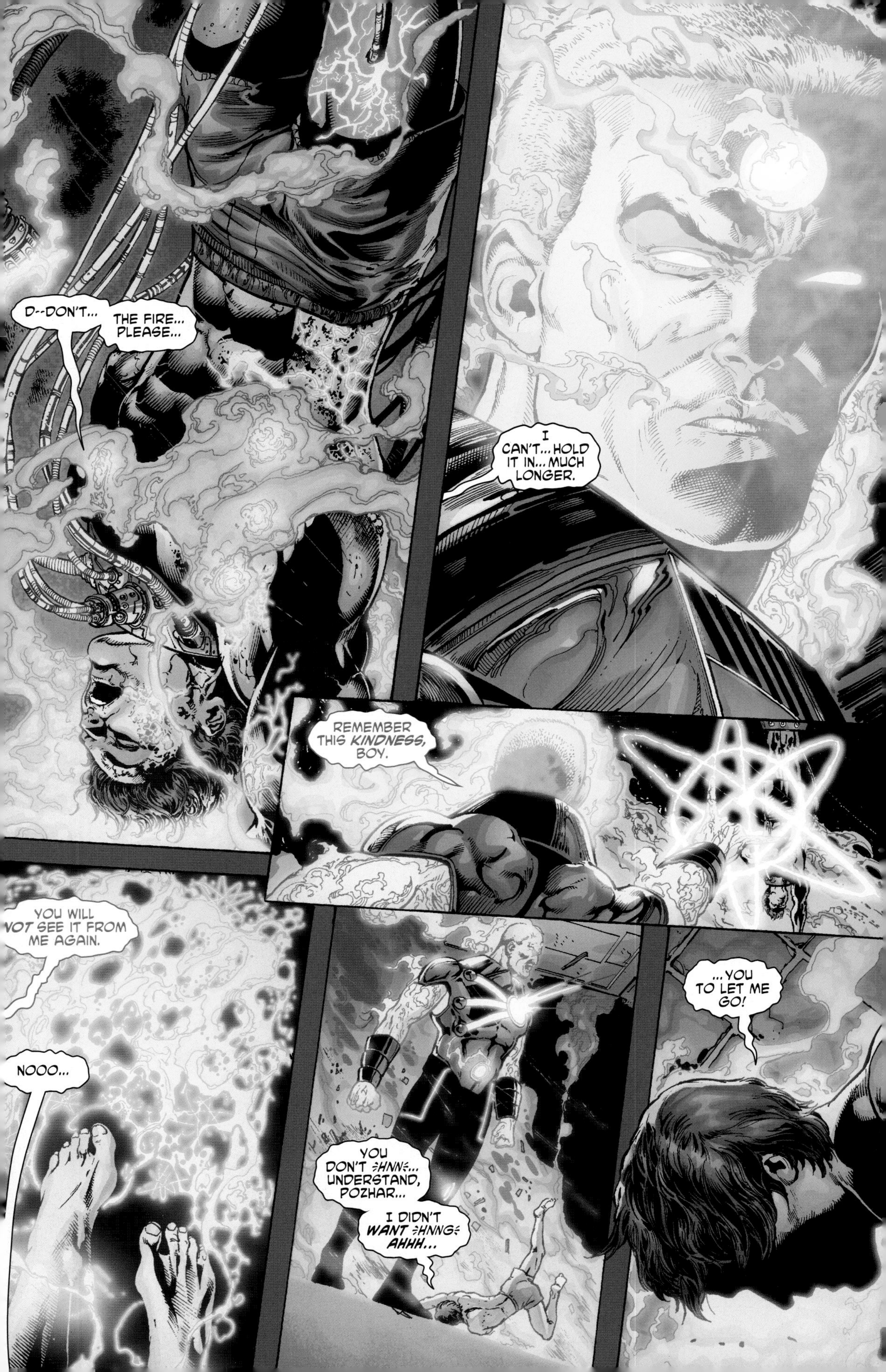
D--DON'T...
THE FIRE... PLEASE...
I CAN'T... HOLD IT IN... MUCH LONGER.
REMEMBER THIS *KINDNESS*, BOY.
YOU WILL *NOT* SEE IT FROM ME AGAIN.
NOOO...
YOU DON'T *HNN*... UNDERSTAND, POZHAR...
I DIDN'T *WANT* *HNNG* *AHHH...*
...YOU TO LET ME GO!

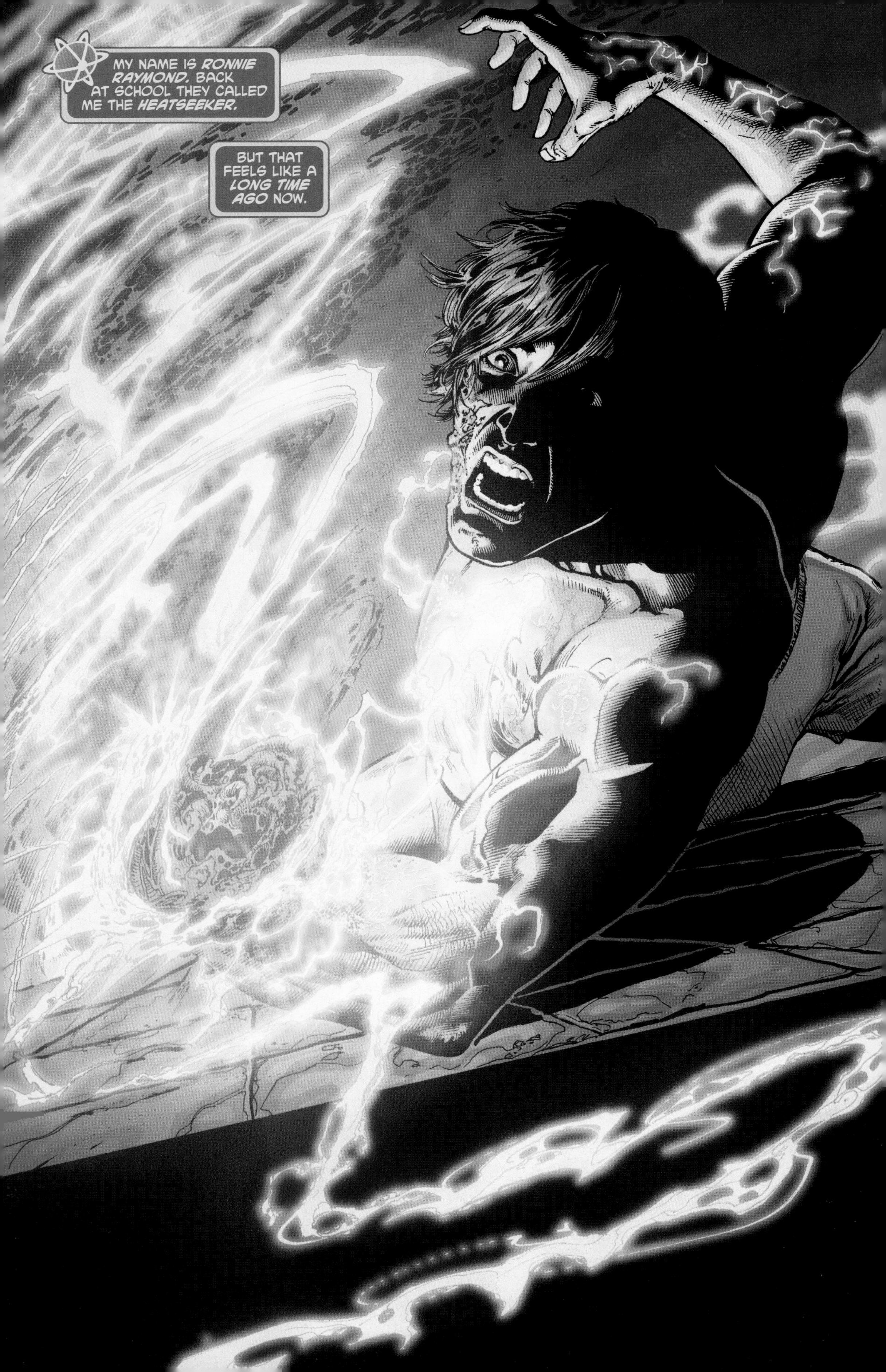
MY NAME IS RONNIE RAYMOND. BACK AT SCHOOL THEY CALLED ME THE HEATSEEKER.
BUT THAT FEELS LIKE A LONG TIME AGO NOW.

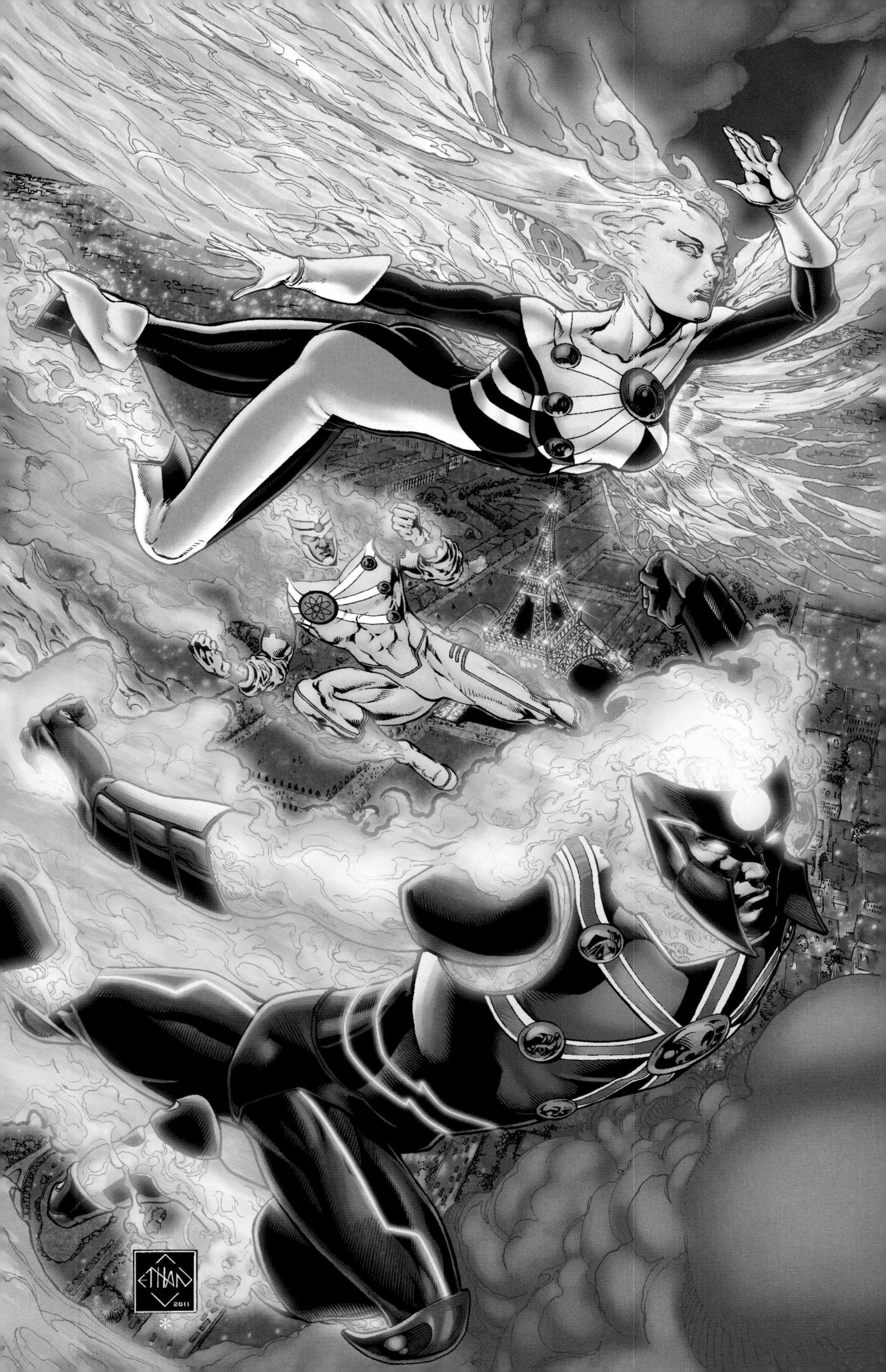

SOPHISTICATED TRAVELLERS

ETHAN VAN SCIVER & JOE HARRIS plot **JOE HARRIS** script **ETHAN VAN SCIVER** artist
cover by **ETHAN VAN SCIVER** with **HI-FI**

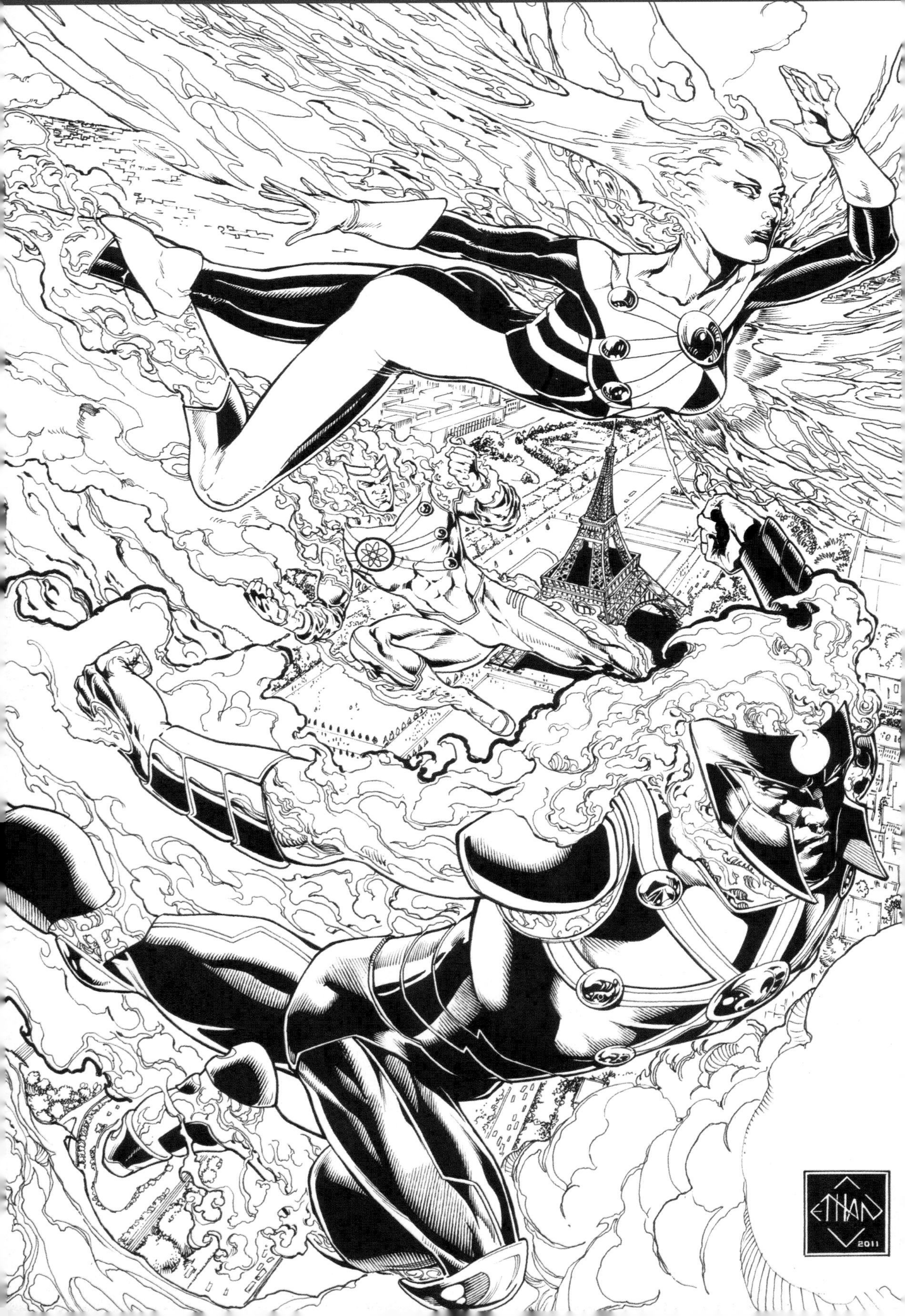
ETHAN
2011

RONALD? RONALD RAYMOND...?

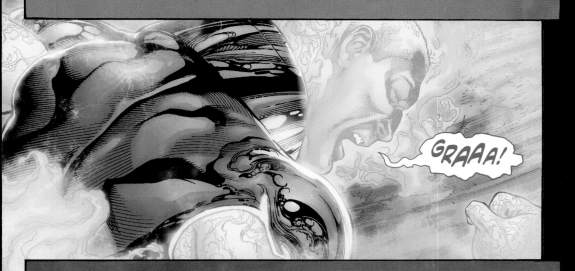

GRAAA!

CAN YOU *HEAR* ME...?

HNN...

I HOPE YOU ARE NOT DEAD *YET,* BOY...

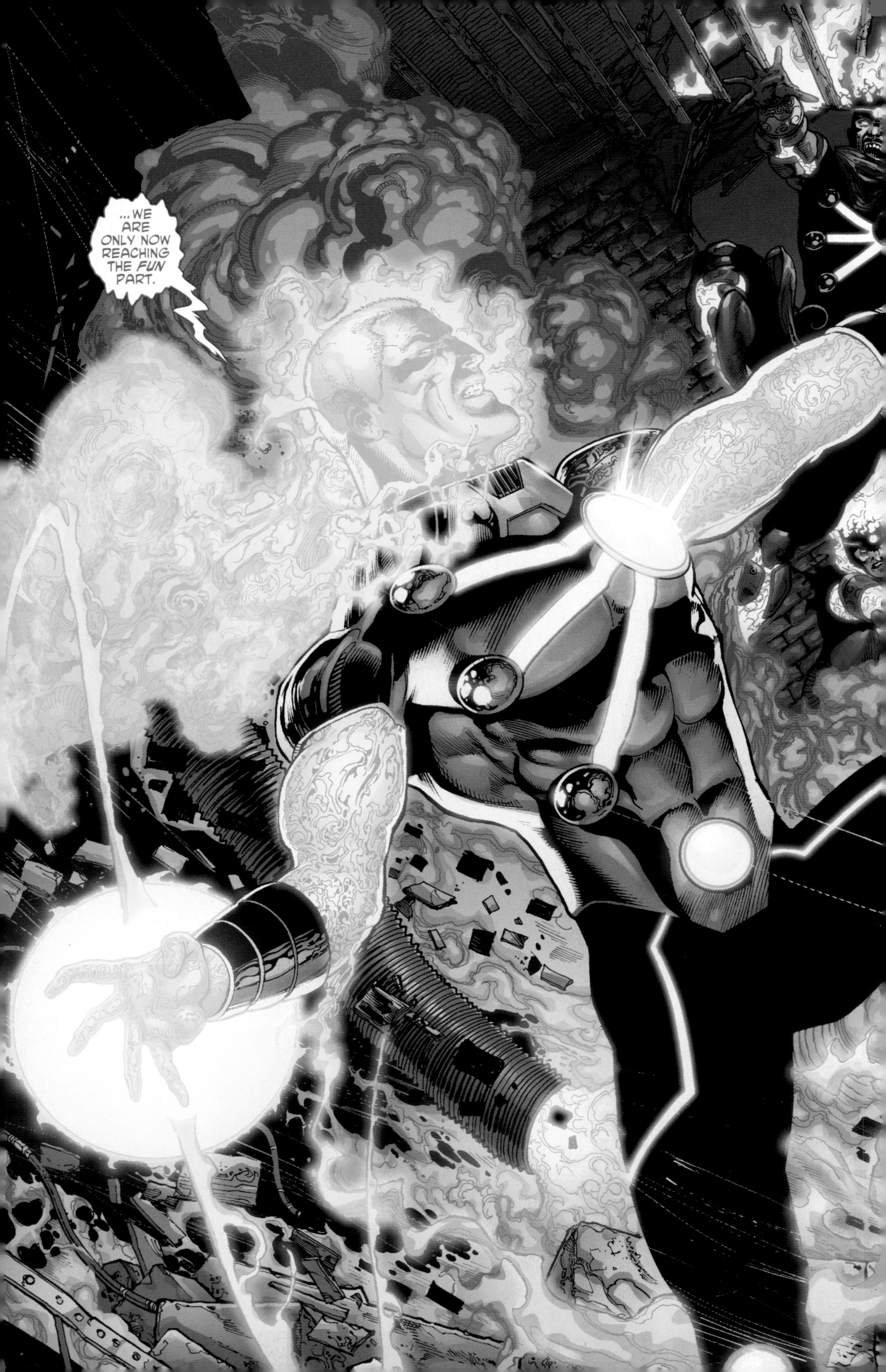
...WE ARE ONLY NOW REACHING THE FUN PART.

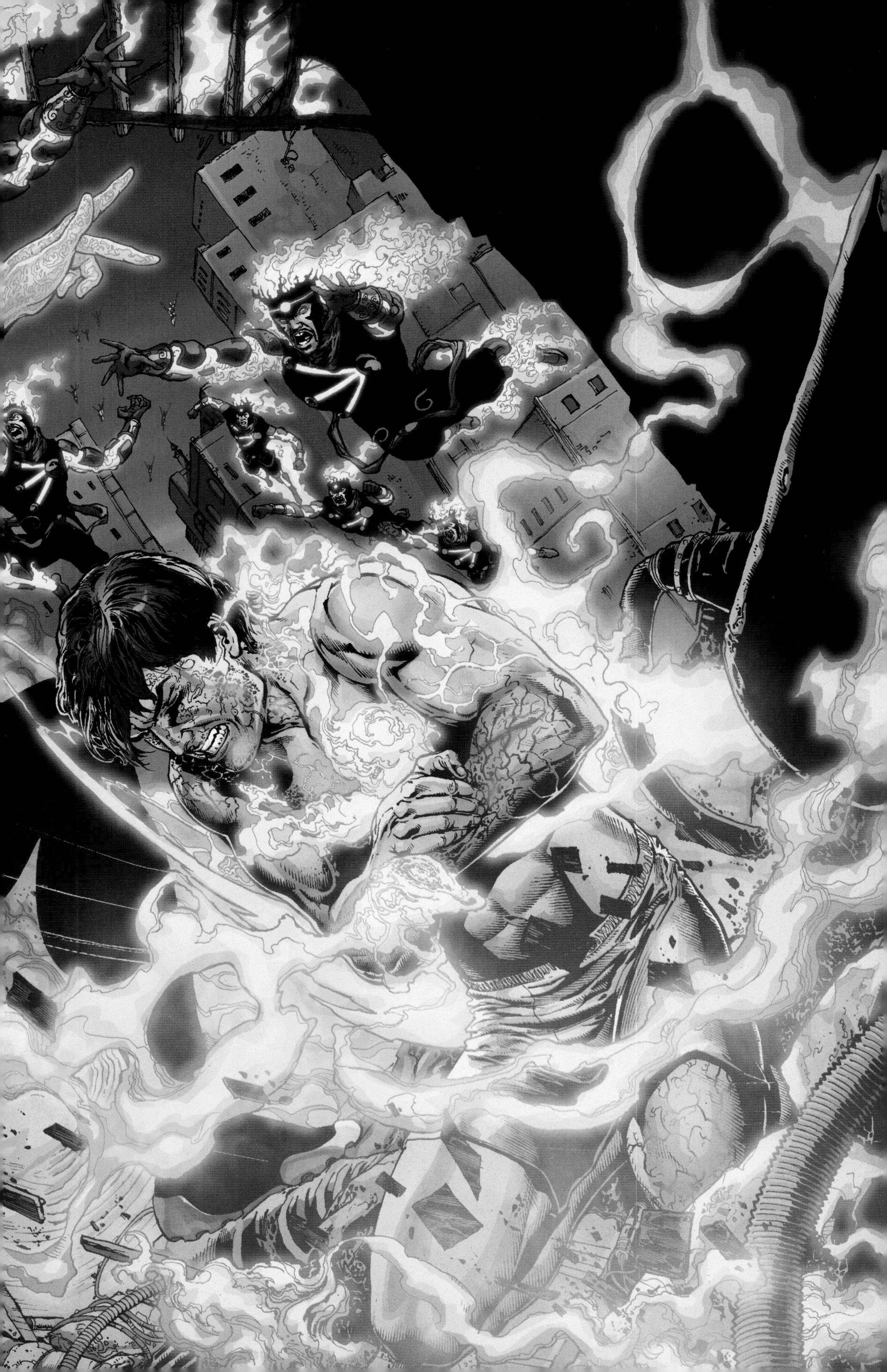

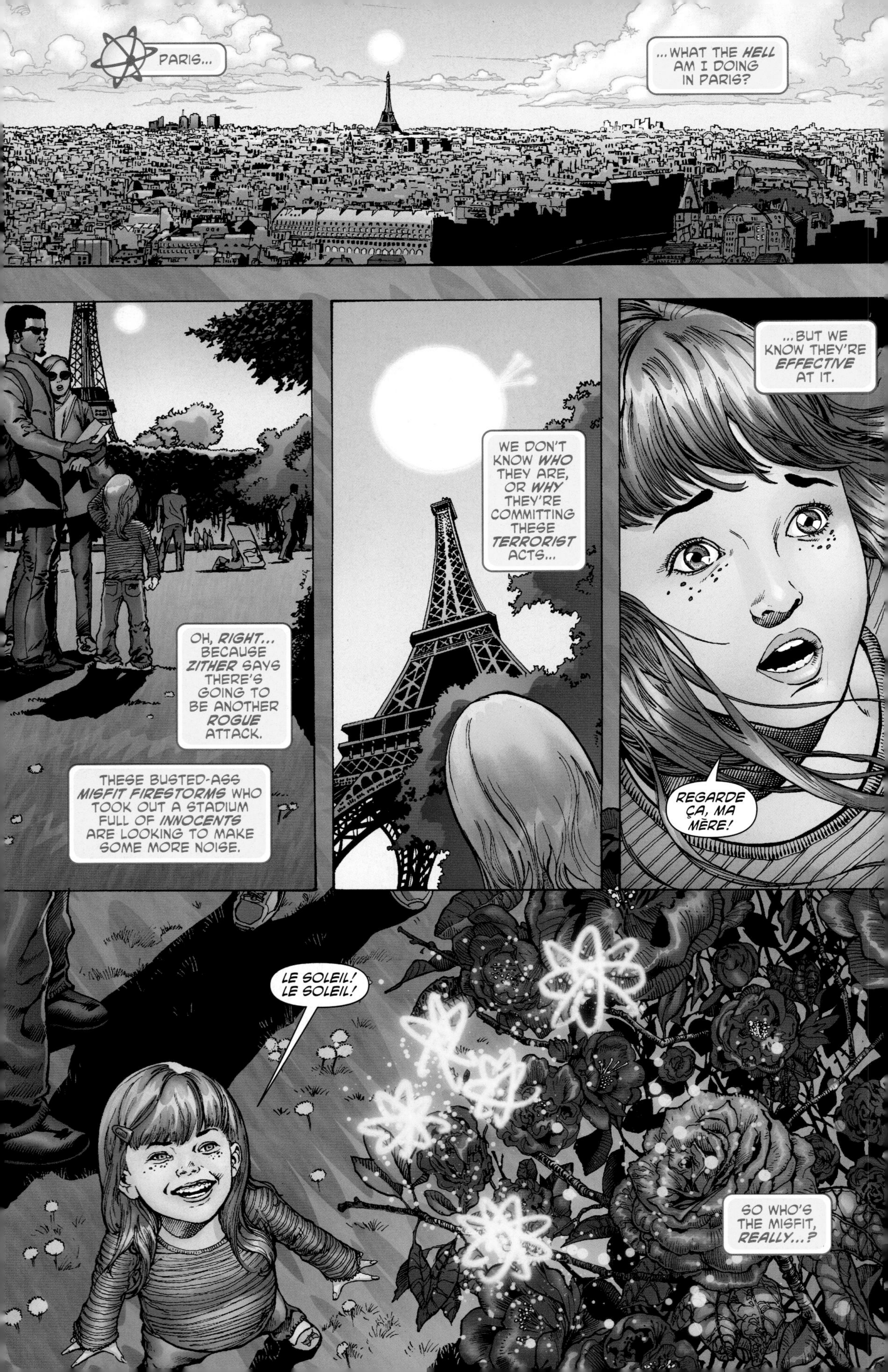
PARIS...
...WHAT THE HELL AM I DOING IN PARIS?
OH, RIGHT... BECAUSE ZITHER SAYS THERE'S GOING TO BE ANOTHER ROGUE ATTACK.
THESE BUSTED-ASS MISFIT FIRESTORMS WHO TOOK OUT A STADIUM FULL OF INNOCENTS ARE LOOKING TO MAKE SOME MORE NOISE.
WE DON'T KNOW WHO THEY ARE, OR WHY THEY'RE COMMITTING THESE TERRORIST ACTS...
...BUT WE KNOW THEY'RE EFFECTIVE AT IT.
REGARDE ÇA, MA MÈRE!
LE SOLEIL! LE SOLEIL!
SO WHO'S THE MISFIT, REALLY...?

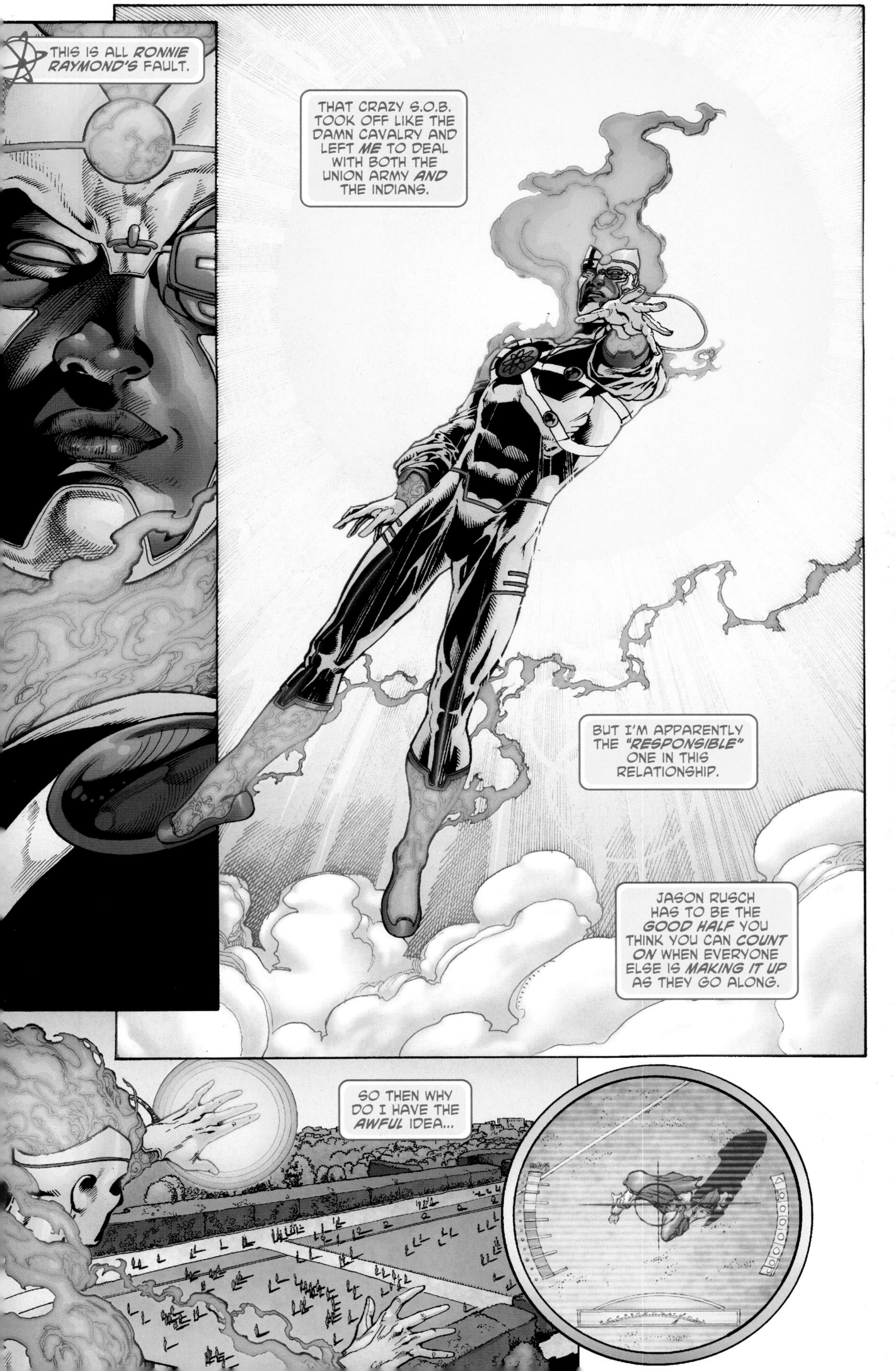
THIS IS ALL RONNIE RAYMOND'S FAULT.
THAT CRAZY S.O.B. TOOK OFF LIKE THE DAMN CAVALRY AND LEFT ME TO DEAL WITH BOTH THE UNION ARMY AND THE INDIANS.
BUT I'M APPARENTLY THE "RESPONSIBLE" ONE IN THIS RELATIONSHIP.
JASON RUSCH HAS TO BE THE GOOD HALF YOU THINK YOU CAN COUNT ON WHEN EVERYONE ELSE IS MAKING IT UP AS THEY GO ALONG.
SO THEN WHY DO I HAVE THE AWFUL IDEA...

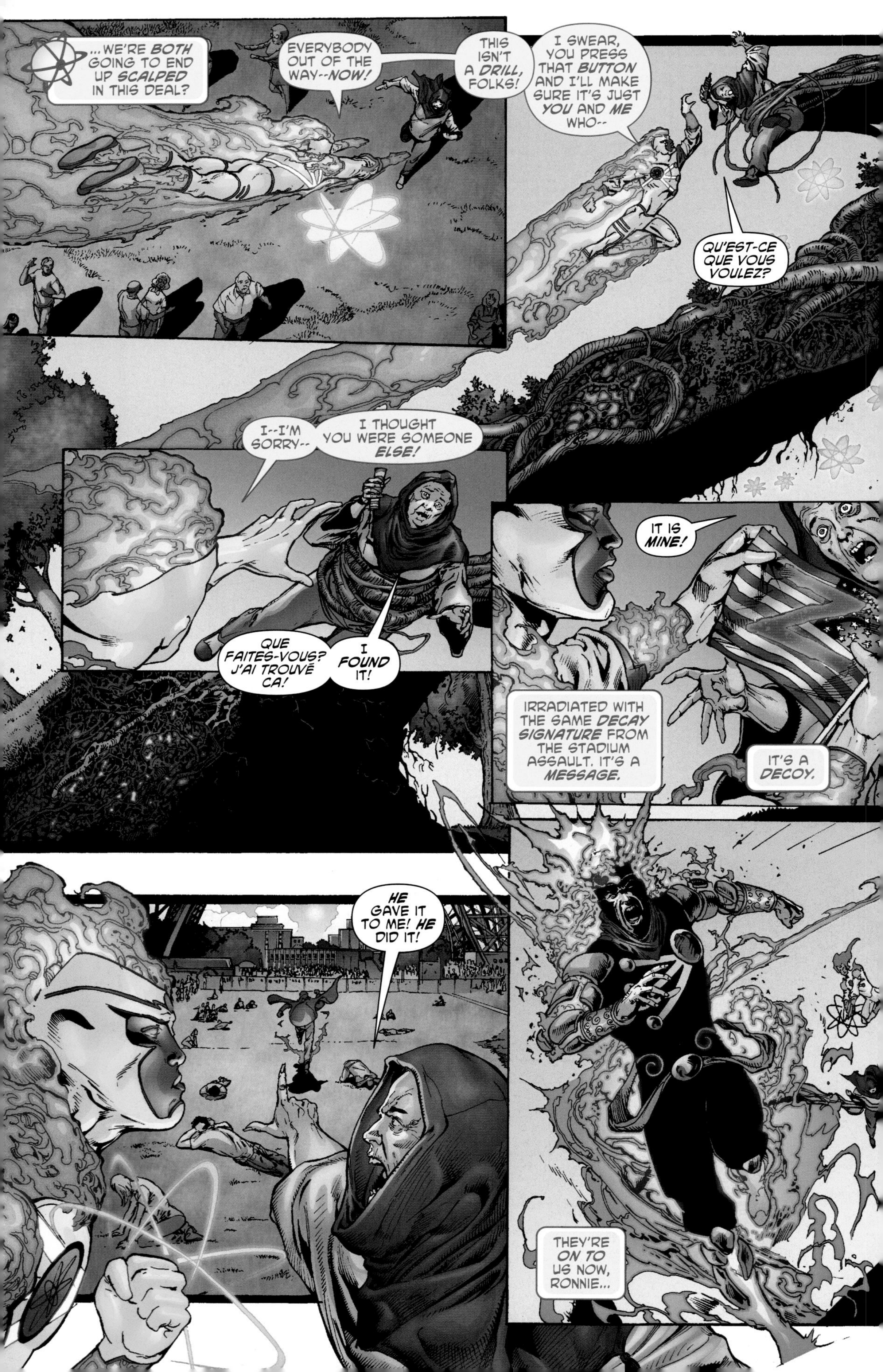
...WE'RE BOTH GOING TO END UP SCALPED IN THIS DEAL?
EVERYBODY OUT OF THE WAY--NOW!
THIS ISN'T A DRILL, FOLKS!
I SWEAR, YOU PRESS THAT BUTTON AND I'LL MAKE SURE IT'S JUST YOU AND ME WHO--
QU'EST-CE QUE VOUS VOULEZ?
I--I'M SORRY--
I THOUGHT YOU WERE SOMEONE ELSE!
QUE FAITES-VOUS? J'AI TROUVÉ ÇA!
I FOUND IT!
IT IS MINE!
IRRADIATED WITH THE SAME DECAY SIGNATURE FROM THE STADIUM ASSAULT. IT'S A MESSAGE.
IT'S A DECOY.
HE GAVE IT TO ME! HE DID IT!
THEY'RE ON TO US NOW, RONNIE...

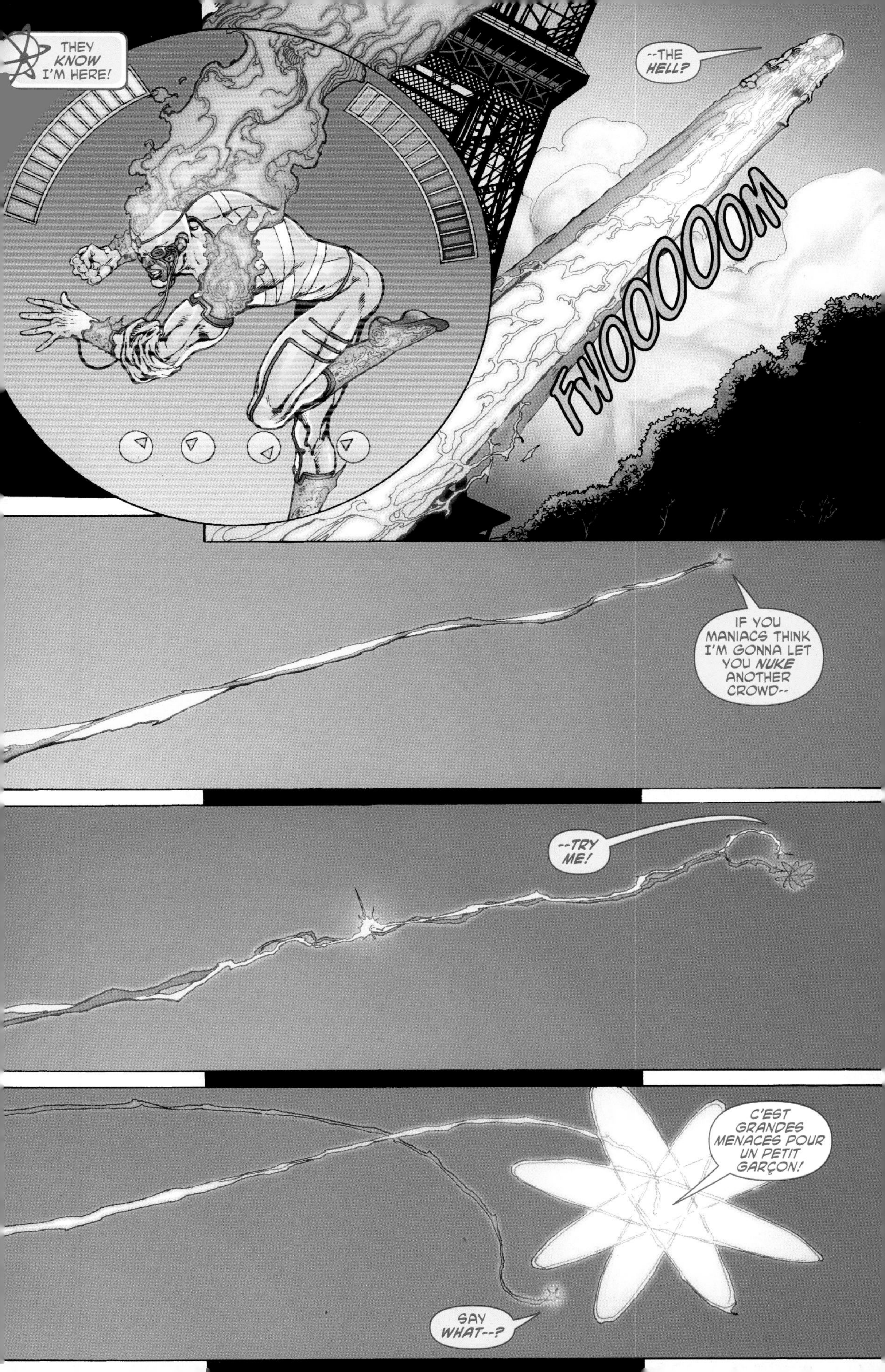
THEY KNOW I'M HERE!
--THE HELL?
FWOOOOOOM
IF YOU MANIACS THINK I'M GONNA LET YOU NUKE ANOTHER CROWD--
--TRY ME!
C'EST GRANDES MENACES POUR UN PETIT GARÇON!
SAY WHAT--?

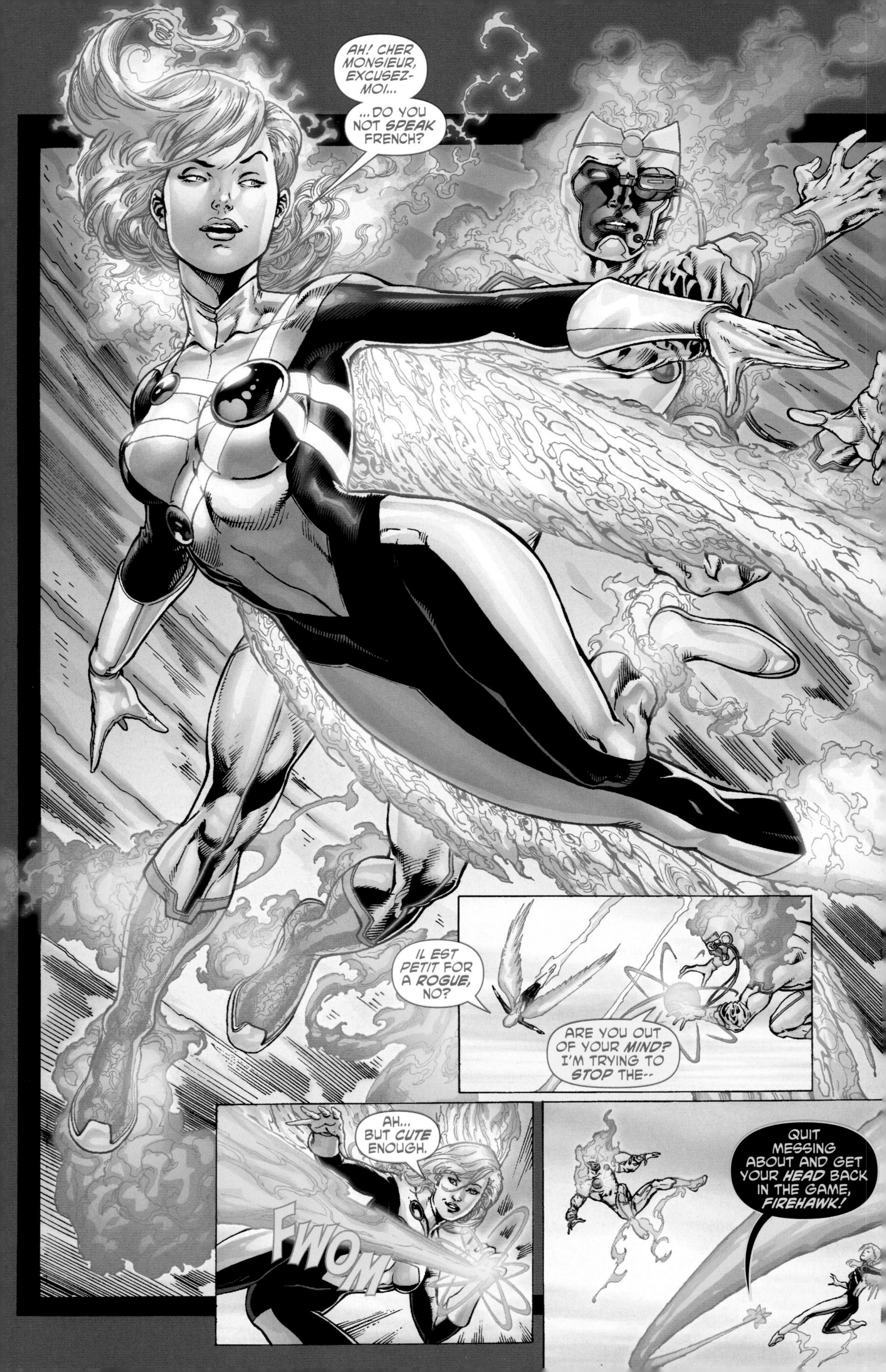
AH! CHER MONSIEUR, EXCUSEZ-MOI...
...DO YOU NOT SPEAK FRENCH?
IL EST PETIT FOR A ROGUE, NO?
ARE YOU OUT OF YOUR MIND? I'M TRYING TO STOP THE--
AH... BUT CUTE ENOUGH.
FWOM
QUIT MESSING ABOUT AND GET YOUR HEAD BACK IN THE GAME, FIREHAWK!

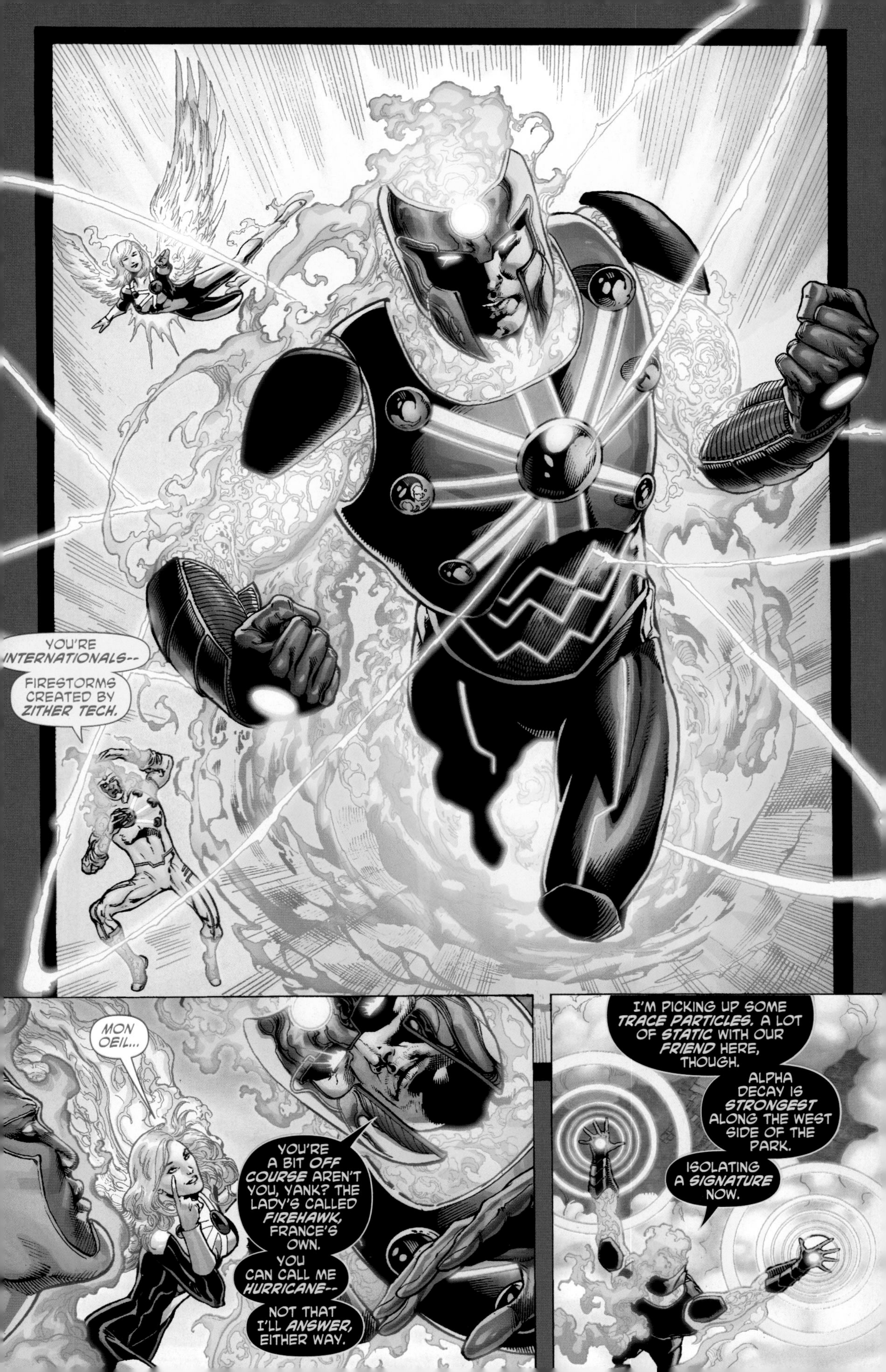
YOU'RE INTERNATIONALS--
FIRESTORMS CREATED BY ZITHER TECH.
MON OEIL...
YOU'RE A BIT OFF COURSE AREN'T YOU, YANK? THE LADY'S CALLED FIREHAWK, FRANCE'S OWN.
YOU CAN CALL ME HURRICANE--
NOT THAT I'LL ANSWER, EITHER WAY.
I'M PICKING UP SOME TRACE PARTICLES. A LOT OF STATIC WITH OUR FRIEND HERE, THOUGH.
ALPHA DECAY IS STRONGEST ALONG THE WEST SIDE OF THE PARK.
ISOLATING A SIGNATURE NOW.

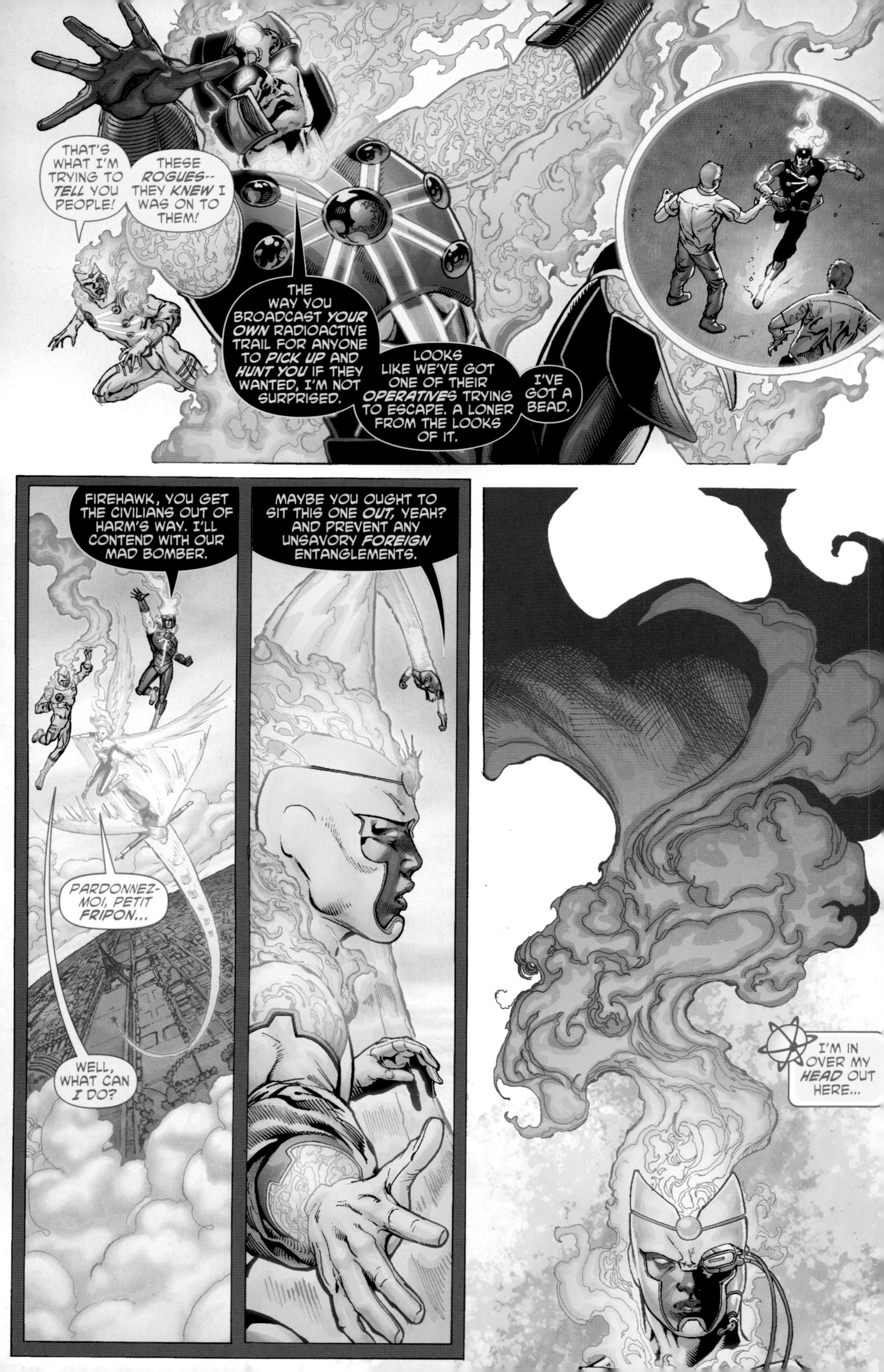
THAT'S WHAT I'M TRYING TO TELL YOU PEOPLE!
THESE ROGUES-- THEY KNEW I WAS ON TO THEM!
THE WAY YOU BROADCAST YOUR OWN RADIOACTIVE TRAIL FOR ANYONE TO PICK UP AND HUNT YOU IF THEY WANTED, I'M NOT SURPRISED.
LOOKS LIKE WE'VE GOT ONE OF THEIR OPERATIVES TRYING TO ESCAPE. A LONER FROM THE LOOKS OF IT.
I'VE GOT A BEAD.
FIREHAWK, YOU GET THE CIVILIANS OUT OF HARM'S WAY. I'LL CONTEND WITH OUR MAD BOMBER.
PARDONNEZ-MOI, PETIT FRIPON...
WELL, WHAT CAN I DO?
MAYBE YOU OUGHT TO SIT THIS ONE OUT, YEAH? AND PREVENT ANY UNSAVORY FOREIGN ENTANGLEMENTS.
I'M IN OVER MY HEAD OUT HERE...

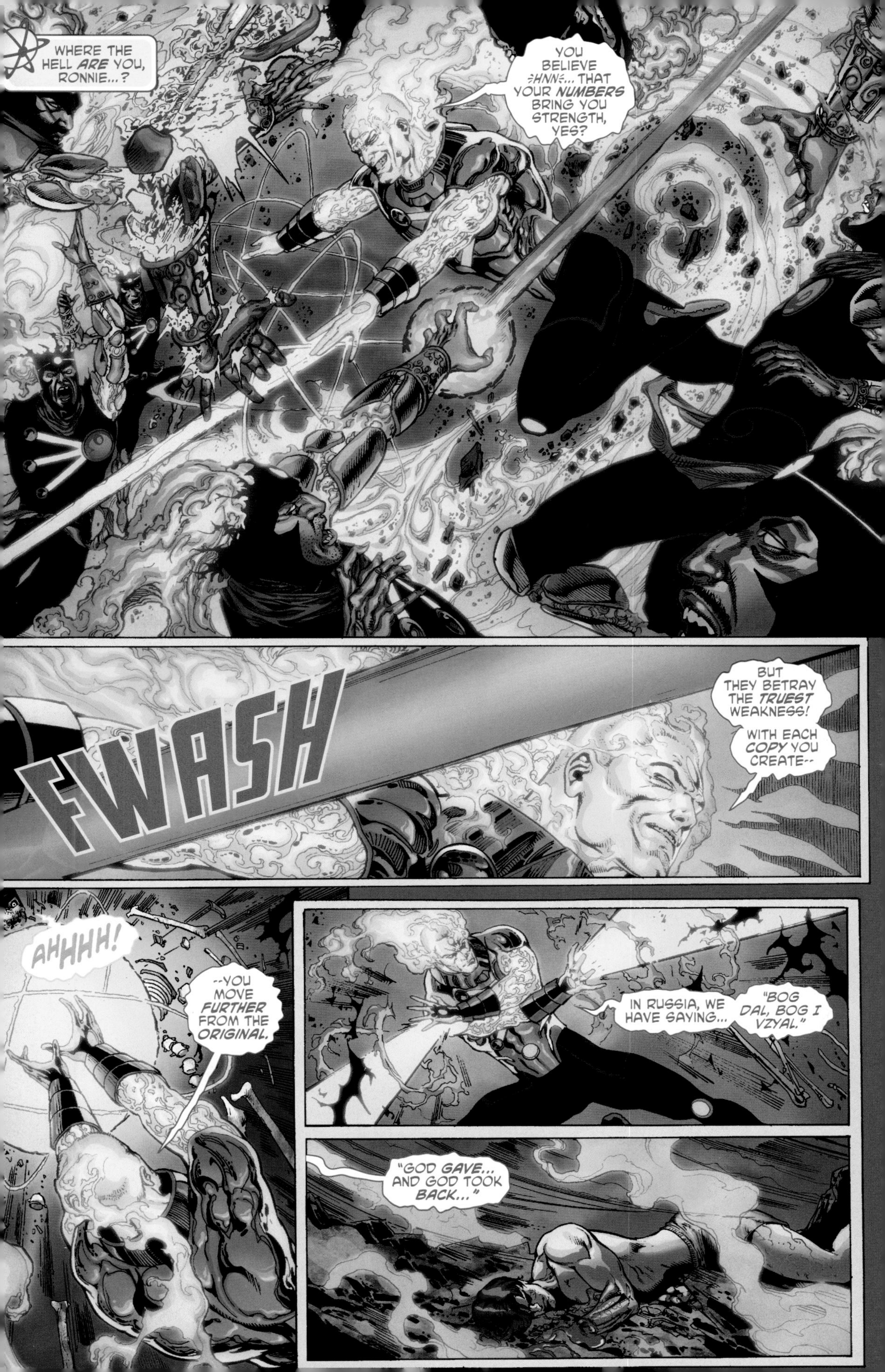
WHERE THE HELL *ARE* YOU, RONNIE...?
YOU BELIEVE *HNN*... THAT YOUR *NUMBERS* BRING YOU STRENGTH, YES?
FWASH
BUT THEY BETRAY THE *TRUEST* WEAKNESS!
WITH EACH *COPY* YOU CREATE--
AHHHH!
--YOU MOVE *FURTHER* FROM THE *ORIGINAL.*
IN RUSSIA, WE HAVE SAYING...
"BOG DAL, BOG I VZYAL."
"GOD *GAVE*... AND GOD TOOK *BACK*..."

YOU NEED TO *FOCUS,* RONALD...

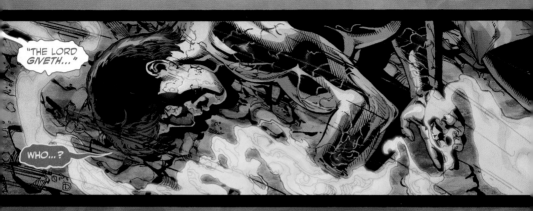

"THE LORD *GIVETH...*"

WHO...?

CONCENTRATE!

"...AND HE *TAKETH* AWAY!"

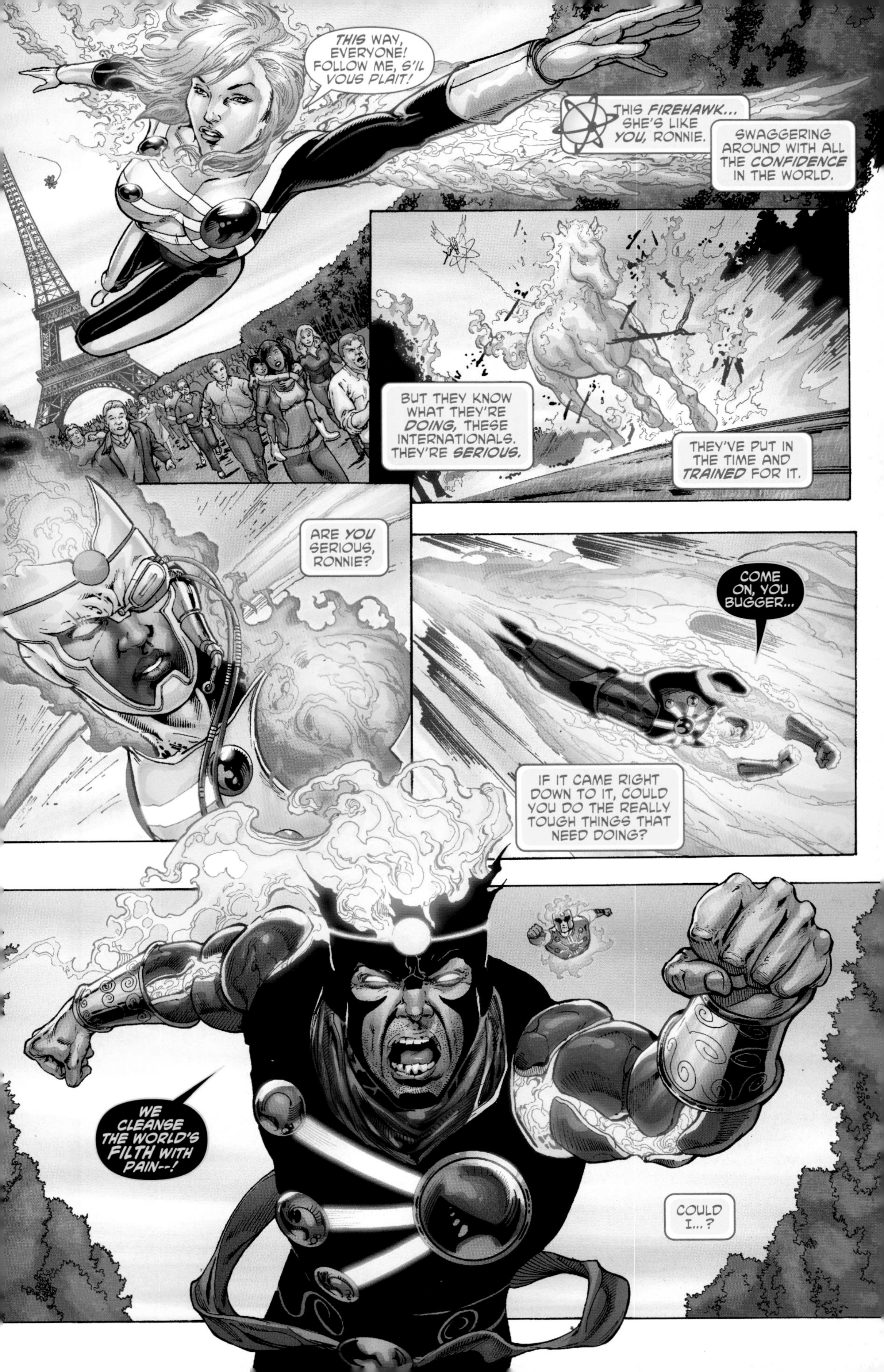
THIS WAY, EVERYONE! FOLLOW ME, S'IL VOUS PLAIT!
THIS FIREHAWK... SHE'S LIKE YOU, RONNIE.
SWAGGERING AROUND WITH ALL THE CONFIDENCE IN THE WORLD.
BUT THEY KNOW WHAT THEY'RE DOING, THESE INTERNATIONALS. THEY'RE SERIOUS.
THEY'VE PUT IN THE TIME AND TRAINED FOR IT.
ARE YOU SERIOUS, RONNIE?
COME ON, YOU BUGGER...
IF IT CAME RIGHT DOWN TO IT, COULD YOU DO THE REALLY TOUGH THINGS THAT NEED DOING?
WE CLEANSE THE WORLD'S FILTH WITH PAIN--!
COULD I...?

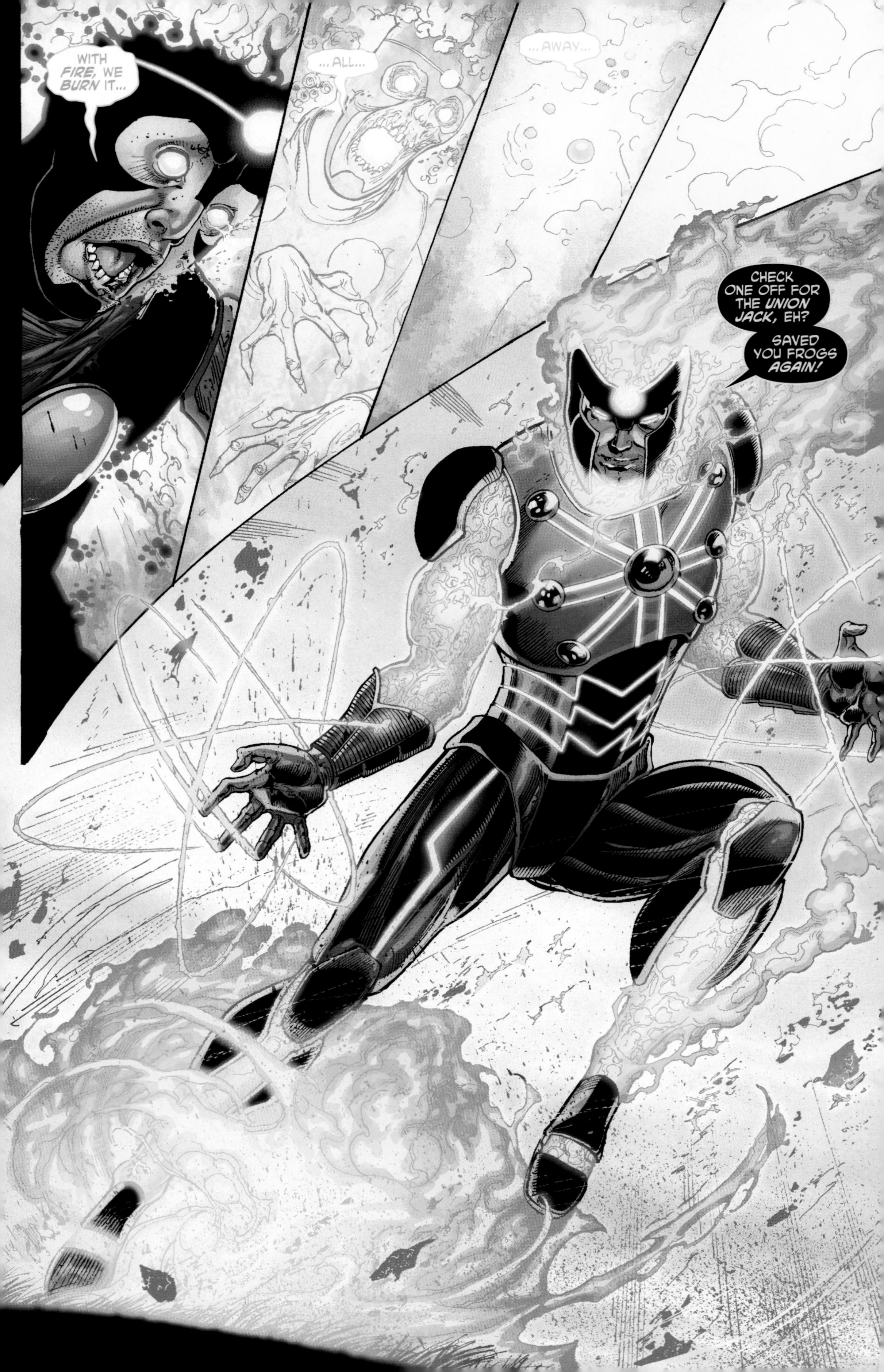
WITH FIRE, WE BURN IT...
...ALL...
...AWAY...
CHECK ONE OFF FOR THE UNION JACK, EH?
SAVED YOU FROGS AGAIN!

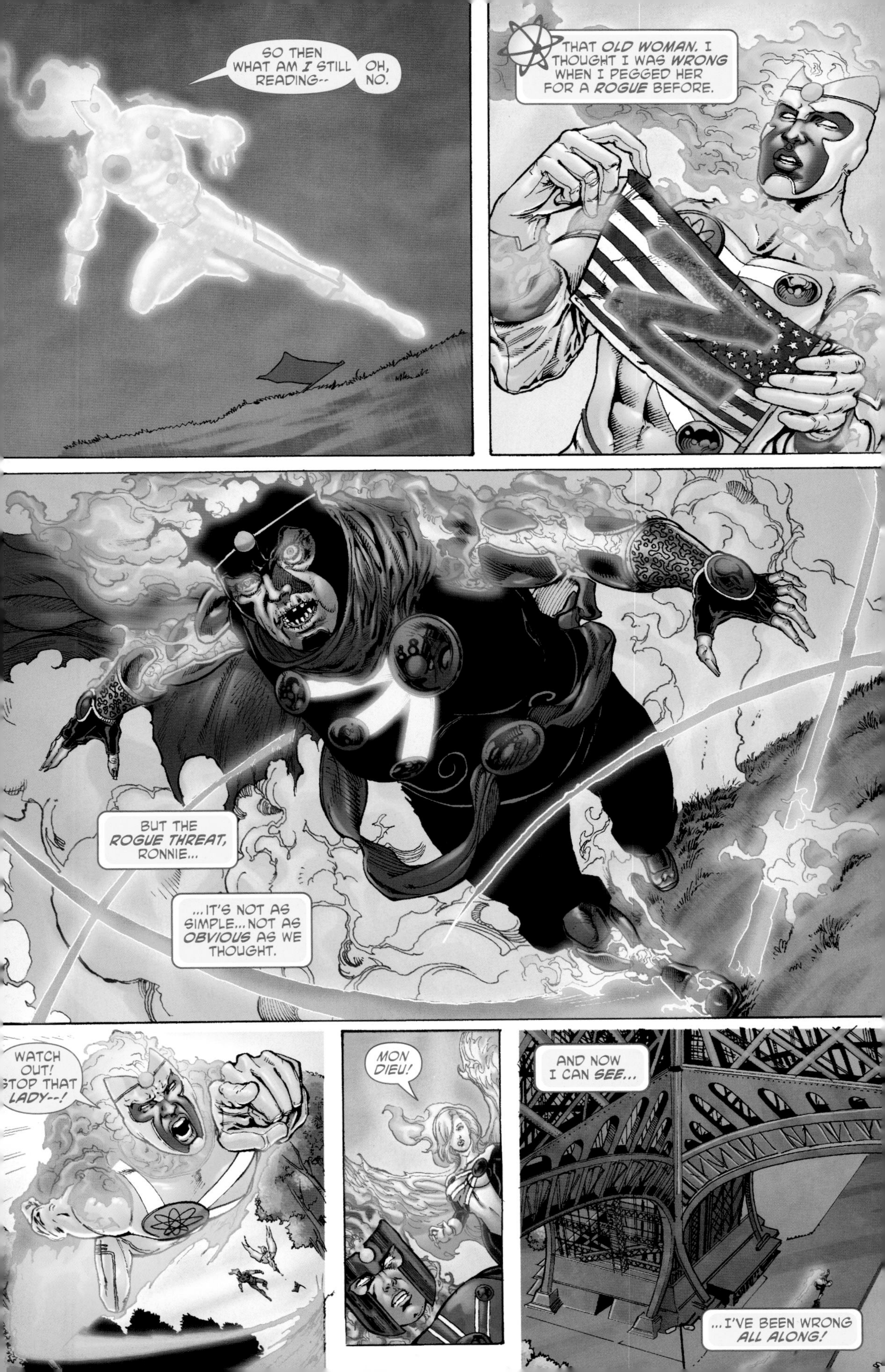

SO THEN WHAT AM I STILL READING--
OH, NO.
THAT OLD WOMAN. I THOUGHT I WAS WRONG WHEN I PEGGED HER FOR A ROGUE BEFORE.
BUT THE ROGUE THREAT, RONNIE...
...IT'S NOT AS SIMPLE...NOT AS OBVIOUS AS WE THOUGHT.
WATCH OUT! STOP THAT LADY--!
MON DIEU!
AND NOW I CAN SEE...
...I'VE BEEN WRONG ALL ALONG!

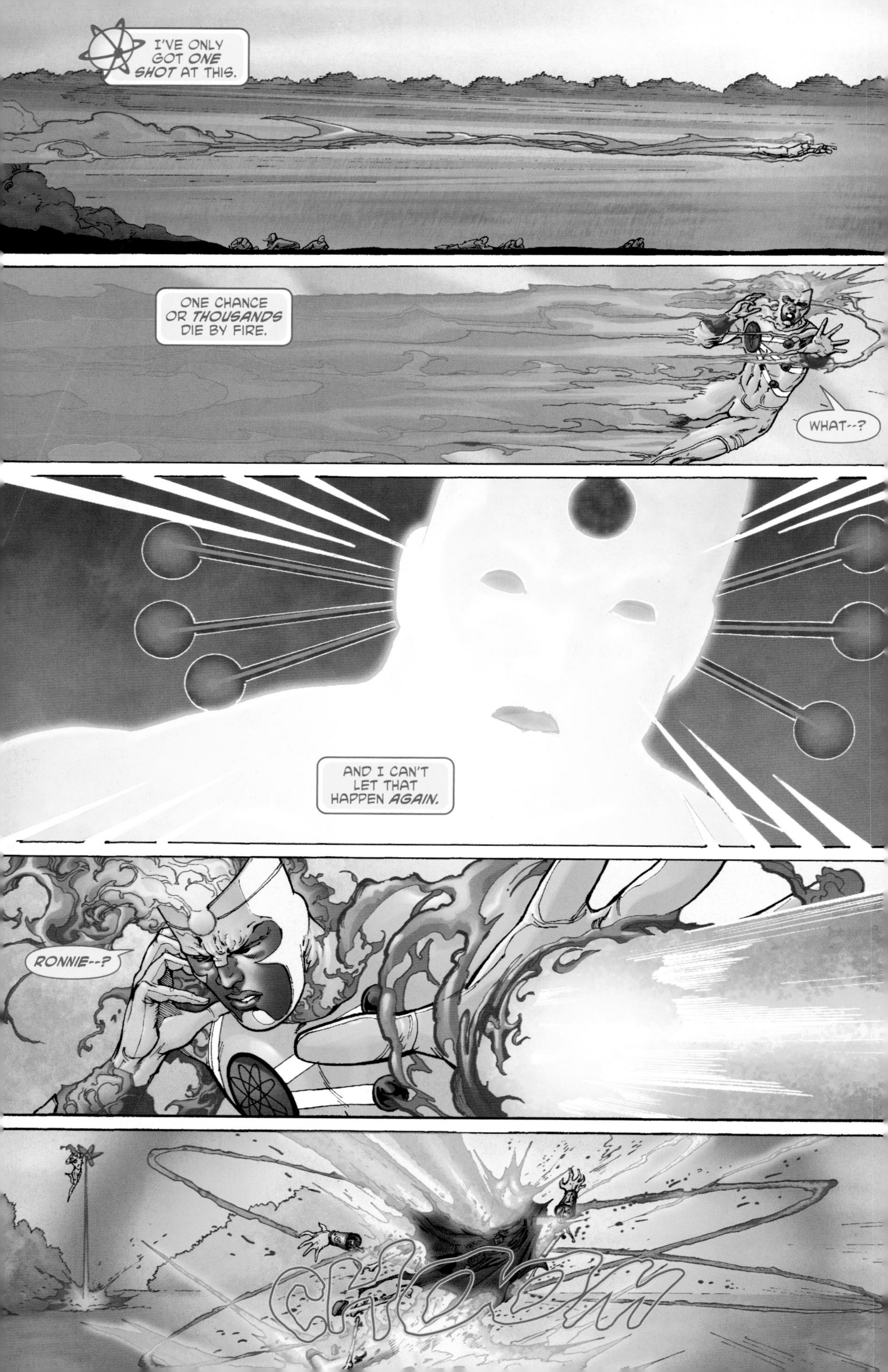
I'VE ONLY GOT *ONE SHOT* AT THIS.
ONE CHANCE OR *THOUSANDS* DIE BY FIRE.
WHAT--?
AND I CAN'T LET THAT HAPPEN *AGAIN.*
RONNIE--?
CHOOOM

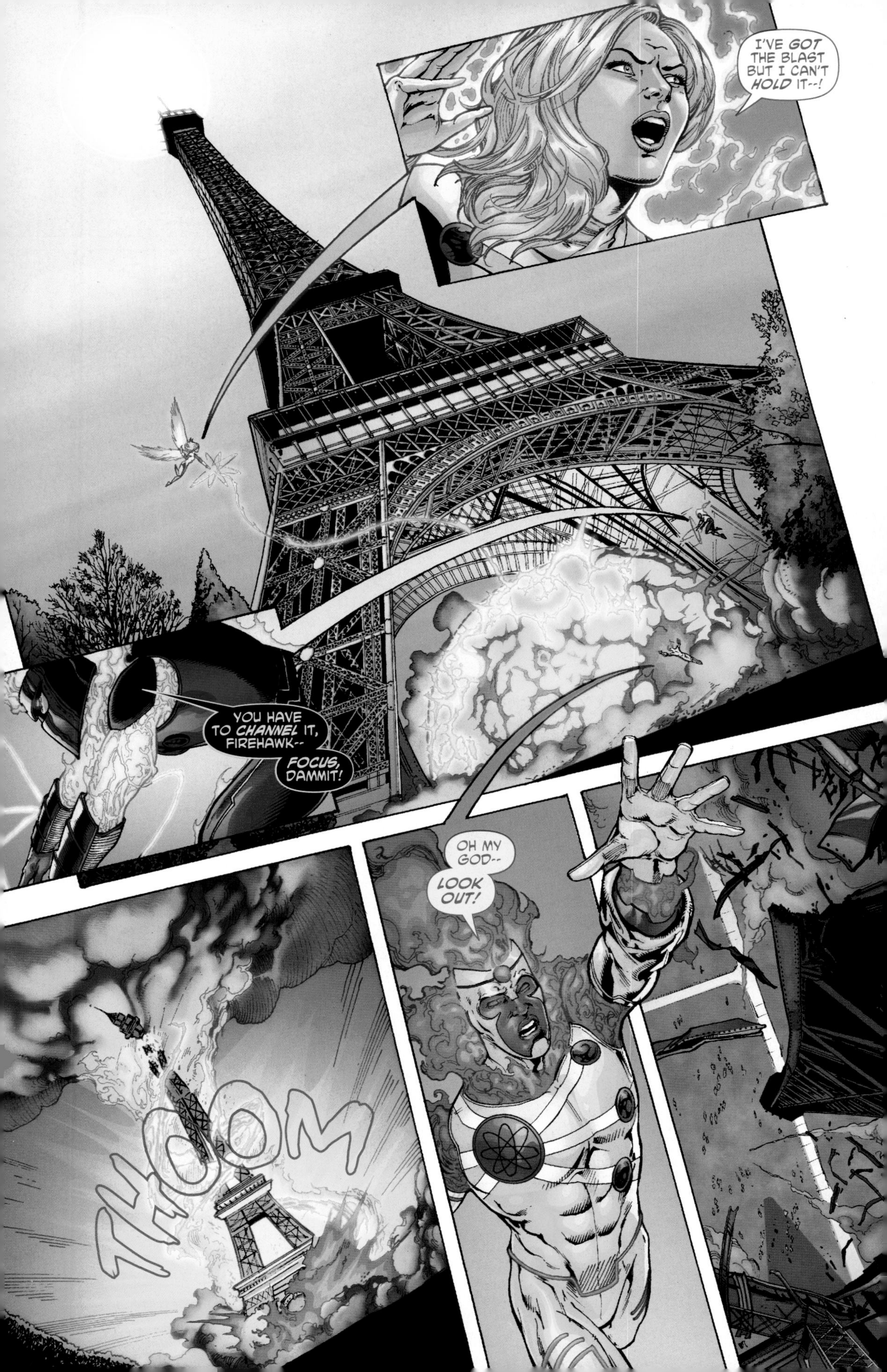
I'VE GOT THE BLAST BUT I CAN'T HOLD IT--!
YOU HAVE TO CHANNEL IT, FIREHAWK--
FOCUS, DAMMIT!
THOOM
OH MY GOD--
LOOK OUT!

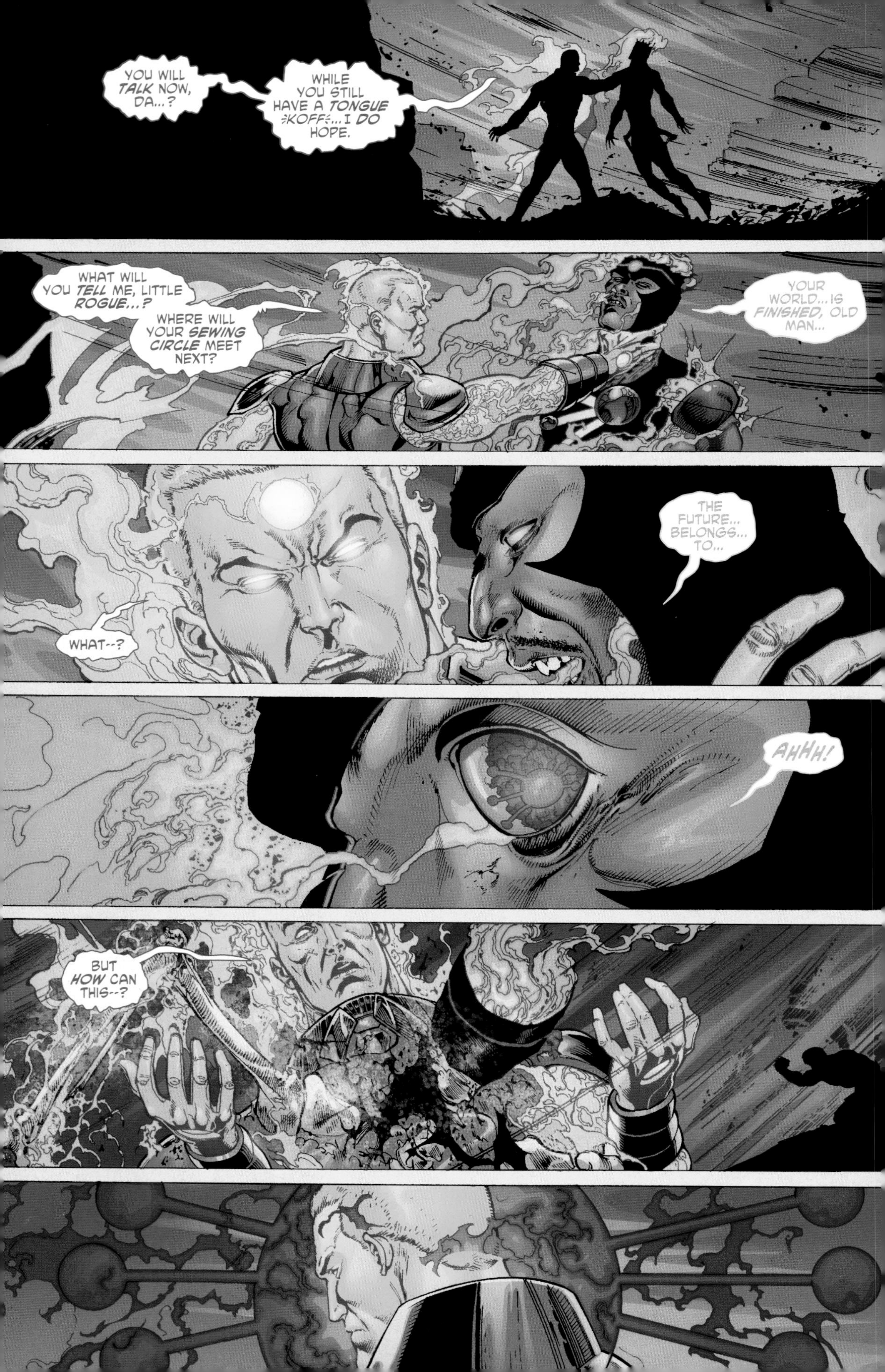
YOU WILL TALK NOW, DA...?
WHILE YOU STILL HAVE A TONGUE ≠KOFF≠...I DO HOPE.
WHAT WILL YOU TELL ME, LITTLE ROGUE...?
WHERE WILL YOUR SEWING CIRCLE MEET NEXT?
YOUR WORLD...IS FINISHED, OLD MAN...
THE FUTURE... BELONGS... TO...
WHAT--?
AHHH!
BUT HOW CAN THIS--?

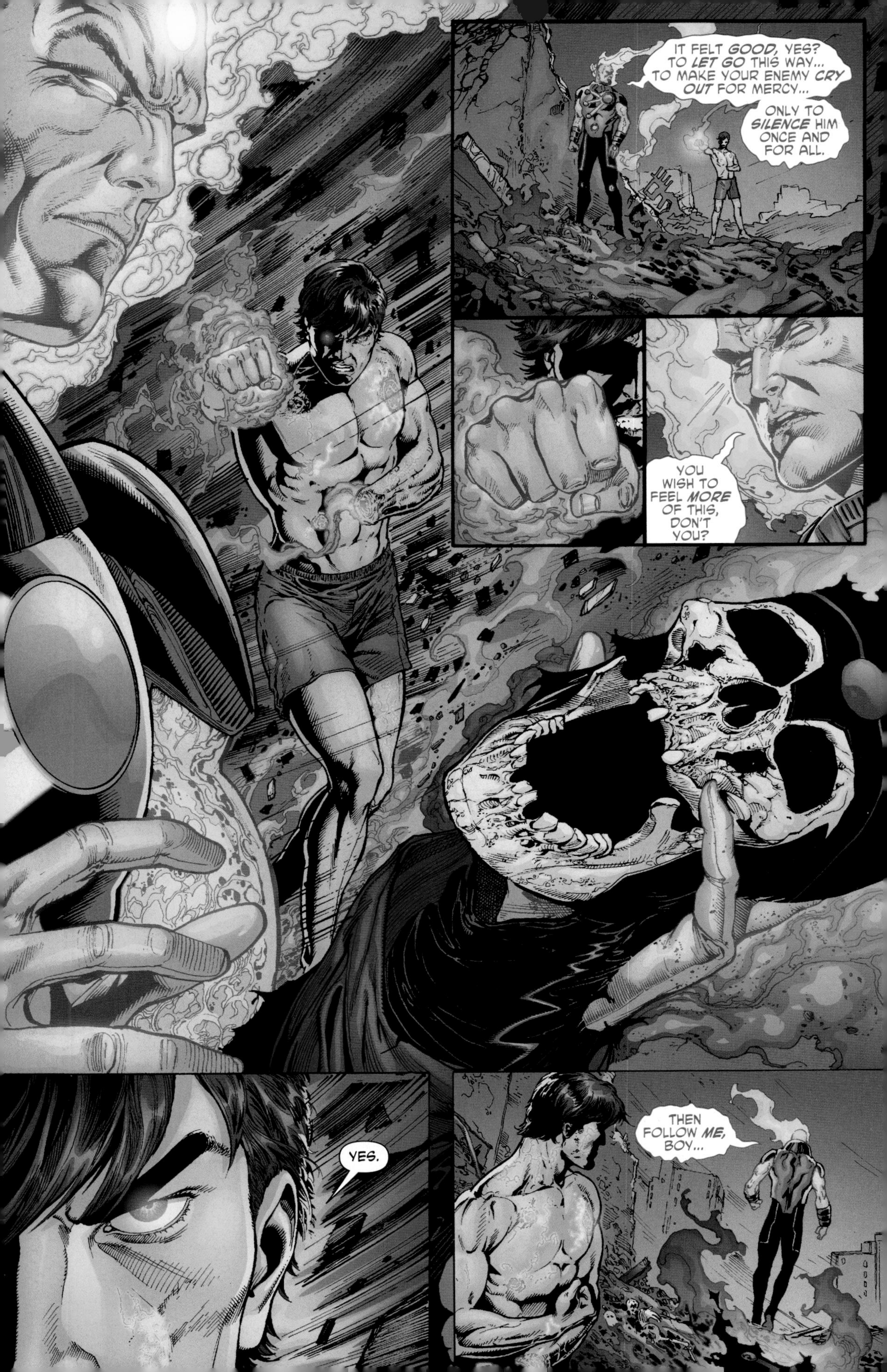
IT FELT GOOD, YES? TO LET GO THIS WAY... TO MAKE YOUR ENEMY CRY OUT FOR MERCY...
ONLY TO SILENCE HIM ONCE AND FOR ALL.
YOU WISH TO FEEL MORE OF THIS, DON'T YOU?
YES.
THEN FOLLOW ME, BOY...

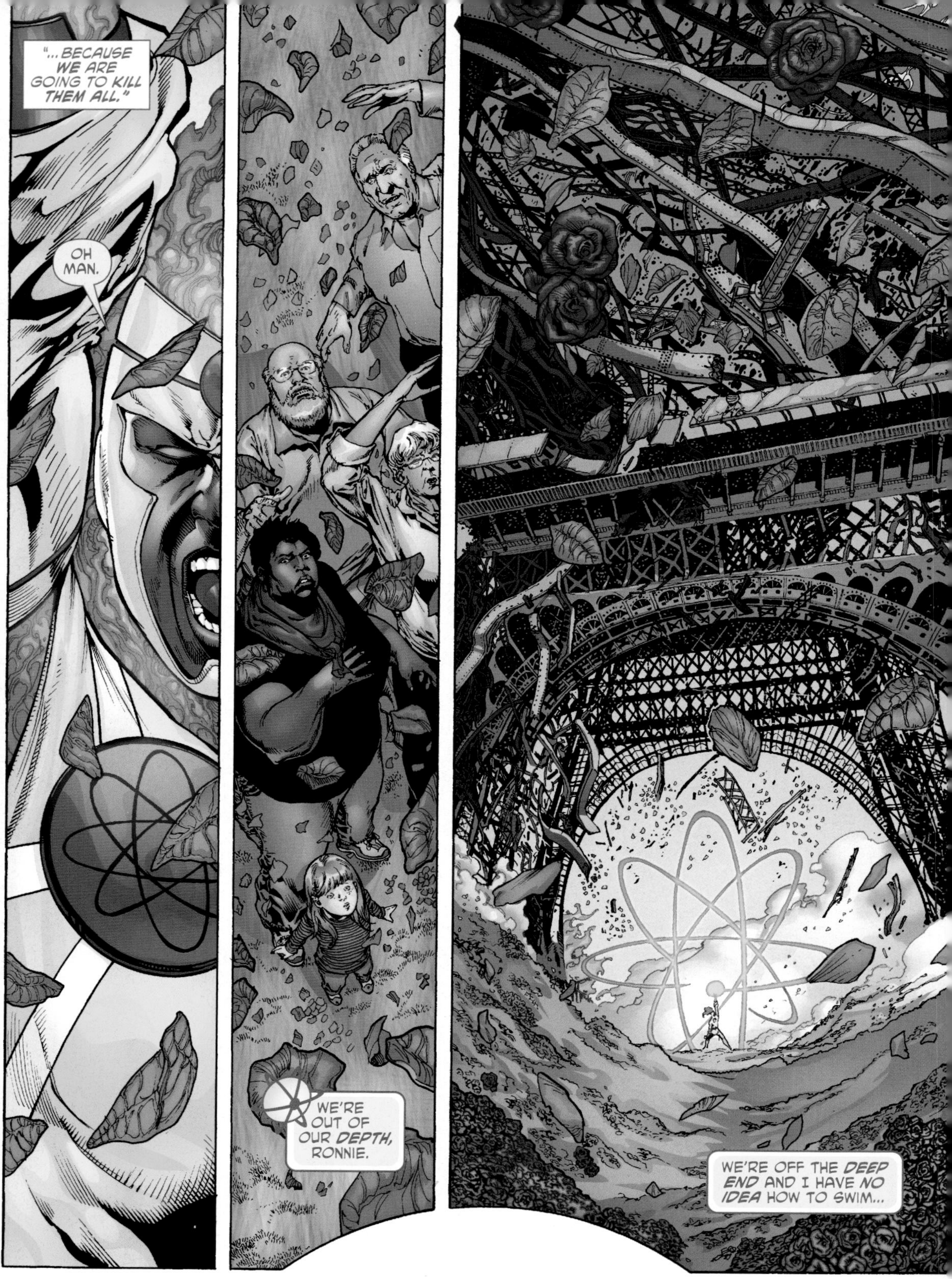
"...BECAUSE WE ARE GOING TO KILL THEM ALL."
OH MAN.
WE'RE OUT OF OUR DEPTH, RONNIE.
WE'RE OFF THE DEEP END AND I HAVE NO IDEA HOW TO SWIM...

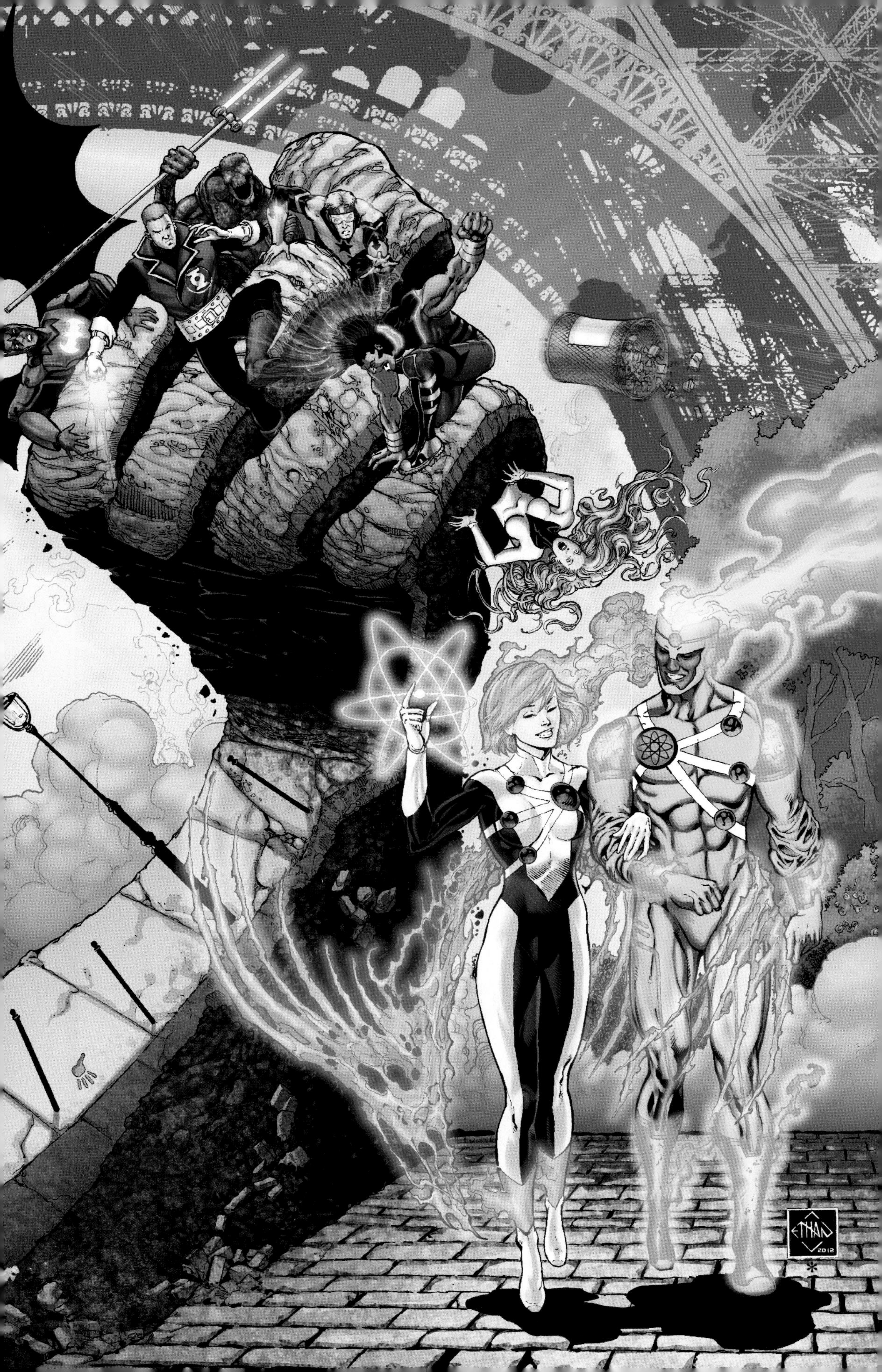
ETHAN
2012

INTERNATIONAL INCIDENT

ETHAN VAN SCIVER & JOE HARRIS plot **JOE HARRIS** script **YILDIRAY CINAR** penciller **MARLO ALQUIZA & NORM RAPMUND** inkers
cover by **ETHAN VAN SCIVER** with **HI-FI**

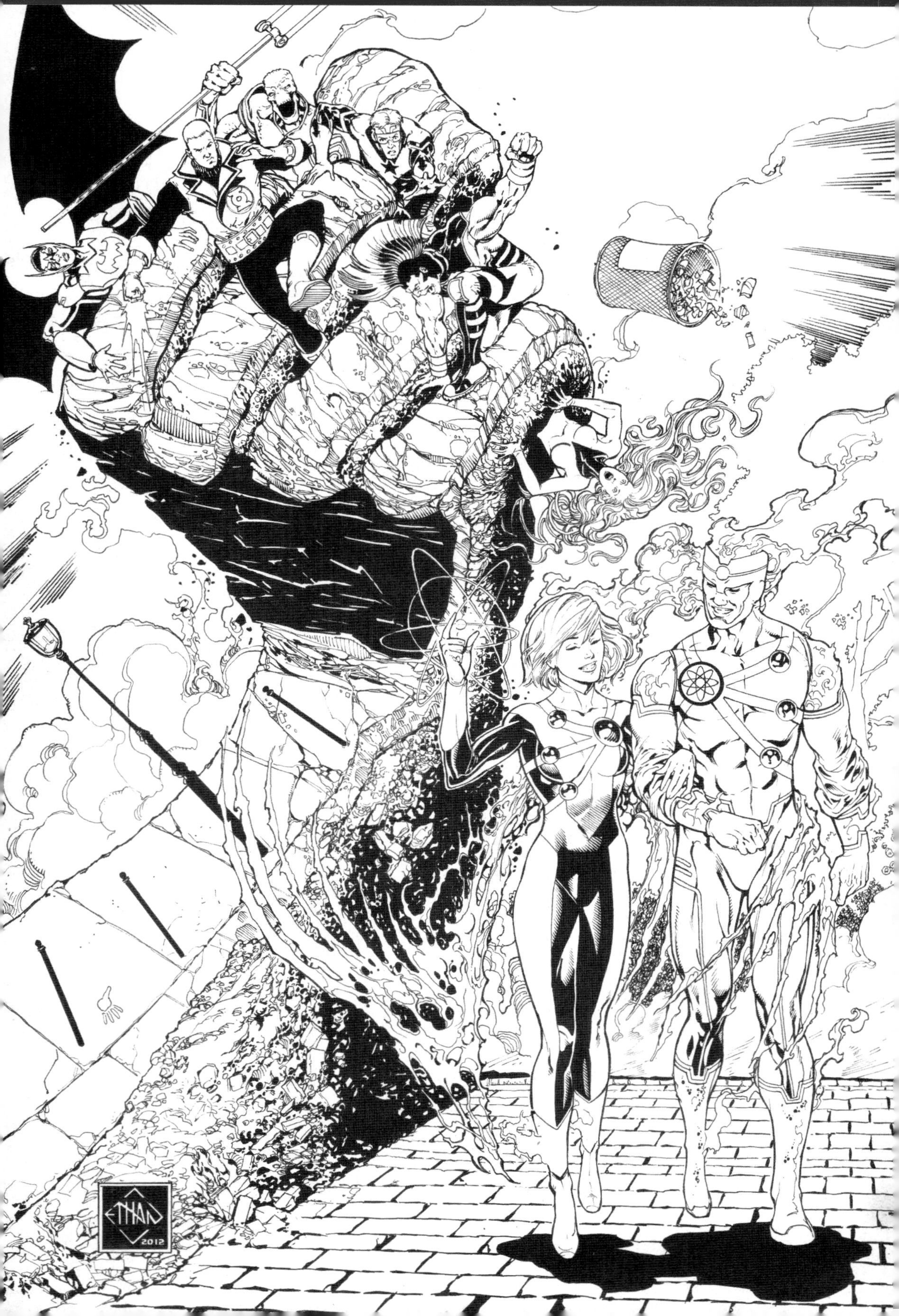
ETHAN
2012

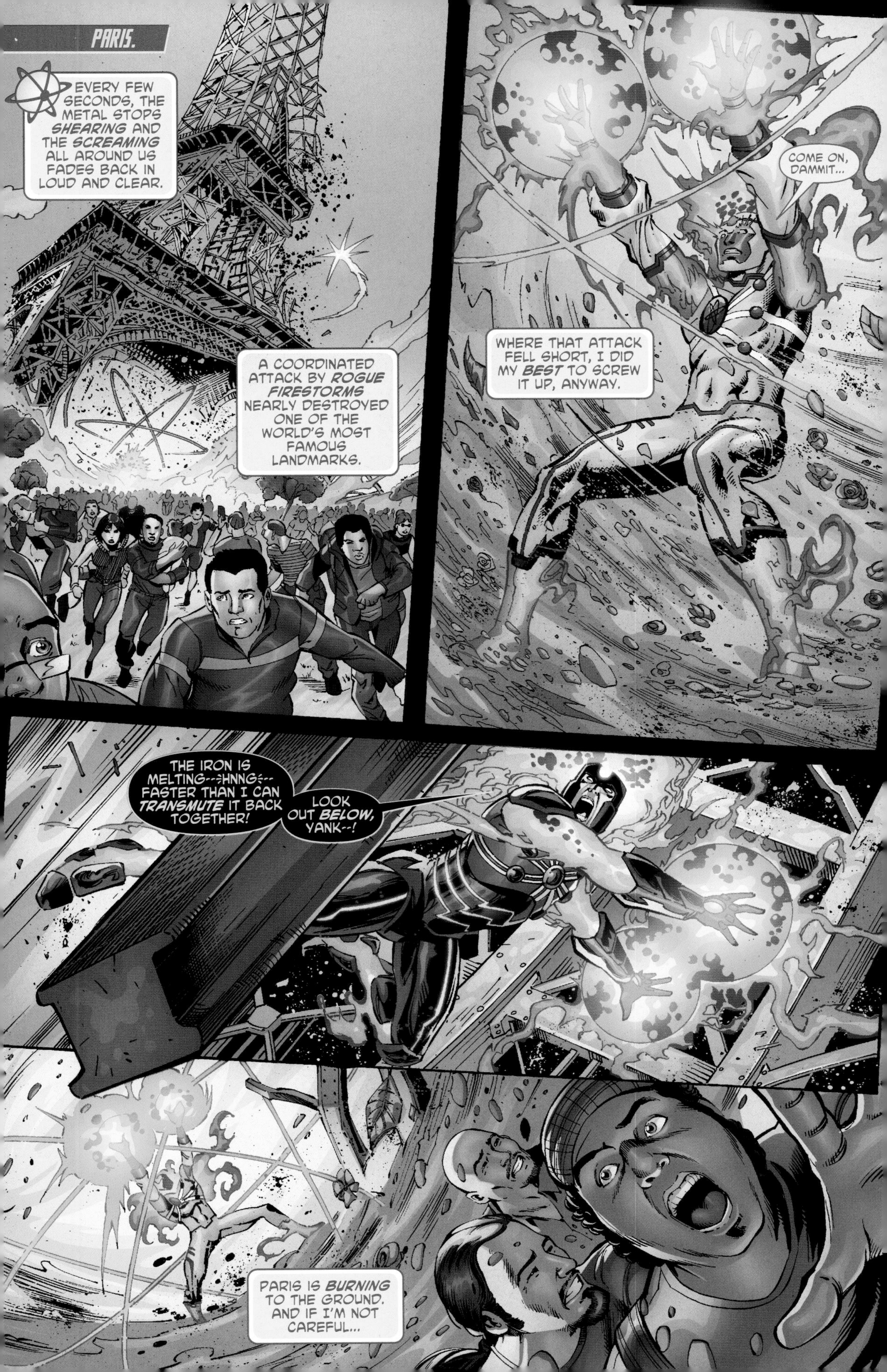
PARIS.
EVERY FEW SECONDS, THE METAL STOPS SHEARING AND THE SCREAMING ALL AROUND US FADES BACK IN LOUD AND CLEAR.
A COORDINATED ATTACK BY ROGUE FIRESTORMS NEARLY DESTROYED ONE OF THE WORLD'S MOST FAMOUS LANDMARKS.
COME ON, DAMMIT...
WHERE THAT ATTACK FELL SHORT, I DID MY BEST TO SCREW IT UP, ANYWAY.
THE IRON IS MELTING--HHNG--FASTER THAN I CAN TRANSMUTE IT BACK TOGETHER!
LOOK OUT BELOW, YANK--!
PARIS IS BURNING TO THE GROUND. AND IF I'M NOT CAREFUL...

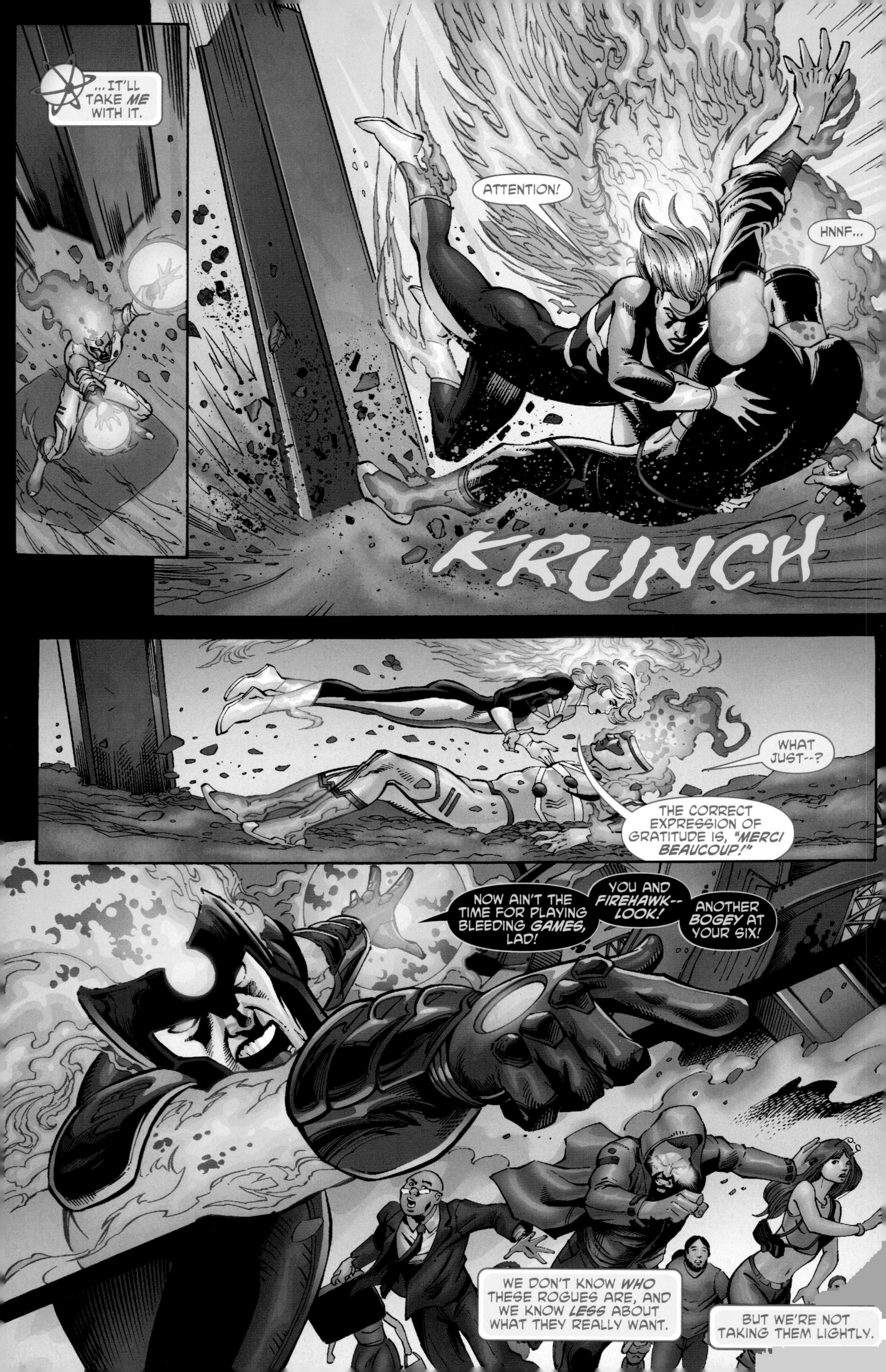
...IT'LL TAKE ME WITH IT.
ATTENTION!
HNNF...
KRUNCH
WHAT JUST--?
THE CORRECT EXPRESSION OF GRATITUDE IS, "MERCI BEAUCOUP!"
NOW AIN'T THE TIME FOR PLAYING BLEEDING GAMES, LAD!
YOU AND FIREHAWK-- LOOK!
ANOTHER BOGEY AT YOUR SIX!
WE DON'T KNOW WHO THESE ROGUES ARE, AND WE KNOW LESS ABOUT WHAT THEY REALLY WANT.
BUT WE'RE NOT TAKING THEM LIGHTLY.

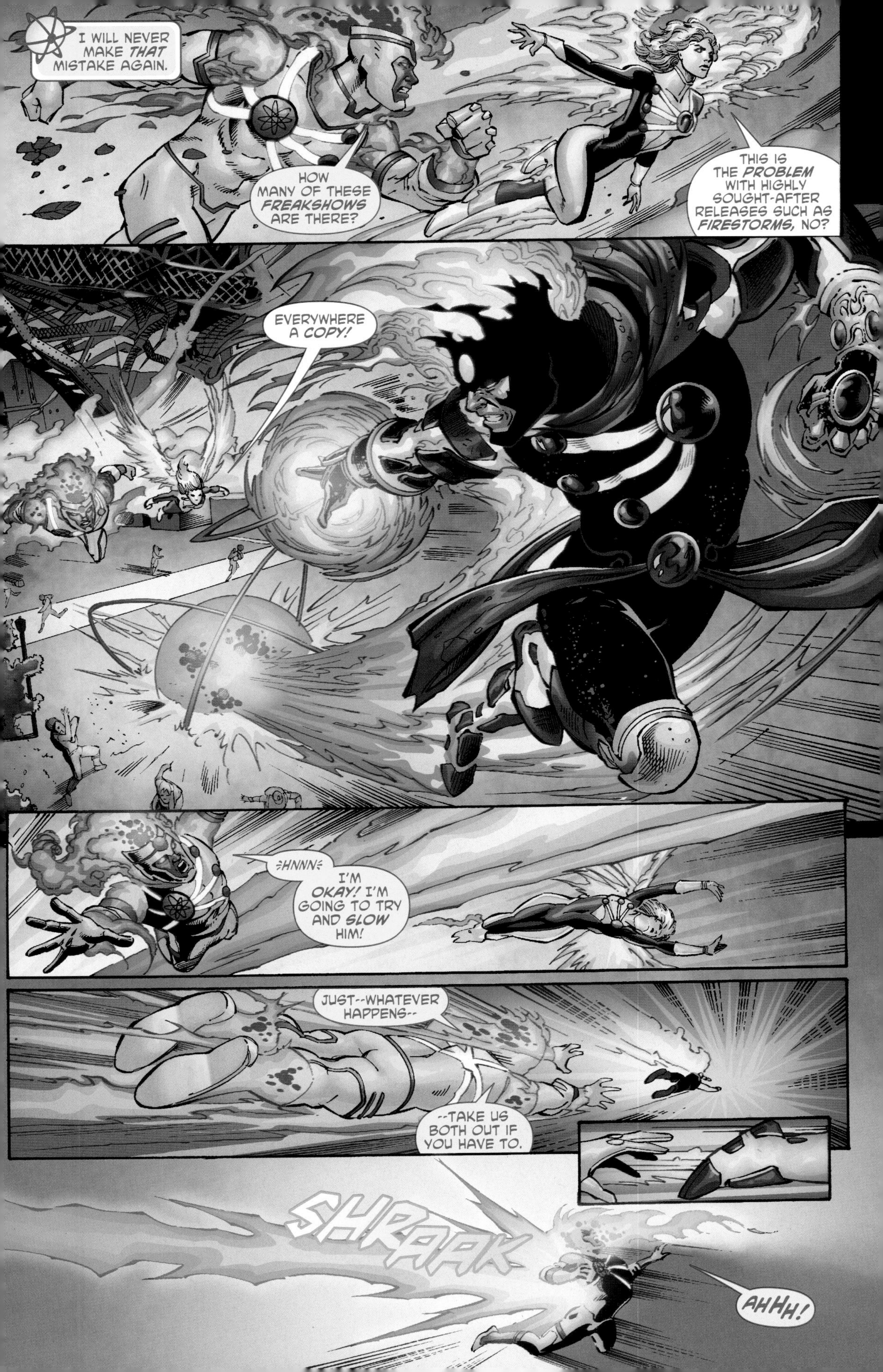
I WILL NEVER MAKE THAT MISTAKE AGAIN.
HOW MANY OF THESE FREAKSHOWS ARE THERE?
THIS IS THE PROBLEM WITH HIGHLY SOUGHT-AFTER RELEASES SUCH AS FIRESTORMS, NO?
EVERYWHERE A COPY!
HNNN
I'M OKAY! I'M GOING TO TRY AND SLOW HIM!
JUST--WHATEVER HAPPENS--
--TAKE US BOTH OUT IF YOU HAVE TO.
SHRAAK
AHHH!

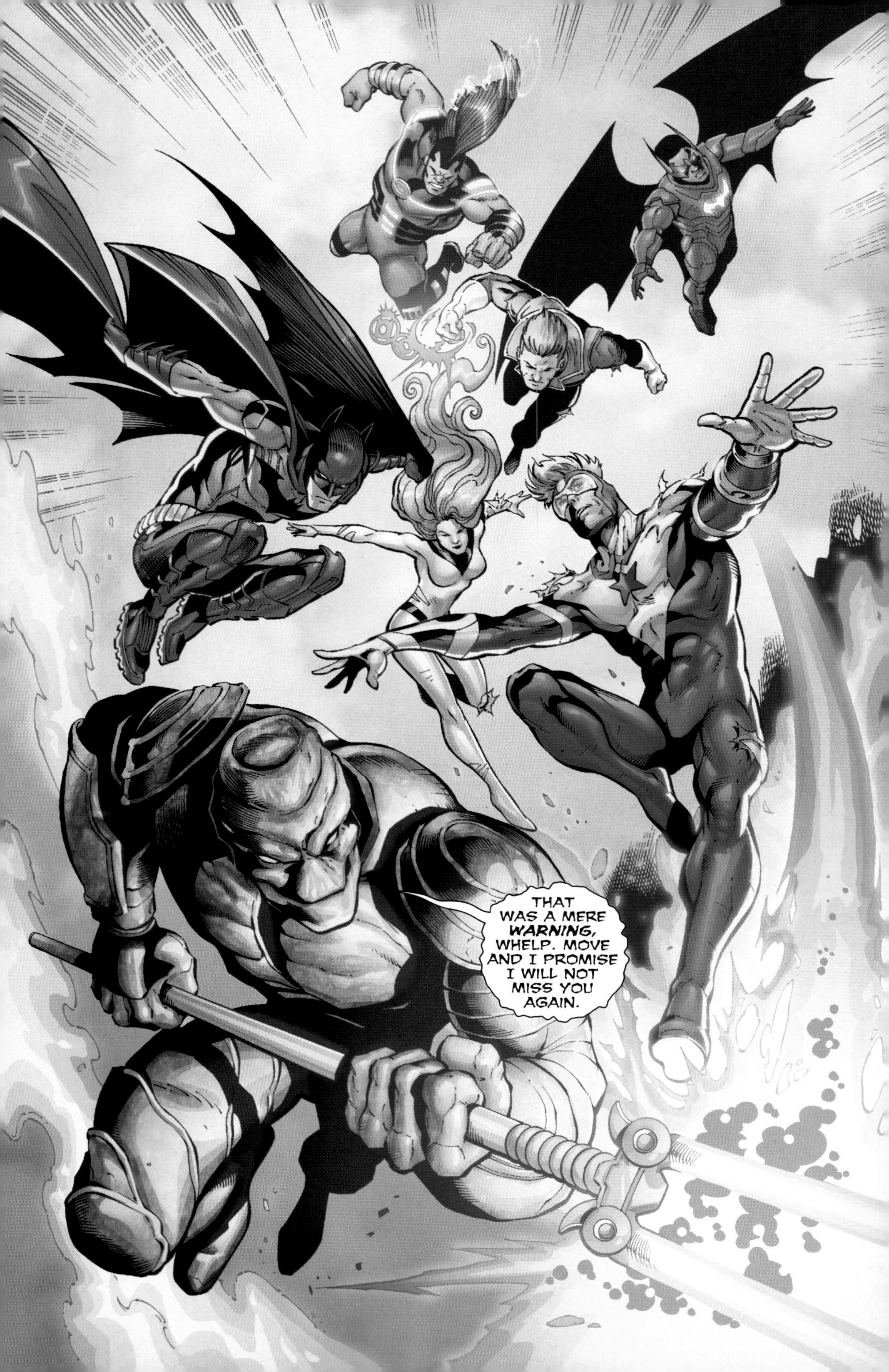
THAT WAS A MERE **WARNING**, WHELP. MOVE AND I PROMISE I WILL NOT MISS YOU AGAIN.

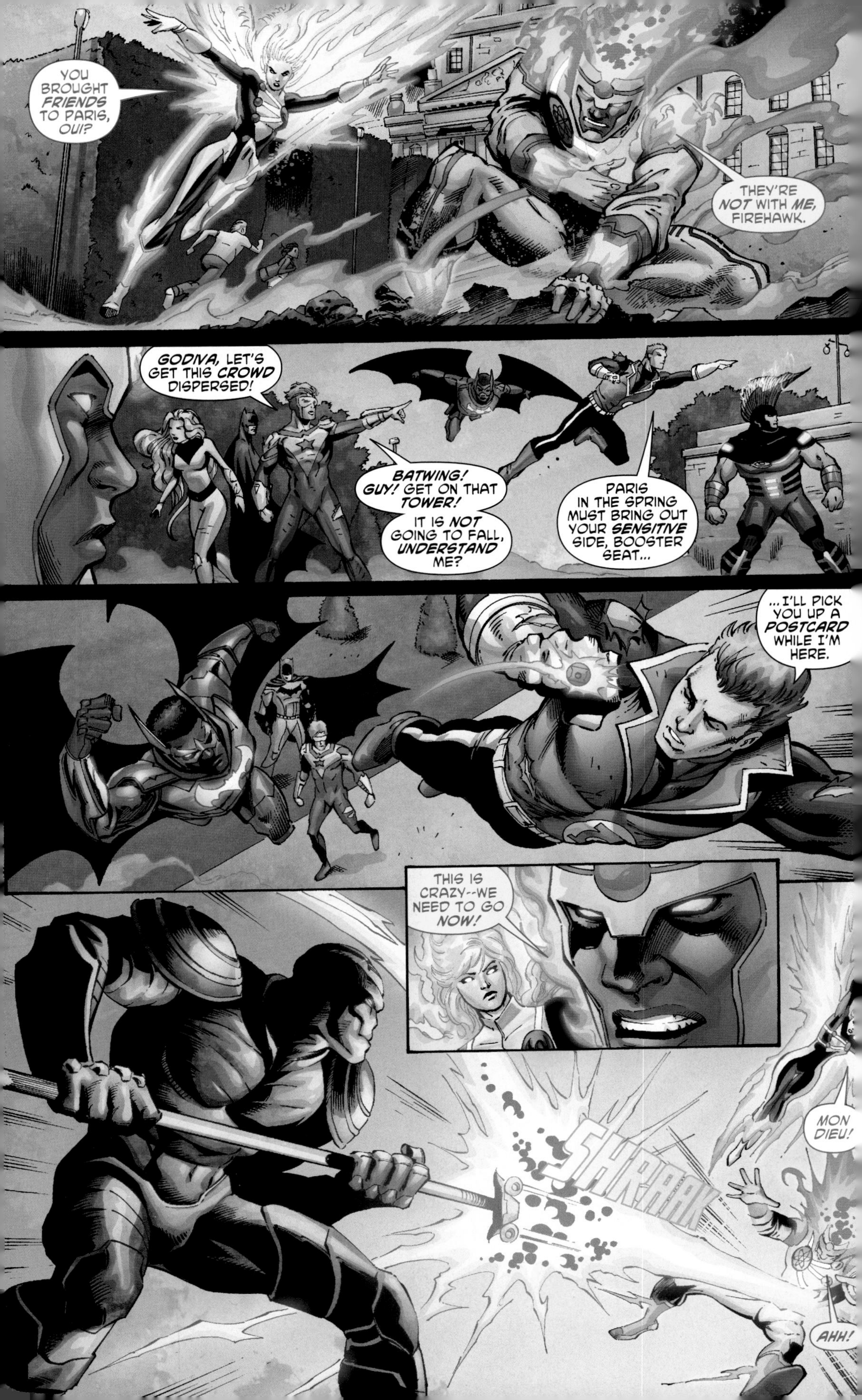
YOU BROUGHT *FRIENDS* TO PARIS, *OUI?*
THEY'RE *NOT* WITH *ME,* FIREHAWK.
GODIVA, LET'S GET THIS *CROWD* DISPERSED!
BATWING! GUY! GET ON THAT *TOWER!*
IT IS *NOT* GOING TO FALL, *UNDERSTAND* ME?
PARIS IN THE SPRING MUST BRING OUT YOUR *SENSITIVE* SIDE, BOOSTER SEAT...
...I'LL PICK YOU UP A *POSTCARD* WHILE I'M HERE.
THIS IS CRAZY--WE NEED TO GO *NOW!*
SHRAAK
MON DIEU!
AHH!

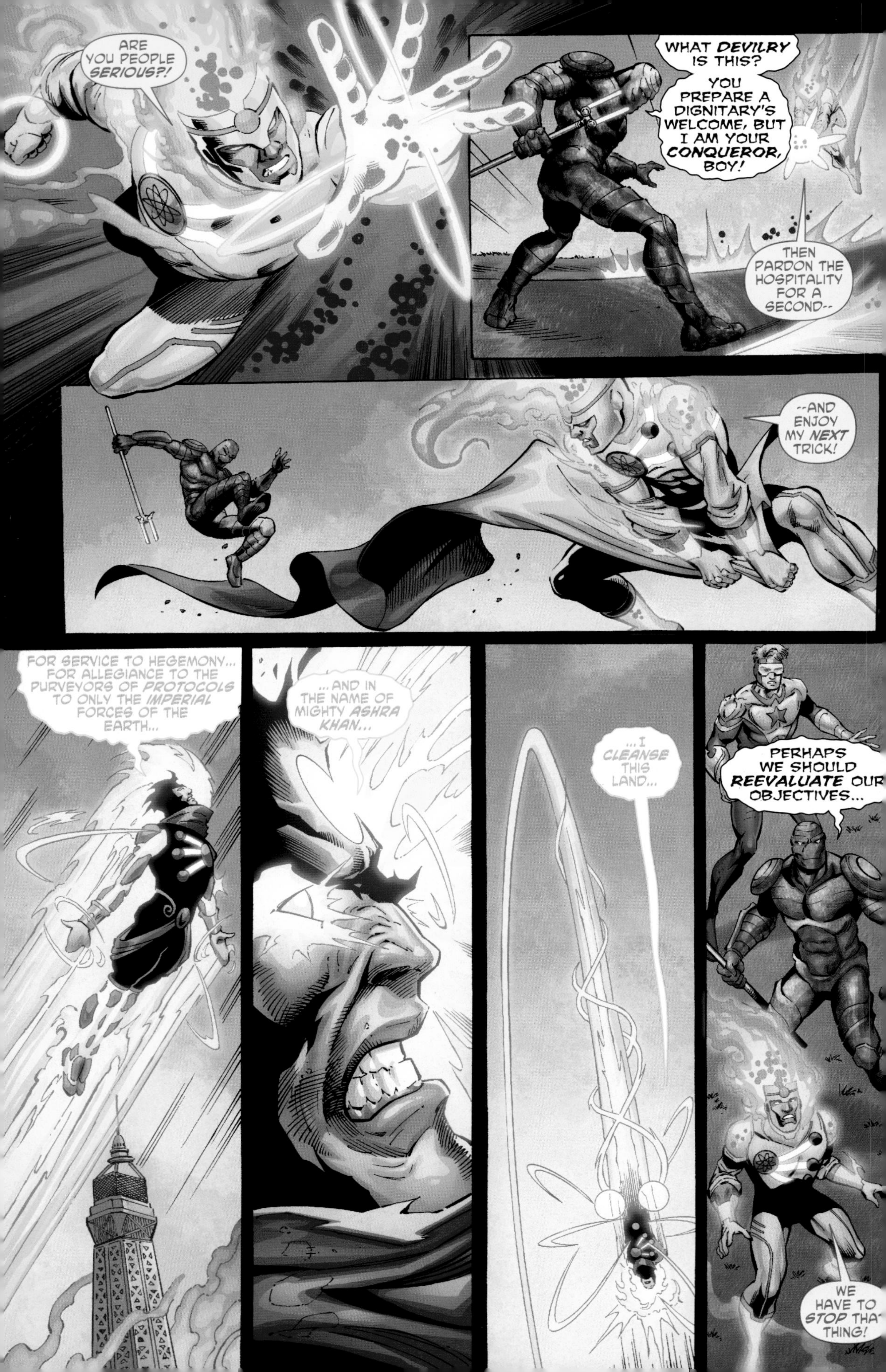

ARE YOU PEOPLE SERIOUS?!
WHAT DEVILRY IS THIS?
YOU PREPARE A DIGNITARY'S WELCOME, BUT I AM YOUR CONQUEROR, BOY!
THEN PARDON THE HOSPITALITY FOR A SECOND--
--AND ENJOY MY NEXT TRICK!
FOR SERVICE TO HEGEMONY... FOR ALLEGIANCE TO THE PURVEYORS OF PROTOCOLS TO ONLY THE IMPERIAL FORCES OF THE EARTH...
...AND IN THE NAME OF MIGHTY ASHRA KHAN...
...I CLEANSE THIS LAND...
PERHAPS WE SHOULD REEVALUATE OUR OBJECTIVES...
WE HAVE TO STOP THAT THING!

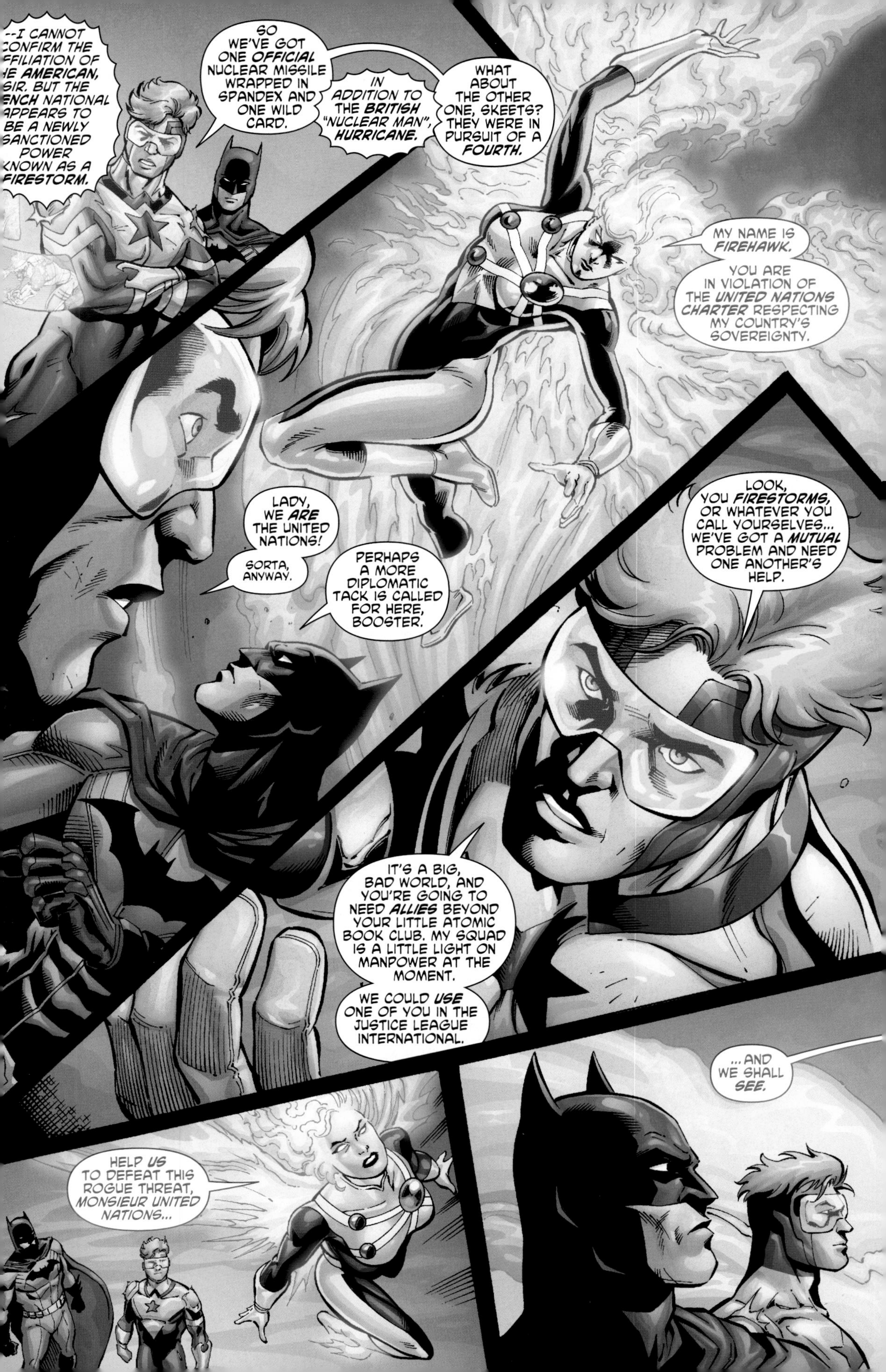
--I CANNOT CONFIRM THE AFFILIATION OF THE AMERICAN, SIR. BUT THE FRENCH NATIONAL APPEARS TO BE A NEWLY SANCTIONED POWER KNOWN AS A FIRESTORM.
SO WE'VE GOT ONE OFFICIAL NUCLEAR MISSILE WRAPPED IN SPANDEX AND ONE WILD CARD.
IN ADDITION TO THE BRITISH "NUCLEAR MAN", HURRICANE.
WHAT ABOUT THE OTHER ONE, SKEETS? THEY WERE IN PURSUIT OF A FOURTH.
MY NAME IS FIREHAWK.
YOU ARE IN VIOLATION OF THE UNITED NATIONS CHARTER RESPECTING MY COUNTRY'S SOVEREIGNTY.
LADY, WE ARE THE UNITED NATIONS!
SORTA, ANYWAY.
PERHAPS A MORE DIPLOMATIC TACK IS CALLED FOR HERE, BOOSTER.
LOOK, YOU FIRESTORMS, OR WHATEVER YOU CALL YOURSELVES... WE'VE GOT A MUTUAL PROBLEM AND NEED ONE ANOTHER'S HELP.
IT'S A BIG, BAD WORLD, AND YOU'RE GOING TO NEED ALLIES BEYOND YOUR LITTLE ATOMIC BOOK CLUB. MY SQUAD IS A LITTLE LIGHT ON MANPOWER AT THE MOMENT.
WE COULD USE ONE OF YOU IN THE JUSTICE LEAGUE INTERNATIONAL.
HELP US TO DEFEAT THIS ROGUE THREAT, MONSIEUR UNITED NATIONS...
...AND WE SHALL SEE.

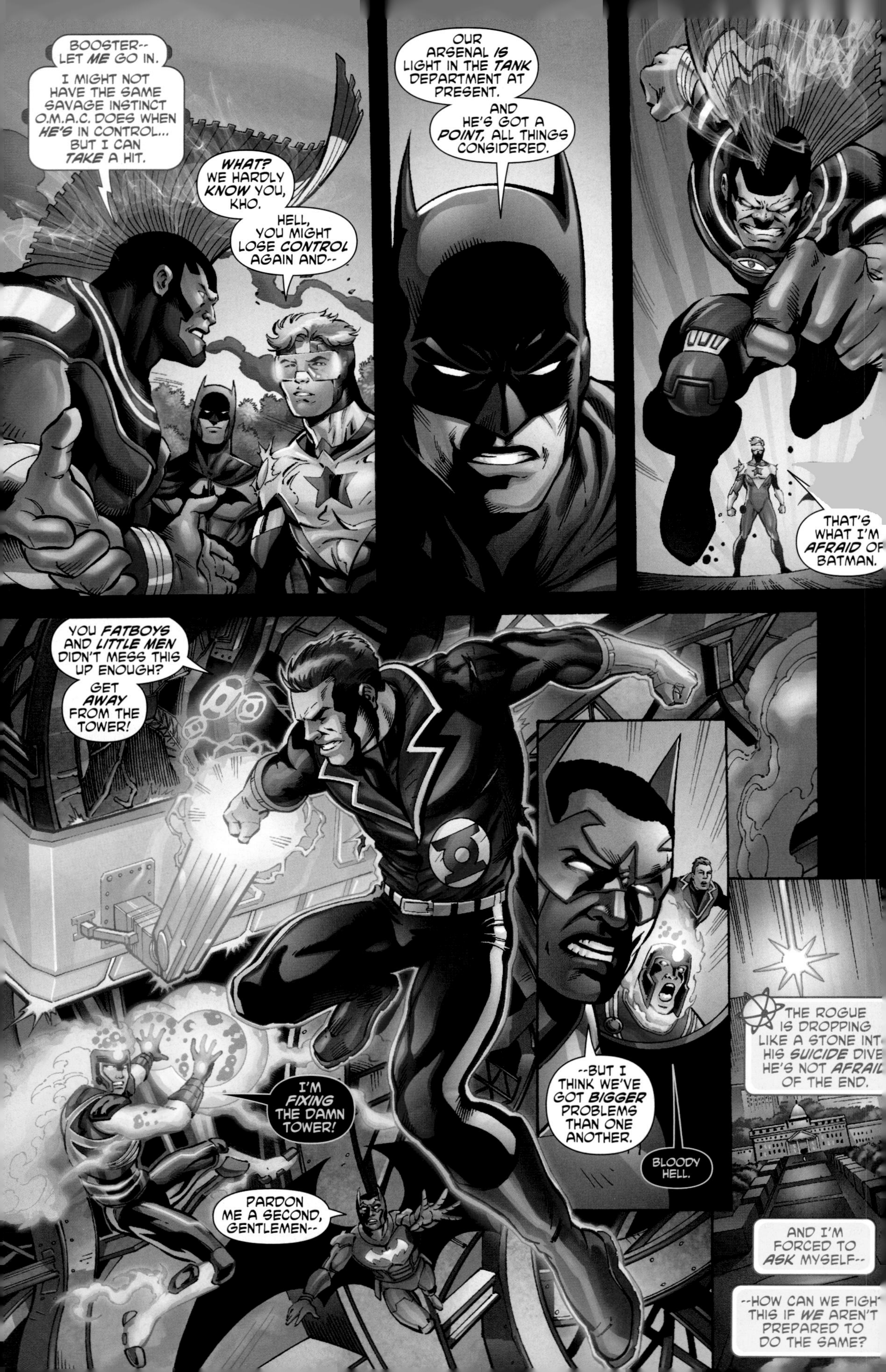
BOOSTER-- LET ME GO IN.
I MIGHT NOT HAVE THE SAME SAVAGE INSTINCT O.M.A.C. DOES WHEN HE'S IN CONTROL... BUT I CAN TAKE A HIT.
WHAT? WE HARDLY KNOW YOU, KHO.
HELL, YOU MIGHT LOSE CONTROL AGAIN AND--
OUR ARSENAL IS LIGHT IN THE TANK DEPARTMENT AT PRESENT.
AND HE'S GOT A POINT, ALL THINGS CONSIDERED.
THAT'S WHAT I'M AFRAID OF, BATMAN.
YOU FATBOYS AND LITTLE MEN DIDN'T MESS THIS UP ENOUGH?
GET AWAY FROM THE TOWER!
I'M FIXING THE DAMN TOWER!
PARDON ME A SECOND, GENTLEMEN--
--BUT I THINK WE'VE GOT BIGGER PROBLEMS THAN ONE ANOTHER.
BLOODY HELL.
THE ROGUE IS DROPPING LIKE A STONE INT HIS SUICIDE DIVE HE'S NOT AFRAI OF THE END.
AND I'M FORCED TO ASK MYSELF--
--HOW CAN WE FIGH THIS IF WE AREN'T PREPARED TO DO THE SAME?

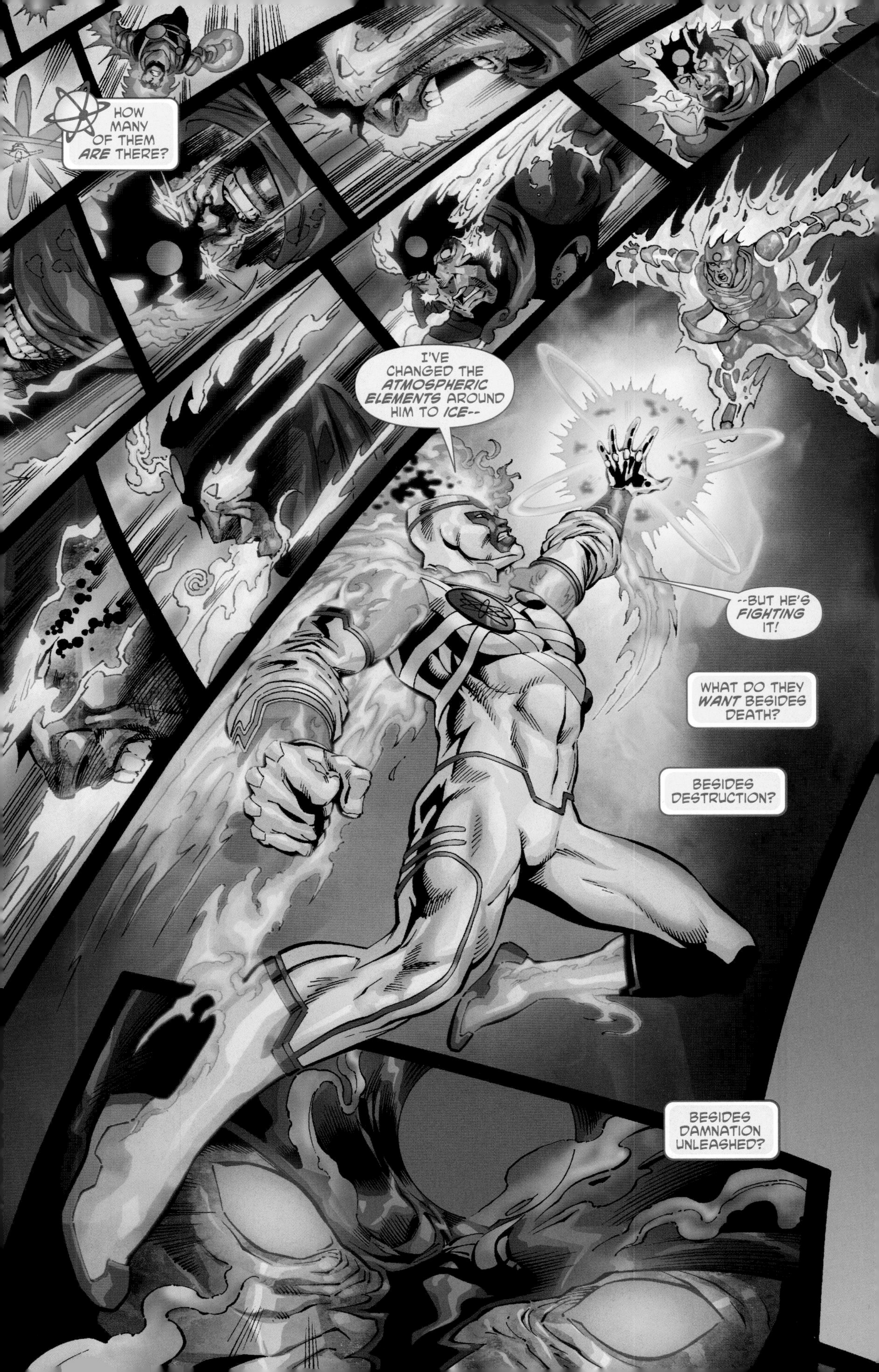
HOW MANY OF THEM *ARE* THERE?
I'VE CHANGED THE *ATMOSPHERIC ELEMENTS* AROUND HIM TO *ICE*--
--BUT HE'S *FIGHTING* IT!
WHAT DO THEY *WANT* BESIDES DEATH?
BESIDES DESTRUCTION?
BESIDES DAMNATION UNLEASHED?

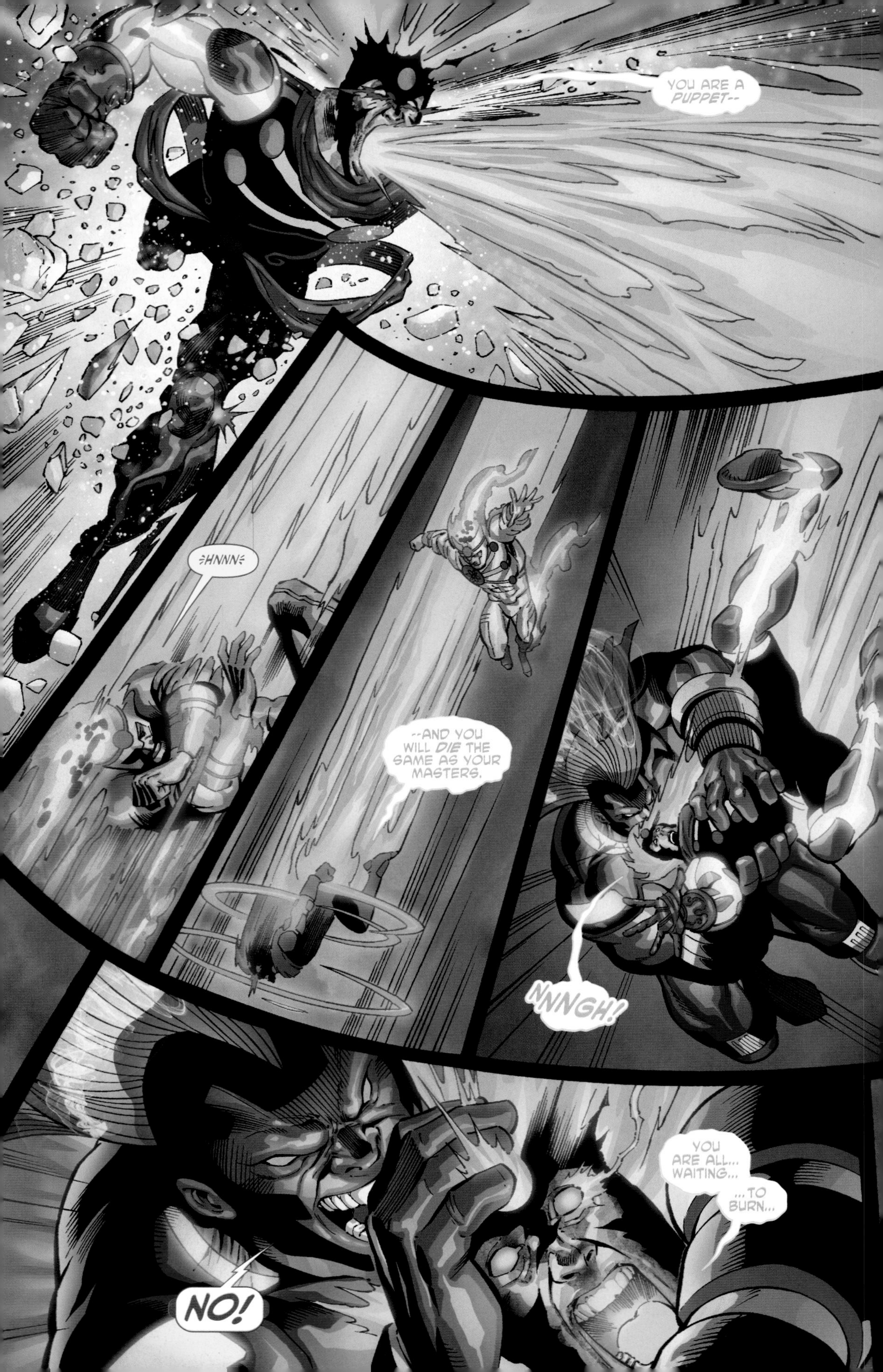
YOU ARE A PUPPET--
HNNN
--AND YOU WILL DIE THE SAME AS YOUR MASTERS.
NNNGH!
YOU ARE ALL... WAITING...
...TO BURN...
NO!

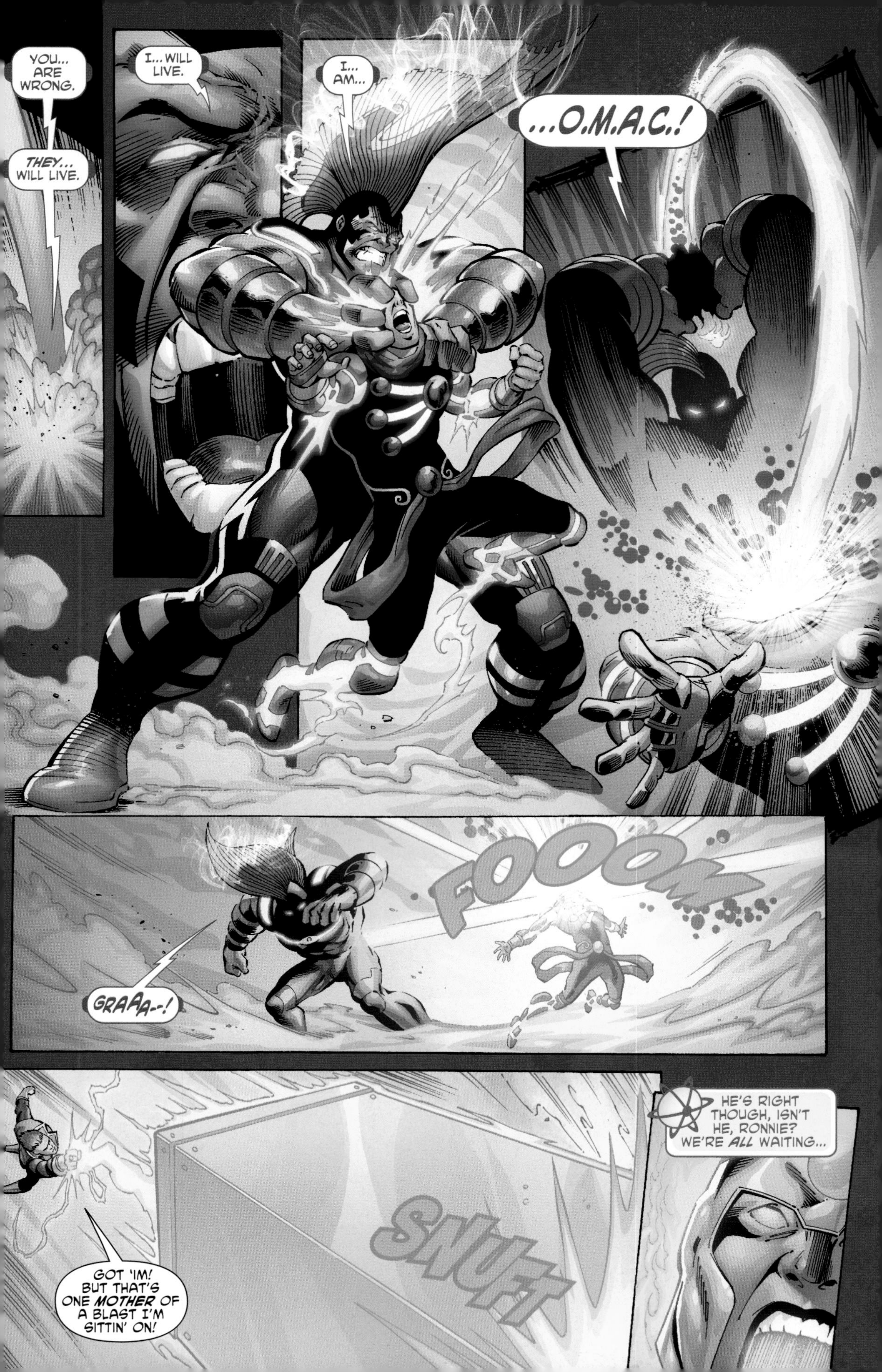
YOU... ARE WRONG.
THEY... WILL LIVE.
I... WILL LIVE.
I... AM...
...O.M.A.C.!
FOOOM
GRAAA--!
HE'S RIGHT THOUGH, ISN'T HE, RONNIE? WE'RE ALL WAITING...
SNUFT
GOT 'IM! BUT THAT'S ONE MOTHER OF A BLAST I'M SITTIN' ON!

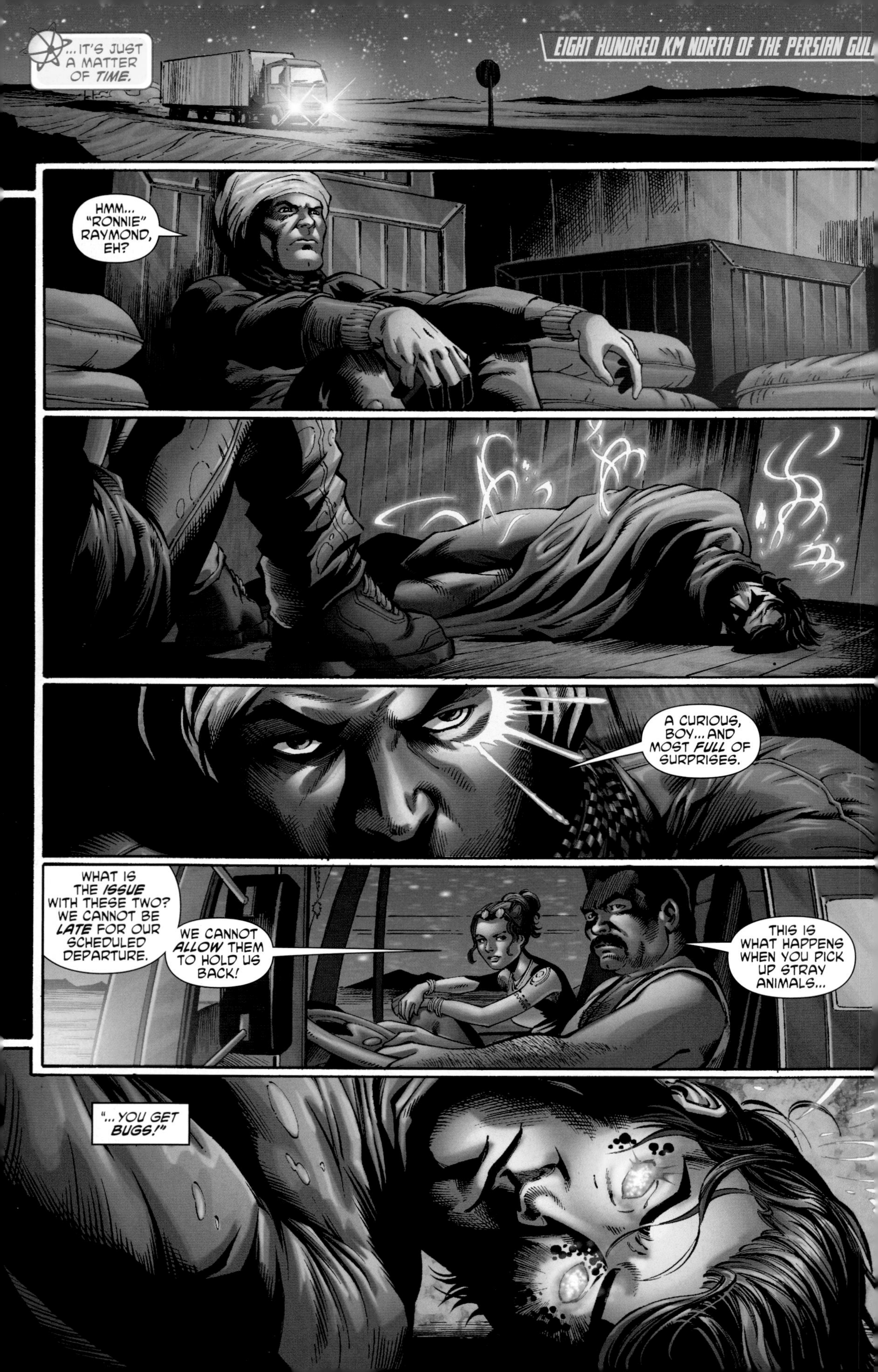
...IT'S JUST A MATTER OF TIME.
EIGHT HUNDRED KM NORTH OF THE PERSIAN GUL
HMM... "RONNIE" RAYMOND, EH?
A CURIOUS, BOY... AND MOST FULL OF SURPRISES.
WHAT IS THE ISSUE WITH THESE TWO? WE CANNOT BE LATE FOR OUR SCHEDULED DEPARTURE.
WE CANNOT ALLOW THEM TO HOLD US BACK!
THIS IS WHAT HAPPENS WHEN YOU PICK UP STRAY ANIMALS...
"...YOU GET BUGS!"

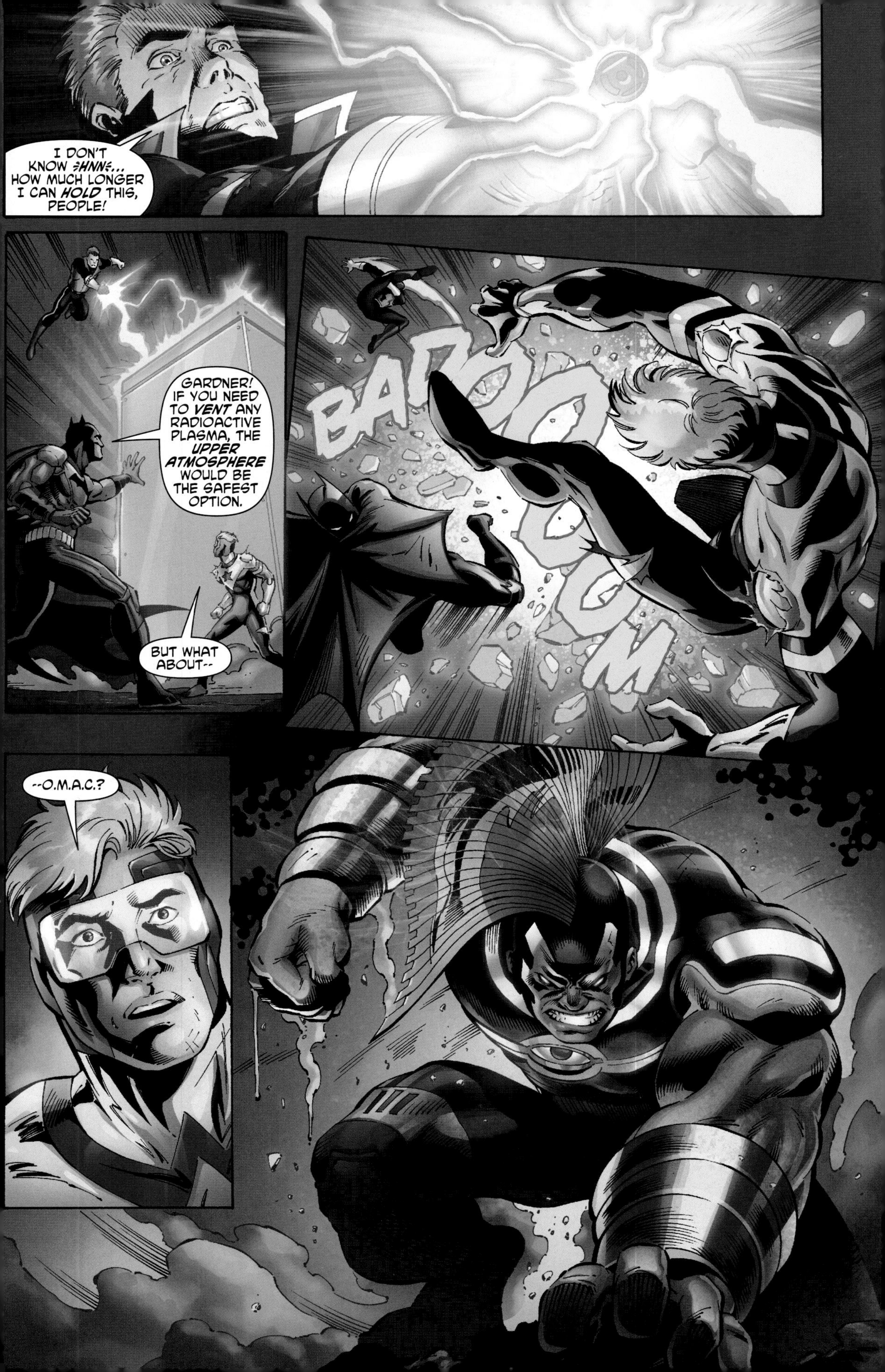

I DON'T KNOW =HNN=... HOW MUCH LONGER I CAN HOLD THIS, PEOPLE!
GARDNER! IF YOU NEED TO VENT ANY RADIOACTIVE PLASMA, THE UPPER ATMOSPHERE WOULD BE THE SAFEST OPTION.
BUT WHAT ABOUT--
BADOOOOM
--O.M.A.C.?

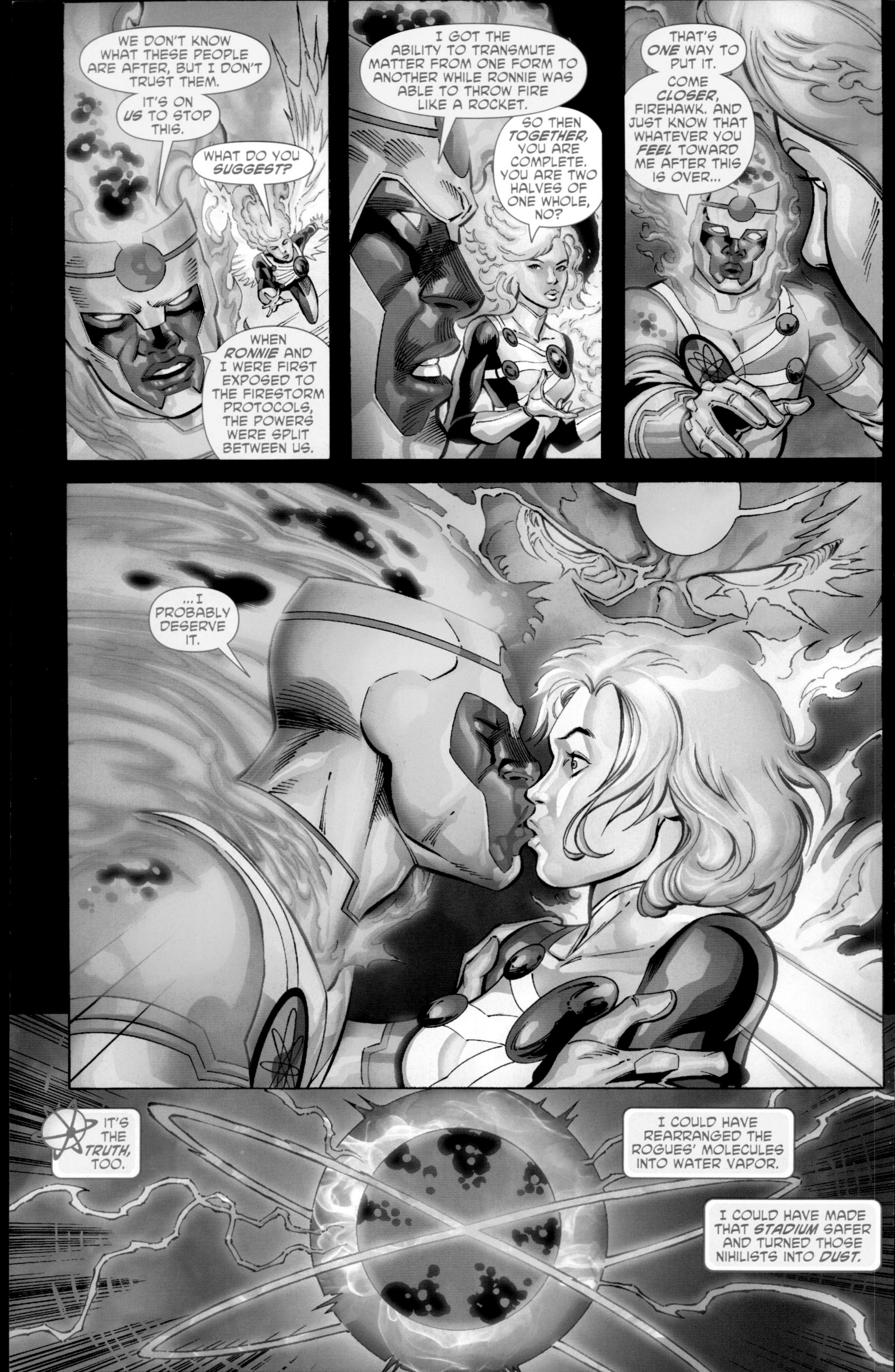
WE DON'T KNOW WHAT THESE PEOPLE ARE AFTER, BUT I DON'T TRUST THEM.
IT'S ON US TO STOP THIS.
WHAT DO YOU SUGGEST?
WHEN RONNIE AND I WERE FIRST EXPOSED TO THE FIRESTORM PROTOCOLS, THE POWERS WERE SPLIT BETWEEN US.
I GOT THE ABILITY TO TRANSMUTE MATTER FROM ONE FORM TO ANOTHER WHILE RONNIE WAS ABLE TO THROW FIRE LIKE A ROCKET.
SO THEN TOGETHER, YOU ARE COMPLETE. YOU ARE TWO HALVES OF ONE WHOLE, NO?
THAT'S ONE WAY TO PUT IT.
COME CLOSER, FIREHAWK. AND JUST KNOW THAT WHATEVER YOU FEEL TOWARD ME AFTER THIS IS OVER...
...I PROBABLY DESERVE IT.
IT'S THE TRUTH, TOO.
I COULD HAVE REARRANGED THE ROGUES' MOLECULES INTO WATER VAPOR.
I COULD HAVE MADE THAT STADIUM SAFER AND TURNED THOSE NIHILISTS INTO DUST.

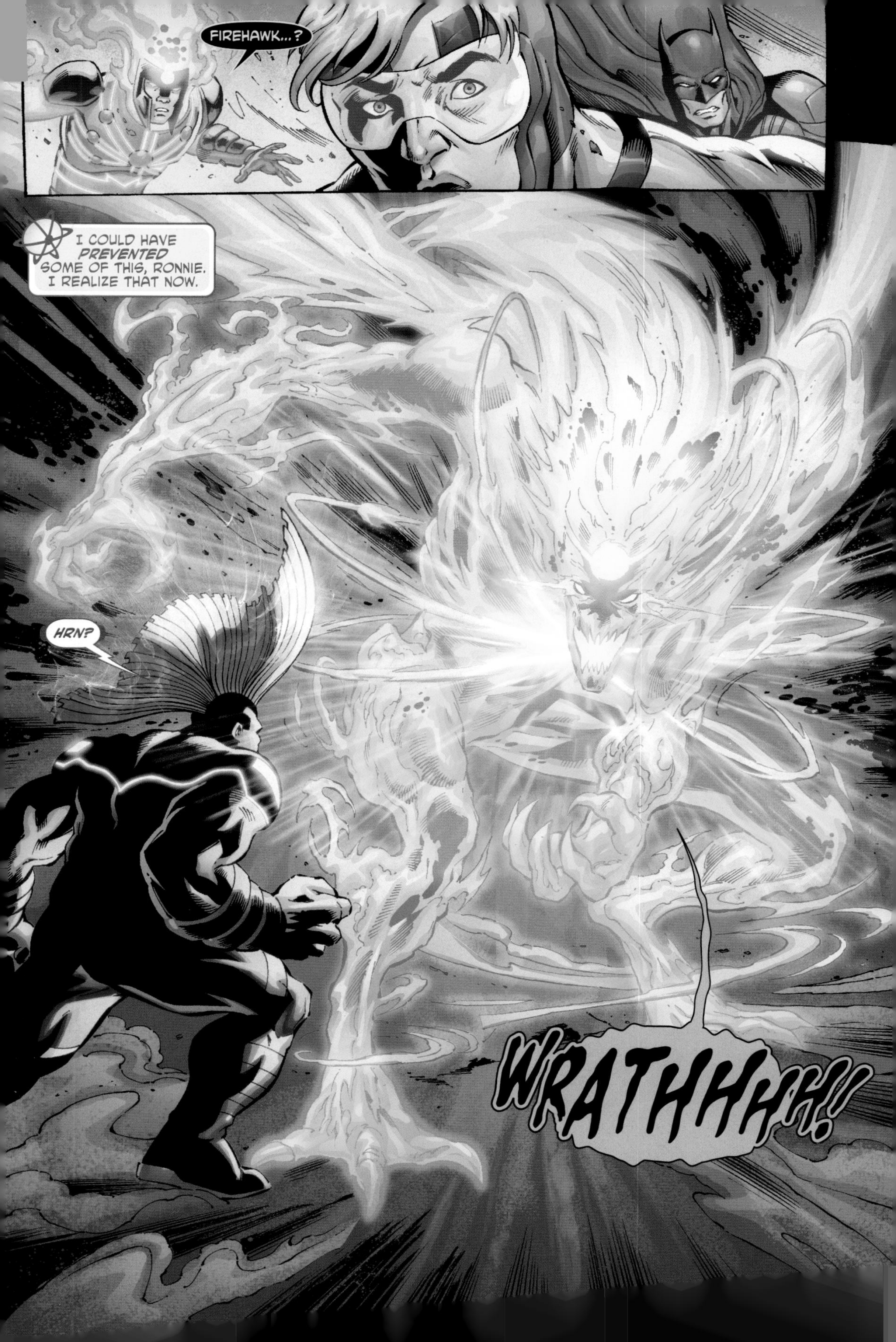
FIREHAWK...?
I COULD HAVE *PREVENTED* SOME OF THIS, RONNIE. I REALIZE THAT NOW.
HRN?
WRATHHHH!!

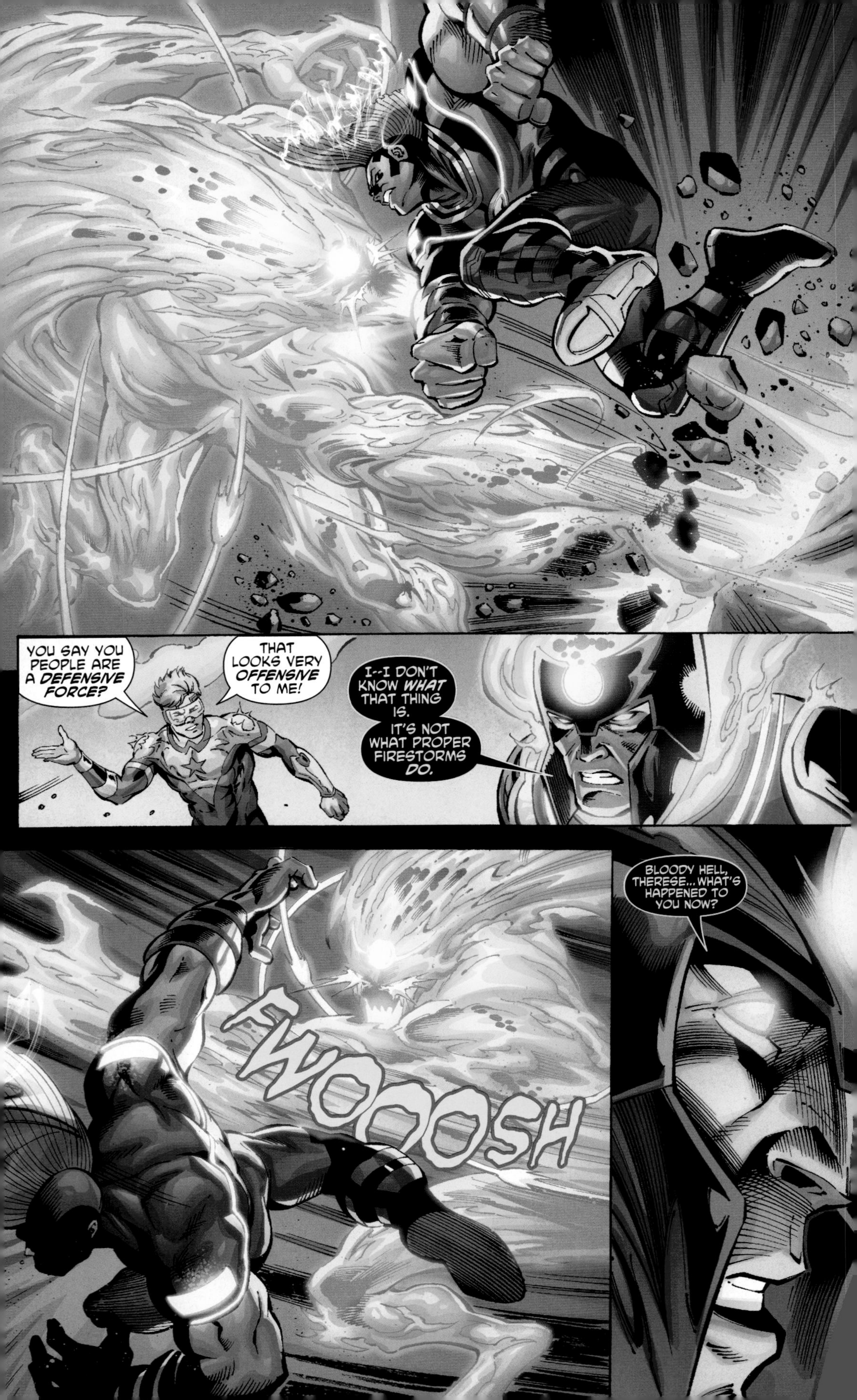
YOU SAY YOU PEOPLE ARE A DEFENSIVE FORCE?
THAT LOOKS VERY OFFENSIVE TO ME!
I--I DON'T KNOW WHAT THAT THING IS.
IT'S NOT WHAT PROPER FIRESTORMS DO.
FWOOOSH
BLOODY HELL, THERESE... WHAT'S HAPPENED TO YOU NOW?

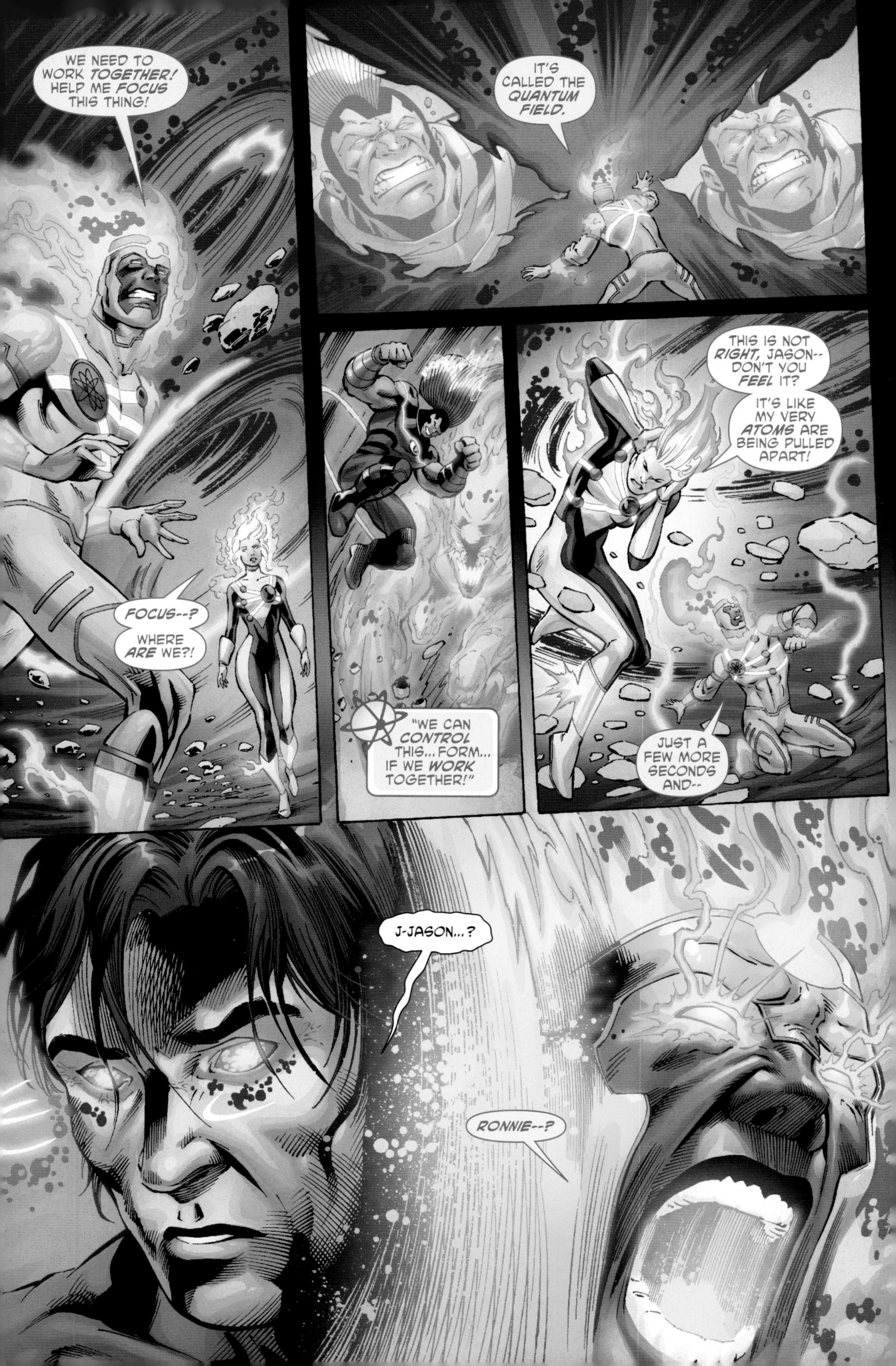
WE NEED TO WORK TOGETHER! HELP ME FOCUS THIS THING!
IT'S CALLED THE QUANTUM FIELD.
FOCUS--?
WHERE ARE WE?!
"WE CAN CONTROL THIS...FORM... IF WE WORK TOGETHER!"
THIS IS NOT RIGHT, JASON--DON'T YOU FEEL IT?
IT'S LIKE MY VERY ATOMS ARE BEING PULLED APART!
JUST A FEW MORE SECONDS AND--
J-JASON...?
RONNIE--?

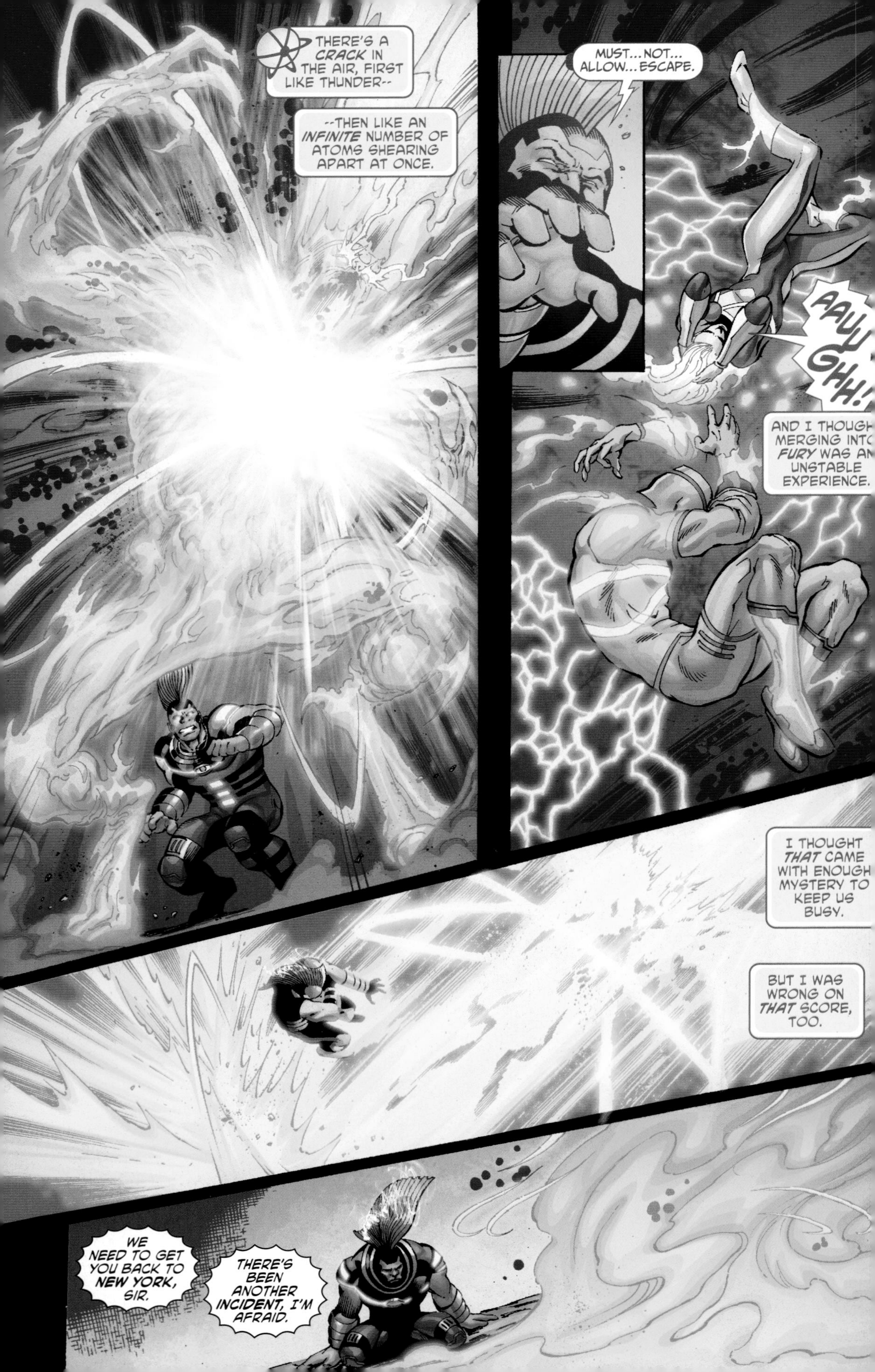
THERE'S A CRACK IN THE AIR, FIRST LIKE THUNDER--
--THEN LIKE AN INFINITE NUMBER OF ATOMS SHEARING APART AT ONCE.
MUST...NOT... ALLOW...ESCAPE.
AAUGHH!!
AND I THOUGHT MERGING INTO FURY WAS AN UNSTABLE EXPERIENCE.
I THOUGHT THAT CAME WITH ENOUGH MYSTERY TO KEEP US BUSY.
BUT I WAS WRONG ON THAT SCORE, TOO.
WE NEED TO GET YOU BACK TO NEW YORK, SIR.
THERE'S BEEN ANOTHER INCIDENT, I'M AFRAID.

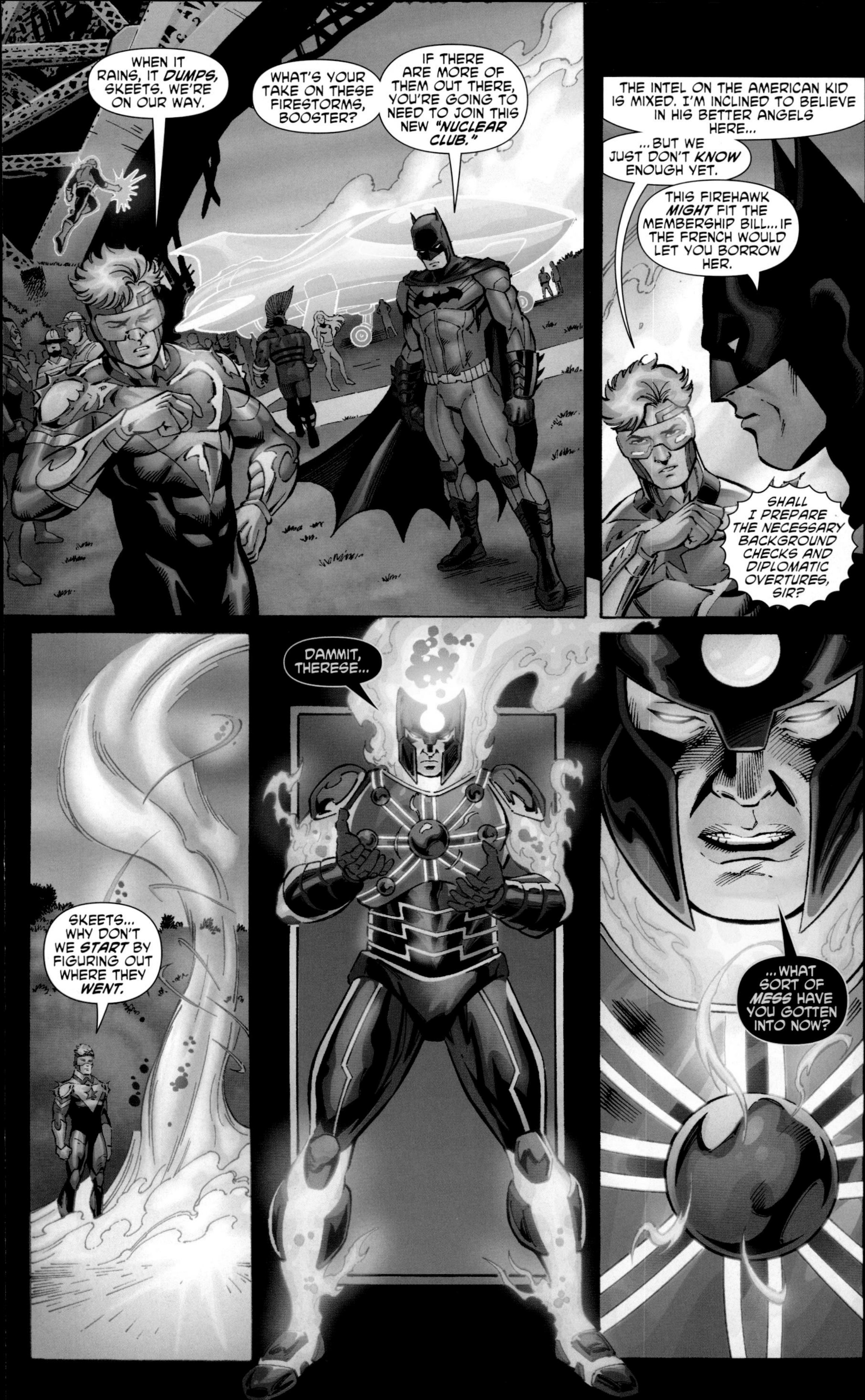
WHEN IT RAINS, IT DUMPS, SKEETS. WE'RE ON OUR WAY.
WHAT'S YOUR TAKE ON THESE FIRESTORMS, BOOSTER?
IF THERE ARE MORE OF THEM OUT THERE, YOU'RE GOING TO NEED TO JOIN THIS NEW "NUCLEAR CLUB."
THE INTEL ON THE AMERICAN KID IS MIXED. I'M INCLINED TO BELIEVE IN HIS BETTER ANGELS HERE...
...BUT WE JUST DON'T KNOW ENOUGH YET.
THIS FIREHAWK MIGHT FIT THE MEMBERSHIP BILL...IF THE FRENCH WOULD LET YOU BORROW HER.
SHALL I PREPARE THE NECESSARY BACKGROUND CHECKS AND DIPLOMATIC OVERTURES, SIR?
SKEETS... WHY DON'T WE START BY FIGURING OUT WHERE THEY WENT.
DAMMIT, THERESE...
...WHAT SORT OF MESS HAVE YOU GOTTEN INTO NOW?

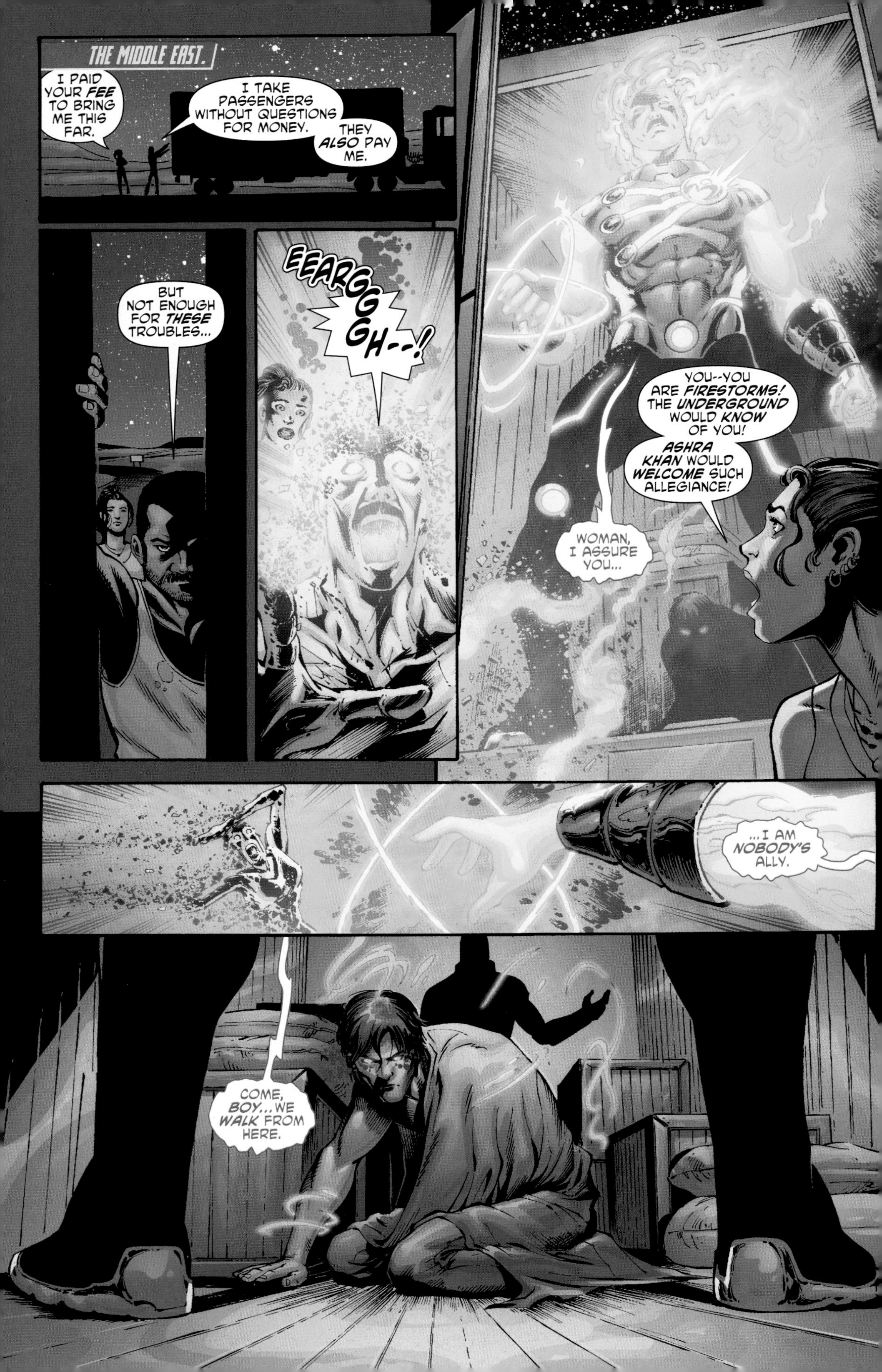
THE MIDDLE EAST.
I PAID YOUR *FEE* TO BRING ME THIS FAR.
I TAKE PASSENGERS WITHOUT QUESTIONS FOR MONEY.
THEY *ALSO* PAY ME.
BUT NOT ENOUGH FOR *THESE* TROUBLES...
EEARGGGH--!
YOU--YOU ARE *FIRESTORMS!* THE *UNDERGROUND* WOULD *KNOW* OF YOU!
ASHRA KHAN WOULD *WELCOME* SUCH ALLEGIANCE!
WOMAN, I ASSURE YOU...
...I AM *NOBODY'S* ALLY.
COME, *BOY*... WE *WALK* FROM HERE.

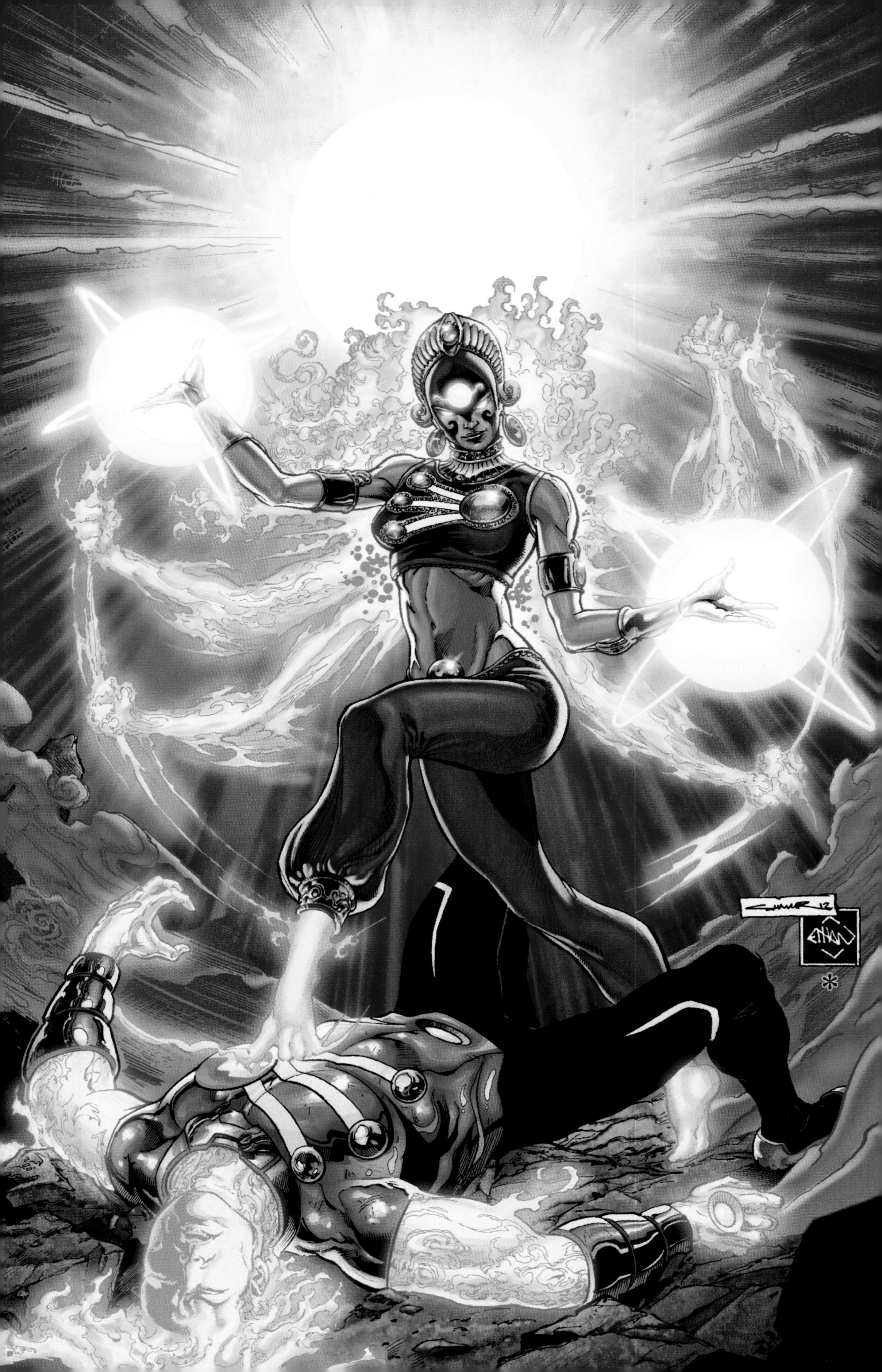

POWER APPLICATION

ETHAN VAN SCIVER & JOE HARRIS plot **JOE HARRIS** script **YILDIRAY CINAR** penciller **MARLO ALQUIZA** inker

cover by **YILDIRAY CINAR & ETHAN VAN SCIVER** with **HI-FI**

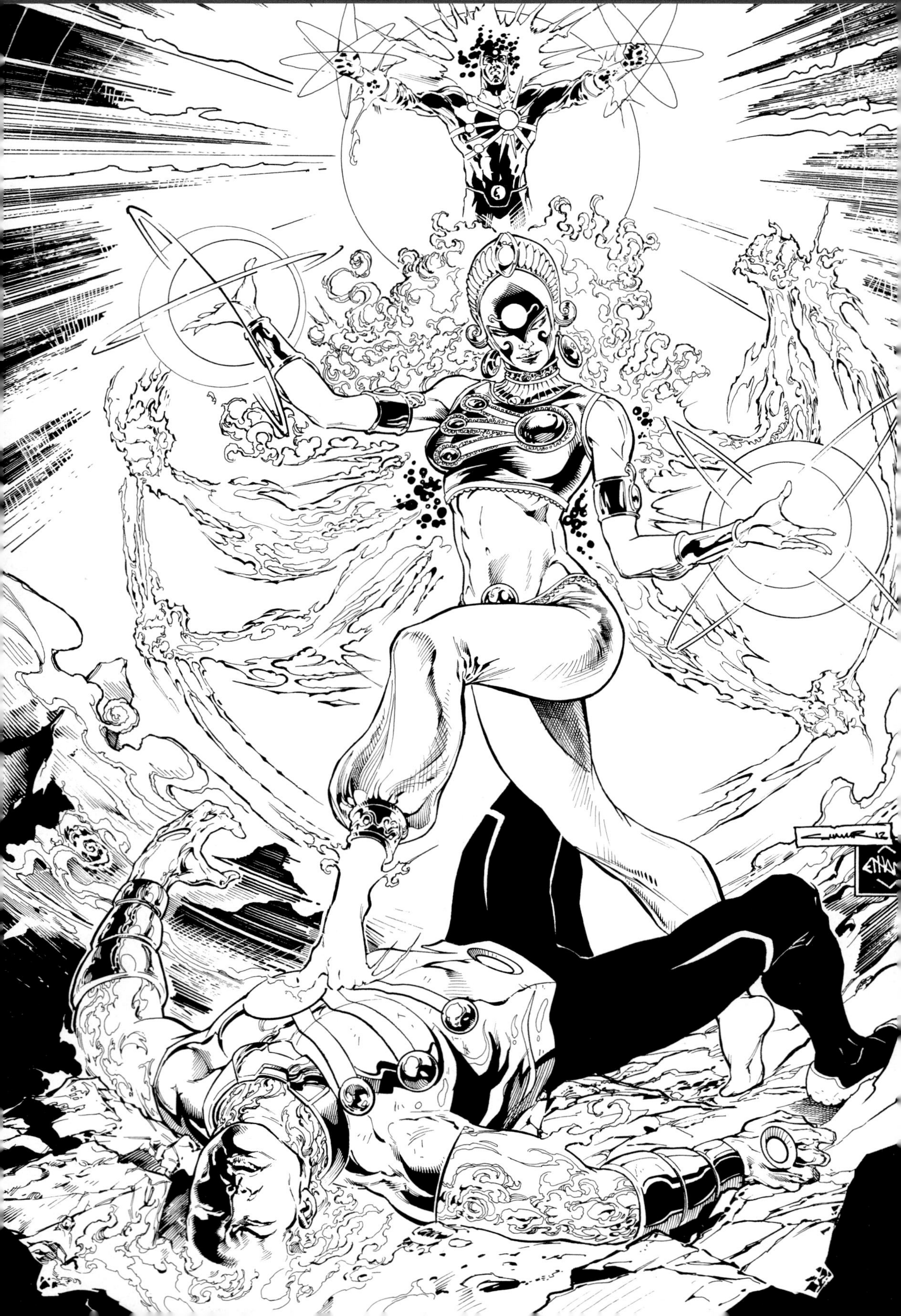

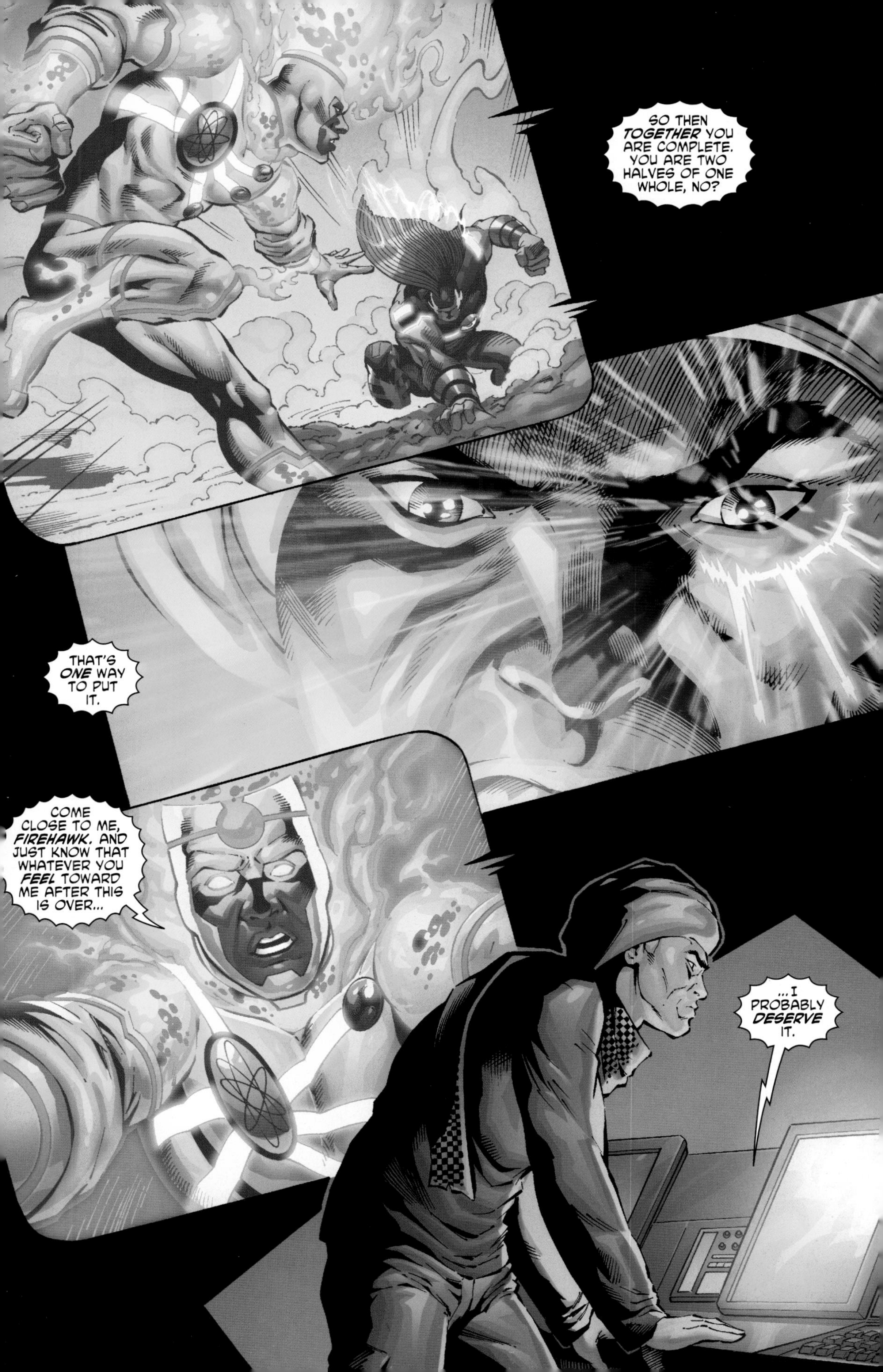
SO THEN TOGETHER YOU ARE COMPLETE. YOU ARE TWO HALVES OF ONE WHOLE, NO?
THAT'S ONE WAY TO PUT IT.
COME CLOSE TO ME, FIREHAWK. AND JUST KNOW THAT WHATEVER YOU FEEL TOWARD ME AFTER THIS IS OVER...
...I PROBABLY DESERVE IT.

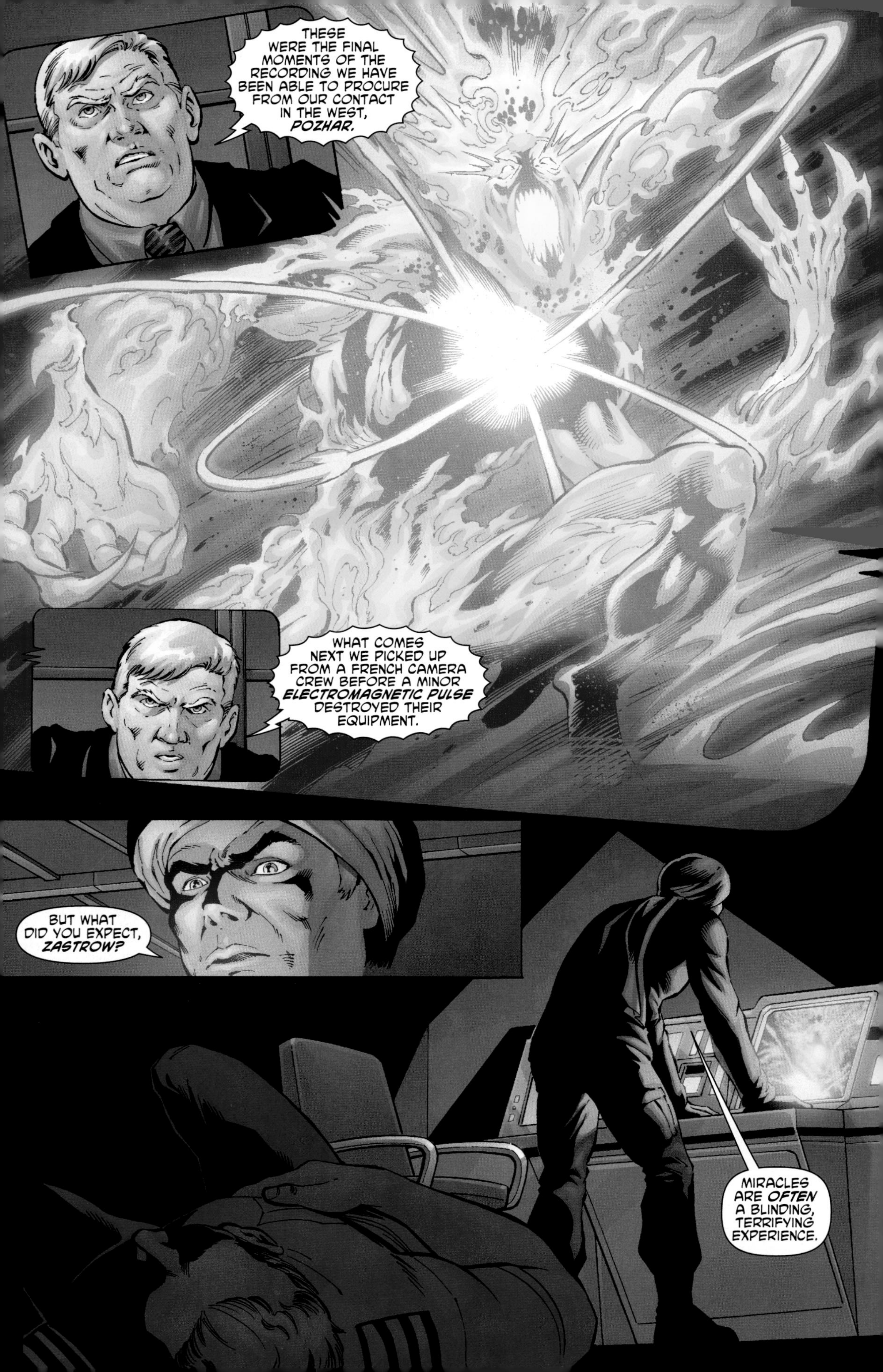
THESE WERE THE FINAL MOMENTS OF THE RECORDING WE HAVE BEEN ABLE TO PROCURE FROM OUR CONTACT IN THE WEST, *POZHAR.*
WHAT COMES NEXT WE PICKED UP FROM A FRENCH CAMERA CREW BEFORE A MINOR *ELECTROMAGNETIC PULSE* DESTROYED THEIR EQUIPMENT.
BUT WHAT DID YOU EXPECT, *ZASTROW?*
MIRACLES ARE *OFTEN* A BLINDING, TERRIFYING EXPERIENCE.

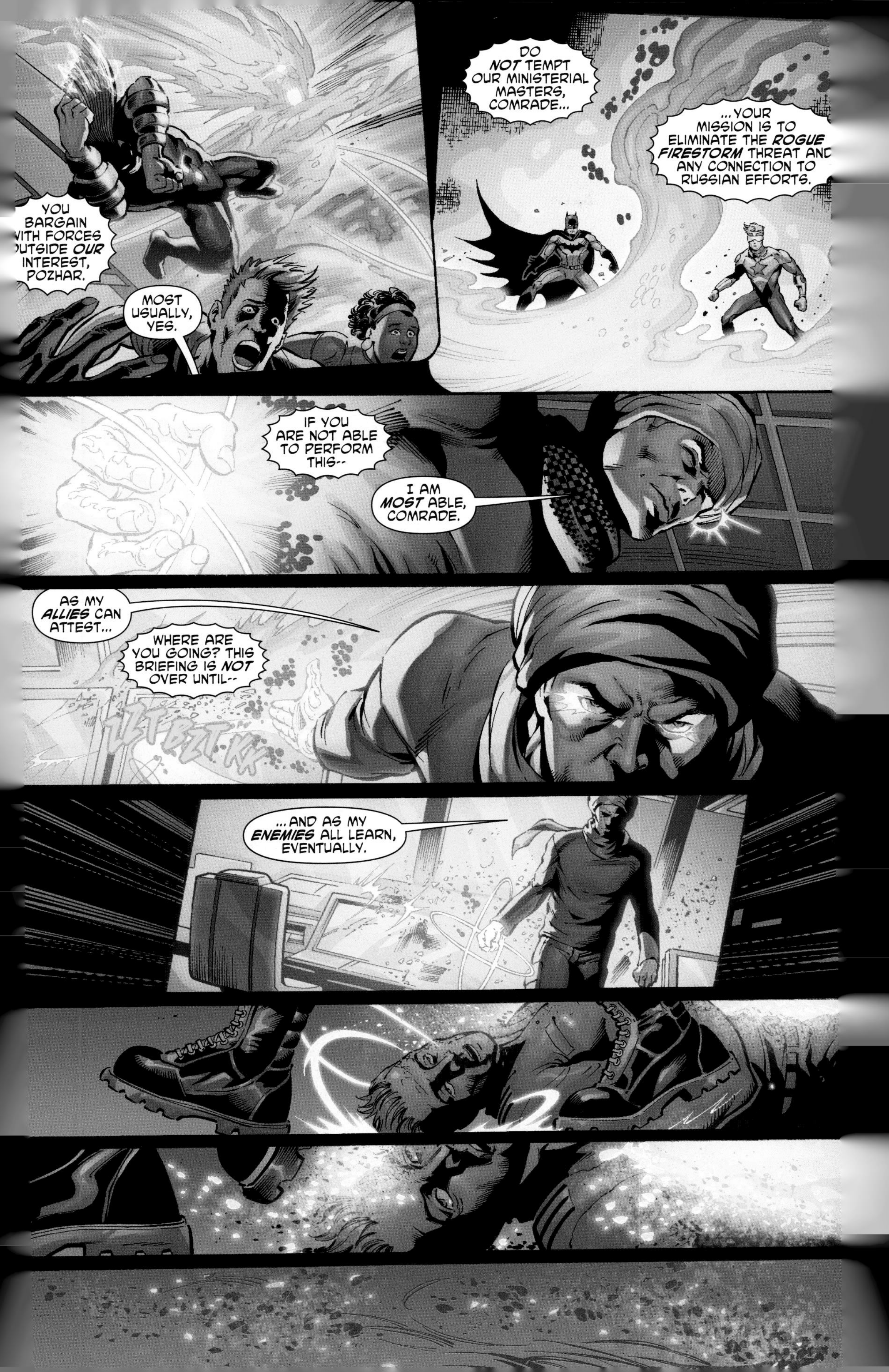
YOU BARGAIN WITH FORCES OUTSIDE OUR INTEREST, POZHAR.
MOST USUALLY, YES.
DO NOT TEMPT OUR MINISTERIAL MASTERS, COMRADE...
...YOUR MISSION IS TO ELIMINATE THE ROGUE FIRESTORM THREAT AND ANY CONNECTION TO RUSSIAN EFFORTS.
IF YOU ARE NOT ABLE TO PERFORM THIS--
I AM MOST ABLE, COMRADE.
AS MY ALLIES CAN ATTEST...
WHERE ARE YOU GOING? THIS BRIEFING IS NOT OVER UNTIL--
ZZT BZT KK
...AND AS MY ENEMIES ALL LEARN, EVENTUALLY.

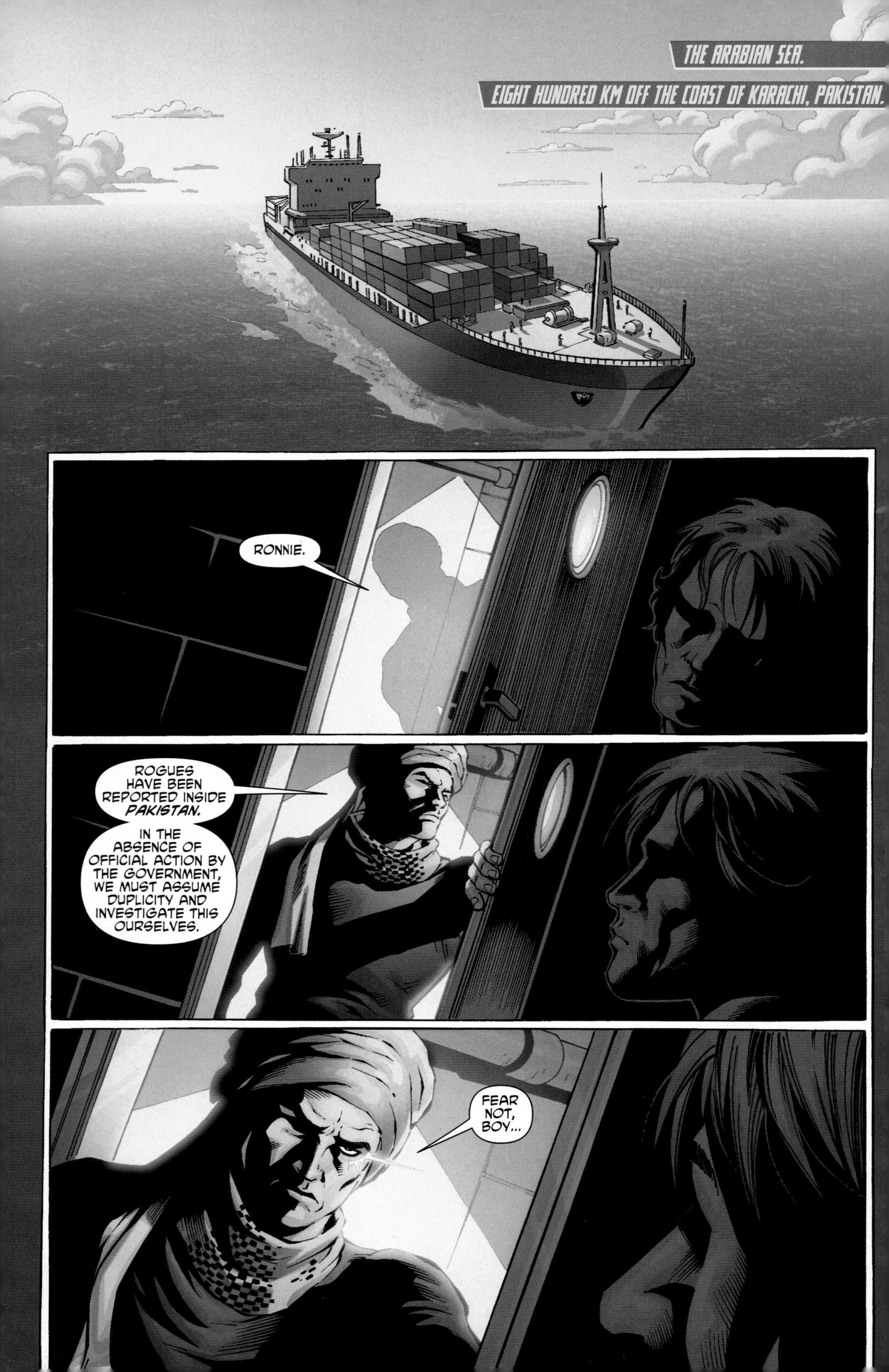
THE ARABIAN SEA.
EIGHT HUNDRED KM OFF THE COAST OF KARACHI, PAKISTAN.
RONNIE.
ROGUES HAVE BEEN REPORTED INSIDE *PAKISTAN.*
IN THE ABSENCE OF OFFICIAL ACTION BY THE GOVERNMENT, WE MUST ASSUME DUPLICITY AND INVESTIGATE THIS OURSELVES.
FEAR NOT, BOY...

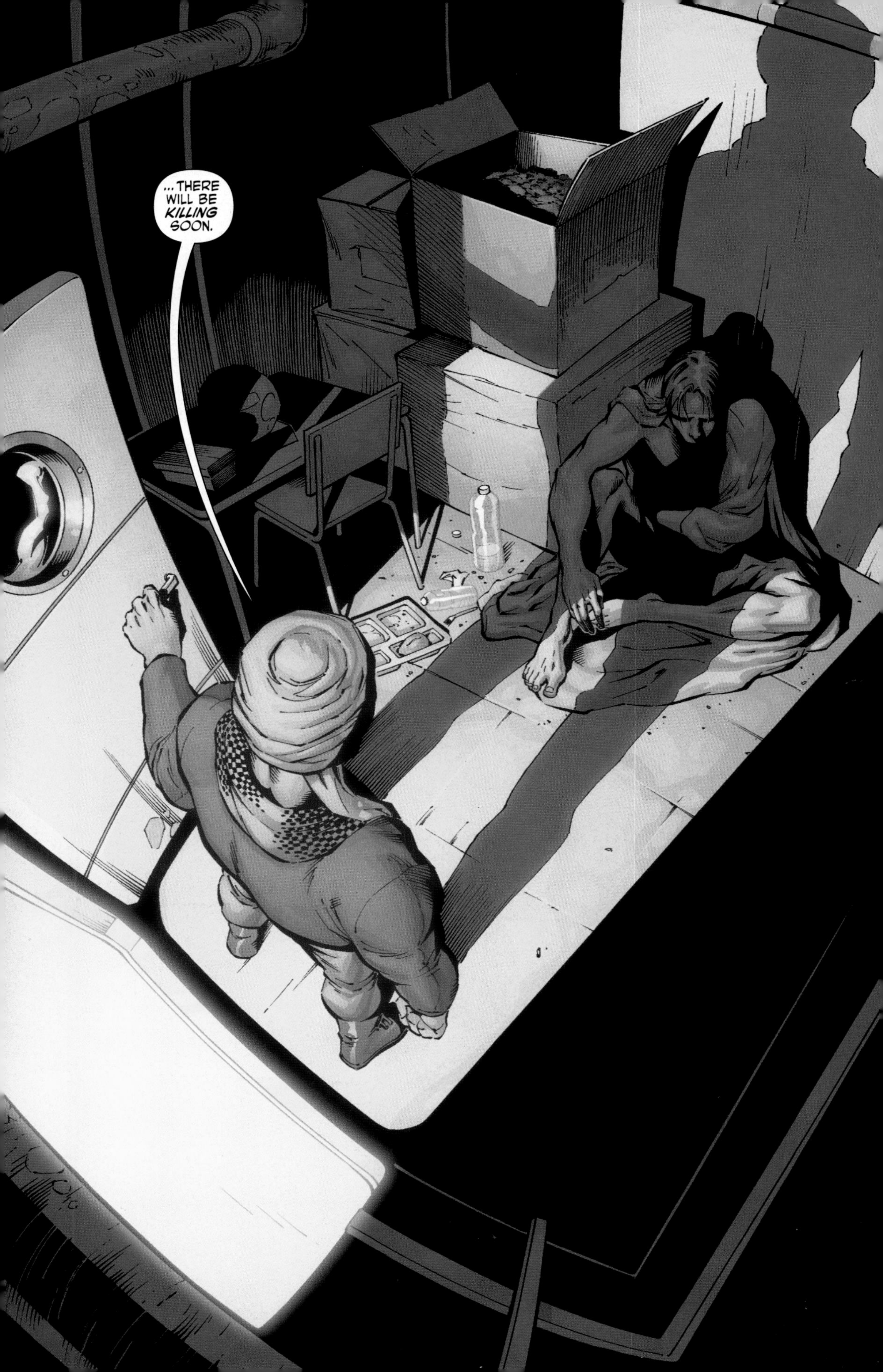
...THERE WILL BE KILLING SOON.

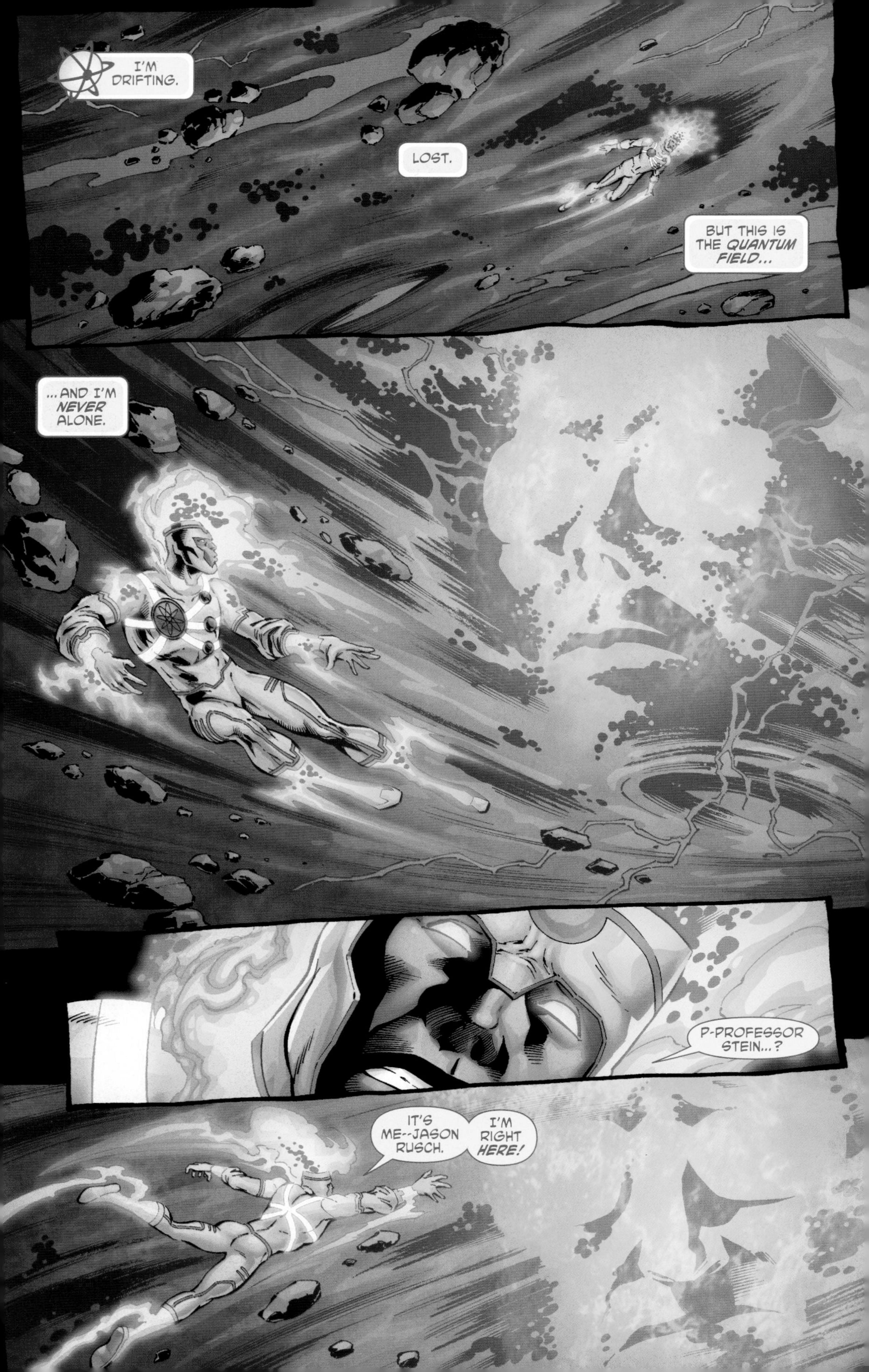
I'M DRIFTING.
LOST.
BUT THIS IS THE QUANTUM FIELD...
...AND I'M NEVER ALONE.
P-PROFESSOR STEIN...?
IT'S ME--JASON RUSCH.
I'M RIGHT HERE!

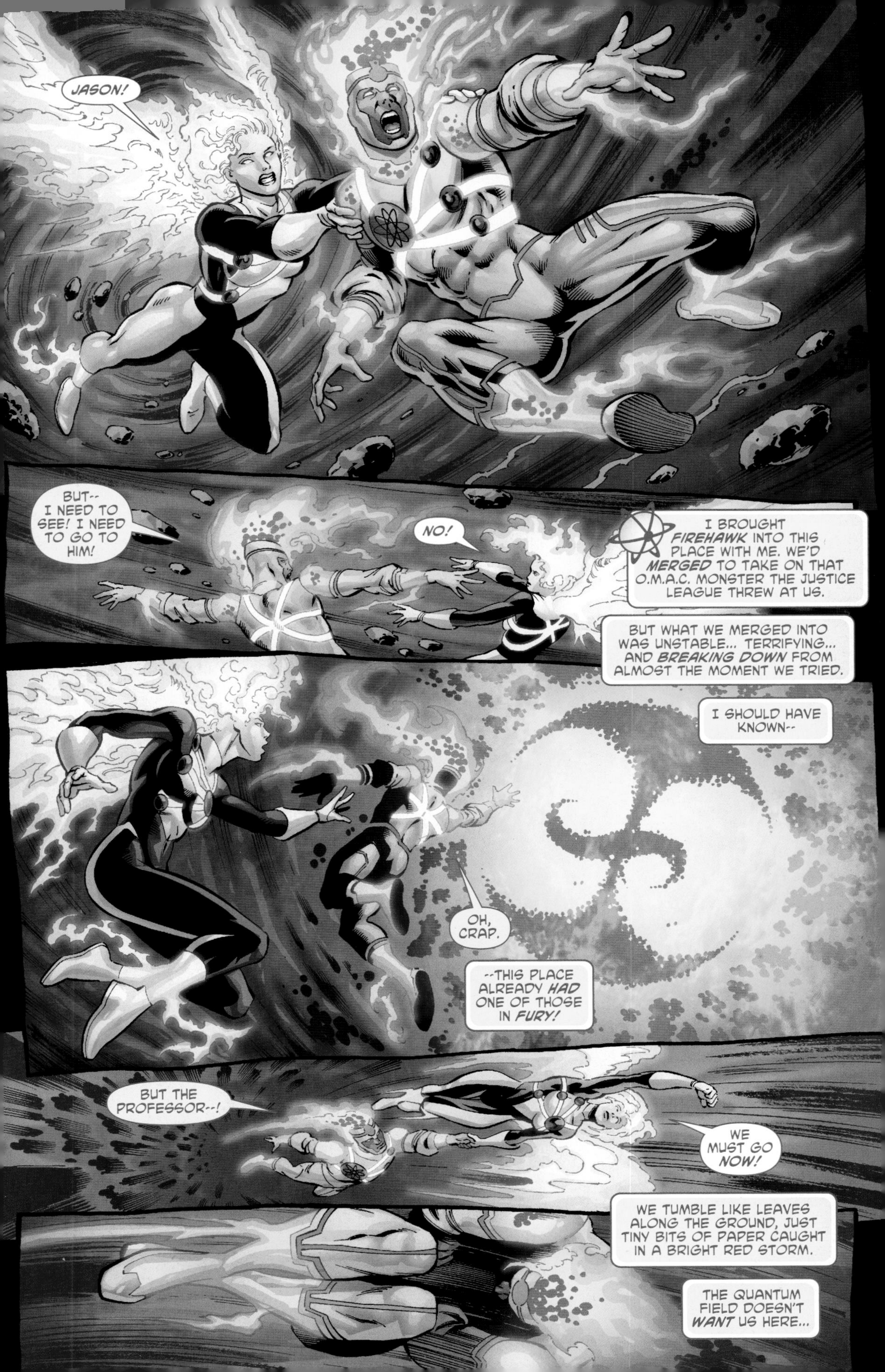
JASON!
BUT-- I NEED TO SEE! I NEED TO GO TO HIM!
NO!
I BROUGHT FIREHAWK INTO THIS PLACE WITH ME. WE'D MERGED TO TAKE ON THAT O.M.A.C. MONSTER THE JUSTICE LEAGUE THREW AT US.
BUT WHAT WE MERGED INTO WAS UNSTABLE... TERRIFYING... AND BREAKING DOWN FROM ALMOST THE MOMENT WE TRIED.
I SHOULD HAVE KNOWN--
OH, CRAP.
--THIS PLACE ALREADY HAD ONE OF THOSE IN FURY!
BUT THE PROFESSOR--!
WE MUST GO NOW!
WE TUMBLE LIKE LEAVES ALONG THE GROUND, JUST TINY BITS OF PAPER CAUGHT IN A BRIGHT RED STORM.
THE QUANTUM FIELD DOESN'T WANT US HERE...

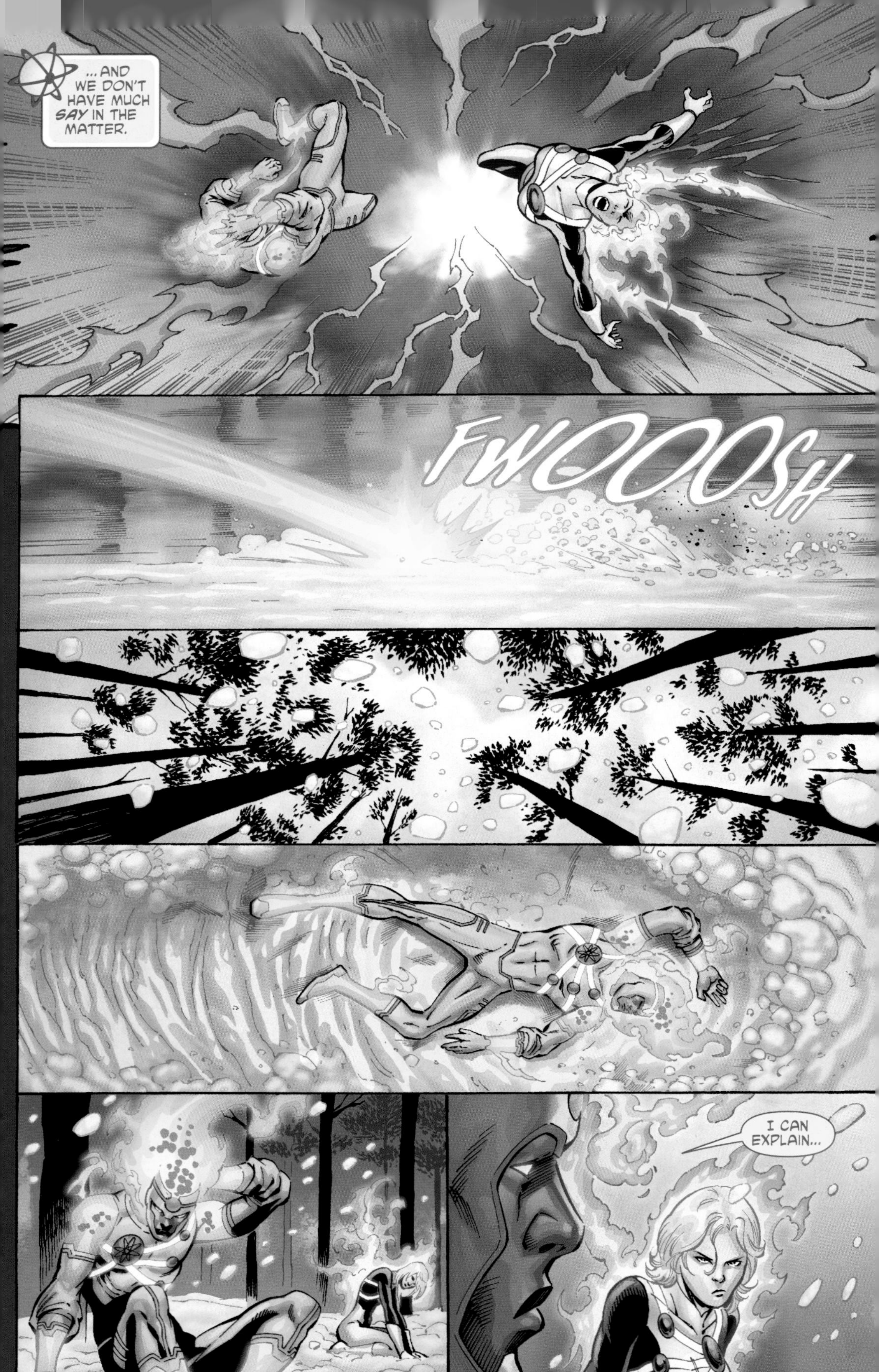
...AND WE DON'T HAVE MUCH SAY IN THE MATTER.
FWOOOOSH
I CAN EXPLAIN...

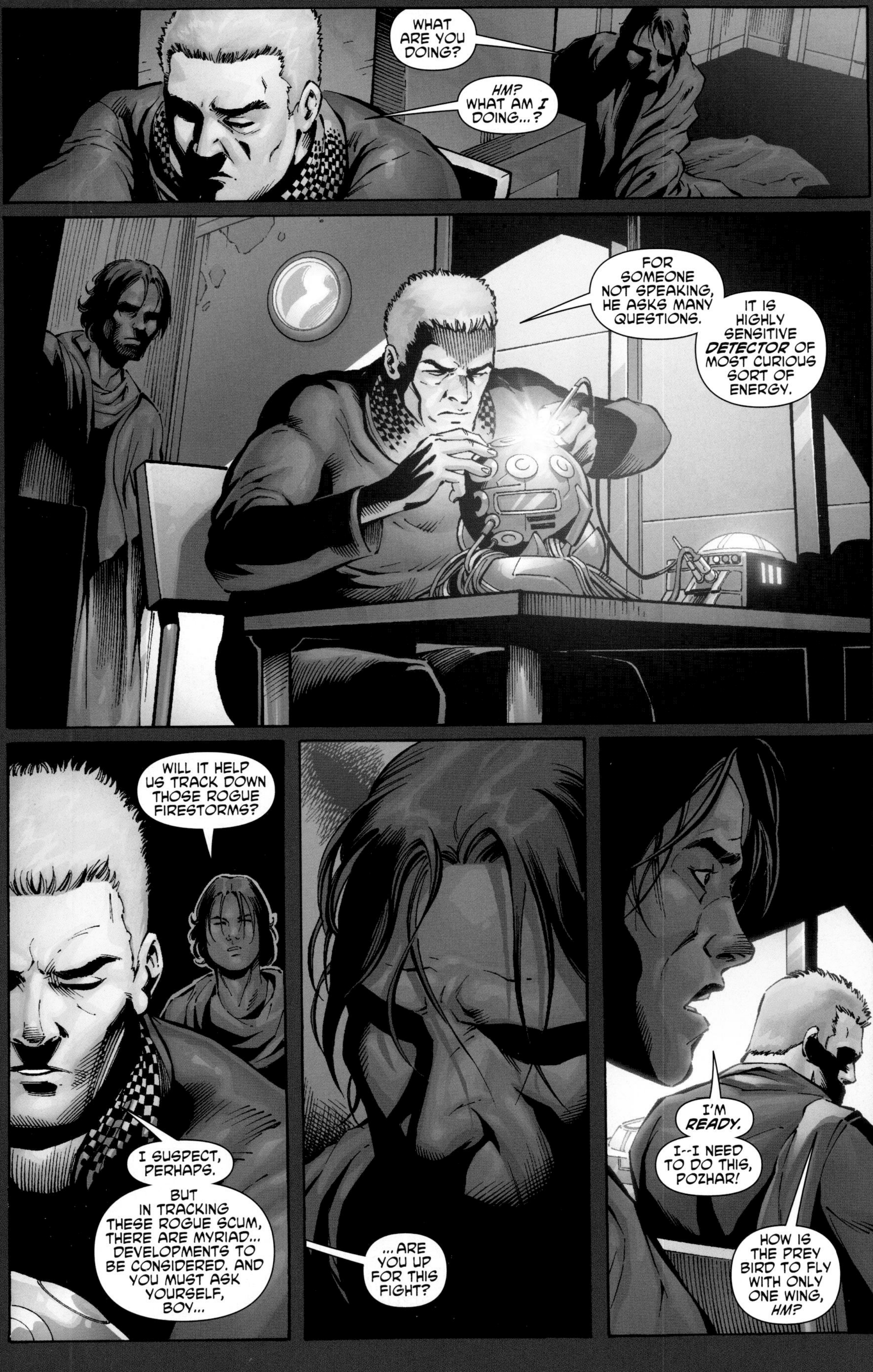
WHAT ARE YOU DOING?
HM? WHAT AM I DOING...?
FOR SOMEONE NOT SPEAKING, HE ASKS MANY QUESTIONS.
IT IS HIGHLY SENSITIVE DETECTOR OF MOST CURIOUS SORT OF ENERGY.
WILL IT HELP US TRACK DOWN THOSE ROGUE FIRESTORMS?
I SUSPECT, PERHAPS.
BUT IN TRACKING THESE ROGUE SCUM, THERE ARE MYRIAD... DEVELOPMENTS TO BE CONSIDERED. AND YOU MUST ASK YOURSELF, BOY...
...ARE YOU UP FOR THIS FIGHT?
I'M READY.
I--I NEED TO DO THIS, POZHAR!
HOW IS THE PREY BIRD TO FLY WITH ONLY ONE WING, HM?

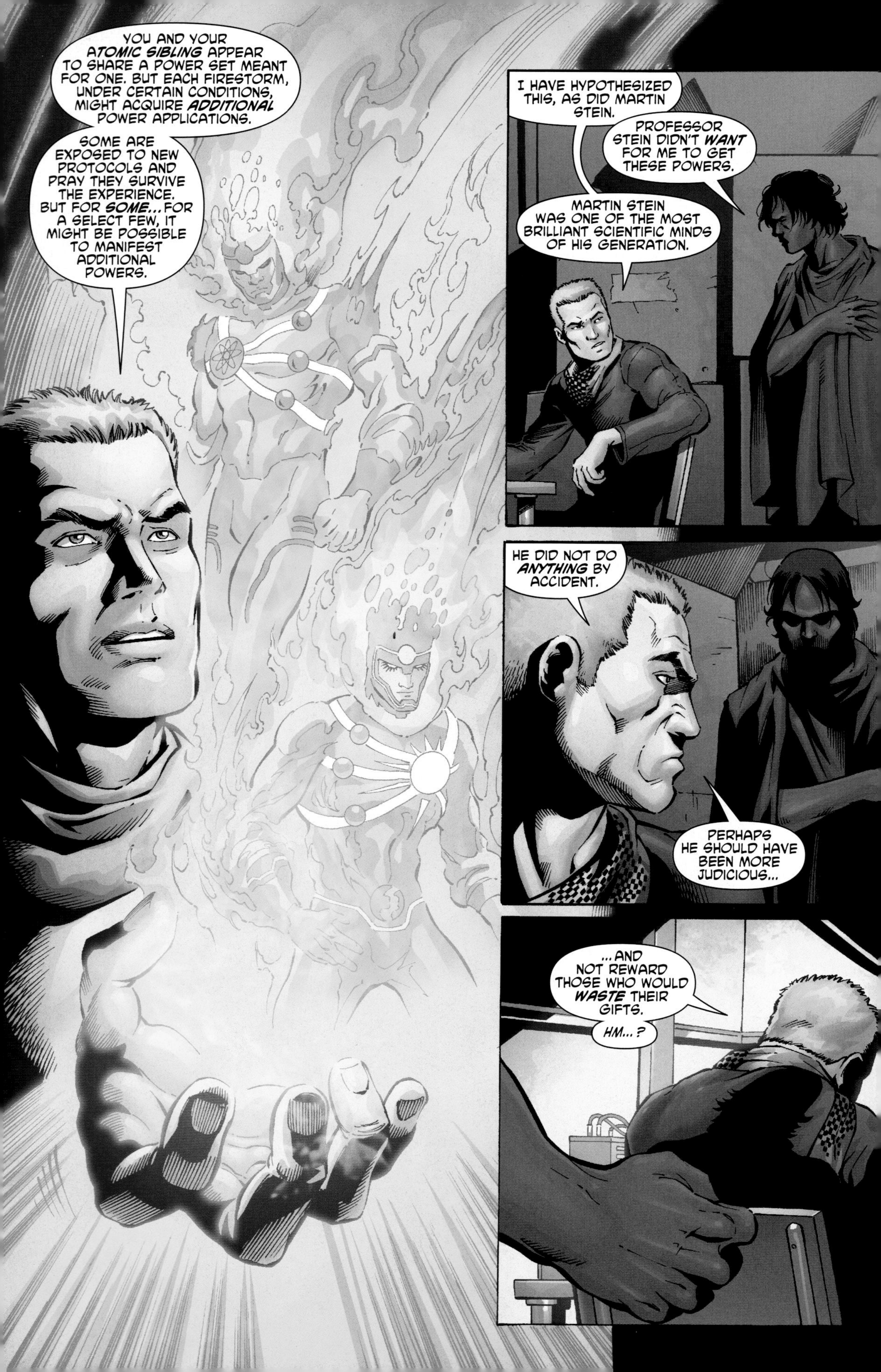
YOU AND YOUR ATOMIC SIBLING APPEAR TO SHARE A POWER SET MEANT FOR ONE. BUT EACH FIRESTORM, UNDER CERTAIN CONDITIONS, MIGHT ACQUIRE ADDITIONAL POWER APPLICATIONS.
SOME ARE EXPOSED TO NEW PROTOCOLS AND PRAY THEY SURVIVE THE EXPERIENCE. BUT FOR SOME... FOR A SELECT FEW, IT MIGHT BE POSSIBLE TO MANIFEST ADDITIONAL POWERS.
I HAVE HYPOTHESIZED THIS, AS DID MARTIN STEIN.
PROFESSOR STEIN DIDN'T WANT FOR ME TO GET THESE POWERS.
MARTIN STEIN WAS ONE OF THE MOST BRILLIANT SCIENTIFIC MINDS OF HIS GENERATION.
HE DID NOT DO ANYTHING BY ACCIDENT.
PERHAPS HE SHOULD HAVE BEEN MORE JUDICIOUS...
...AND NOT REWARD THOSE WHO WOULD WASTE THEIR GIFTS.
HM...?

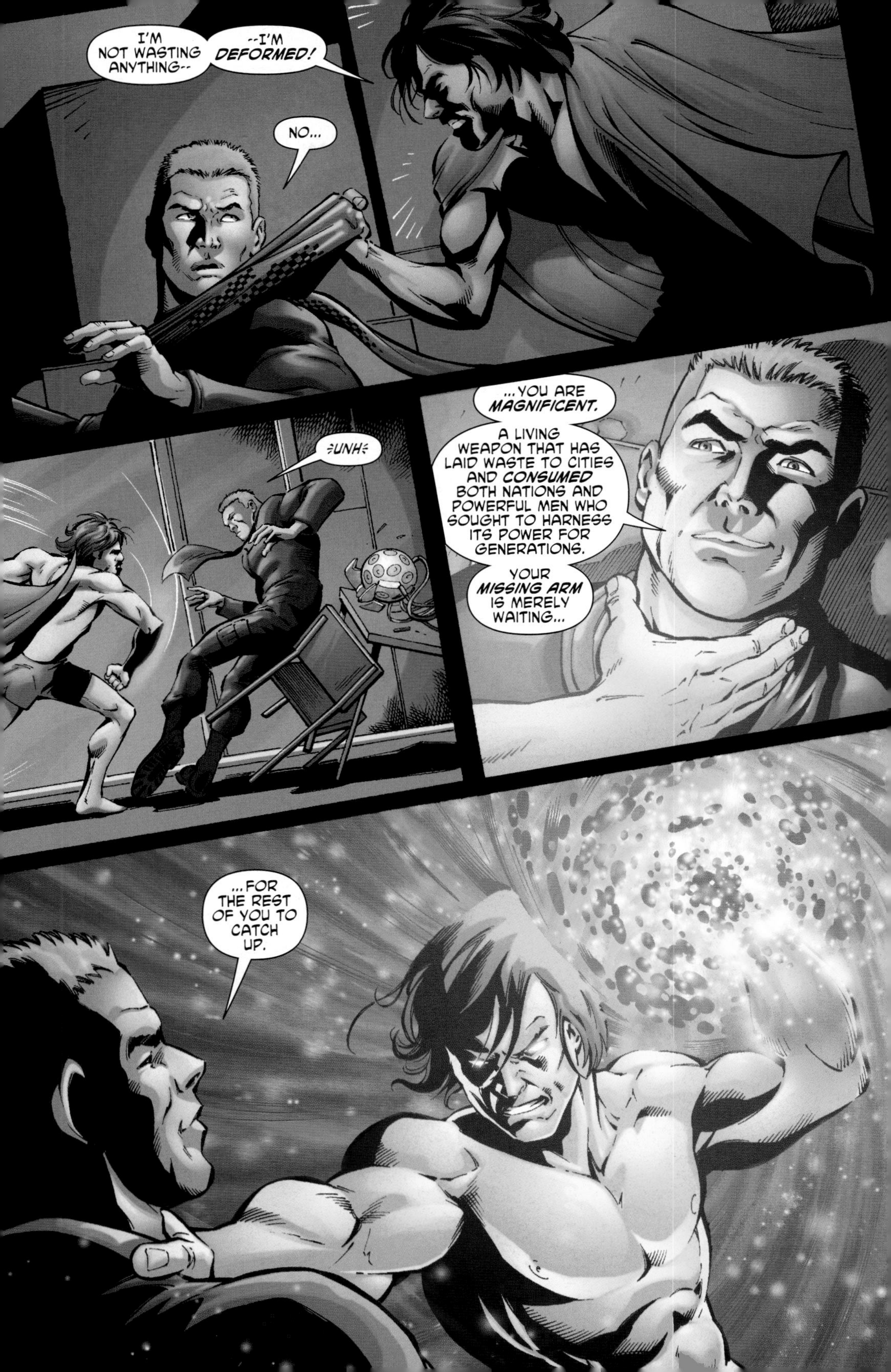
I'M NOT WASTING ANYTHING--
--I'M DEFORMED!
NO...
UNH
...YOU ARE MAGNIFICENT.
A LIVING WEAPON THAT HAS LAID WASTE TO CITIES AND CONSUMED BOTH NATIONS AND POWERFUL MEN WHO SOUGHT TO HARNESS ITS POWER FOR GENERATIONS.
YOUR MISSING ARM IS MERELY WAITING...
...FOR THE REST OF YOU TO CATCH UP.

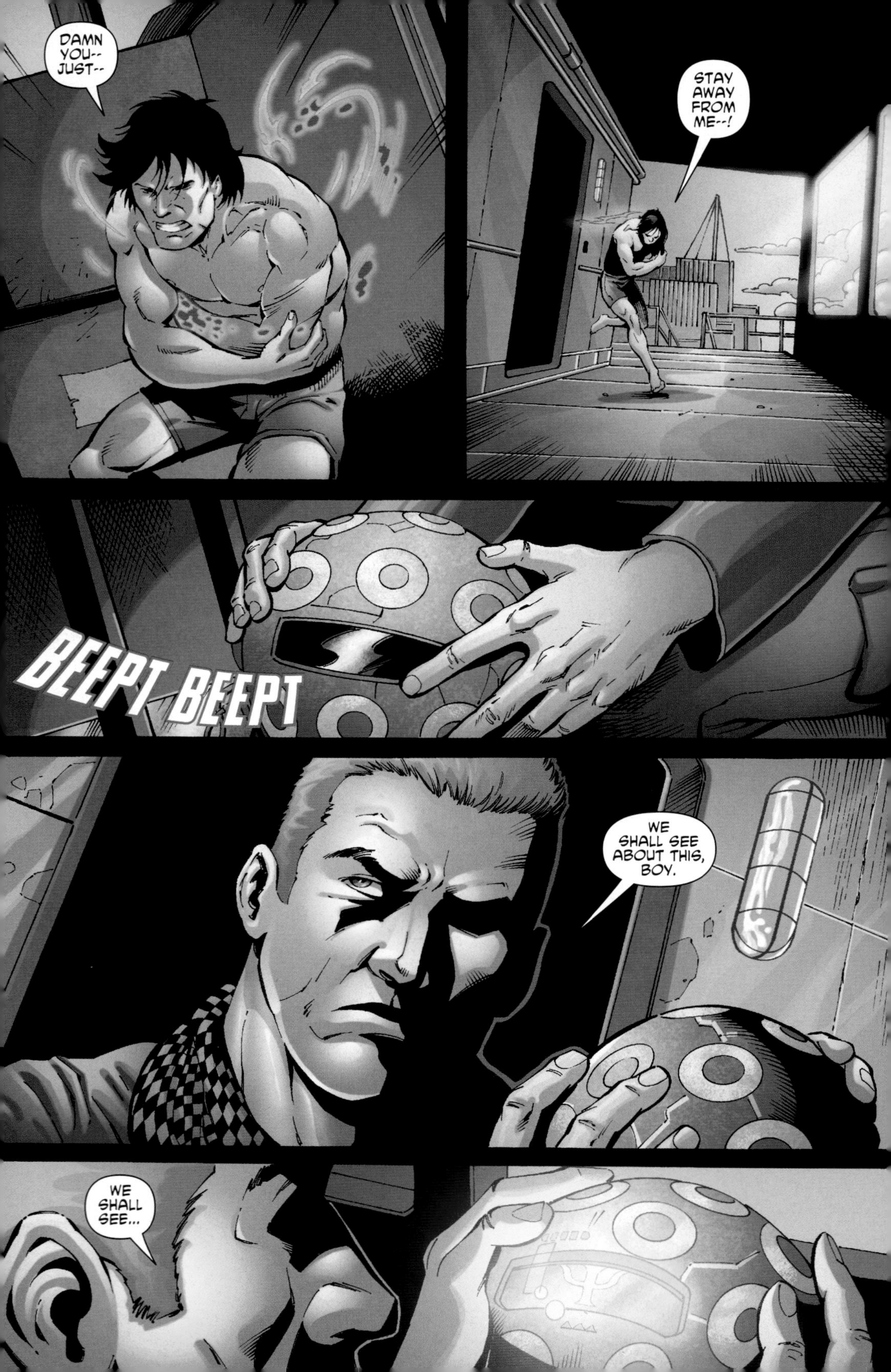
DAMN YOU-- JUST--
STAY AWAY FROM ME--!
BEEPT BEEPT
WE SHALL SEE ABOUT THIS, BOY.
WE SHALL SEE...

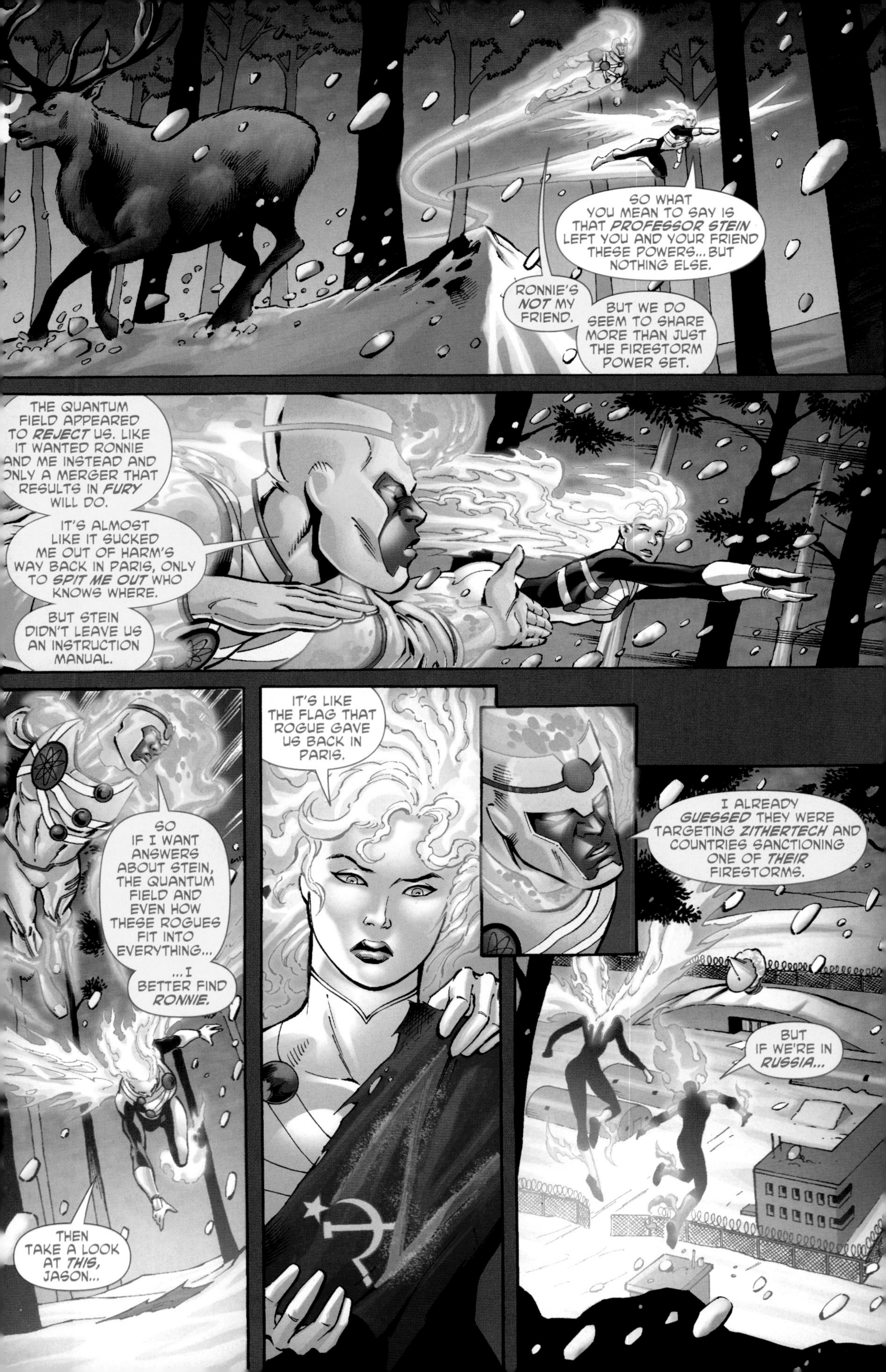
SO WHAT YOU MEAN TO SAY IS THAT PROFESSOR STEIN LEFT YOU AND YOUR FRIEND THESE POWERS... BUT NOTHING ELSE.
RONNIE'S NOT MY FRIEND.
BUT WE DO SEEM TO SHARE MORE THAN JUST THE FIRESTORM POWER SET.
THE QUANTUM FIELD APPEARED TO REJECT US. LIKE IT WANTED RONNIE AND ME INSTEAD AND ONLY A MERGER THAT RESULTS IN FURY WILL DO.
IT'S ALMOST LIKE IT SUCKED ME OUT OF HARM'S WAY BACK IN PARIS, ONLY TO SPIT ME OUT WHO KNOWS WHERE.
BUT STEIN DIDN'T LEAVE US AN INSTRUCTION MANUAL.
SO IF I WANT ANSWERS ABOUT STEIN, THE QUANTUM FIELD AND EVEN HOW THESE ROGUES FIT INTO EVERYTHING...
...I BETTER FIND RONNIE.
THEN TAKE A LOOK AT THIS, JASON...
IT'S LIKE THE FLAG THAT ROGUE GAVE US BACK IN PARIS.
I ALREADY GUESSED THEY WERE TARGETING ZITHERTECH AND COUNTRIES SANCTIONING ONE OF THEIR FIRESTORMS.
BUT IF WE'RE IN RUSSIA...

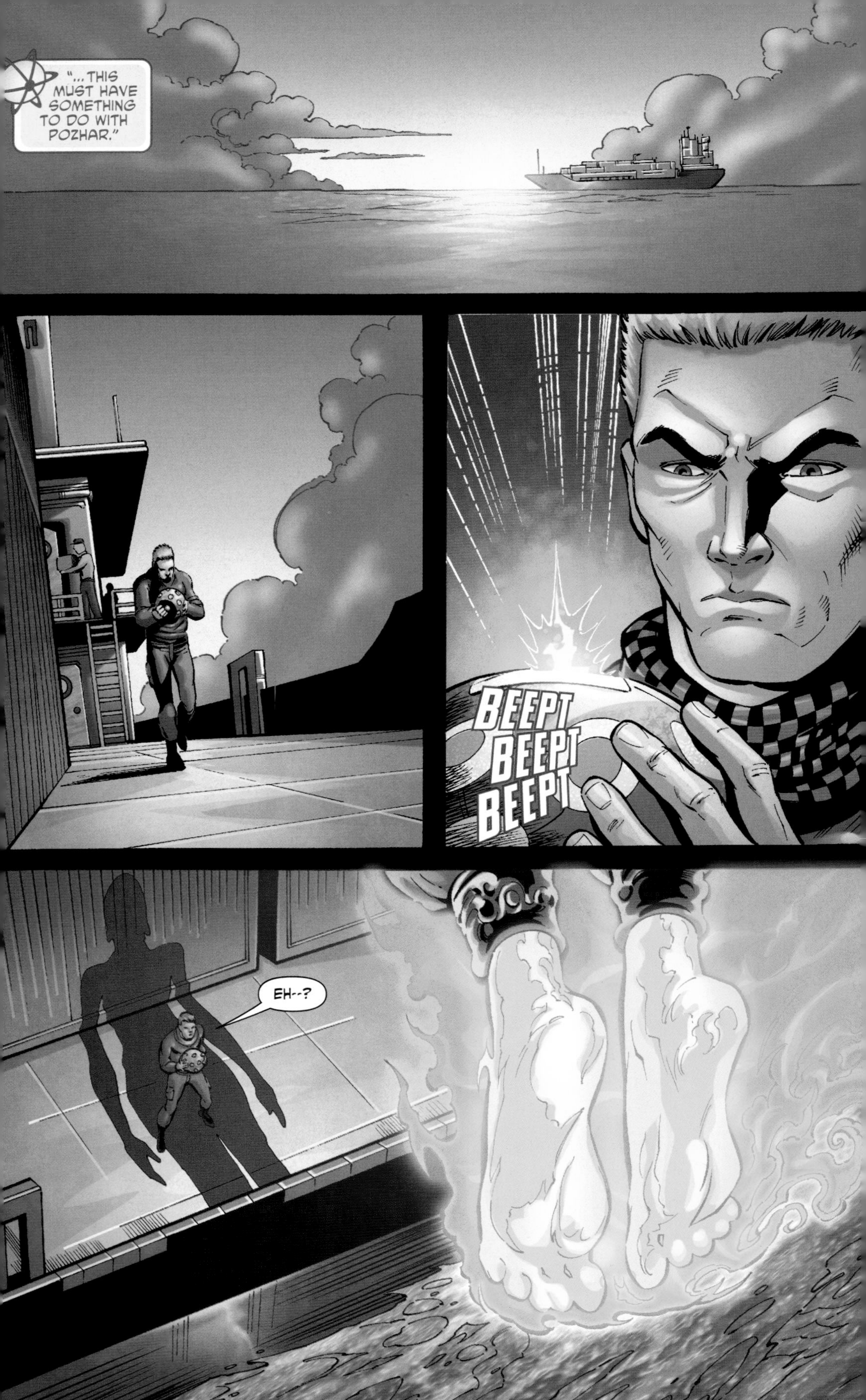
"...THIS MUST HAVE SOMETHING TO DO WITH POZHAR."
BEEPT
BEEPT
BEEPT
EH--?

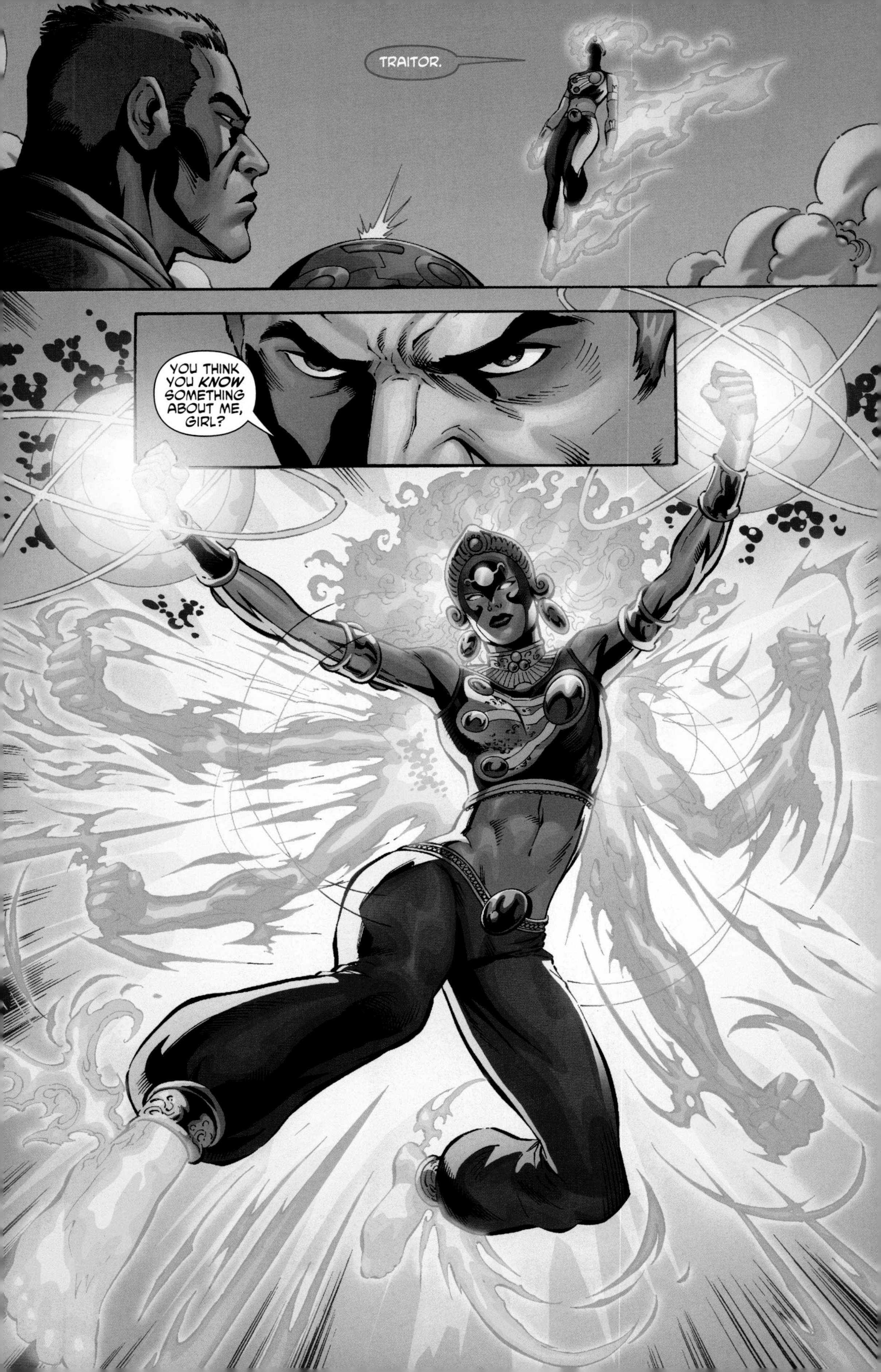
TRAITOR.
YOU THINK YOU *KNOW* SOMETHING ABOUT ME, GIRL?

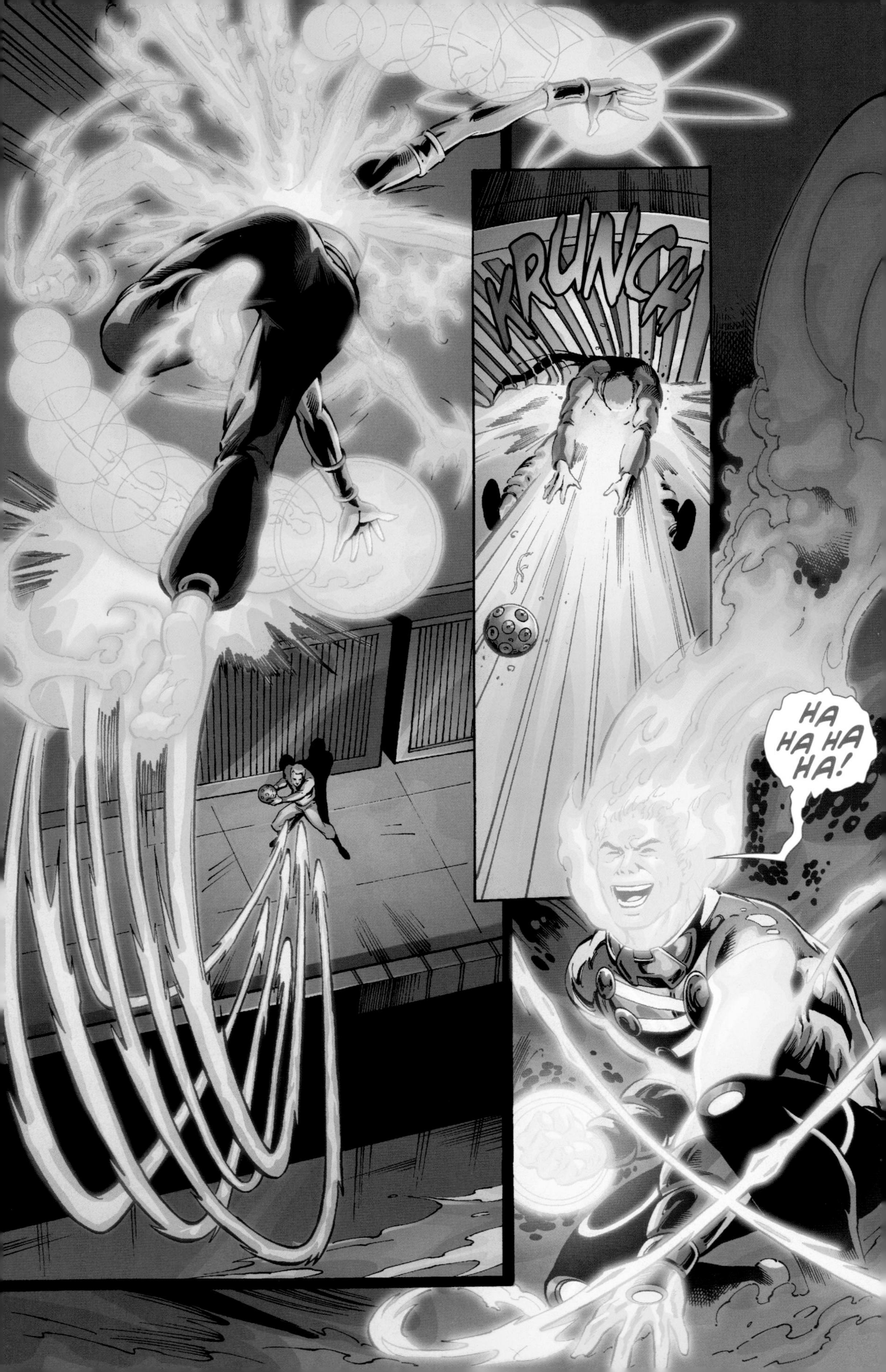
KRUNCH
HA HA HA HA HA!

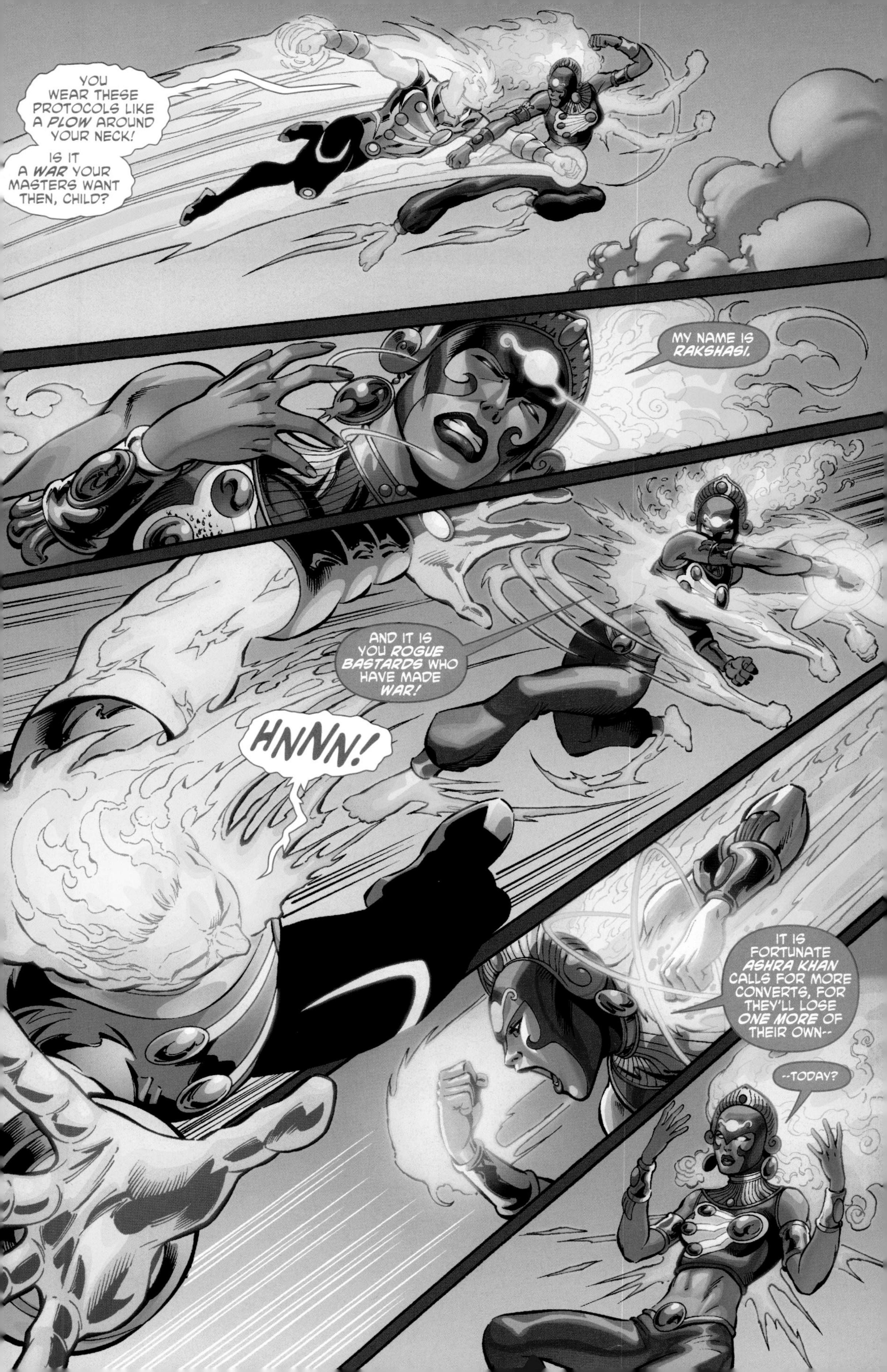

YOU WEAR THESE PROTOCOLS LIKE A *PLOW* AROUND YOUR NECK!
IS IT A *WAR* YOUR MASTERS WANT THEN, CHILD?
MY NAME IS *RAKSHASI.*
AND IT IS YOU *ROGUE BASTARDS* WHO HAVE MADE *WAR!*
HNNN!
IT IS FORTUNATE *ASHRA KHAN* CALLS FOR MORE CONVERTS, FOR THEY'LL LOSE *ONE MORE* OF THEIR OWN--
--TODAY?

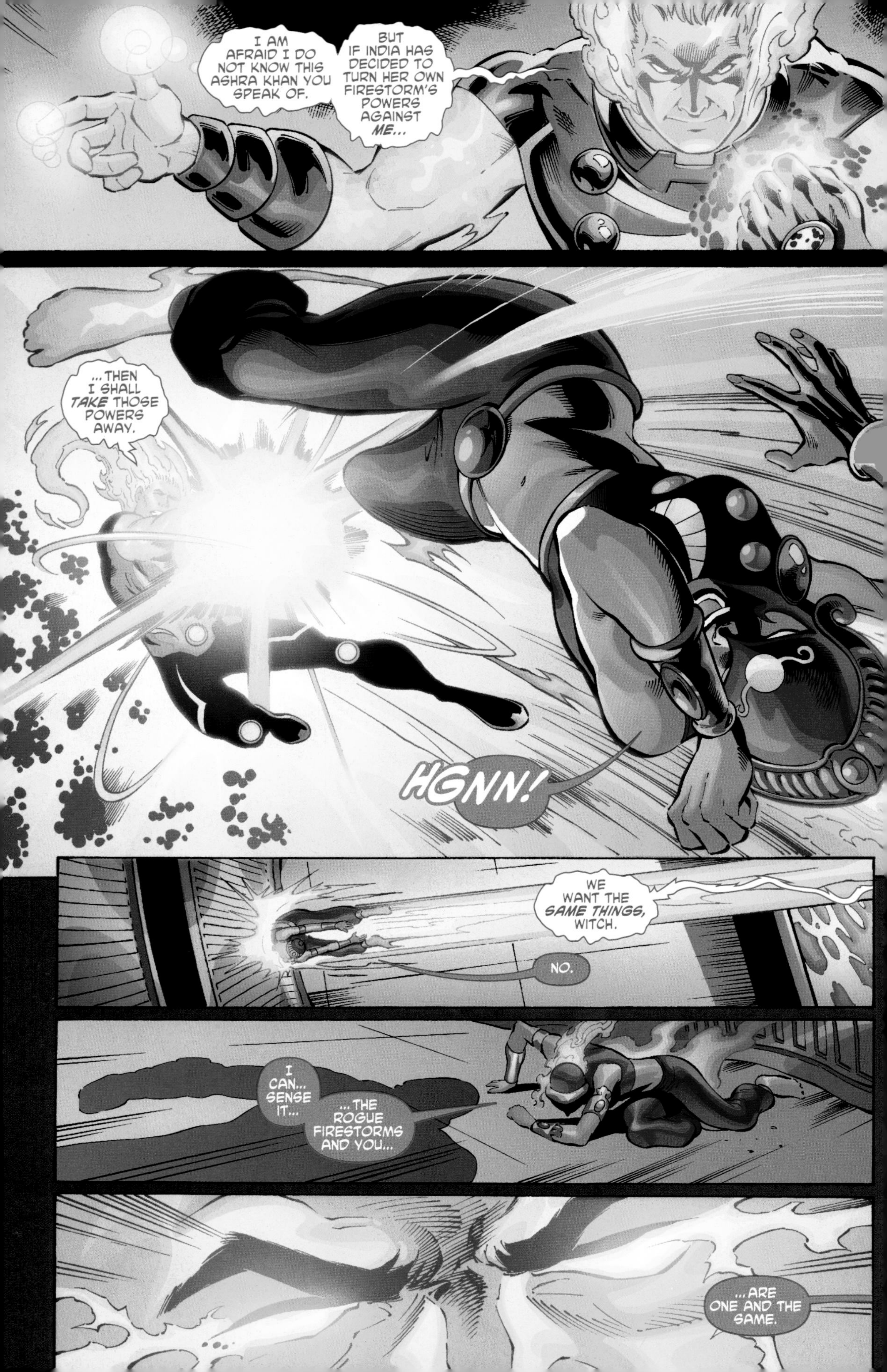
I AM AFRAID I DO NOT KNOW THIS ASHRA KHAN YOU SPEAK OF.
BUT IF INDIA HAS DECIDED TO TURN HER OWN FIRESTORM'S POWERS AGAINST ME...
...THEN I SHALL TAKE THOSE POWERS AWAY.
HGNN!
WE WANT THE SAME THINGS, WITCH.
NO.
I CAN... SENSE IT...
...THE ROGUE FIRESTORMS AND YOU...
...ARE ONE AND THE SAME.

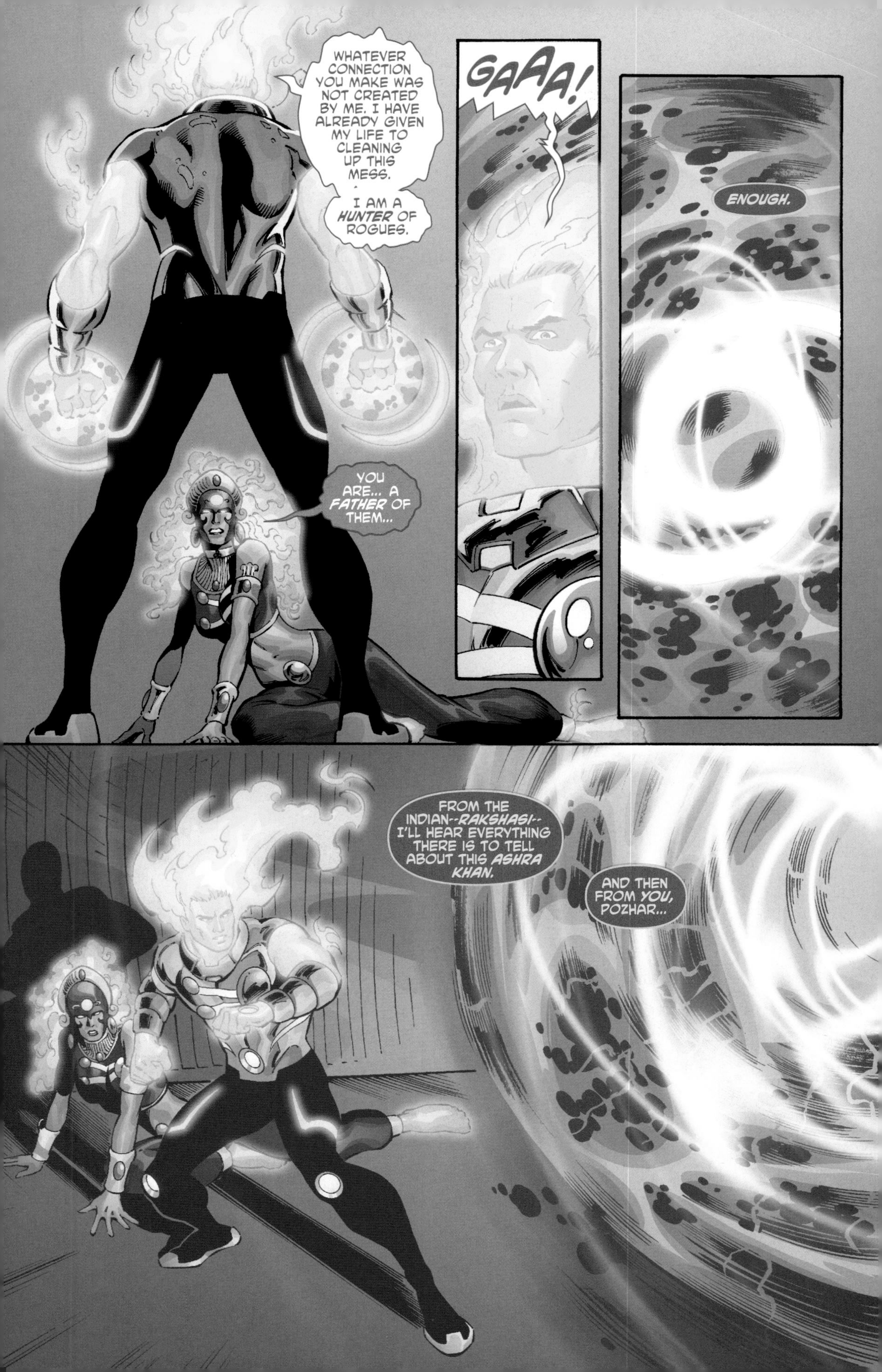
WHATEVER CONNECTION YOU MAKE WAS NOT CREATED BY ME. I HAVE ALREADY GIVEN MY LIFE TO CLEANING UP THIS MESS.
I AM A HUNTER OF ROGUES.
YOU ARE... A FATHER OF THEM...
GAAA!
ENOUGH.
FROM THE INDIAN--RAKSHASI--I'LL HEAR EVERYTHING THERE IS TO TELL ABOUT THIS ASHRA KHAN.
AND THEN FROM YOU, POZHAR...

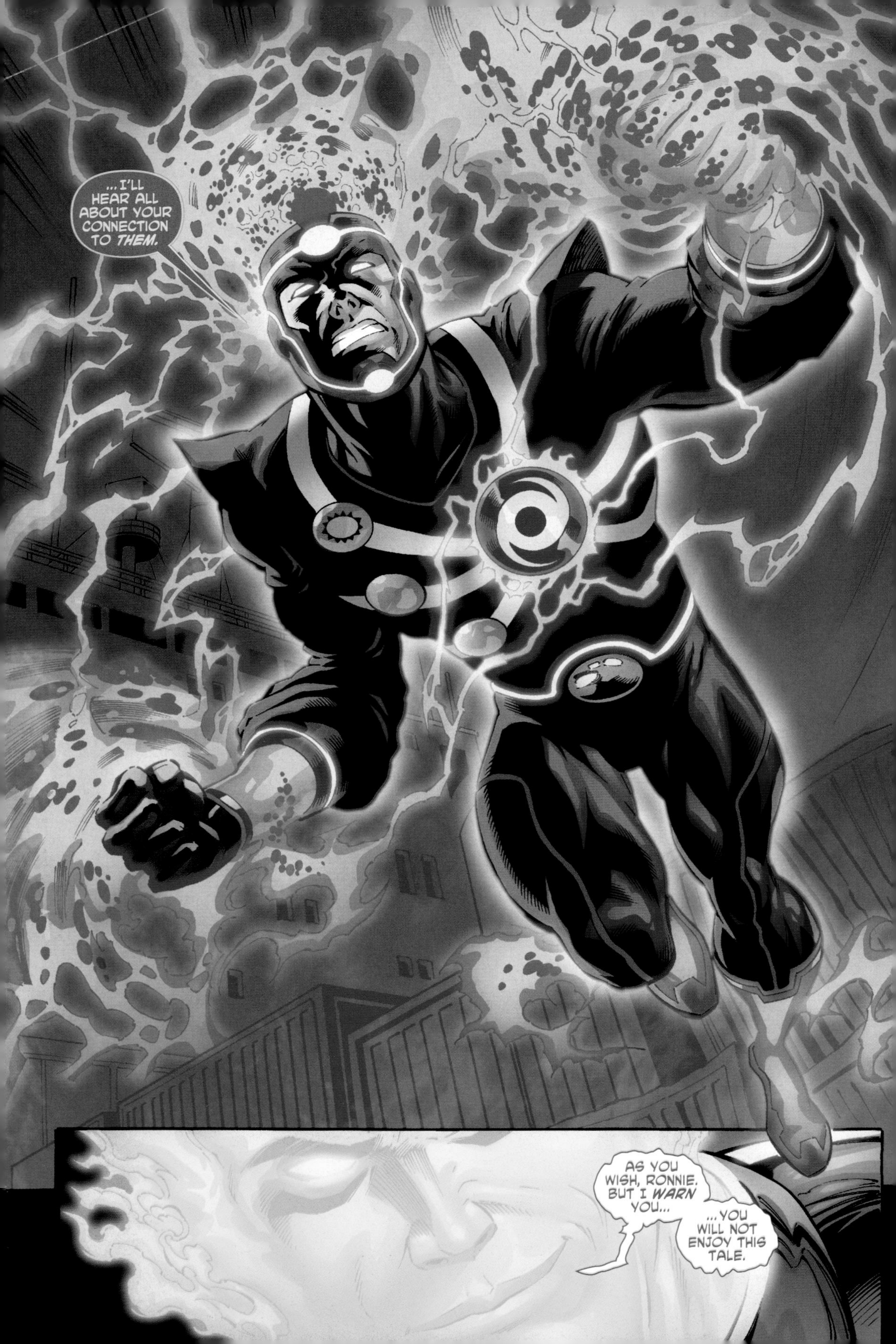
...I'LL HEAR ALL ABOUT YOUR CONNECTION TO THEM.
AS YOU WISH, RONNIE. BUT I WARN YOU...
...YOU WILL NOT ENJOY THIS TALE.

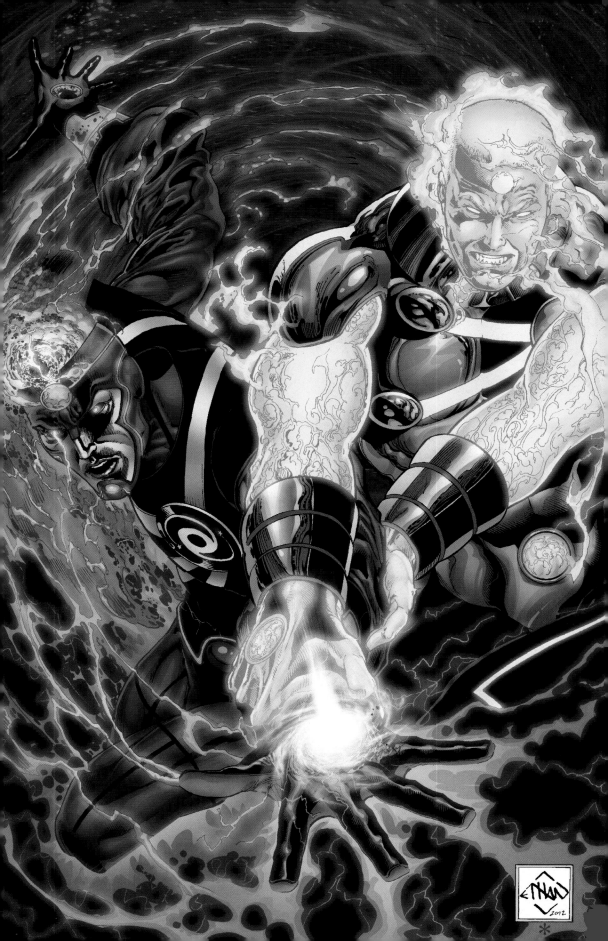

DARK MATTER

JOE HARRIS writer **YILDIRAY CINAR** penciller **MARLO ALQUIZA** inker
cover by **ETHAN VAN SCIVER** with **HI-FI**

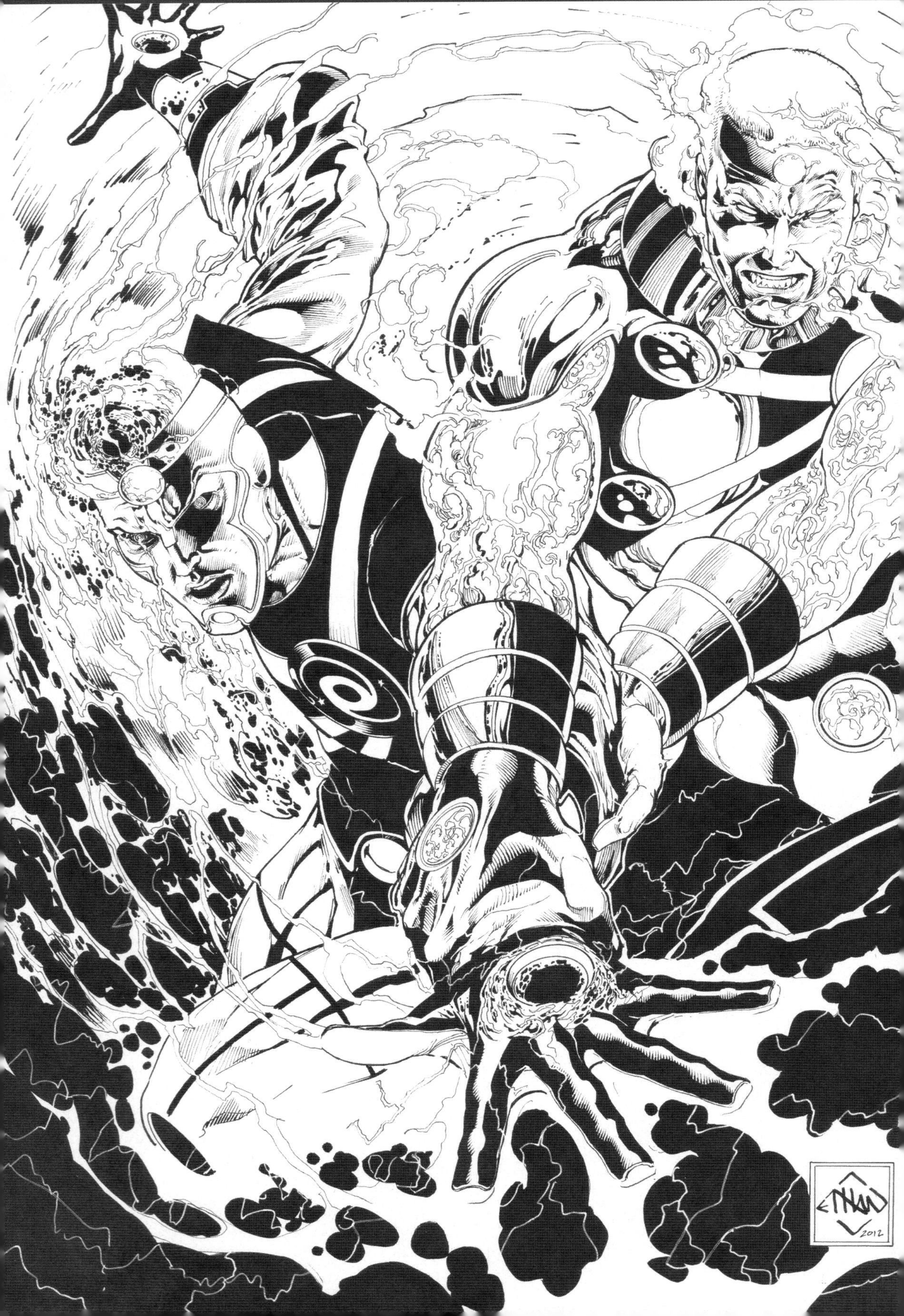
ETHAN
2012

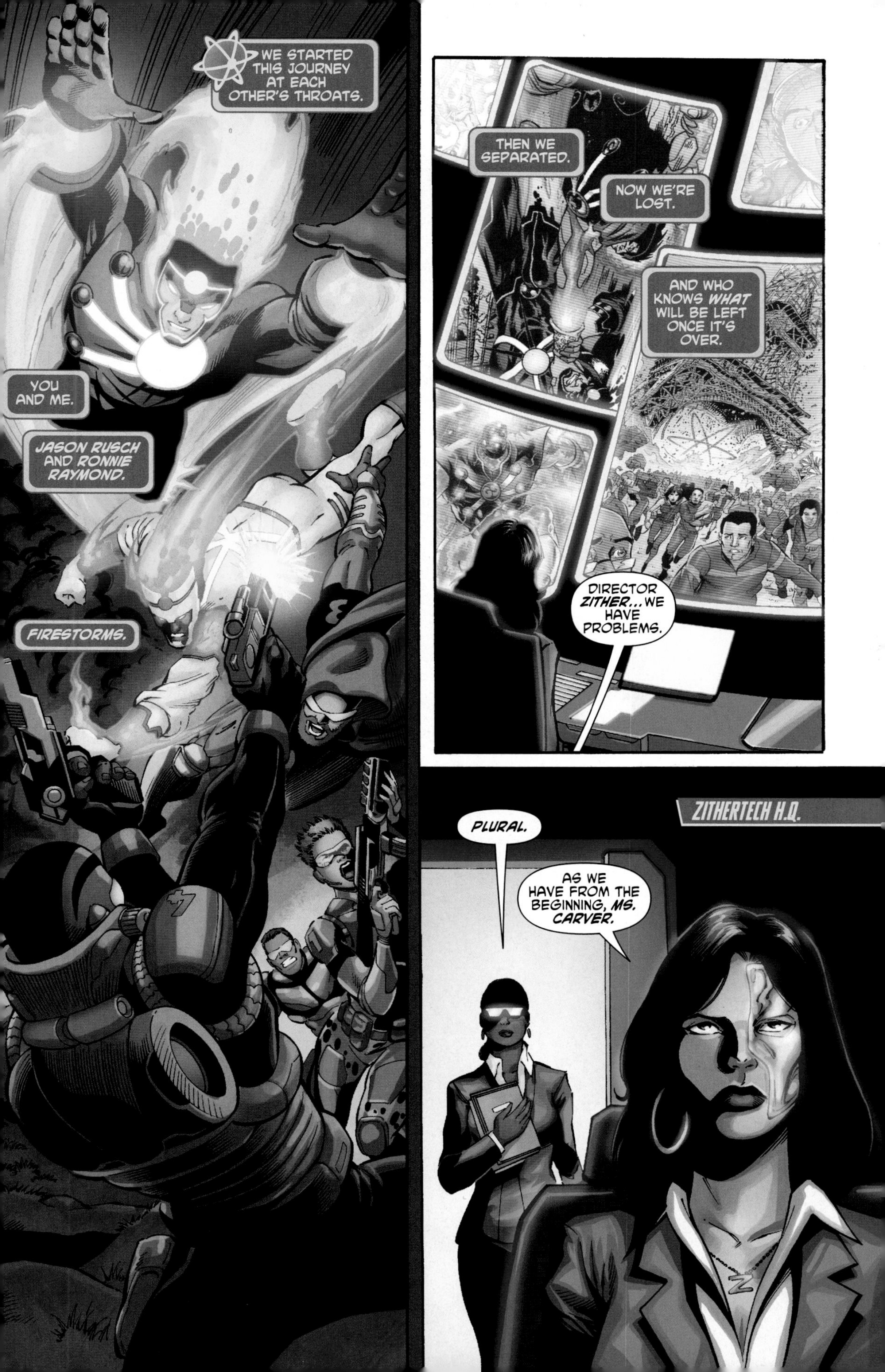
WE STARTED THIS JOURNEY AT EACH OTHER'S THROATS.
YOU AND ME.
JASON RUSCH AND RONNIE RAYMOND.
FIRESTORMS.
THEN WE SEPARATED.
NOW WE'RE LOST.
AND WHO KNOWS WHAT WILL BE LEFT ONCE IT'S OVER.
DIRECTOR ZITHER... WE HAVE PROBLEMS.
ZITHERTECH H.Q.
PLURAL.
AS WE HAVE FROM THE BEGINNING, MS. CARVER.

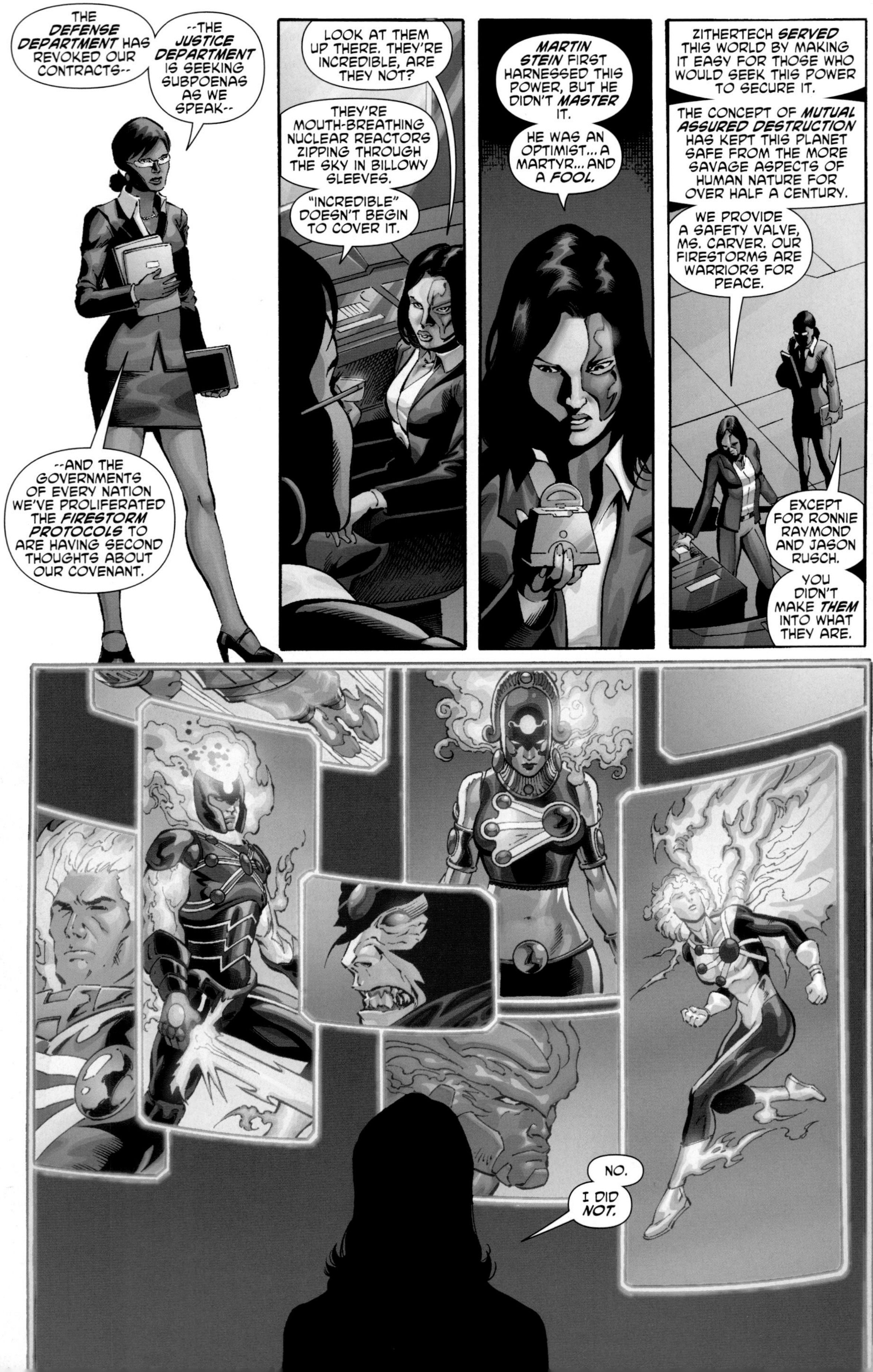
THE DEFENSE DEPARTMENT HAS REVOKED OUR CONTRACTS--
--THE JUSTICE DEPARTMENT IS SEEKING SUBPOENAS AS WE SPEAK--
--AND THE GOVERNMENTS OF EVERY NATION WE'VE PROLIFERATED THE FIRESTORM PROTOCOLS TO ARE HAVING SECOND THOUGHTS ABOUT OUR COVENANT.
LOOK AT THEM UP THERE. THEY'RE INCREDIBLE, ARE THEY NOT?
THEY'RE MOUTH-BREATHING NUCLEAR REACTORS ZIPPING THROUGH THE SKY IN BILLOWY SLEEVES.
"INCREDIBLE" DOESN'T BEGIN TO COVER IT.
MARTIN STEIN FIRST HARNESSED THIS POWER, BUT HE DIDN'T MASTER IT.
HE WAS AN OPTIMIST... A MARTYR... AND A FOOL.
ZITHERTECH SERVED THIS WORLD BY MAKING IT EASY FOR THOSE WHO WOULD SEEK THIS POWER TO SECURE IT.
THE CONCEPT OF MUTUAL ASSURED DESTRUCTION HAS KEPT THIS PLANET SAFE FROM THE MORE SAVAGE ASPECTS OF HUMAN NATURE FOR OVER HALF A CENTURY.
WE PROVIDE A SAFETY VALVE, MS. CARVER. OUR FIRESTORMS ARE WARRIORS FOR PEACE.
EXCEPT FOR RONNIE RAYMOND AND JASON RUSCH.
YOU DIDN'T MAKE THEM INTO WHAT THEY ARE.
NO.
I DID NOT.

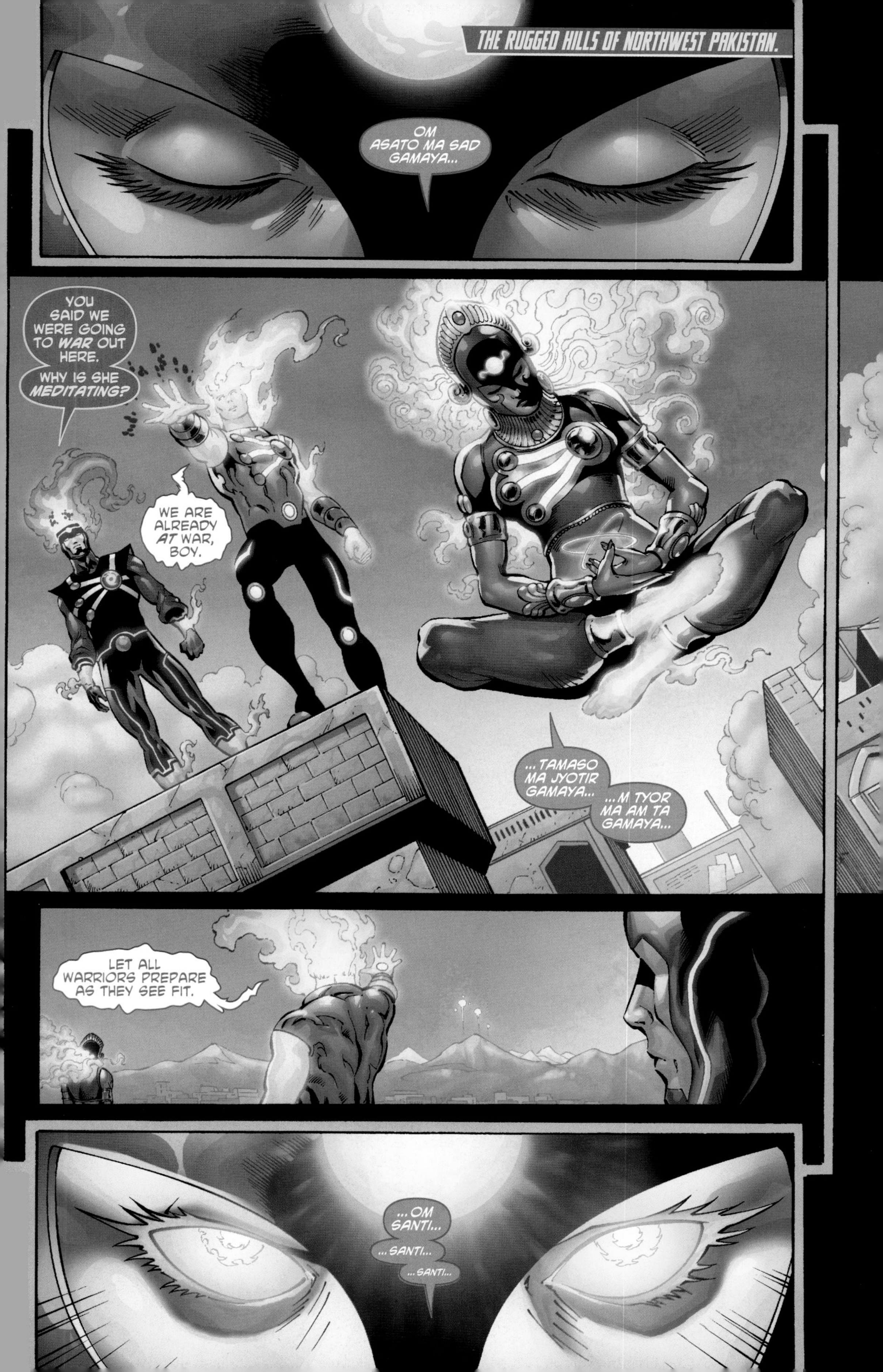
THE RUGGED HILLS OF NORTHWEST PAKISTAN.
OM ASATO MA SAD GAMAYA...
YOU SAID WE WERE GOING TO WAR OUT HERE.
WHY IS SHE MEDITATING?
WE ARE ALREADY AT WAR, BOY.
...TAMASO MA JYOTIR GAMAYA...
...M TYOR MA AM TA GAMAYA...
LET ALL WARRIORS PREPARE AS THEY SEE FIT.
...OM SANTI...
...SANTI...
...SANTI...

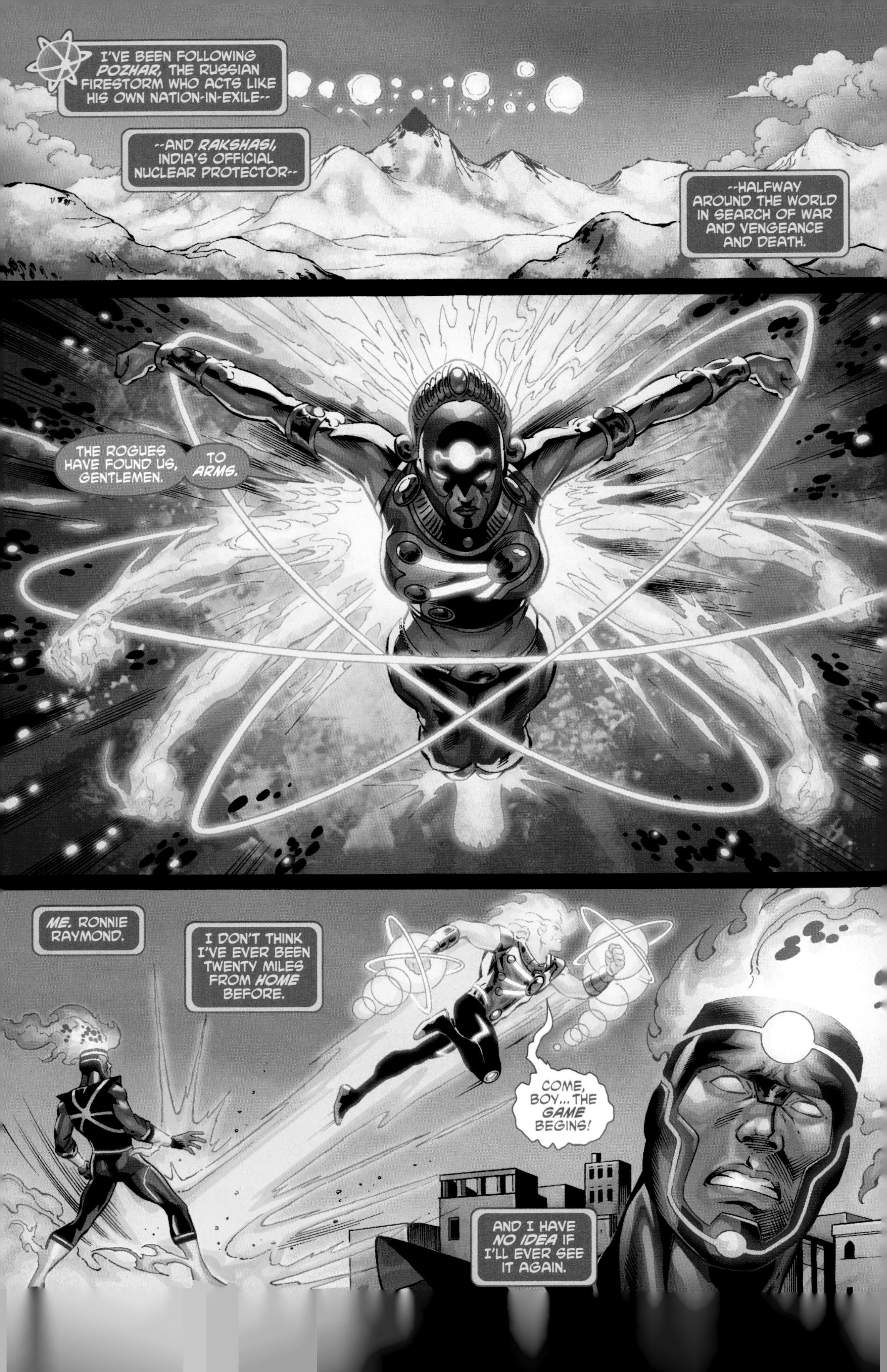
I'VE BEEN FOLLOWING POZHAR, THE RUSSIAN FIRESTORM WHO ACTS LIKE HIS OWN NATION-IN-EXILE--
--AND RAKSHASI, INDIA'S OFFICIAL NUCLEAR PROTECTOR--
--HALFWAY AROUND THE WORLD IN SEARCH OF WAR AND VENGEANCE AND DEATH.
THE ROGUES HAVE FOUND US, GENTLEMEN.
TO ARMS.
ME. RONNIE RAYMOND.
I DON'T THINK I'VE EVER BEEN TWENTY MILES FROM HOME BEFORE.
COME, BOY... THE GAME BEGINS!
AND I HAVE NO IDEA IF I'LL EVER SEE IT AGAIN.

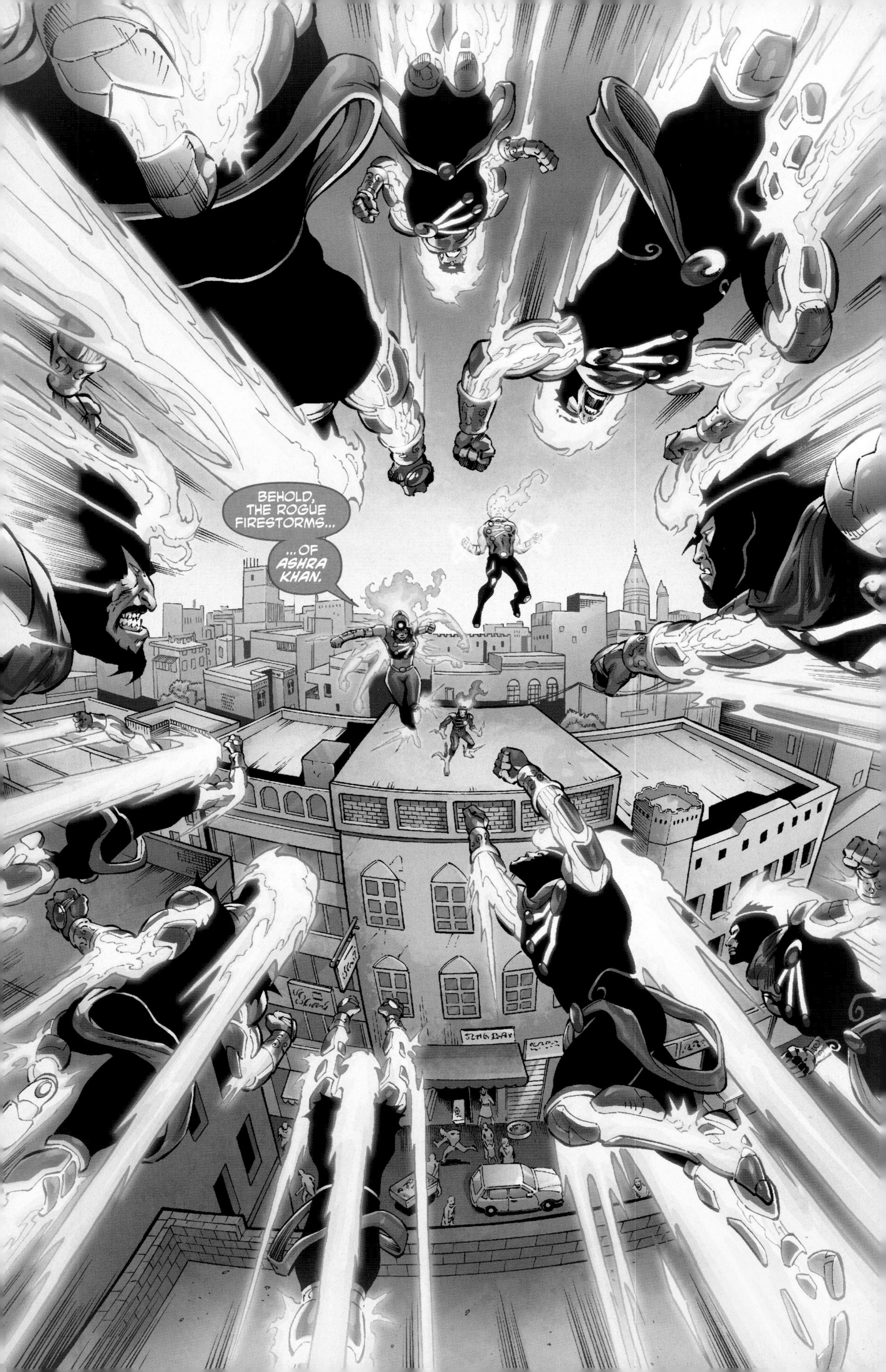

BEHOLD, THE ROGUE FIRESTORMS...
...OF ASHRA KHAN.

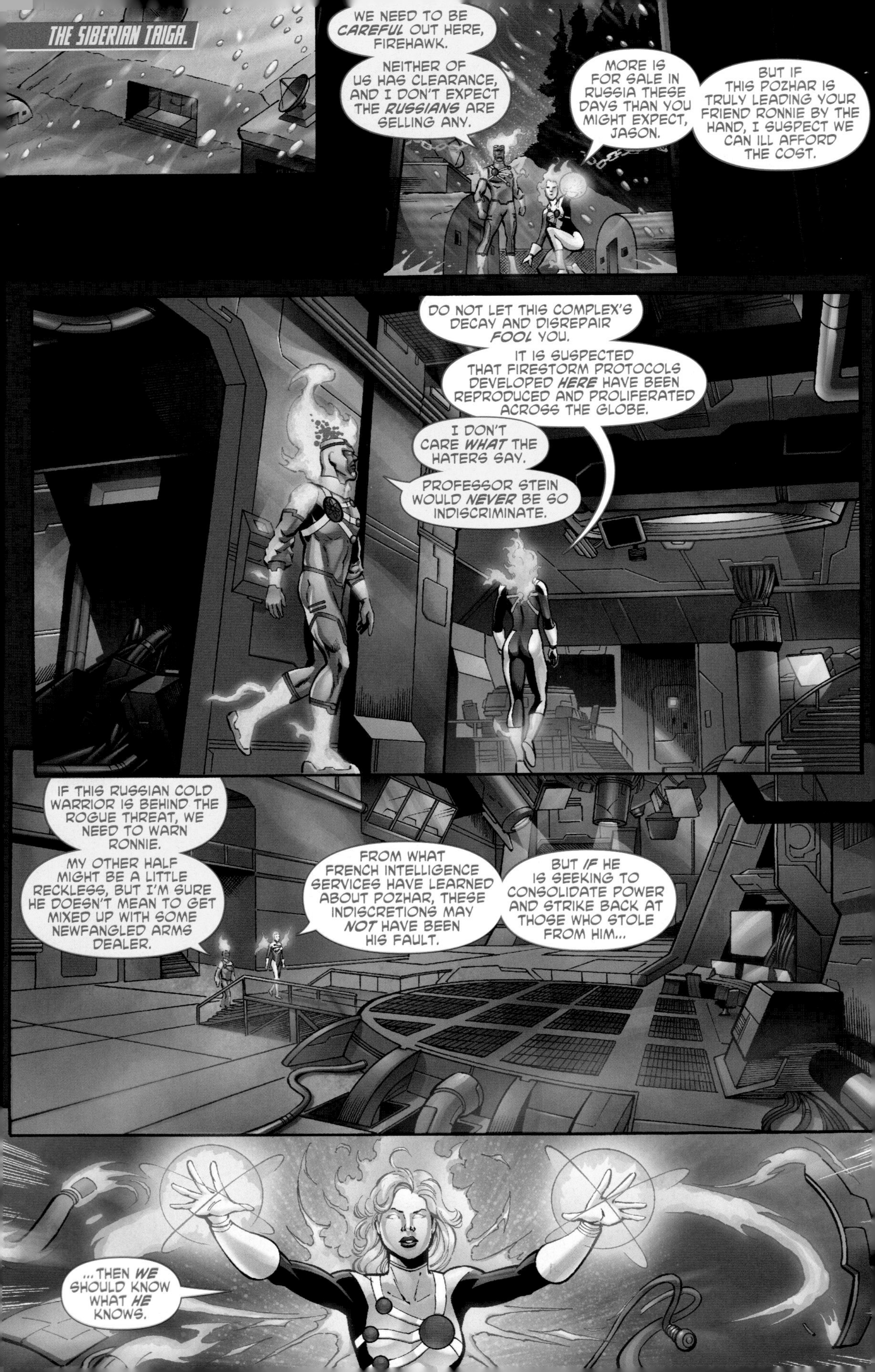
THE SIBERIAN TAIGA.
WE NEED TO BE CAREFUL OUT HERE, FIREHAWK.
NEITHER OF US HAS CLEARANCE, AND I DON'T EXPECT THE RUSSIANS ARE SELLING ANY.
MORE IS FOR SALE IN RUSSIA THESE DAYS THAN YOU MIGHT EXPECT, JASON.
BUT IF THIS POZHAR IS TRULY LEADING YOUR FRIEND RONNIE BY THE HAND, I SUSPECT WE CAN ILL AFFORD THE COST.
DO NOT LET THIS COMPLEX'S DECAY AND DISREPAIR FOOL YOU.
IT IS SUSPECTED THAT FIRESTORM PROTOCOLS DEVELOPED HERE HAVE BEEN REPRODUCED AND PROLIFERATED ACROSS THE GLOBE.
I DON'T CARE WHAT THE HATERS SAY.
PROFESSOR STEIN WOULD NEVER BE SO INDISCRIMINATE.
IF THIS RUSSIAN COLD WARRIOR IS BEHIND THE ROGUE THREAT, WE NEED TO WARN RONNIE.
MY OTHER HALF MIGHT BE A LITTLE RECKLESS, BUT I'M SURE HE DOESN'T MEAN TO GET MIXED UP WITH SOME NEWFANGLED ARMS DEALER.
FROM WHAT FRENCH INTELLIGENCE SERVICES HAVE LEARNED ABOUT POZHAR, THESE INDISCRETIONS MAY NOT HAVE BEEN HIS FAULT.
BUT IF HE IS SEEKING TO CONSOLIDATE POWER AND STRIKE BACK AT THOSE WHO STOLE FROM HIM...
...THEN WE SHOULD KNOW WHAT HE KNOWS.

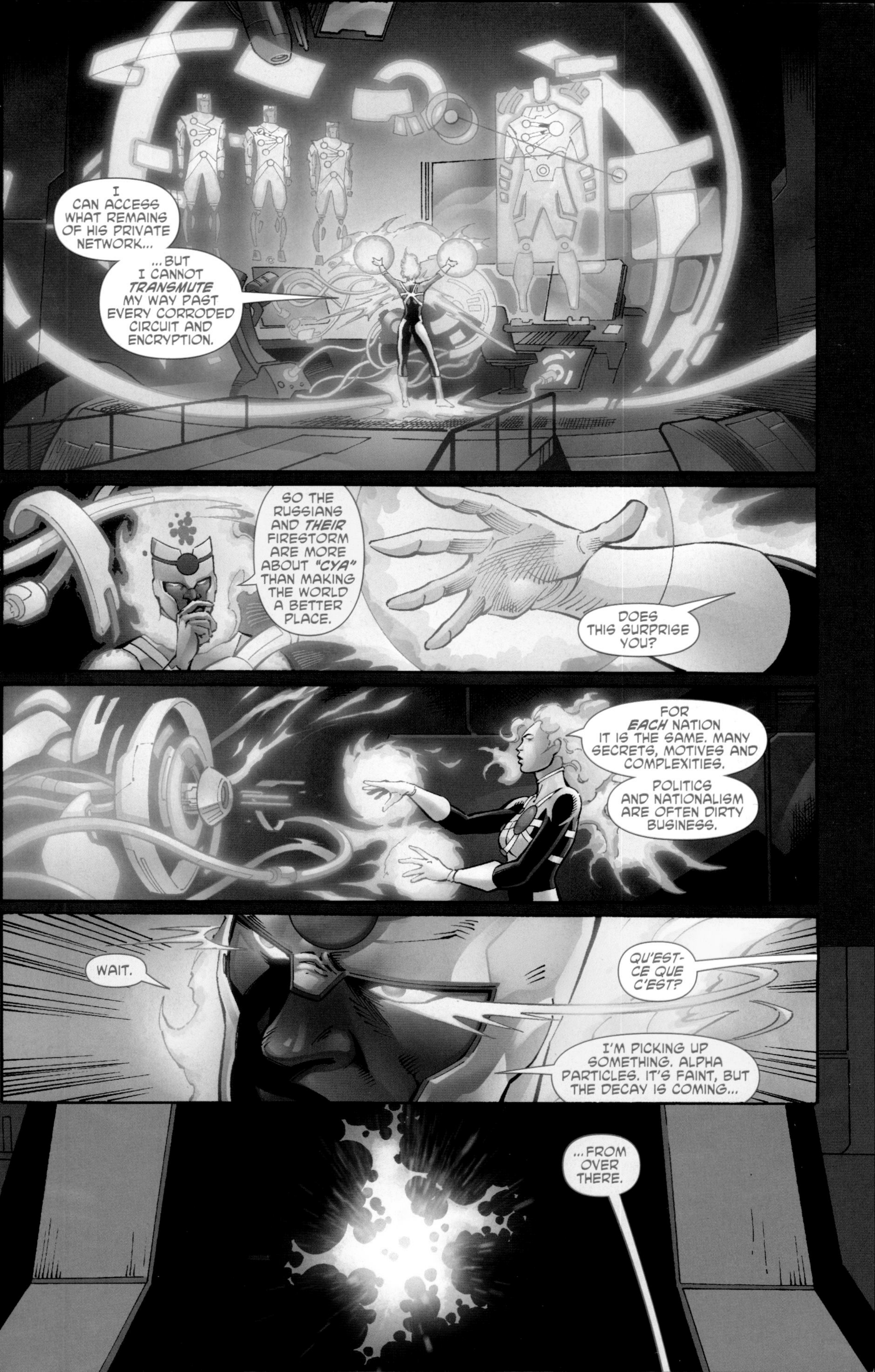
I CAN ACCESS WHAT REMAINS OF HIS PRIVATE NETWORK...
...BUT I CANNOT *TRANSMUTE* MY WAY PAST EVERY CORRODED CIRCUIT AND ENCRYPTION.
SO THE RUSSIANS AND *THEIR* FIRESTORM ARE MORE ABOUT "*CYA*" THAN MAKING THE WORLD A BETTER PLACE.
DOES THIS SURPRISE YOU?
FOR *EACH* NATION IT IS THE SAME. MANY SECRETS, MOTIVES AND COMPLEXITIES.
POLITICS AND NATIONALISM ARE OFTEN DIRTY BUSINESS.
WAIT.
QU'EST-CE QUE C'EST?
I'M PICKING UP SOMETHING. ALPHA PARTICLES. IT'S FAINT, BUT THE DECAY IS COMING...
...FROM OVER THERE.

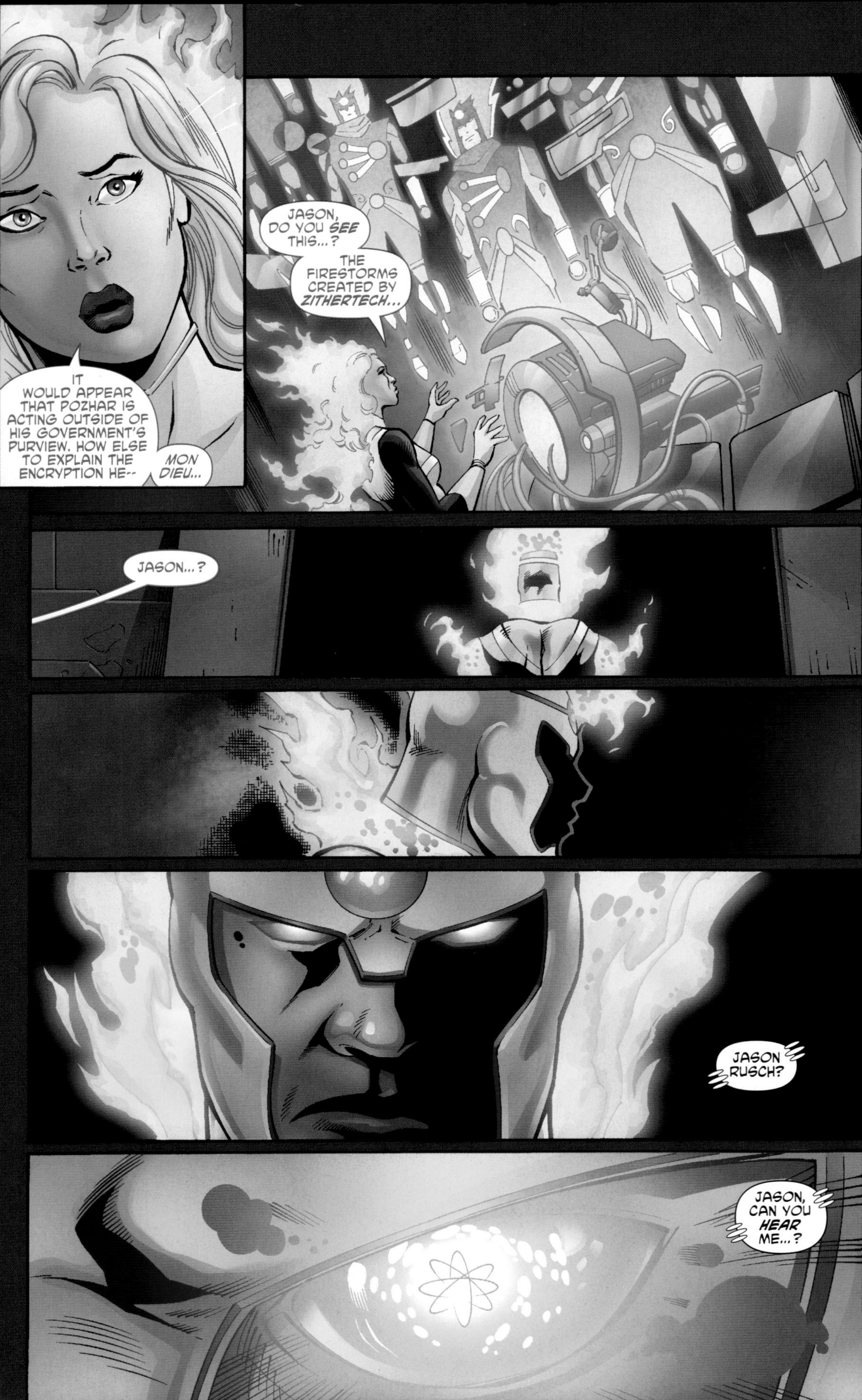
JASON, DO YOU SEE THIS...?
THE FIRESTORMS CREATED BY ZITHERTECH...
IT WOULD APPEAR THAT POZHAR IS ACTING OUTSIDE OF HIS GOVERNMENT'S PURVIEW. HOW ELSE TO EXPLAIN THE ENCRYPTION HE--
MON DIEU...
JASON...?
JASON RUSCH?
JASON, CAN YOU HEAR ME...?

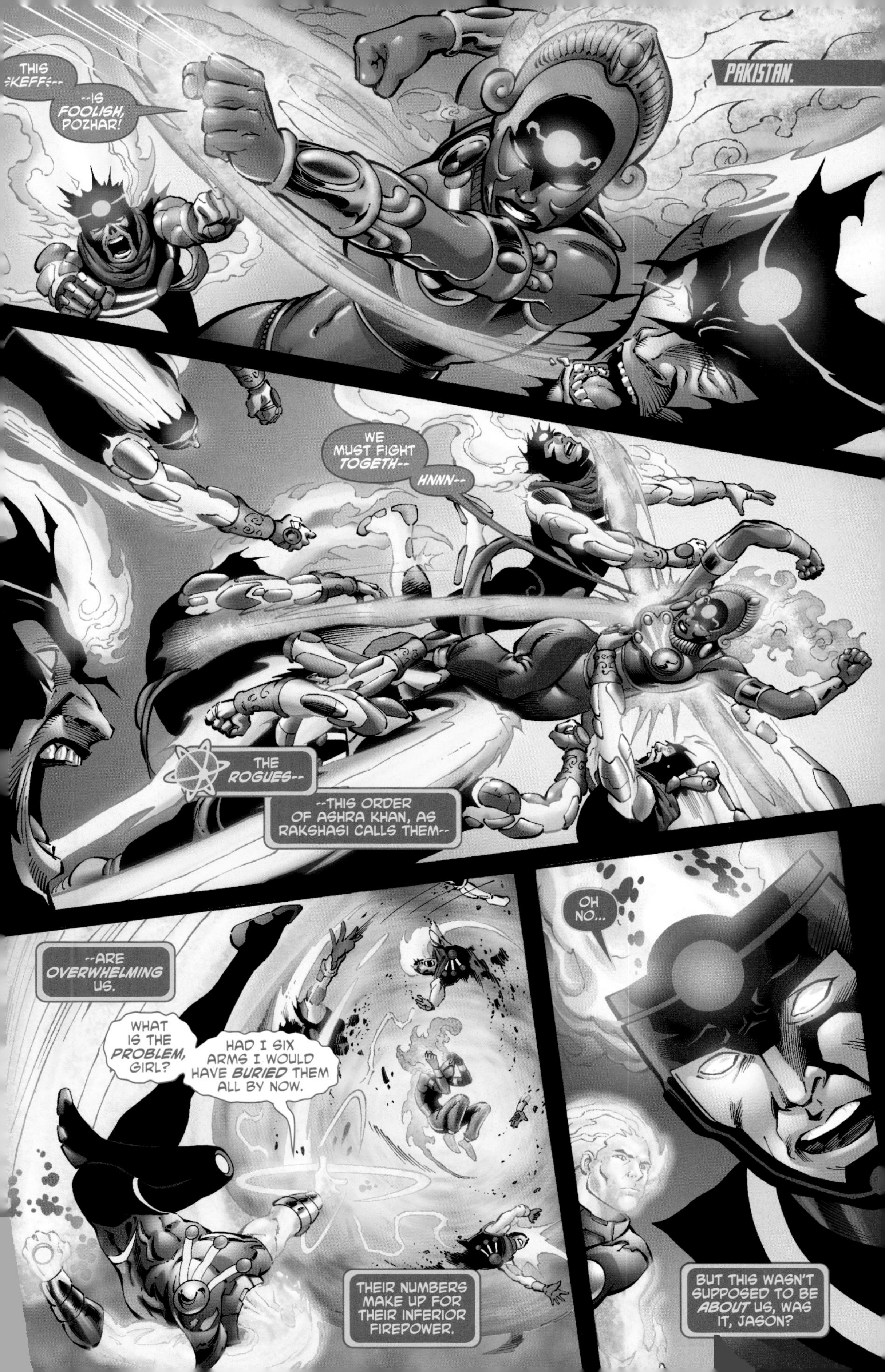
PAKISTAN.
THIS KEFF--
--IS FOOLISH, POZHAR!
WE MUST FIGHT TOGETH--
HNNN--
THE ROGUES--
--THIS ORDER OF ASHRA KHAN, AS RAKSHASI CALLS THEM--
--ARE OVERWHELMING US.
WHAT IS THE PROBLEM, GIRL?
HAD I SIX ARMS I WOULD HAVE BURIED THEM ALL BY NOW.
THEIR NUMBERS MAKE UP FOR THEIR INFERIOR FIREPOWER.
OH NO...
BUT THIS WASN'T SUPPOSED TO BE ABOUT US, WAS IT, JASON?

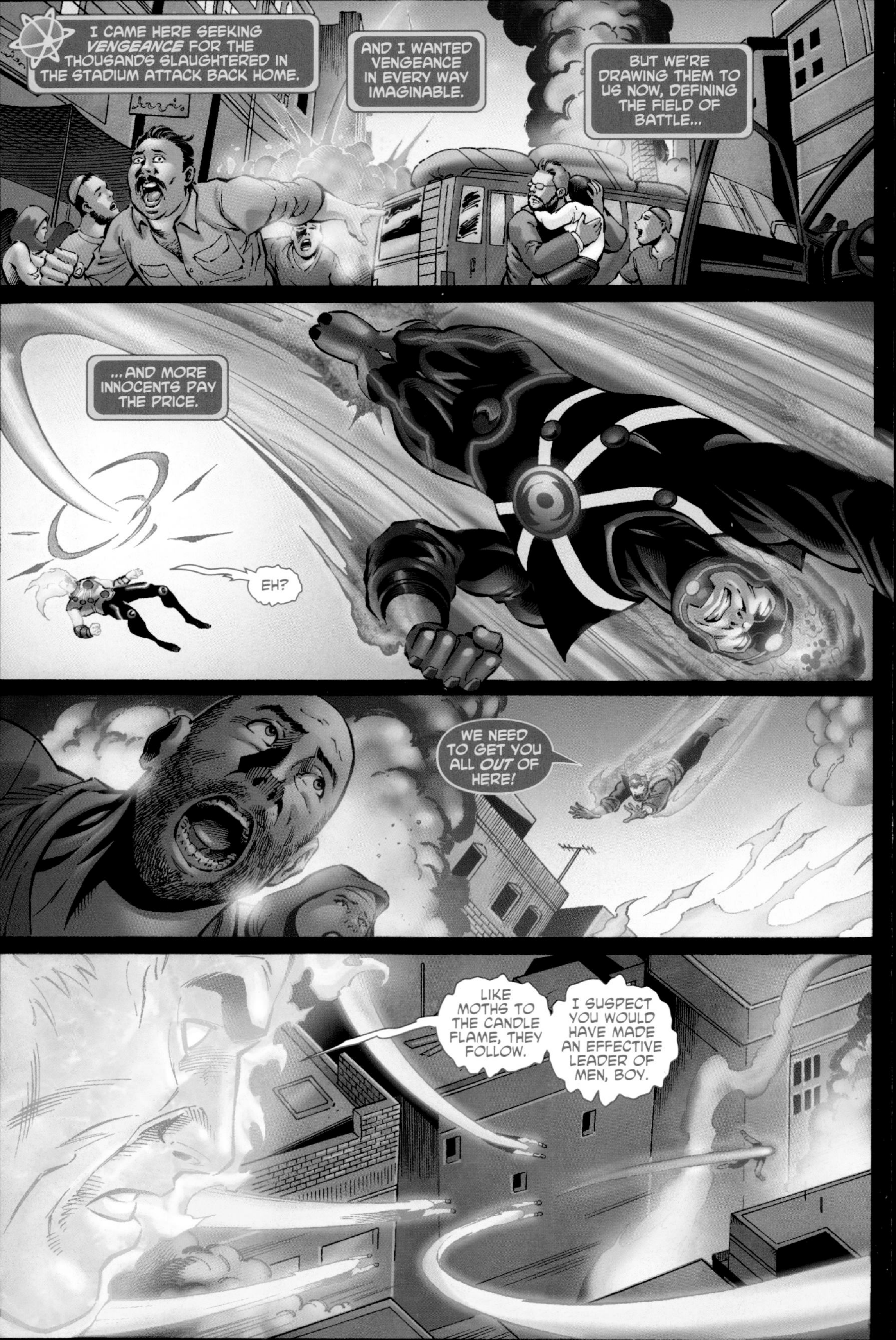
I CAME HERE SEEKING VENGEANCE FOR THE THOUSANDS SLAUGHTERED IN THE STADIUM ATTACK BACK HOME.
AND I WANTED VENGEANCE IN EVERY WAY IMAGINABLE.
BUT WE'RE DRAWING THEM TO US NOW, DEFINING THE FIELD OF BATTLE...
...AND MORE INNOCENTS PAY THE PRICE.
EH?
WE NEED TO GET YOU ALL OUT OF HERE!
LIKE MOTHS TO THE CANDLE FLAME, THEY FOLLOW.
I SUSPECT YOU WOULD HAVE MADE AN EFFECTIVE LEADER OF MEN, BOY.

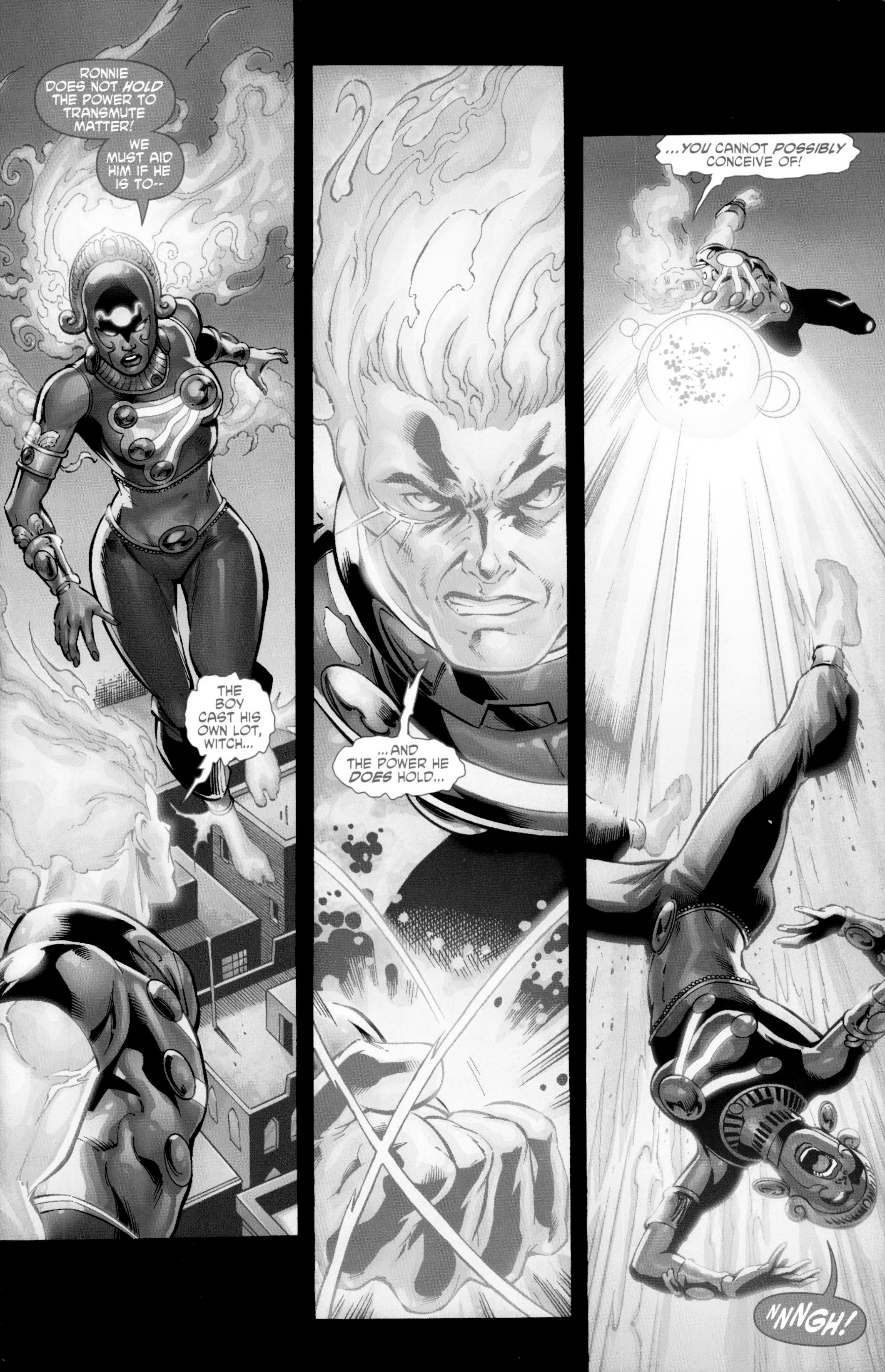
RONNIE DOES NOT *HOLD* THE POWER TO TRANSMUTE MATTER!
WE MUST AID HIM IF HE IS TO--
THE BOY CAST HIS OWN LOT, WITCH...
...AND THE POWER HE *DOES* HOLD...
...*YOU* CANNOT *POSSIBLY* CONCEIVE OF!
NNNGH!

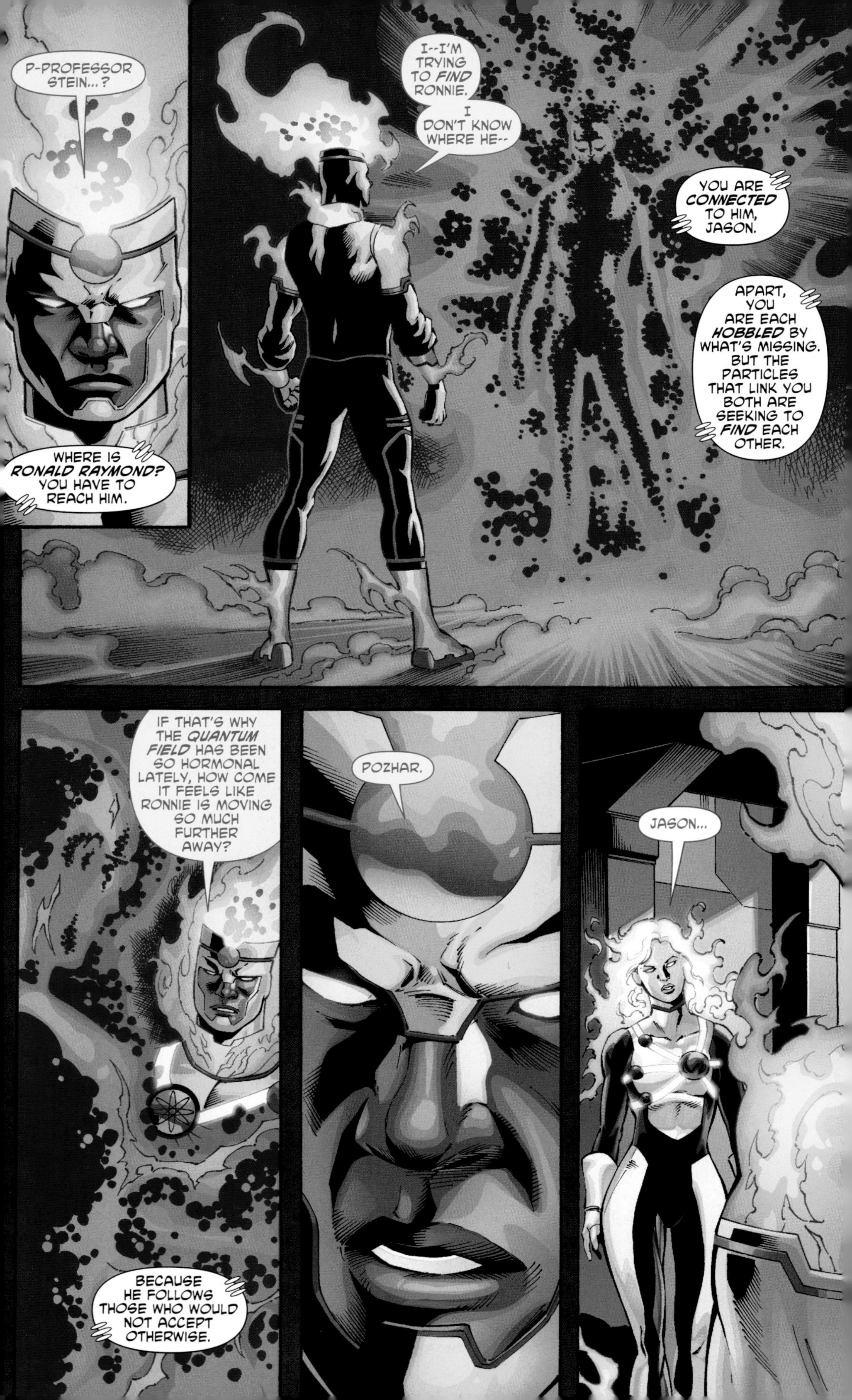
P-PROFESSOR STEIN...?
WHERE IS RONALD RAYMOND? YOU HAVE TO REACH HIM.
I--I'M TRYING TO FIND RONNIE.
I DON'T KNOW WHERE HE--
YOU ARE CONNECTED TO HIM, JASON.
APART, YOU ARE EACH HOBBLED BY WHAT'S MISSING. BUT THE PARTICLES THAT LINK YOU BOTH ARE SEEKING TO FIND EACH OTHER.
IF THAT'S WHY THE QUANTUM FIELD HAS BEEN SO HORMONAL LATELY, HOW COME IT FEELS LIKE RONNIE IS MOVING SO MUCH FURTHER AWAY?
BECAUSE HE FOLLOWS THOSE WHO WOULD NOT ACCEPT OTHERWISE.
POZHAR.
JASON...

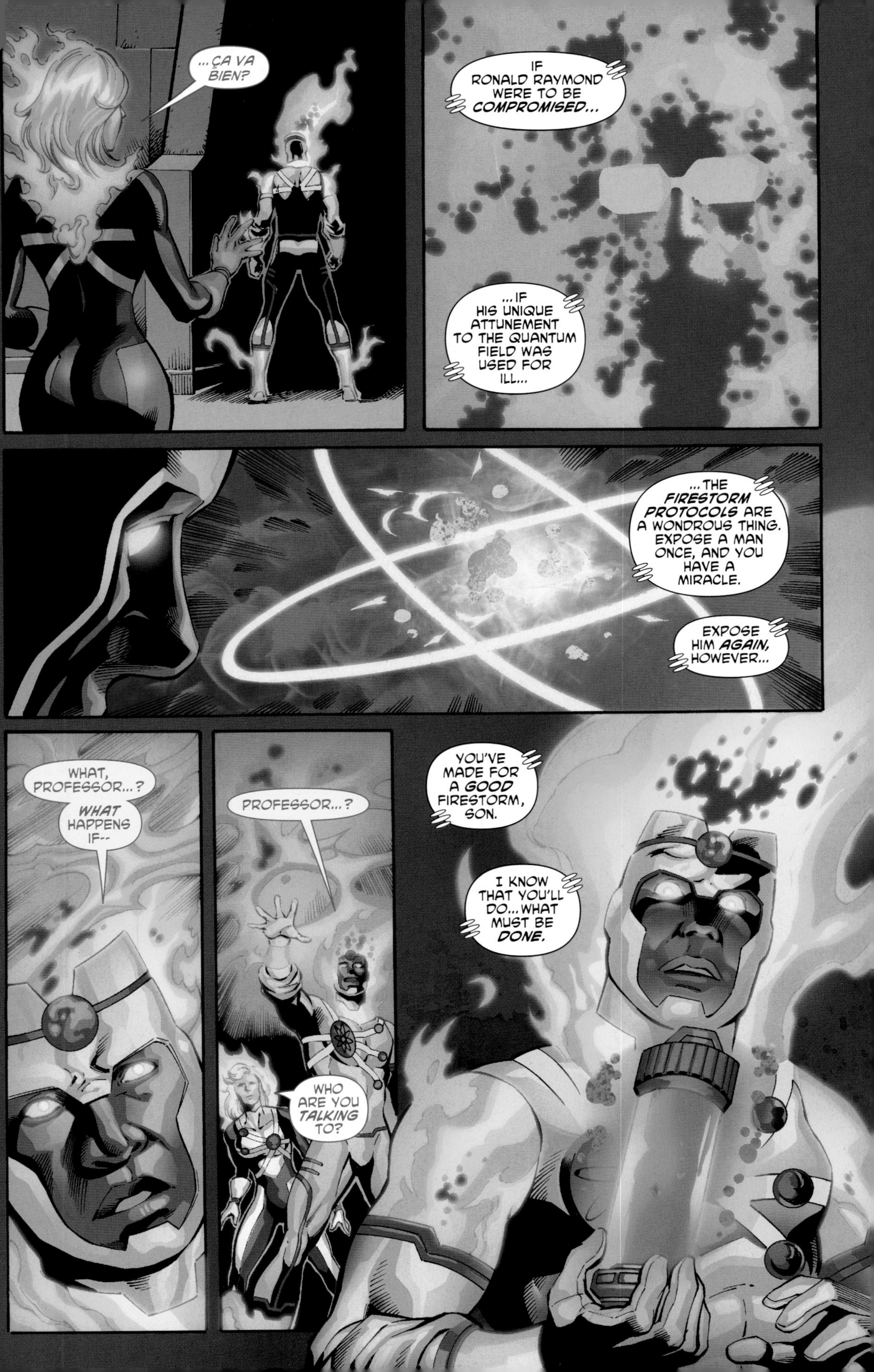
...ÇA VA BIEN?
IF RONALD RAYMOND WERE TO BE COMPROMISED...
...IF HIS UNIQUE ATTUNEMENT TO THE QUANTUM FIELD WAS USED FOR ILL...
...THE FIRESTORM PROTOCOLS ARE A WONDROUS THING. EXPOSE A MAN ONCE, AND YOU HAVE A MIRACLE.
EXPOSE HIM AGAIN, HOWEVER...
WHAT, PROFESSOR...? WHAT HAPPENS IF--
PROFESSOR...?
WHO ARE YOU TALKING TO?
YOU'VE MADE FOR A GOOD FIRESTORM, SON.
I KNOW THAT YOU'LL DO...WHAT MUST BE DONE.

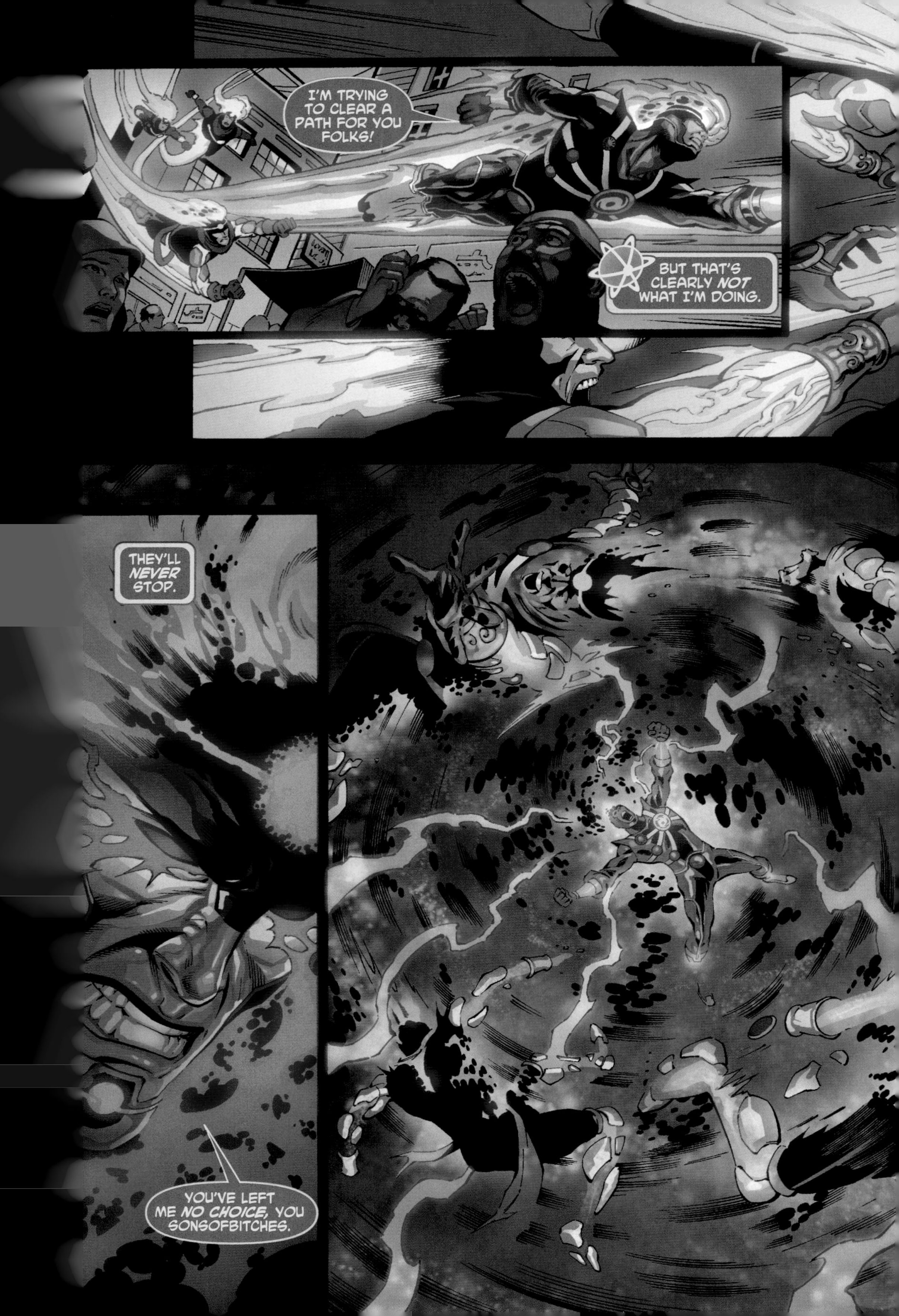
I'M TRYING TO CLEAR A PATH FOR YOU FOLKS!
BUT THAT'S CLEARLY NOT WHAT I'M DOING.
THEY'LL NEVER STOP.
YOU'VE LEFT ME NO CHOICE, YOU SONSOFBITCHES.

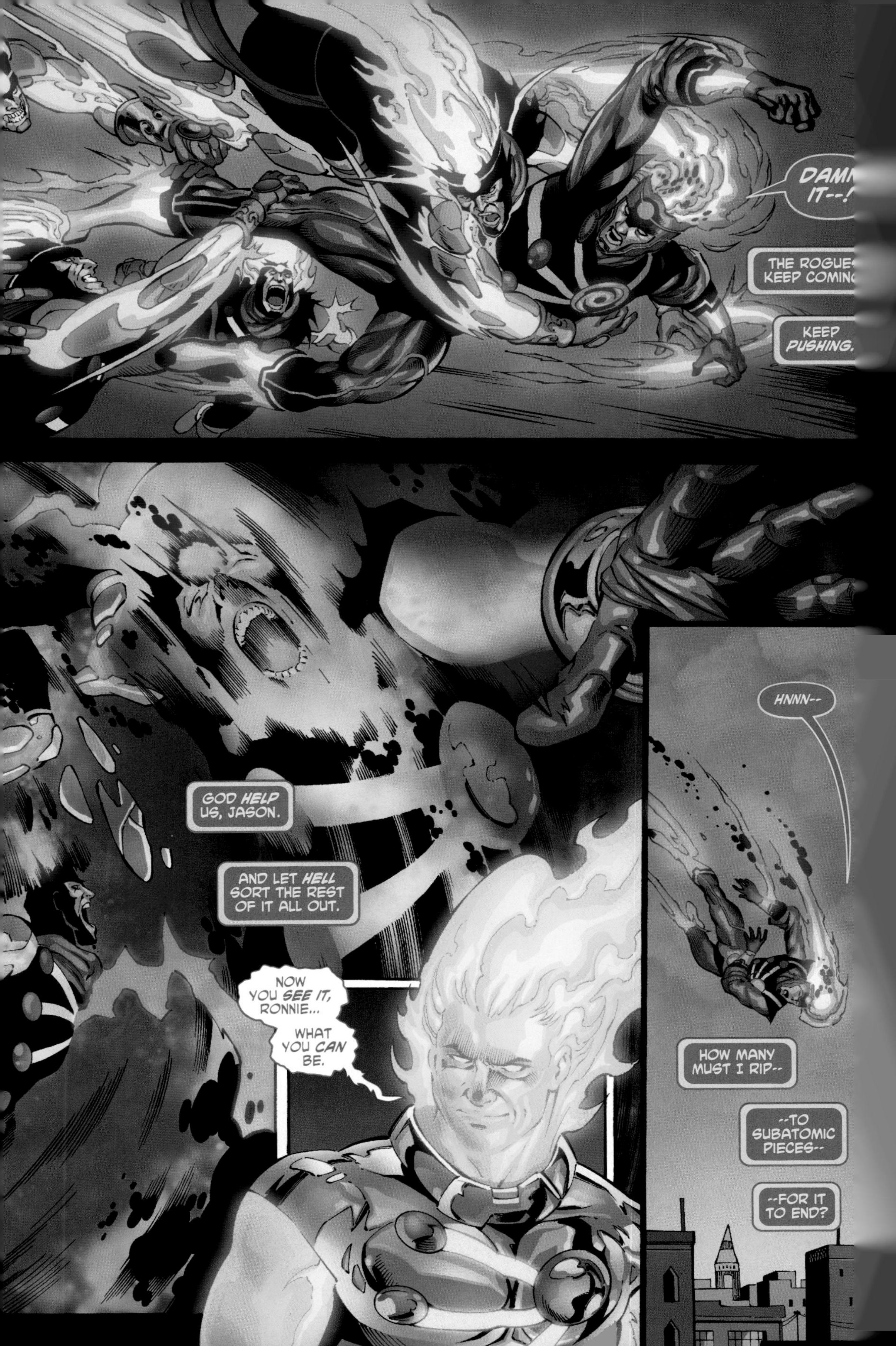
DAMN IT--!
THE ROGUES KEEP COMING
KEEP PUSHING.
GOD HELP US, JASON.
AND LET HELL SORT THE REST OF IT ALL OUT.
NOW YOU SEE IT, RONNIE...
WHAT YOU CAN BE.
HNNN--
HOW MANY MUST I RIP--
--TO SUBATOMIC PIECES--
--FOR IT TO END?

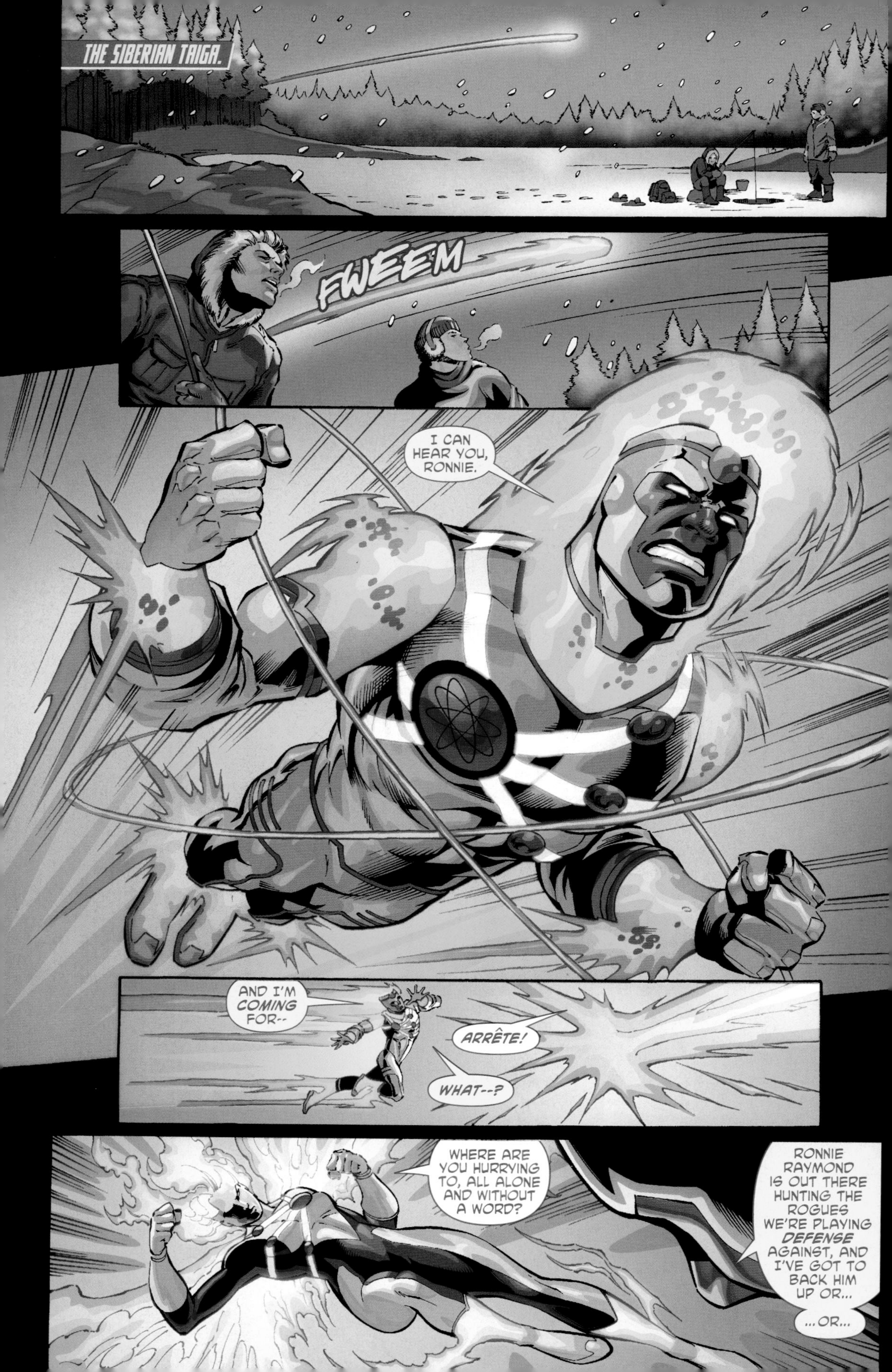
THE SIBERIAN TAIGA.
FWEEM
I CAN HEAR YOU, RONNIE.
AND I'M COMING FOR--
ARRÊTE!
WHAT--?
WHERE ARE YOU HURRYING TO, ALL ALONE AND WITHOUT A WORD?
RONNIE RAYMOND IS OUT THERE HUNTING THE ROGUES WE'RE PLAYING DEFENSE AGAINST, AND I'VE GOT TO BACK HIM UP OR...
...OR...

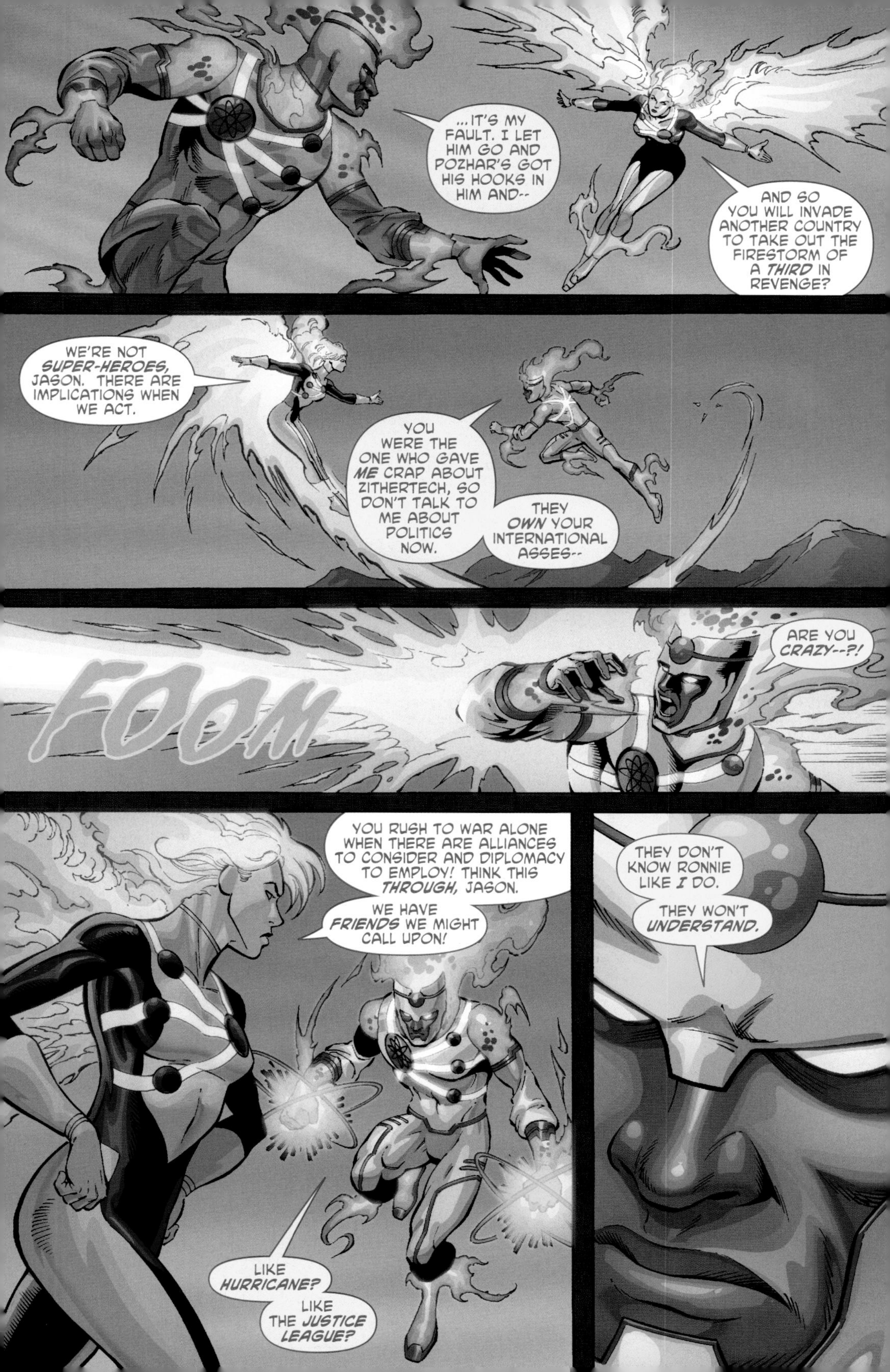
...IT'S MY FAULT. I LET HIM GO AND POZHAR'S GOT HIS HOOKS IN HIM AND--
AND SO YOU WILL INVADE ANOTHER COUNTRY TO TAKE OUT THE FIRESTORM OF A *THIRD* IN REVENGE?
WE'RE NOT *SUPER-HEROES,* JASON. THERE ARE IMPLICATIONS WHEN WE ACT.
YOU WERE THE ONE WHO GAVE *ME* CRAP ABOUT ZITHERTECH, SO DON'T TALK TO ME ABOUT POLITICS NOW.
THEY *OWN* YOUR INTERNATIONAL ASSES--
FOOM
ARE YOU *CRAZY*--?!
YOU RUSH TO WAR ALONE WHEN THERE ARE ALLIANCES TO CONSIDER AND DIPLOMACY TO EMPLOY! THINK THIS *THROUGH,* JASON.
WE HAVE *FRIENDS* WE MIGHT CALL UPON!
LIKE *HURRICANE?*
LIKE THE *JUSTICE LEAGUE?*
THEY DON'T KNOW RONNIE LIKE *I* DO.
THEY WON'T *UNDERSTAND.*

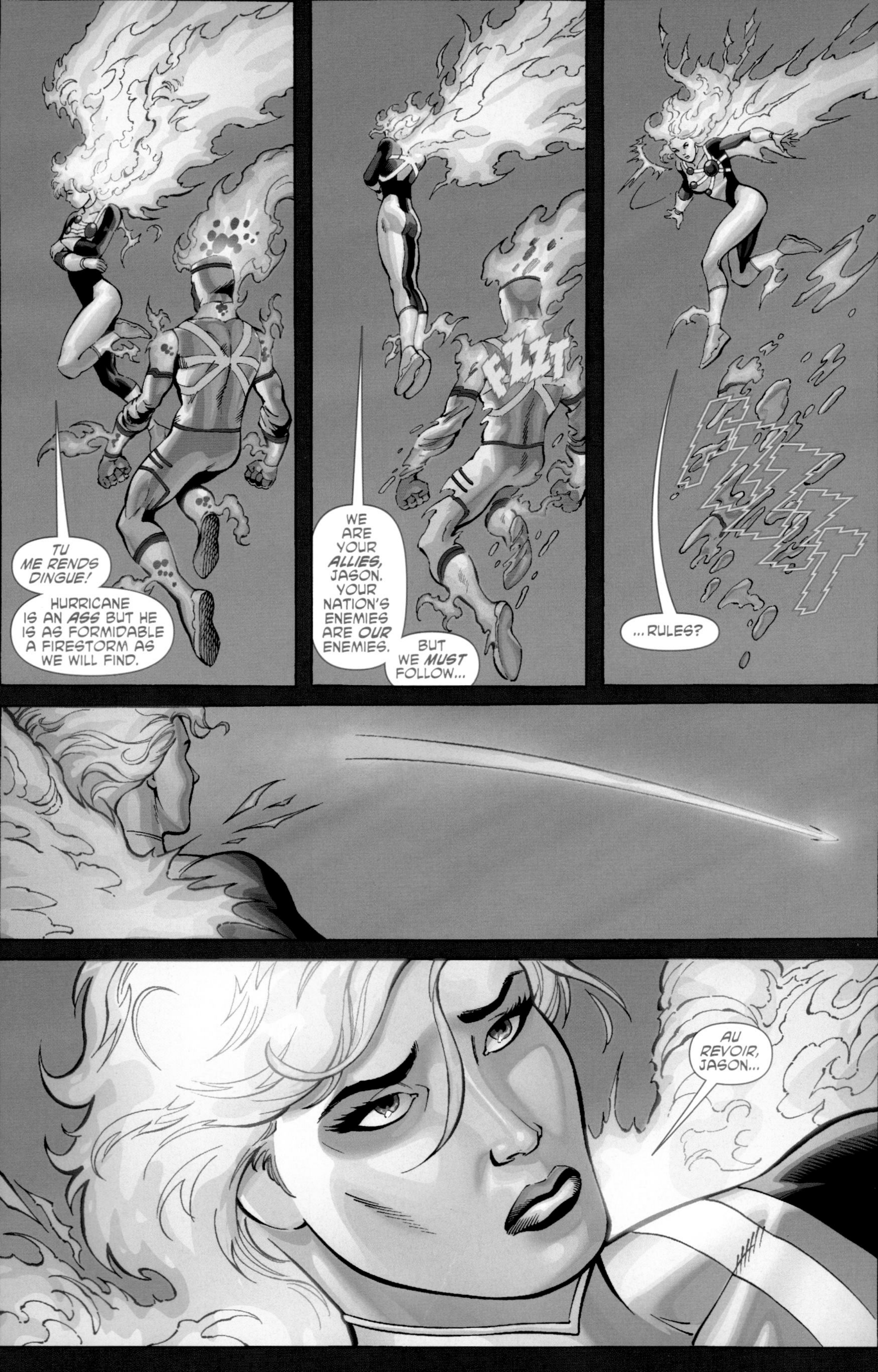

TU ME RENDS DINGUE!
HURRICANE IS AN ASS BUT HE IS AS FORMIDABLE A FIRESTORM AS WE WILL FIND.
WE ARE YOUR ALLIES, JASON. YOUR NATION'S ENEMIES ARE OUR ENEMIES.
BUT WE MUST FOLLOW...
FZZT
...RULES?
FZZT
AU REVOIR, JASON...

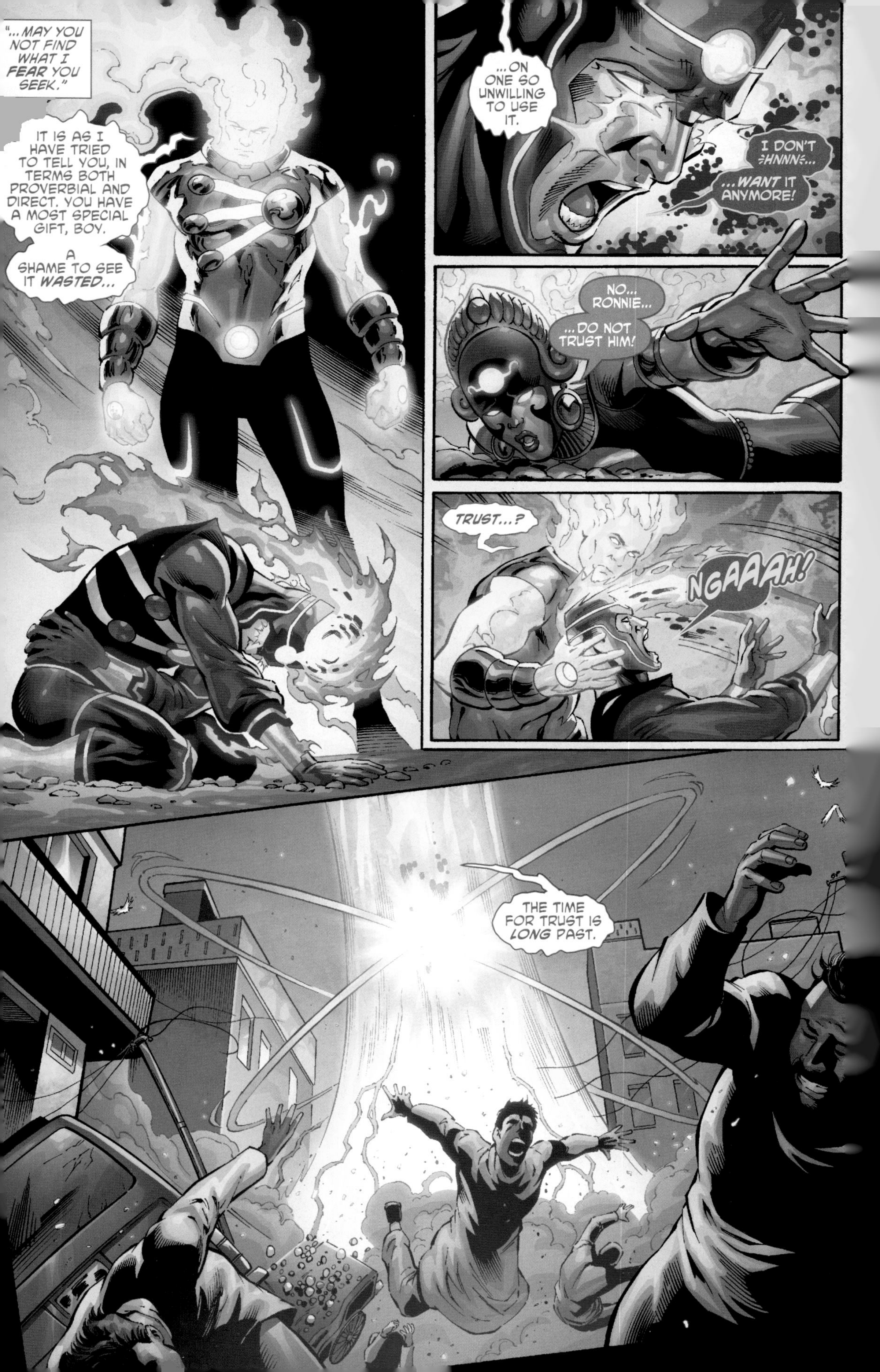
"...MAY YOU NOT FIND WHAT I FEAR YOU SEEK."
IT IS AS I HAVE TRIED TO TELL YOU, IN TERMS BOTH PROVERBIAL AND DIRECT. YOU HAVE A MOST SPECIAL GIFT, BOY.
A SHAME TO SEE IT WASTED...
...ON ONE SO UNWILLING TO USE IT.
I DON'T HNNN...
...WANT IT ANYMORE!
NO... RONNIE...
...DO NOT TRUST HIM!
TRUST...?
NGAAAH!
THE TIME FOR TRUST IS LONG PAST.

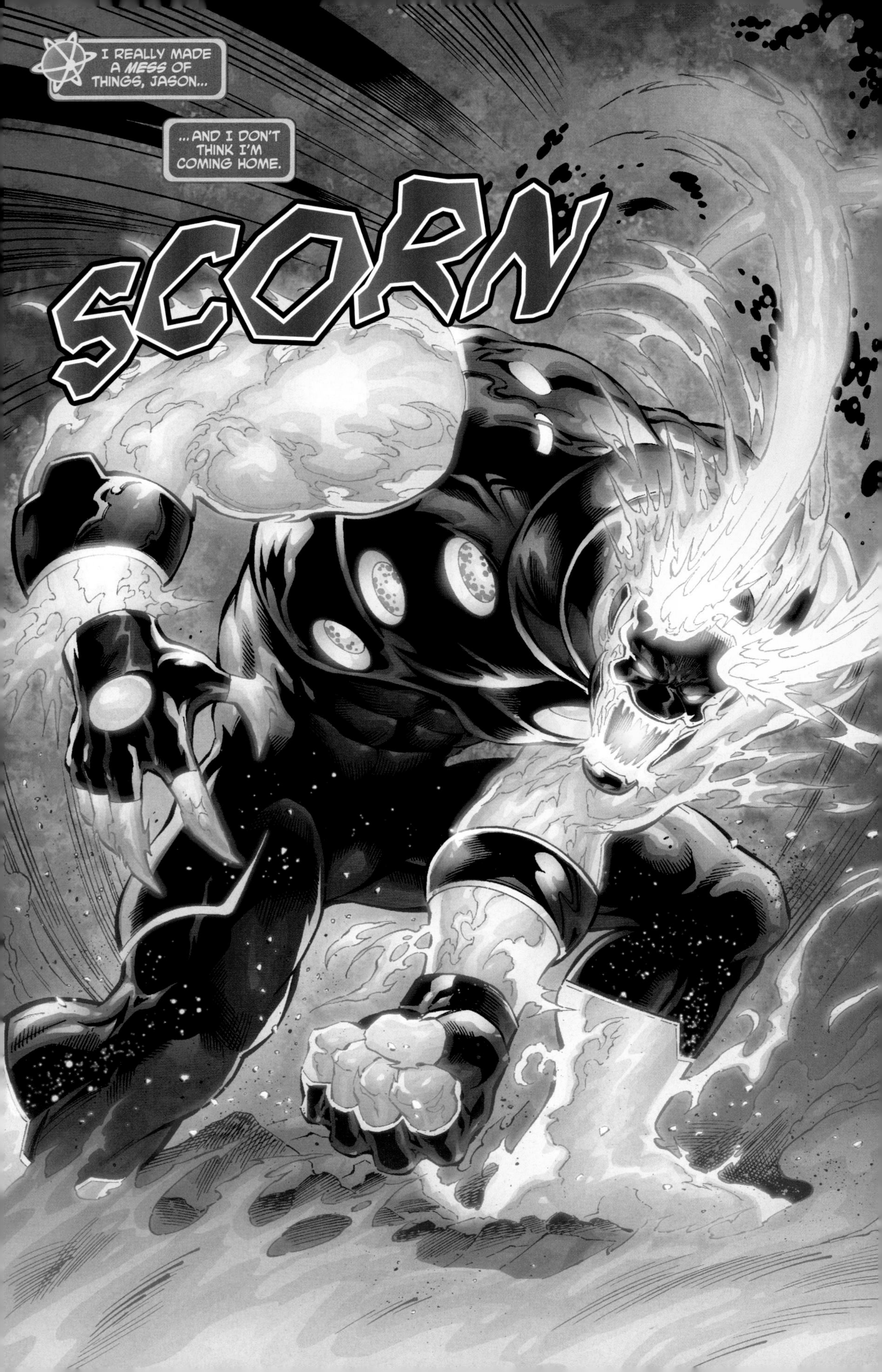
I REALLY MADE A *MESS* OF THINGS, JASON...
...AND I DON'T THINK I'M COMING HOME.
SCORN

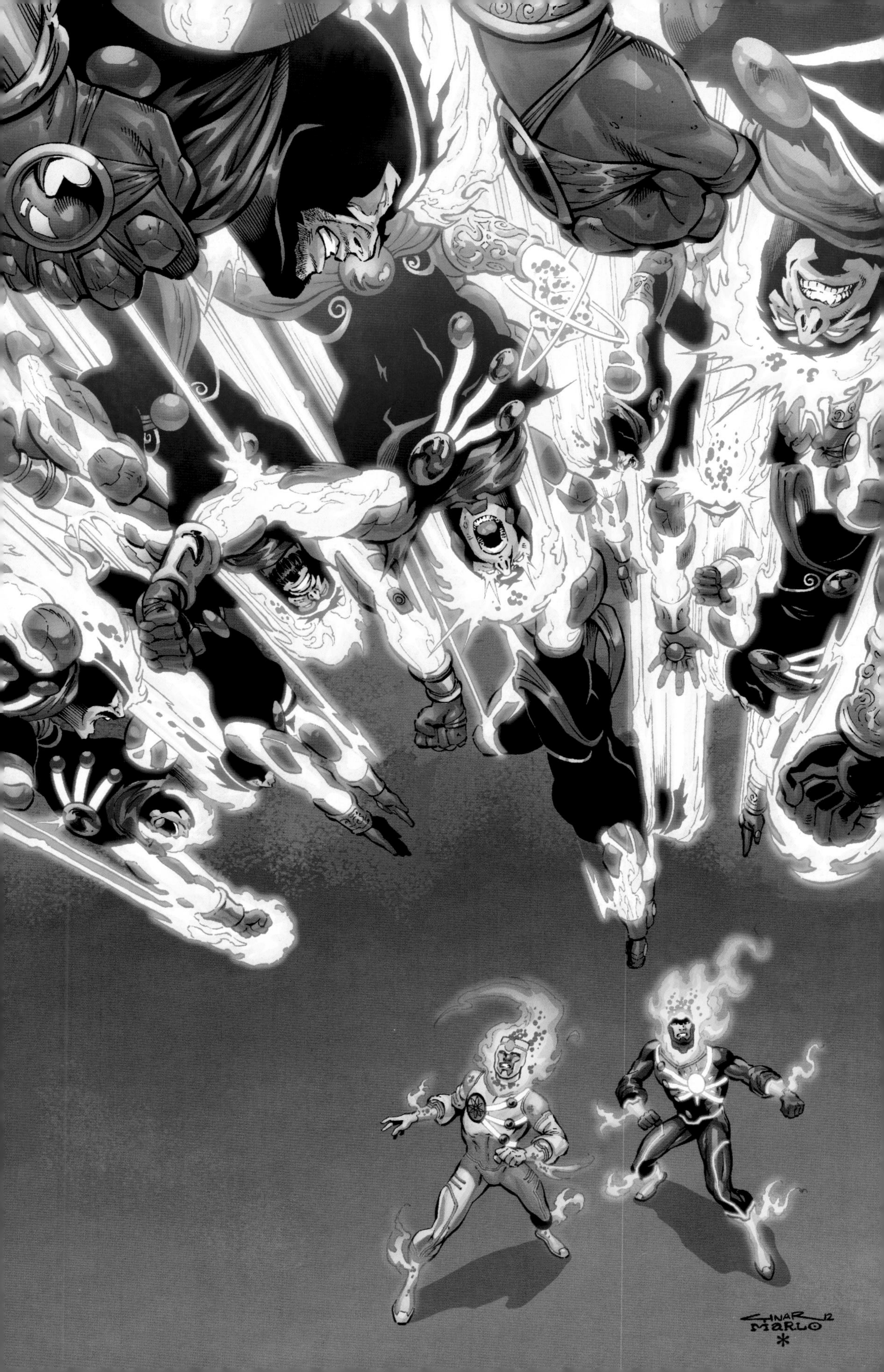
CINAR 12
MARLO

FALLOUT & DECAY

JOE HARRIS writer **YILDIRAY CINAR & DANIEL HDR** pencillers **MARLO ALQUIZA & WALDEN WONG** inkers
cover by **YILDIRAY CINAR & MARLO AQUIZA** with **HI-FI**

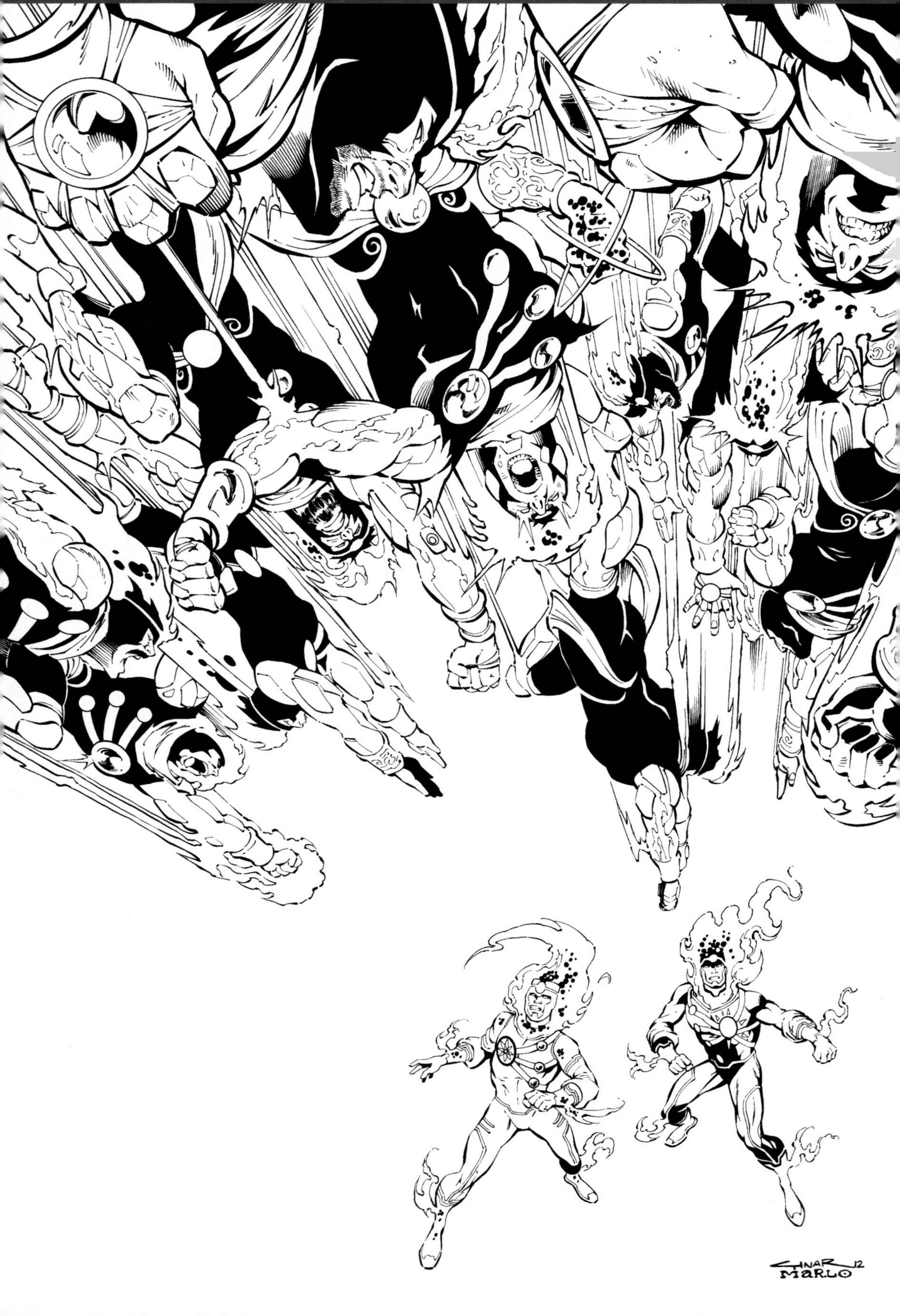

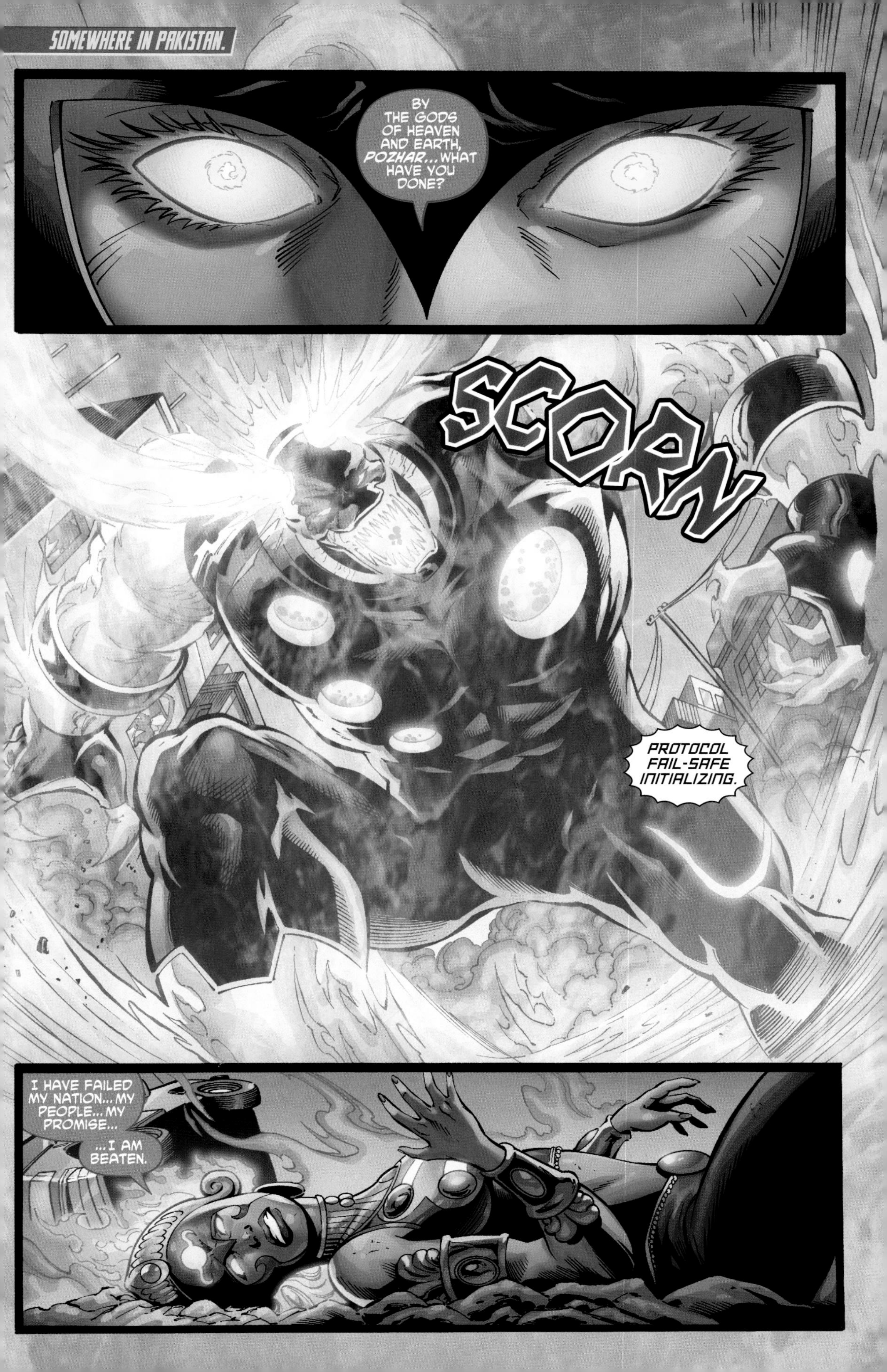
SOMEWHERE IN PAKISTAN.
BY THE GODS OF HEAVEN AND EARTH, POZHAR... WHAT HAVE YOU DONE?
SCORN
PROTOCOL FAIL-SAFE INITIALIZING.
I HAVE FAILED MY NATION... MY PEOPLE... MY PROMISE...
...I AM BEATEN.

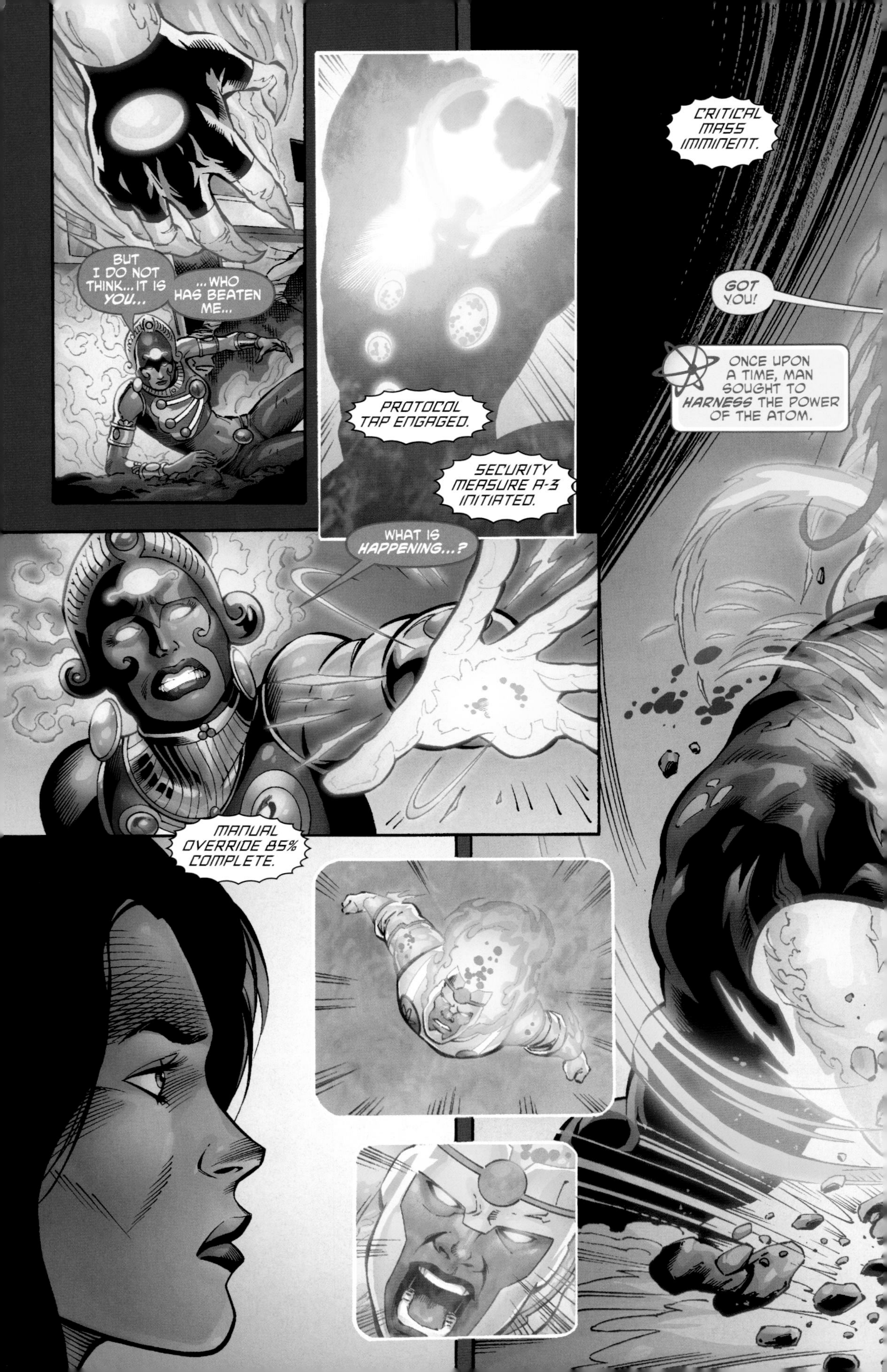

BUT I DO NOT THINK...IT IS YOU...
...WHO HAS BEATEN ME...
PROTOCOL TAP ENGAGED.
SECURITY MEASURE A-3 INITIATED.
CRITICAL MASS IMMINENT.
GOT YOU!
ONCE UPON A TIME, MAN SOUGHT TO HARNESS THE POWER OF THE ATOM.
WHAT IS HAPPENING...?
MANUAL OVERRIDE 85% COMPLETE.

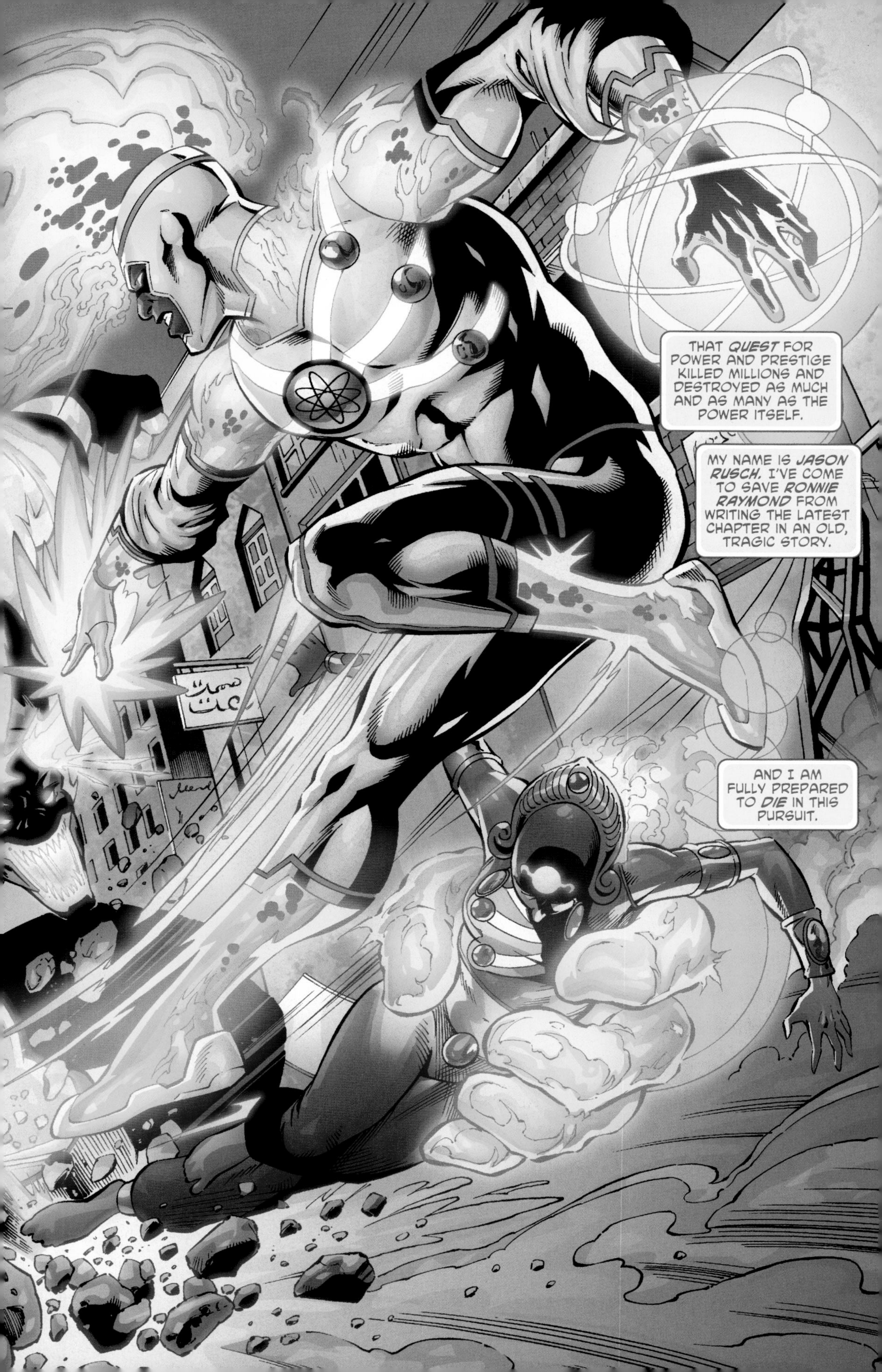
THAT *QUEST* FOR POWER AND PRESTIGE KILLED MILLIONS AND DESTROYED AS MUCH AND AS MANY AS THE POWER ITSELF.
MY NAME IS *JASON RUSCH.* I'VE COME TO SAVE *RONNIE RAYMOND* FROM WRITING THE LATEST CHAPTER IN AN OLD, TRAGIC STORY.
AND I AM FULLY PREPARED TO *DIE* IN THIS PURSUIT.

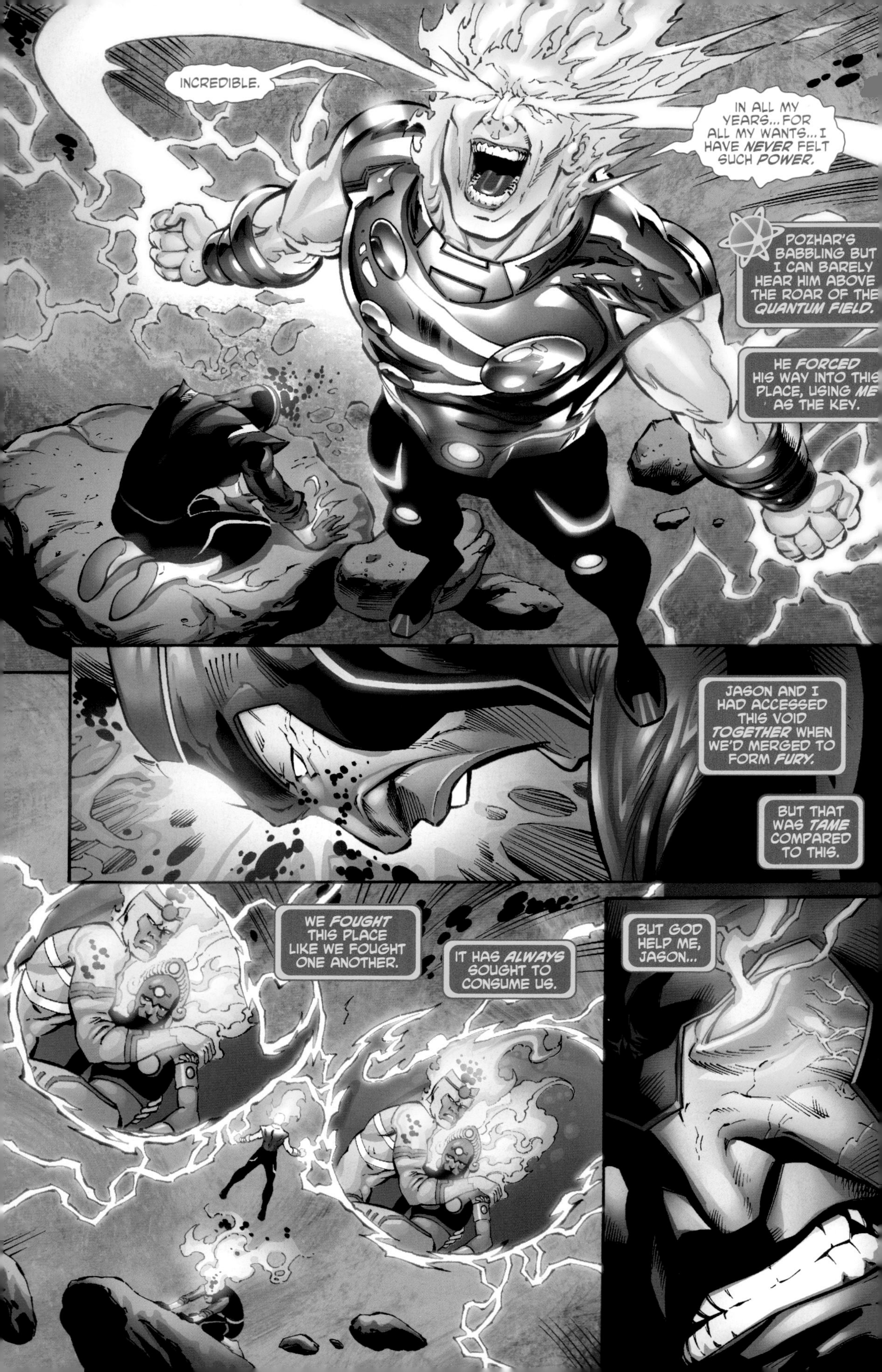
INCREDIBLE.
IN ALL MY YEARS...FOR ALL MY WANTS...I HAVE NEVER FELT SUCH POWER.
POZHAR'S BABBLING BUT I CAN BARELY HEAR HIM ABOVE THE ROAR OF THE QUANTUM FIELD.
HE FORCED HIS WAY INTO THIS PLACE, USING ME AS THE KEY.
JASON AND I HAD ACCESSED THIS VOID TOGETHER WHEN WE'D MERGED TO FORM FURY.
BUT THAT WAS TAME COMPARED TO THIS.
WE FOUGHT THIS PLACE LIKE WE FOUGHT ONE ANOTHER.
IT HAS ALWAYS SOUGHT TO CONSUME US.
BUT GOD HELP ME, JASON...

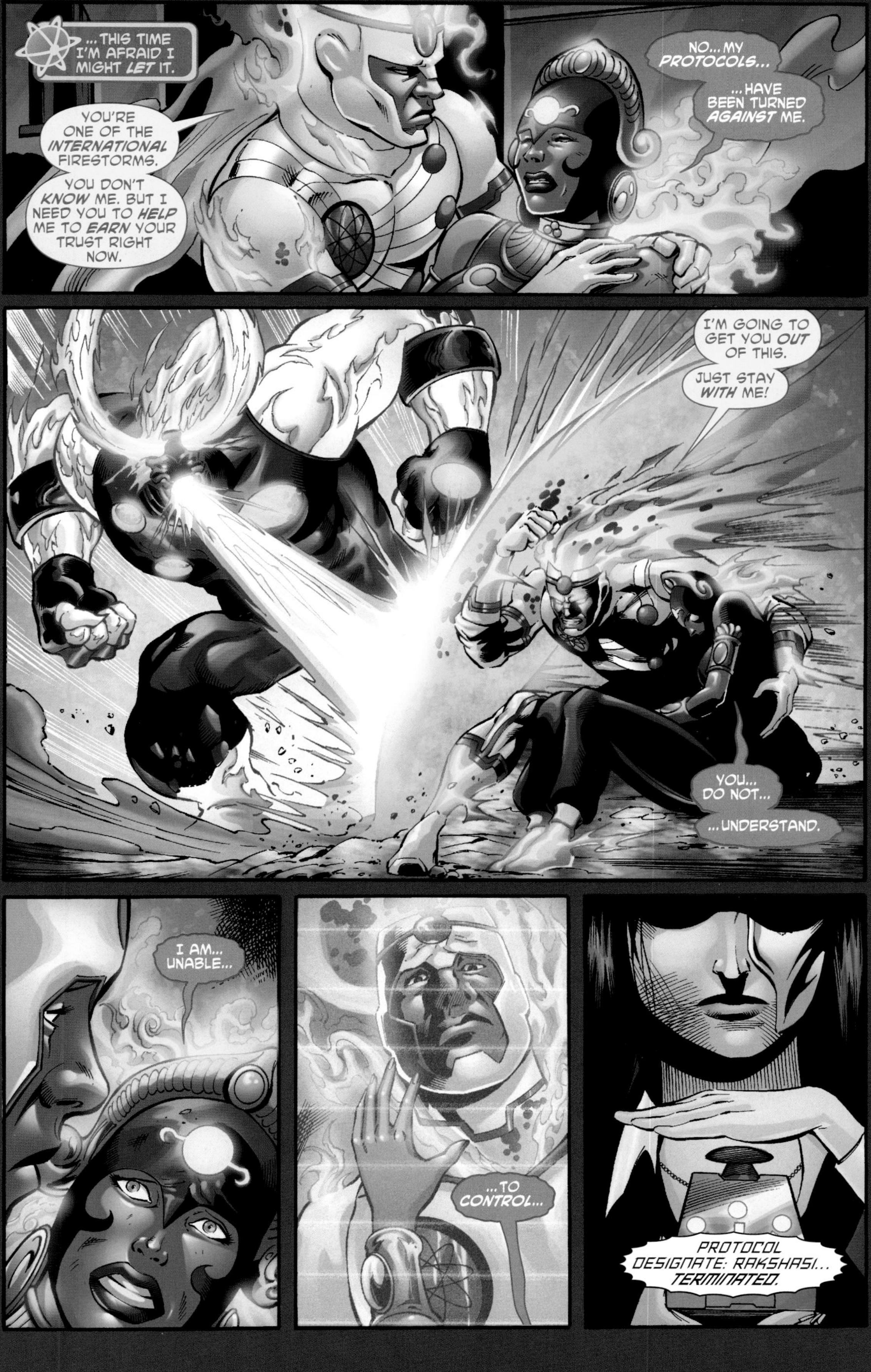
...THIS TIME I'M AFRAID I MIGHT *LET* IT.
NO... MY *PROTOCOLS*...
...HAVE BEEN TURNED *AGAINST* ME.
YOU'RE ONE OF THE *INTERNATIONAL* FIRESTORMS.
YOU DON'T *KNOW* ME. BUT I NEED YOU TO *HELP* ME TO *EARN* YOUR TRUST RIGHT NOW.
I'M GOING TO GET YOU *OUT* OF THIS.
JUST STAY *WITH* ME!
YOU... DO NOT...
...UNDERSTAND.
I AM... UNABLE...
...TO *CONTROL*...
PROTOCOL DESIGNATE: RAKSHASI... *TERMINATED.*

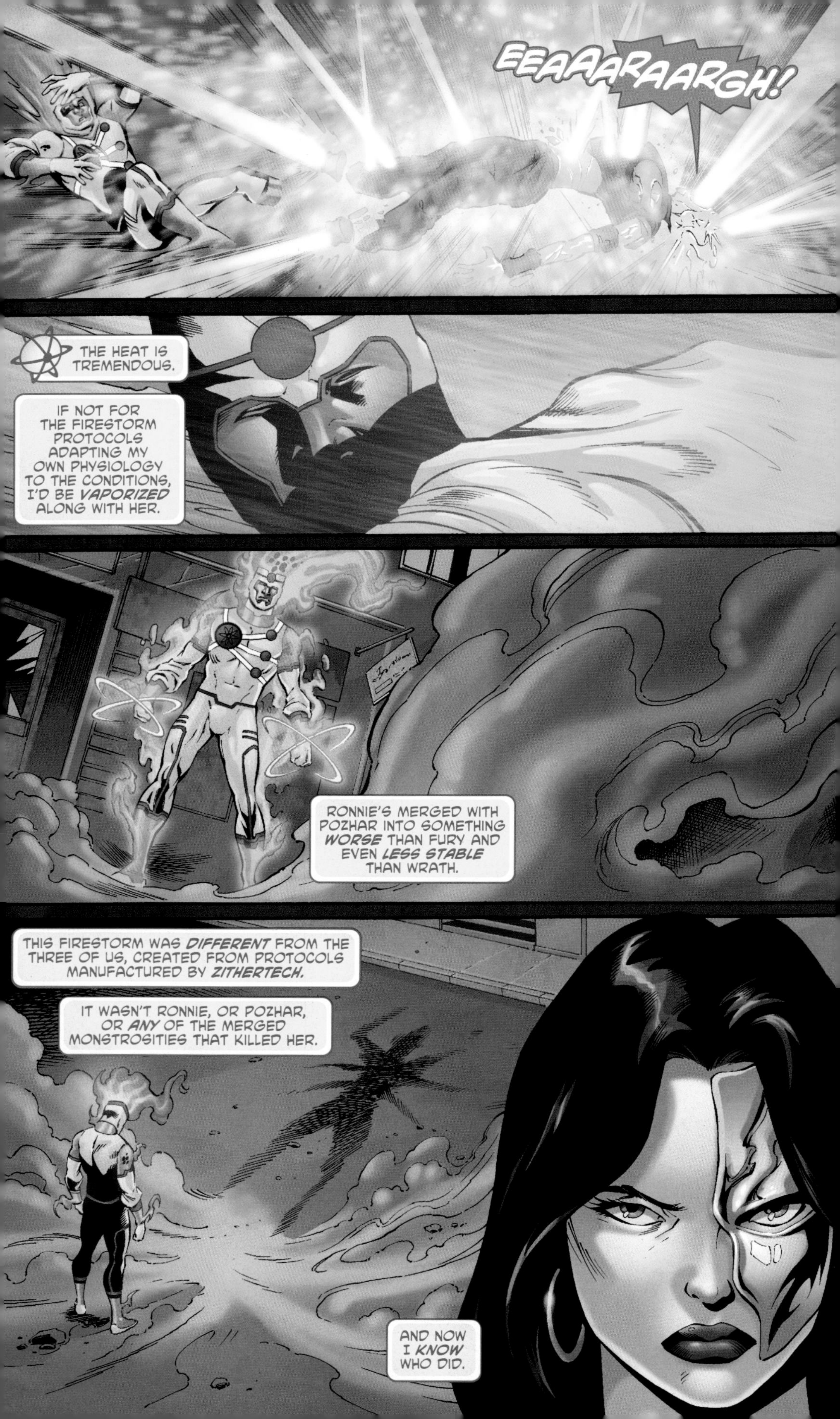
EEAAARAARGH!
THE HEAT IS TREMENDOUS.
IF NOT FOR THE FIRESTORM PROTOCOLS ADAPTING MY OWN PHYSIOLOGY TO THE CONDITIONS, I'D BE *VAPORIZED* ALONG WITH HER.
RONNIE'S MERGED WITH POZHAR INTO SOMETHING *WORSE* THAN FURY AND EVEN *LESS STABLE* THAN WRATH.
THIS FIRESTORM WAS *DIFFERENT* FROM THE THREE OF US, CREATED FROM PROTOCOLS MANUFACTURED BY *ZITHERTECH.*
IT WASN'T RONNIE, OR POZHAR, OR *ANY* OF THE MERGED MONSTROSITIES THAT KILLED HER.
AND NOW I *KNOW* WHO DID.

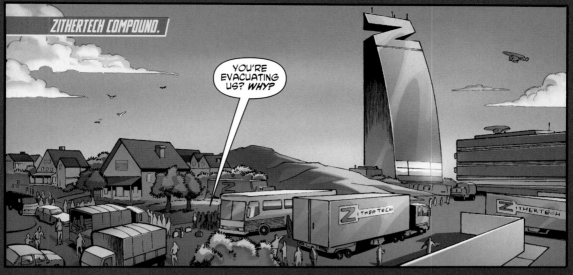

ZITHERTECH COMPOUND.
YOU'RE EVACUATING US? WHY?
ZITHERTECH
ZITHERTECH
THIS ISN'T WHAT WAS PROMISED.
YOU PEOPLE NEED TO PROVIDE SOME CONSISTENCY IF YOU WANT US TO TRUST YOU!
WE NEED TO KNOW WHAT'S GOING ON. ZITHER PROMISED US STABILITY AND ALL WE GET IS UPHEAVAL.
OUR SONS AREN'T NUCLEAR EXPERIMENTS YOU CAN JUST--
MS. RAYMOND... MR. RUSCH...
...DIRECTOR ZITHER IS A LITTLE, SHALL WE SAY, NUCLEAR HERSELF AT THE MOMENT.
ZITHERTECH IS ABOUT TO BE THE SUBJECT OF A MASSIVE CONGRESSIONAL INQUIRY, AND SOME UGLY BUSINESS DETAILS ARE ABOUT TO HIT THE OPEN AIR.
BUT WHAT ABOUT OUR BOYS, MS. CARVER?
WHO'S LOOKING OUT FOR THEM?
AT THIS POINT, MA'AM... I HOPE THEY'RE LOOKING OUT FOR ONE ANOTHER.
"I ASSURE YOU, IT COULD BE A LOT WORSE."

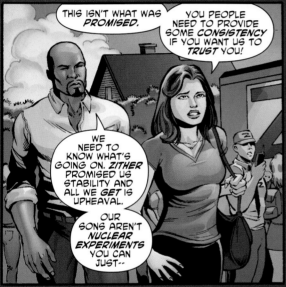

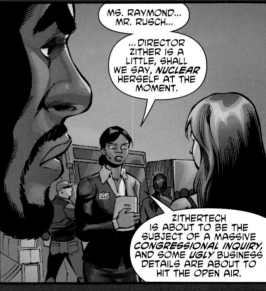

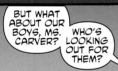

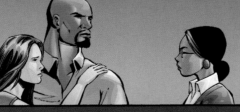

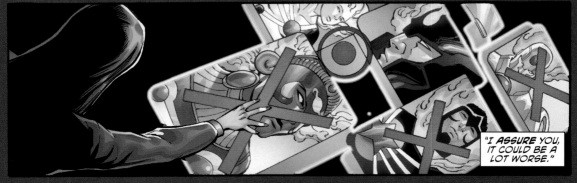

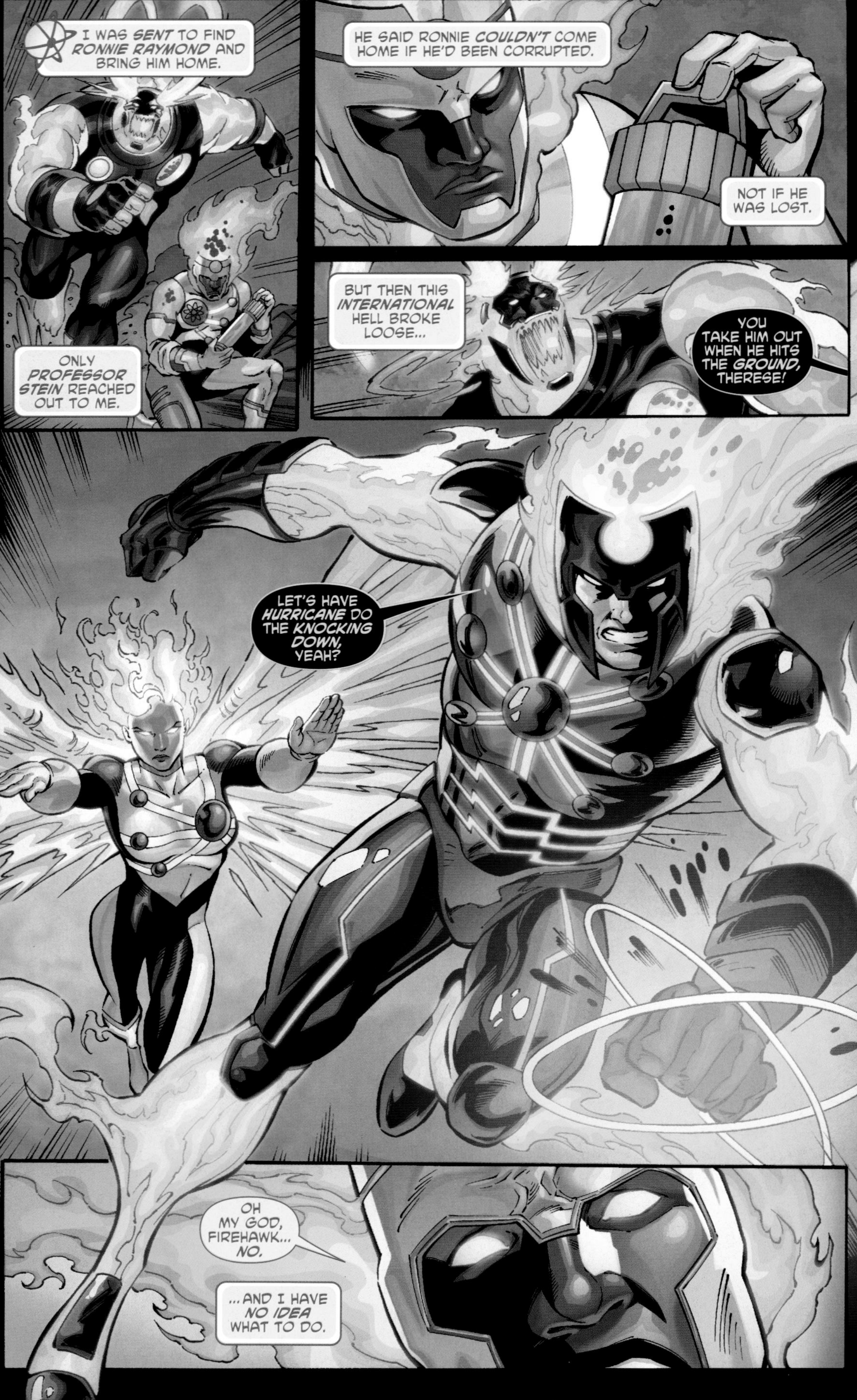
I WAS SENT TO FIND RONNIE RAYMOND AND BRING HIM HOME.
ONLY PROFESSOR STEIN REACHED OUT TO ME.
HE SAID RONNIE COULDN'T COME HOME IF HE'D BEEN CORRUPTED.
NOT IF HE WAS LOST.
BUT THEN THIS INTERNATIONAL HELL BROKE LOOSE...
YOU TAKE HIM OUT WHEN HE HITS THE GROUND, THERESE!
LET'S HAVE HURRICANE DO THE KNOCKING DOWN, YEAH?
OH MY GOD, FIREHAWK... NO.
...AND I HAVE NO IDEA WHAT TO DO.

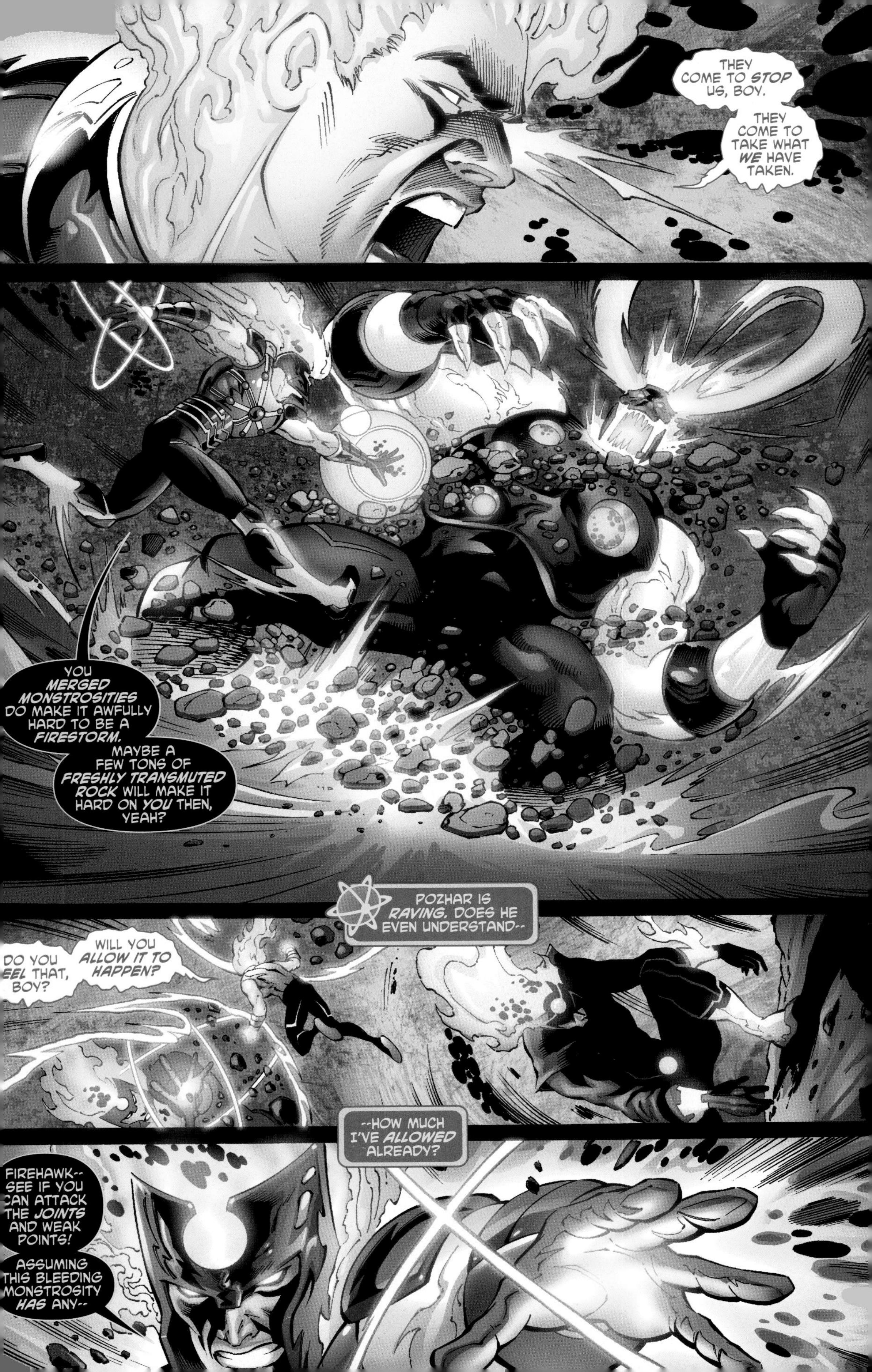

THEY COME TO STOP US, BOY.
THEY COME TO TAKE WHAT WE HAVE TAKEN.
YOU MERGED MONSTROSITIES DO MAKE IT AWFULLY HARD TO BE A FIRESTORM.
MAYBE A FEW TONS OF FRESHLY TRANSMUTED ROCK WILL MAKE IT HARD ON YOU THEN, YEAH?
POZHAR IS RAVING. DOES HE EVEN UNDERSTAND--
DO YOU EEL THAT, BOY?
WILL YOU ALLOW IT TO HAPPEN?
--HOW MUCH I'VE ALLOWED ALREADY?
FIREHAWK-- SEE IF YOU CAN ATTACK THE JOINTS AND WEAK POINTS!
ASSUMING THIS BLEEDING MONSTROSITY HAS ANY--

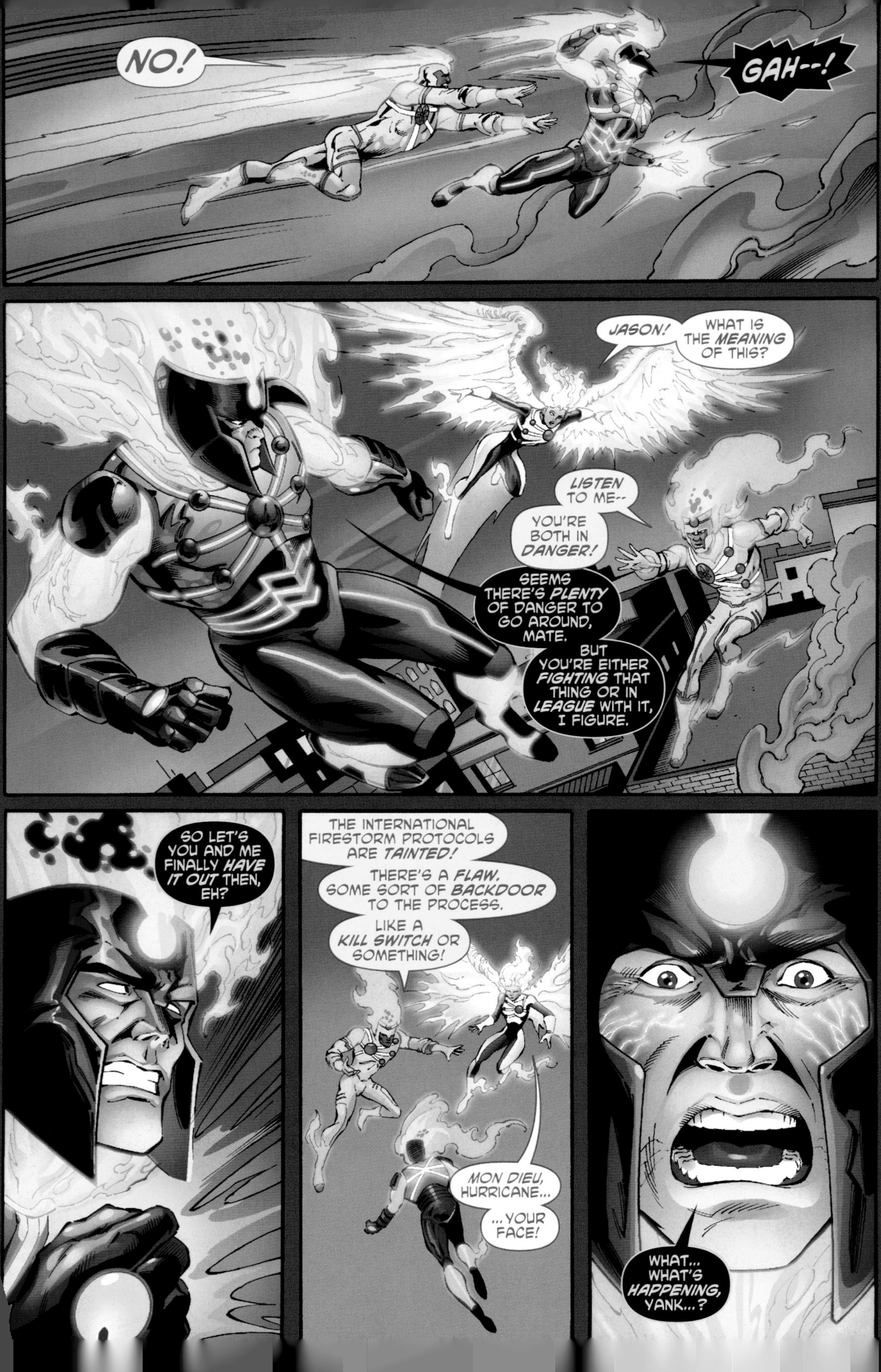
NO!
GAH--!
JASON!
WHAT IS THE MEANING OF THIS?
LISTEN TO ME--
YOU'RE BOTH IN DANGER!
SEEMS THERE'S PLENTY OF DANGER TO GO AROUND, MATE.
BUT YOU'RE EITHER FIGHTING THAT THING OR IN LEAGUE WITH IT, I FIGURE.
SO LET'S YOU AND ME FINALLY HAVE IT OUT THEN, EH?
THE INTERNATIONAL FIRESTORM PROTOCOLS ARE TAINTED!
THERE'S A FLAW. SOME SORT OF BACKDOOR TO THE PROCESS.
LIKE A KILL SWITCH OR SOMETHING!
MON DIEU, HURRICANE...
...YOUR FACE!
WHAT... WHAT'S HAPPENING, YANK...?

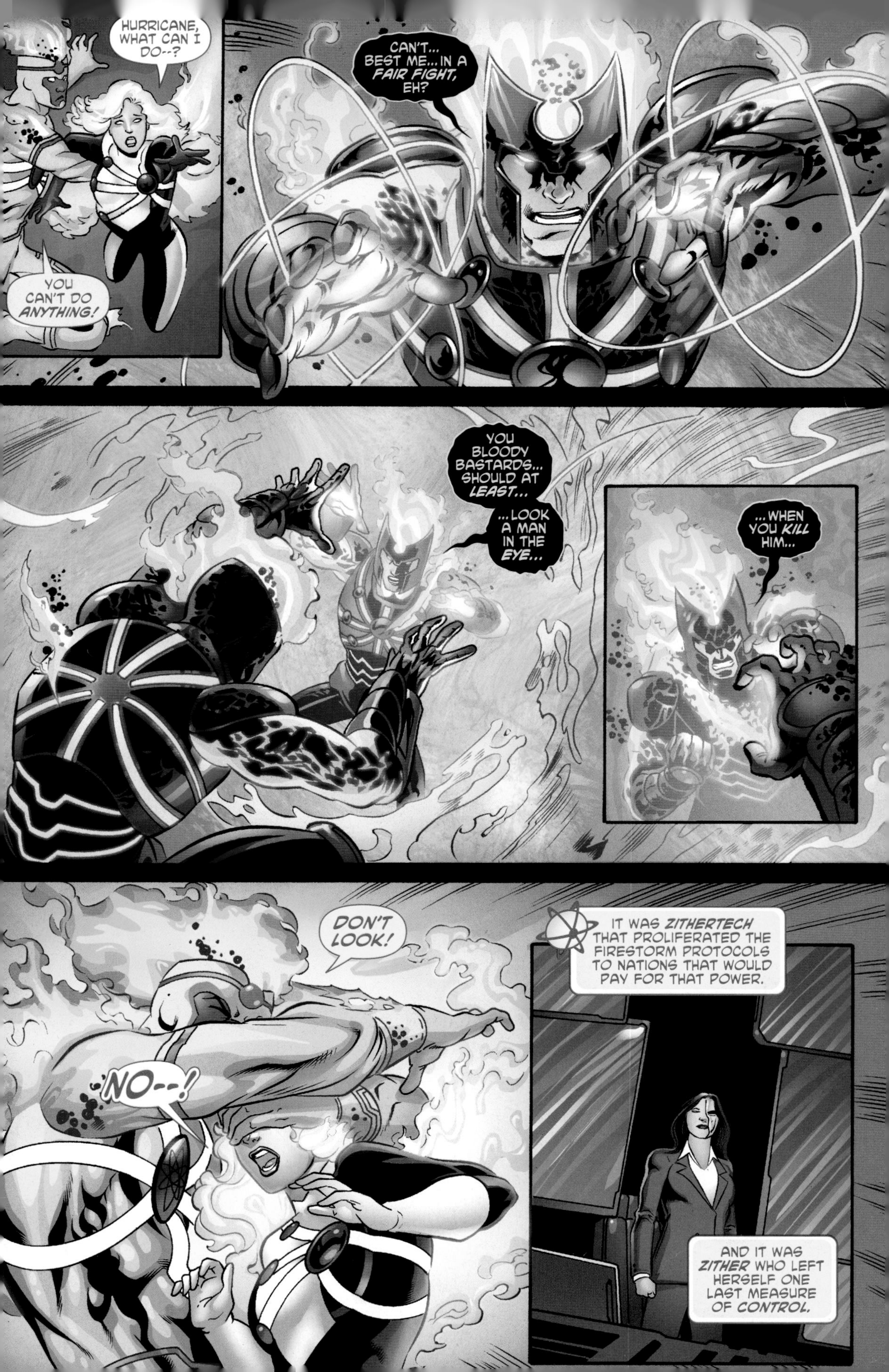
HURRICANE, WHAT CAN I DO--?
YOU CAN'T DO *ANYTHING!*
CAN'T... BEST ME... IN A *FAIR FIGHT,* EH?
YOU BLOODY BASTARDS... SHOULD AT *LEAST*...
...LOOK A MAN IN THE *EYE*...
...WHEN YOU *KILL* HIM...
DON'T LOOK!
NO--!
IT WAS *ZITHERTECH* THAT PROLIFERATED THE FIRESTORM PROTOCOLS TO NATIONS THAT WOULD PAY FOR THAT POWER.
AND IT WAS *ZITHER* WHO LEFT HERSELF ONE LAST MEASURE OF *CONTROL.*

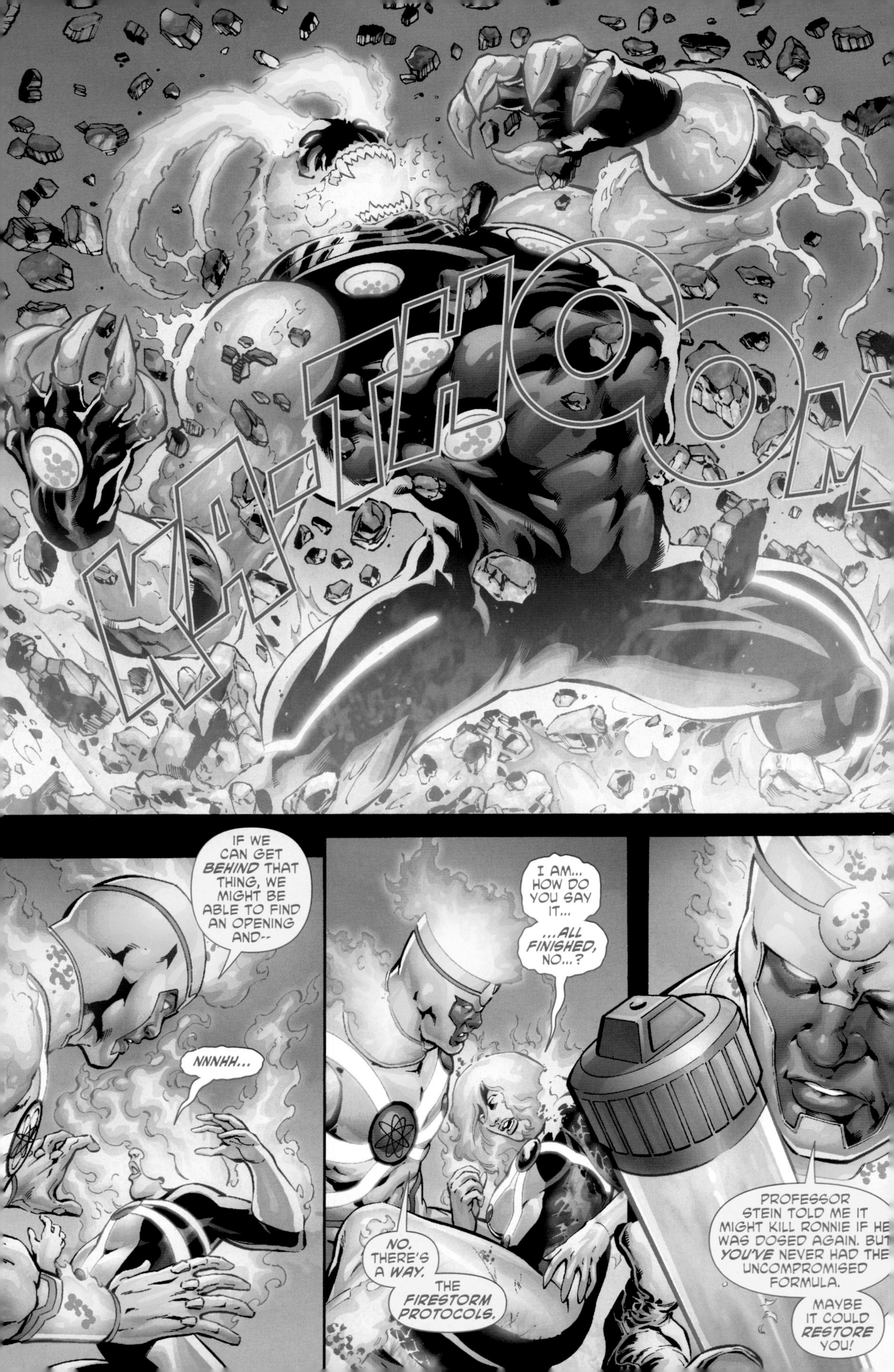
KA-THOOOM
IF WE CAN GET *BEHIND* THAT THING, WE MIGHT BE ABLE TO FIND AN OPENING AND--
NNNHH...
I AM... HOW DO YOU SAY IT...
...*ALL FINISHED,* NO...?
NO. THERE'S A *WAY.*
THE *FIRESTORM PROTOCOLS.*
PROFESSOR STEIN TOLD ME IT MIGHT KILL RONNIE IF HE WAS DOSED AGAIN. BUT *YOU'VE* NEVER HAD THE UNCOMPROMISED FORMULA.
MAYBE IT COULD *RESTORE* YOU!

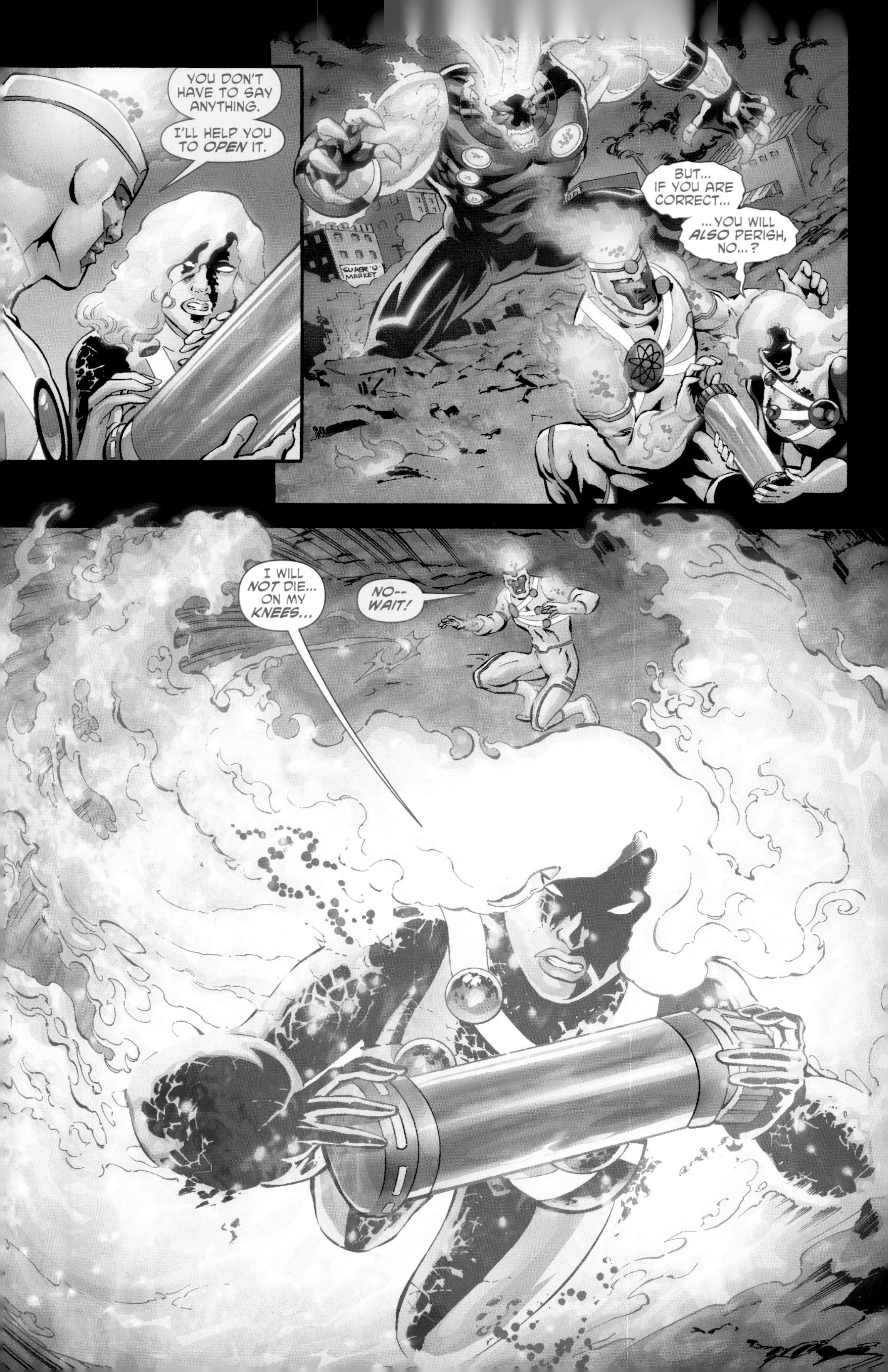
YOU DON'T HAVE TO SAY ANYTHING.
I'LL HELP YOU TO OPEN IT.
SUPER 'Q' MARKET
BUT... IF YOU ARE CORRECT...
...YOU WILL ALSO PERISH, NO...?
I WILL NOT DIE... ON MY KNEES...
NO-- WAIT!

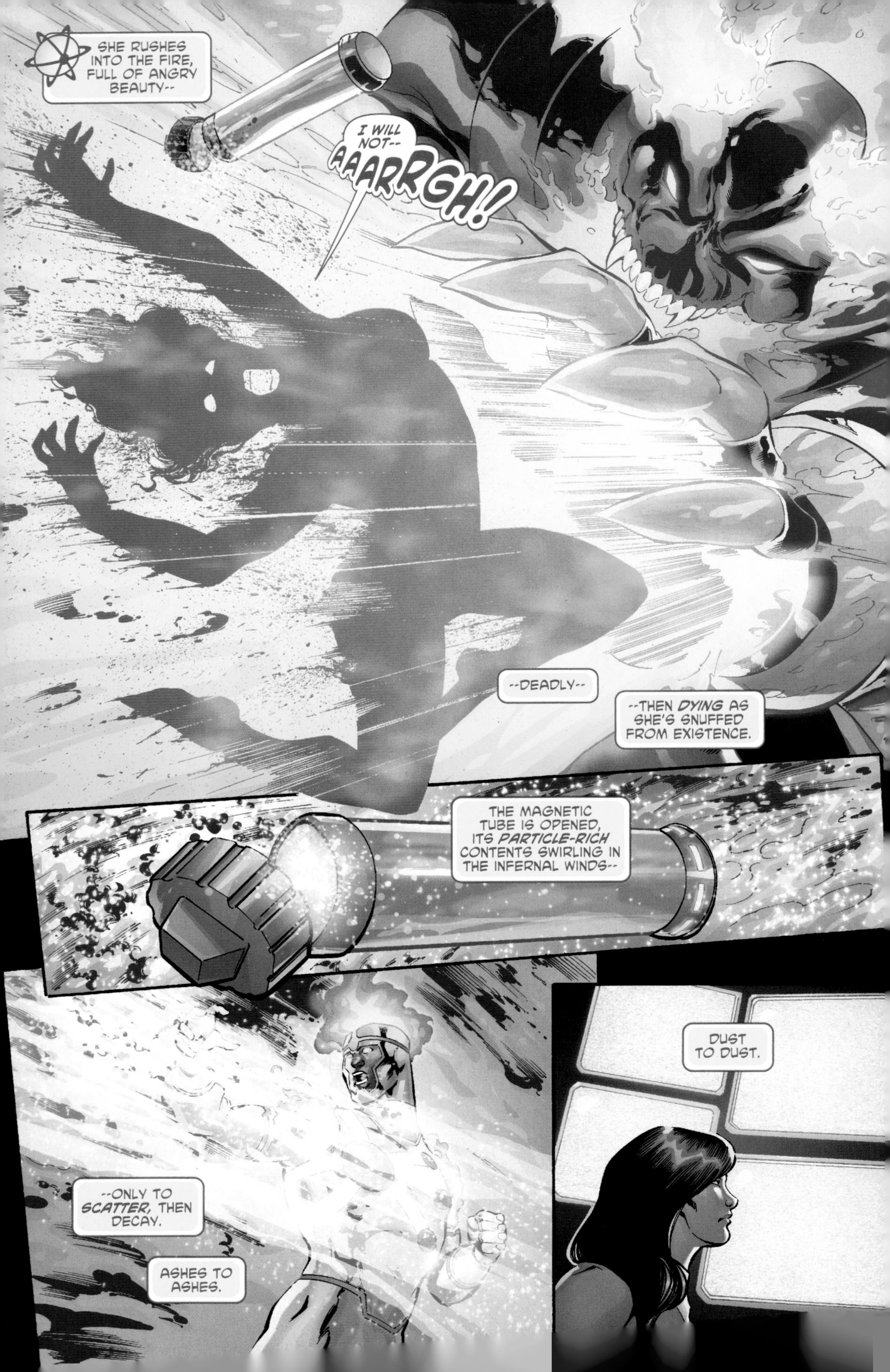
SHE RUSHES INTO THE FIRE, FULL OF ANGRY BEAUTY--
I WILL NOT-- AAARRGH!
--DEADLY--
--THEN *DYING* AS SHE'S SNUFFED FROM EXISTENCE.
THE MAGNETIC TUBE IS OPENED, ITS *PARTICLE-RICH* CONTENTS SWIRLING IN THE INFERNAL WINDS--
--ONLY TO *SCATTER*, THEN DECAY.
ASHES TO ASHES.
DUST TO DUST.

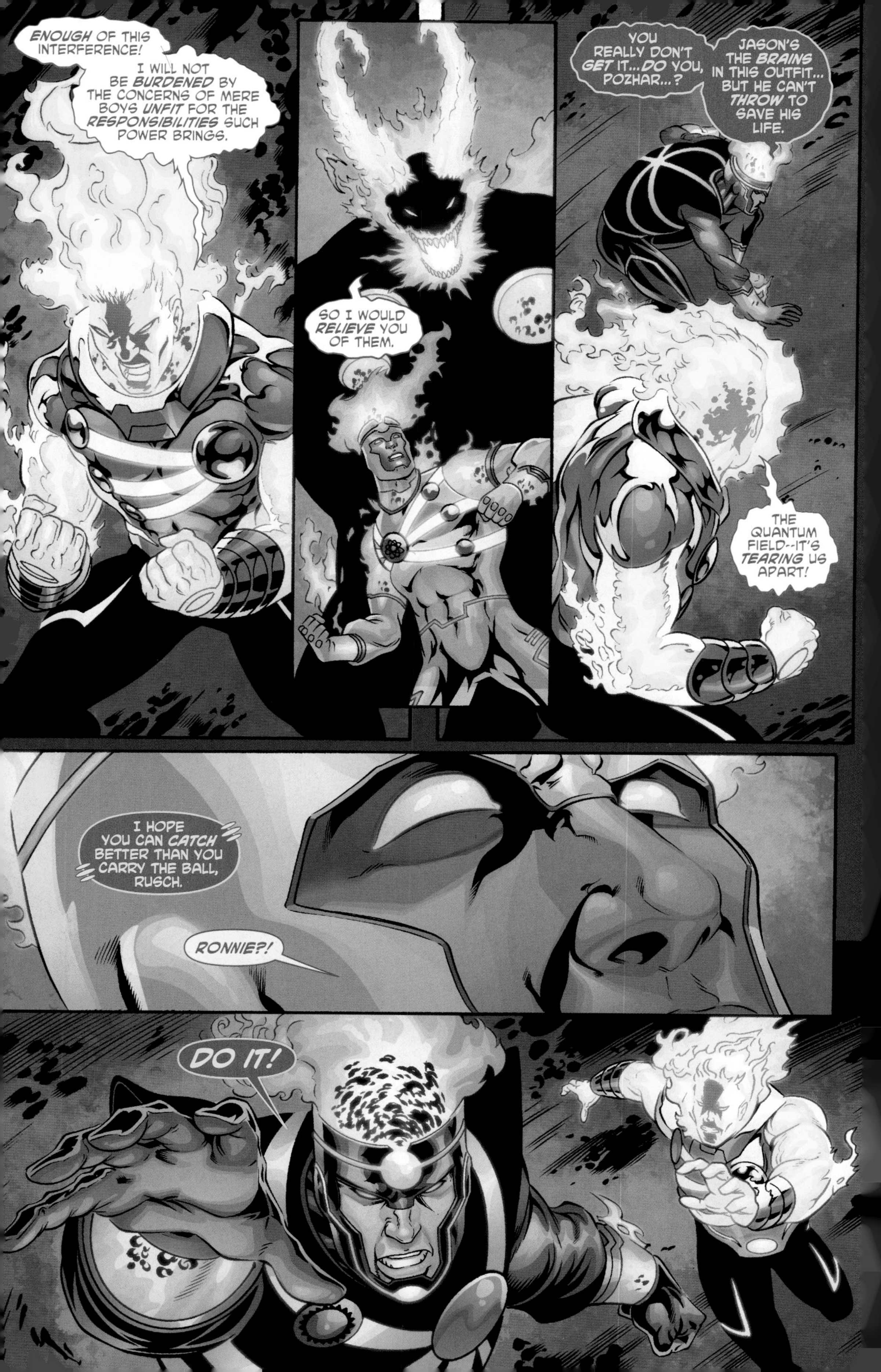
ENOUGH OF THIS INTERFERENCE!
I WILL NOT BE BURDENED BY THE CONCERNS OF MERE BOYS UNFIT FOR THE RESPONSIBILITIES SUCH POWER BRINGS.
SO I WOULD RELIEVE YOU OF THEM.
YOU REALLY DON'T GET IT...DO YOU, POZHAR...?
JASON'S THE BRAINS IN THIS OUTFIT... BUT HE CAN'T THROW TO SAVE HIS LIFE.
THE QUANTUM FIELD--IT'S TEARING US APART!
I HOPE YOU CAN CATCH BETTER THAN YOU CARRY THE BALL, RUSCH.
RONNIE?!
DO IT!

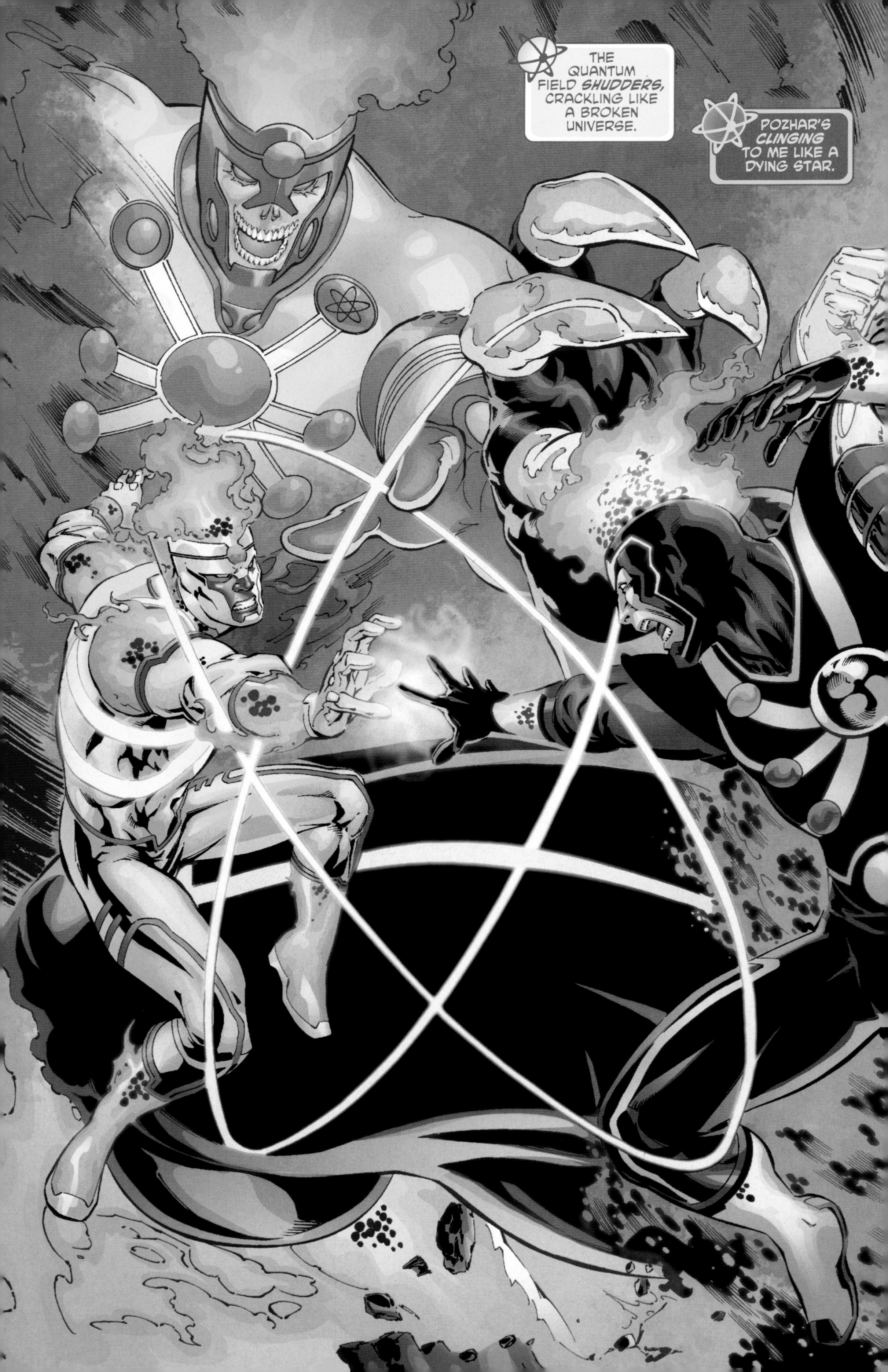

THE QUANTUM FIELD SHUDDERS, CRACKLING LIKE A BROKEN UNIVERSE.
POZHAR'S CLINGING TO ME LIKE A DYING STAR.

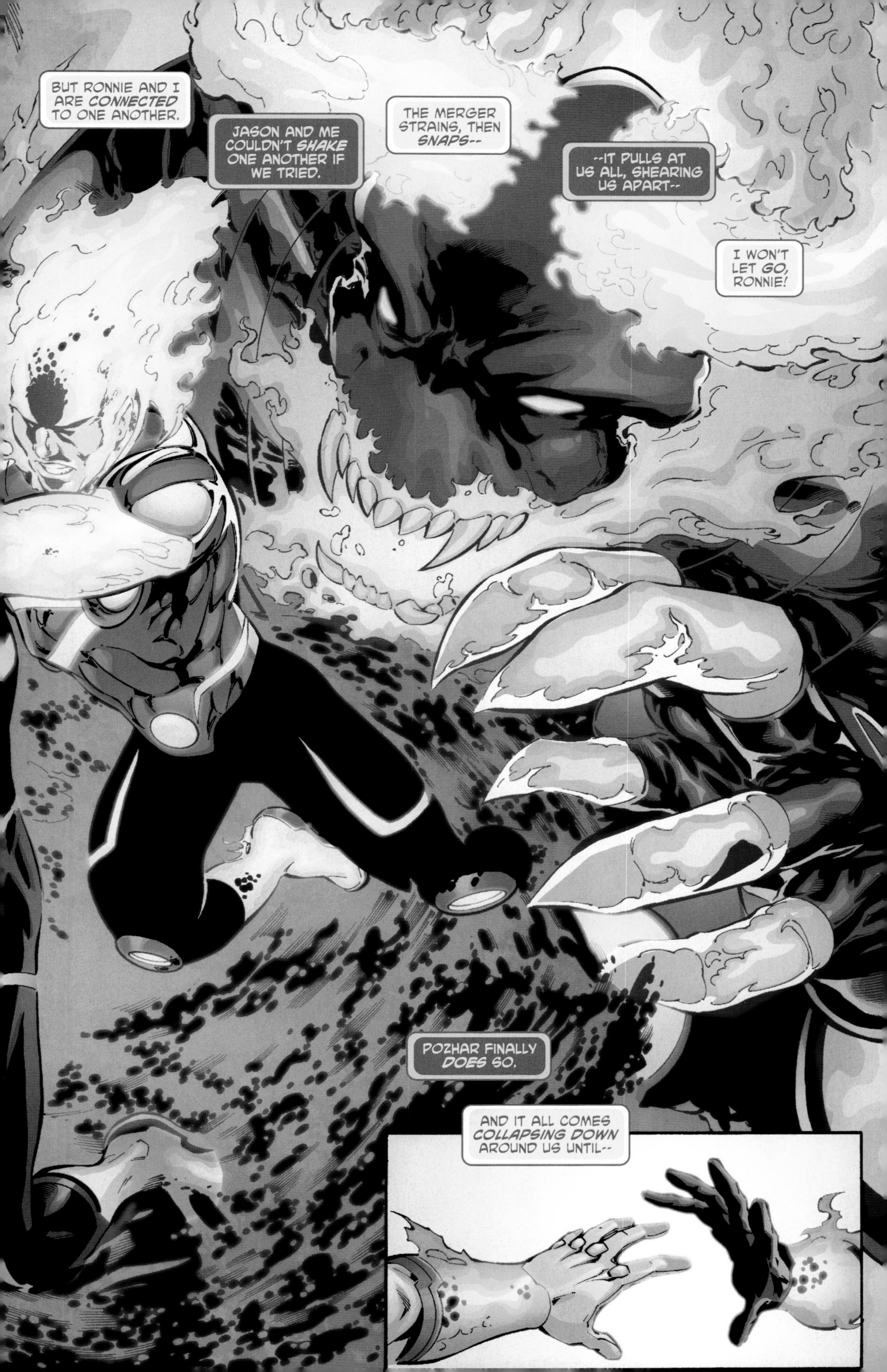
BUT RONNIE AND I ARE *CONNECTED* TO ONE ANOTHER.
JASON AND ME COULDN'T *SHAKE* ONE ANOTHER IF WE TRIED.
THE MERGER STRAINS, THEN *SNAPS*--
--IT PULLS AT US ALL, SHEARING US APART--
I WON'T LET *GO*, RONNIE!
POZHAR FINALLY *DOES* SO.
AND IT ALL COMES *COLLAPSING DOWN* AROUND US UNTIL--

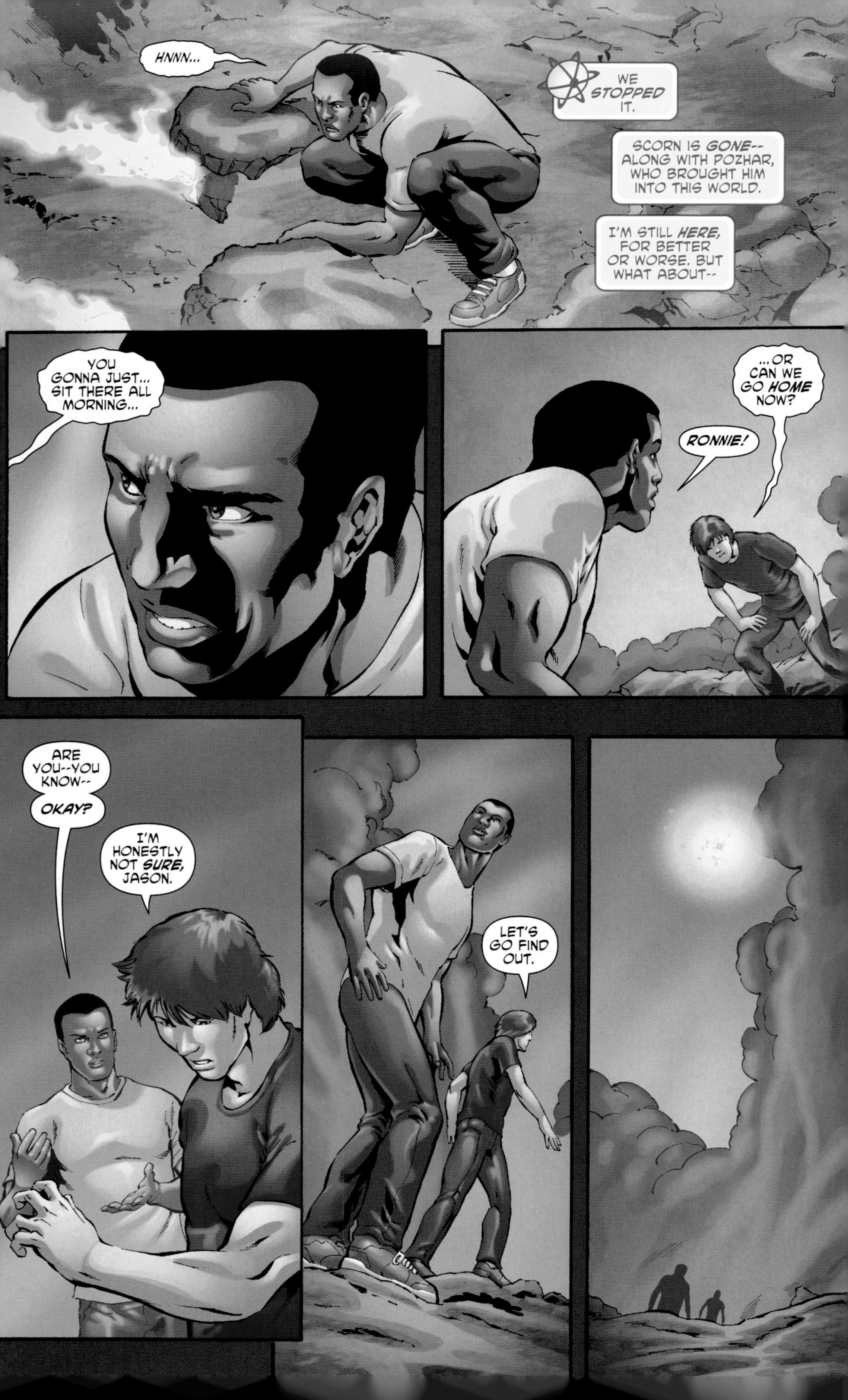
HNNN...
WE STOPPED IT.
SCORN IS GONE-- ALONG WITH POZHAR, WHO BROUGHT HIM INTO THIS WORLD.
I'M STILL HERE, FOR BETTER OR WORSE. BUT WHAT ABOUT--
YOU GONNA JUST... SIT THERE ALL MORNING...
...OR CAN WE GO HOME NOW?
RONNIE!
ARE YOU--YOU KNOW-- OKAY?
I'M HONESTLY NOT SURE, JASON.
LET'S GO FIND OUT.

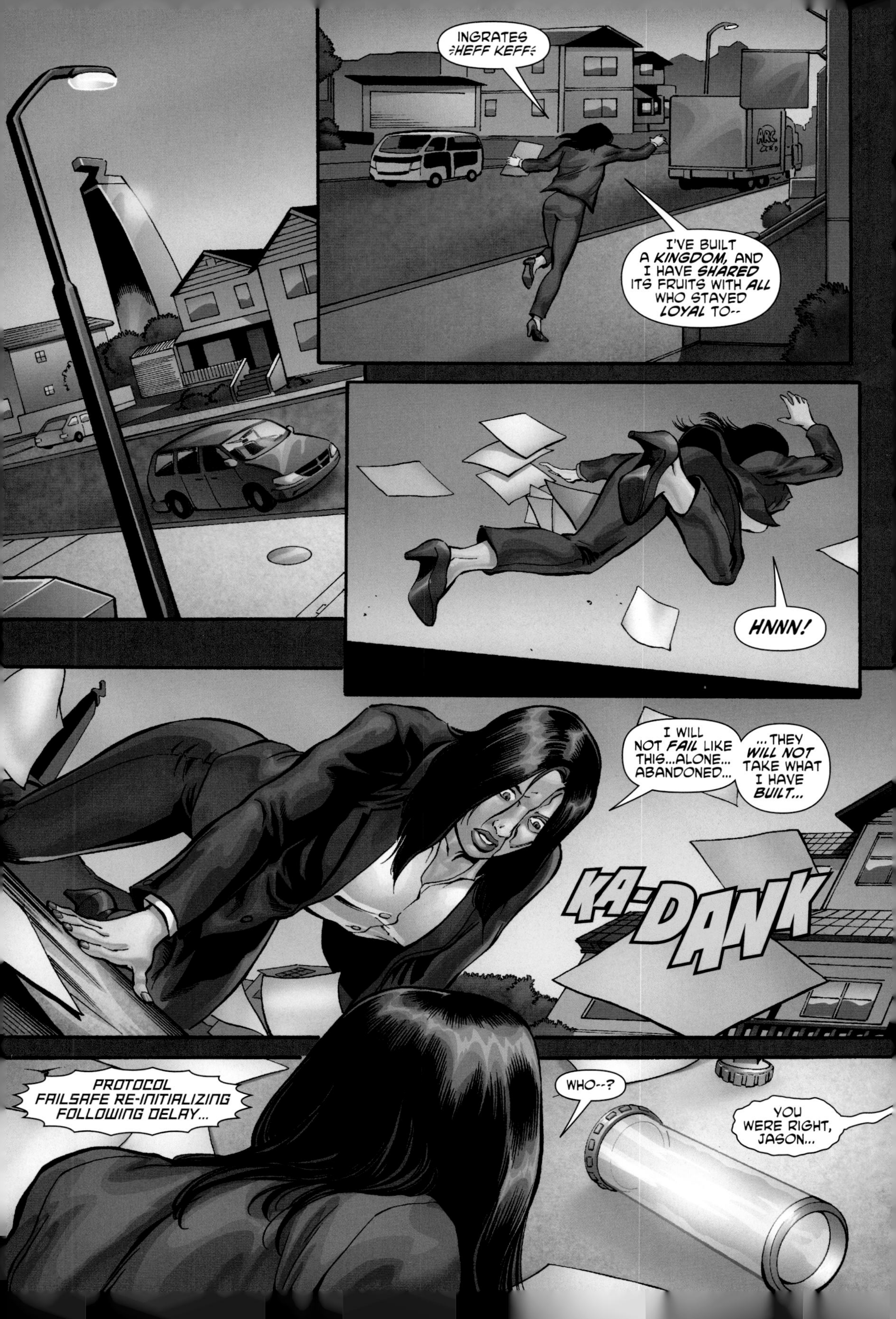
INGRATES
HEFF KEFF
I'VE BUILT A *KINGDOM,* AND I HAVE *SHARED* ITS FRUITS WITH *ALL* WHO STAYED *LOYAL* TO--
HNNN!
I WILL NOT *FAIL* LIKE THIS...ALONE... ABANDONED...
...THEY *WILL NOT* TAKE WHAT I HAVE *BUILT...*
KA-DANK
PROTOCOL FAILSAFE RE-INITIALIZING FOLLOWING DELAY...
WHO--?
YOU WERE RIGHT, JASON...

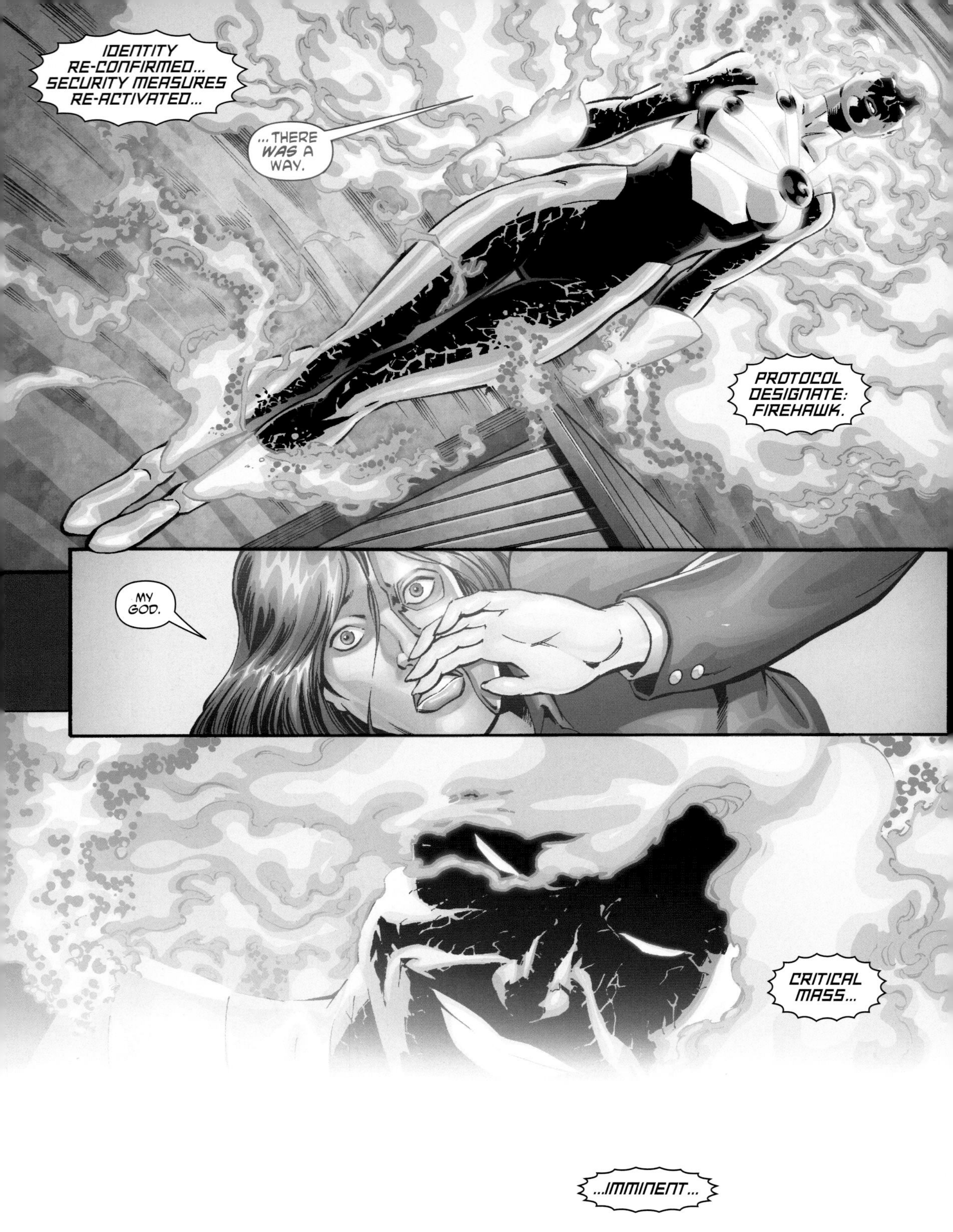
IDENTITY RE-CONFIRMED... SECURITY MEASURES RE-ACTIVATED...
...THERE WAS A WAY.
PROTOCOL DESIGNATE: FIREHAWK.
MY GOD.
CRITICAL MASS...
...IMMINENT...

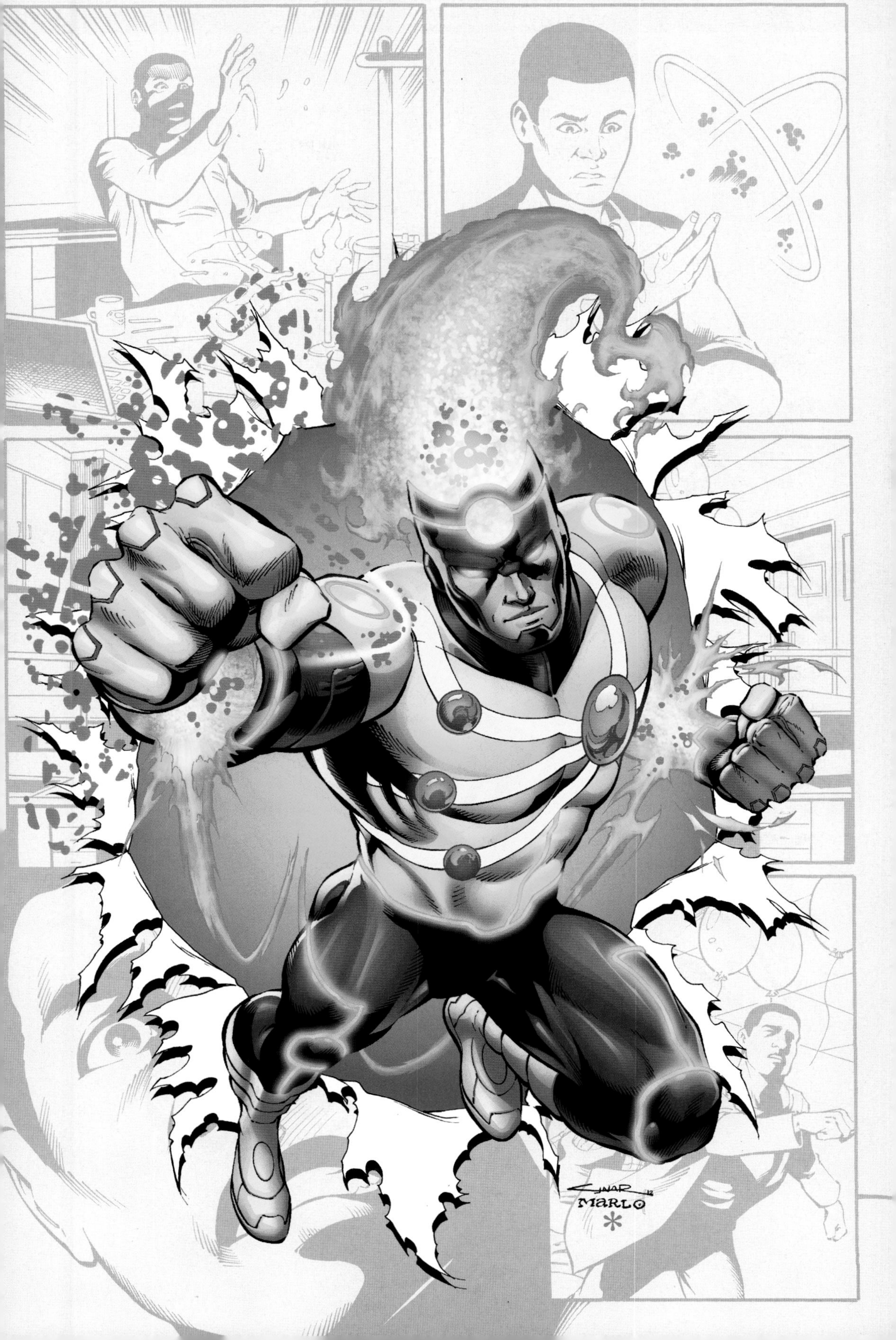
MARLO

COVALENCE

JOE HARRIS writer **YILDIRAY CINAR** penciller **MARLO ALQUIZA** inker
cover by **YILDIRAY CINAR & MARLO ALQUIZA** with **HI-FI**

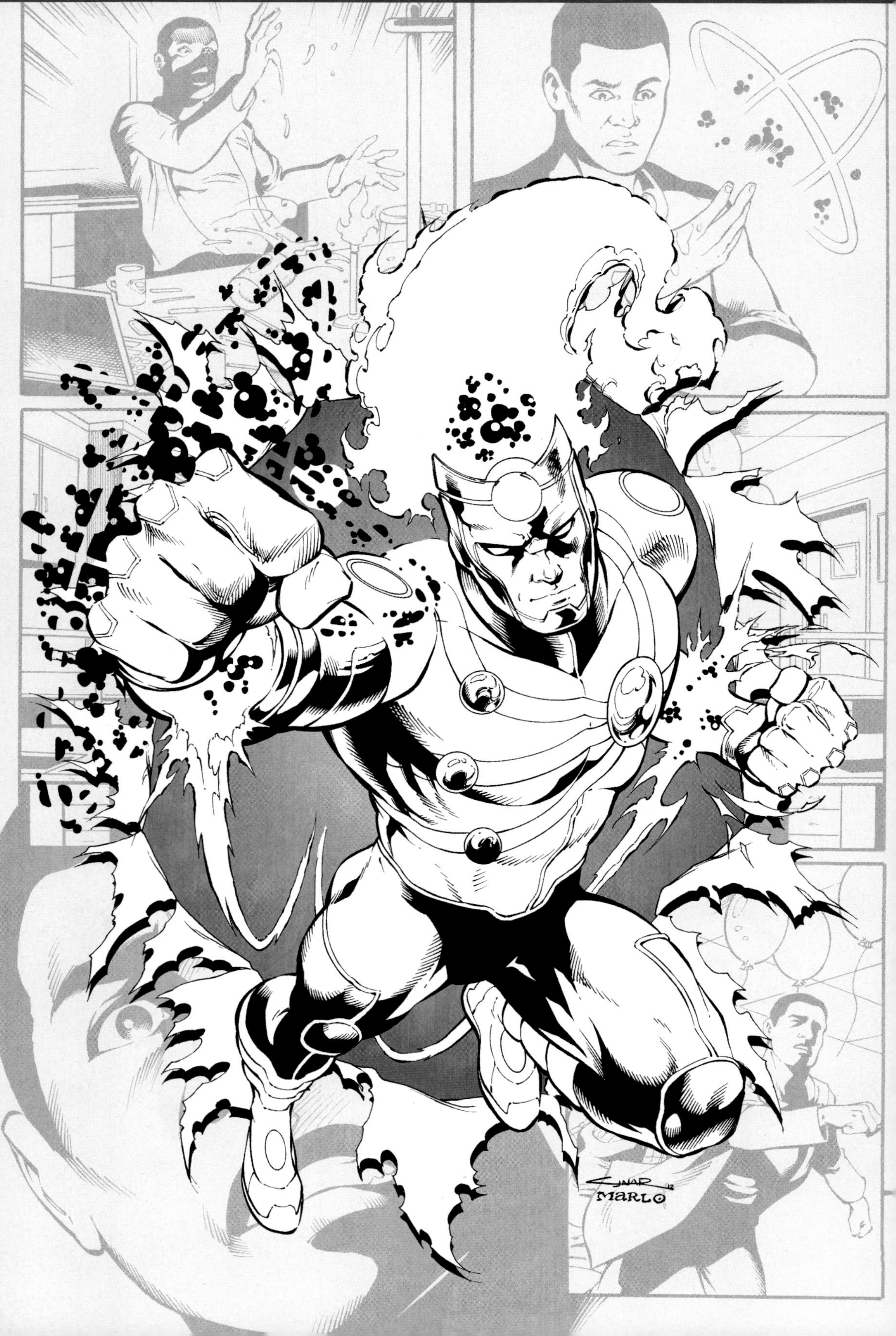
CINAR '12
MARLO

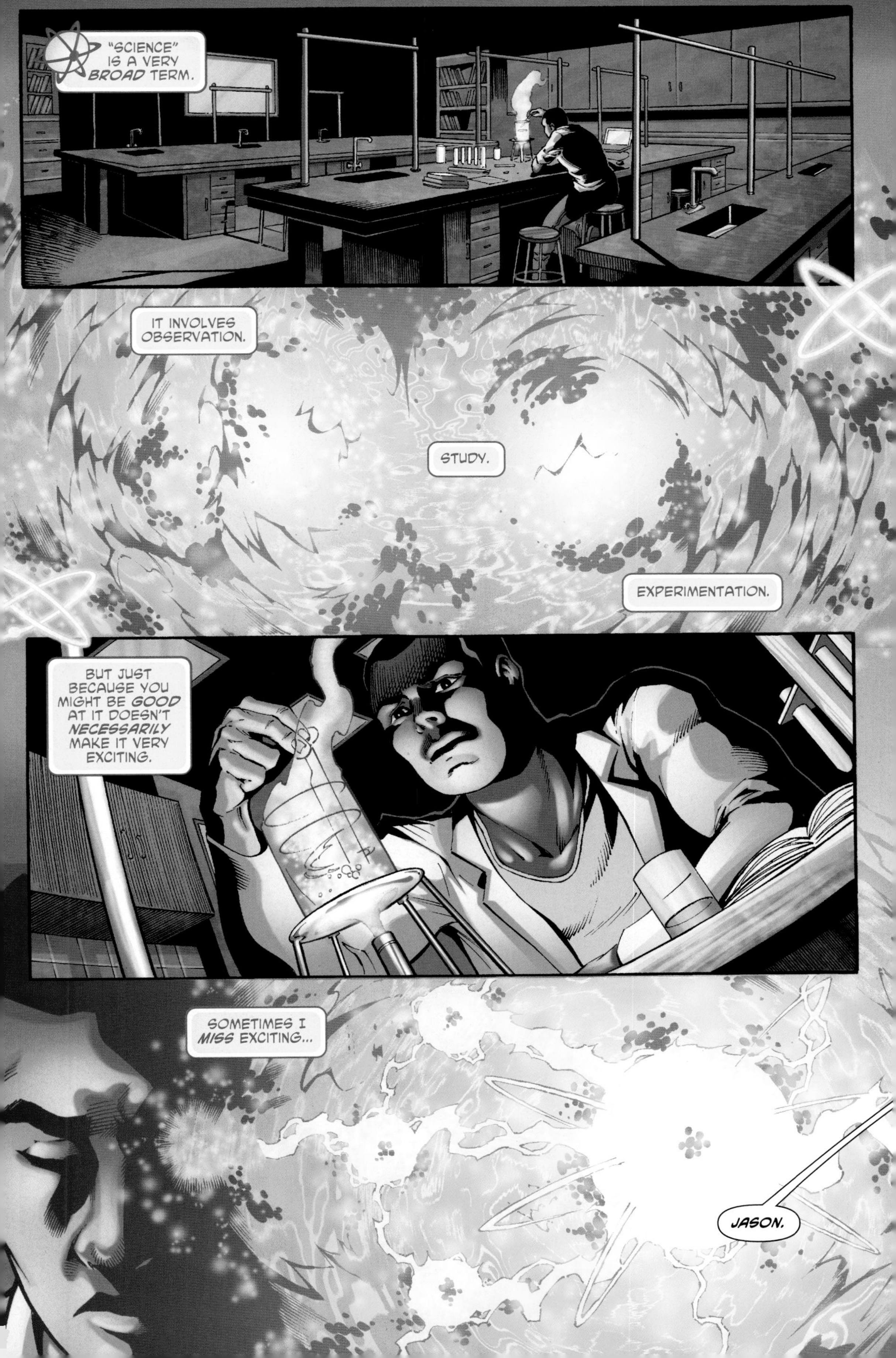
"SCIENCE" IS A VERY BROAD TERM.
IT INVOLVES OBSERVATION.
STUDY.
EXPERIMENTATION.
BUT JUST BECAUSE YOU MIGHT BE GOOD AT IT DOESN'T NECESSARILY MAKE IT VERY EXCITING.
SOMETIMES I MISS EXCITING...
JASON.

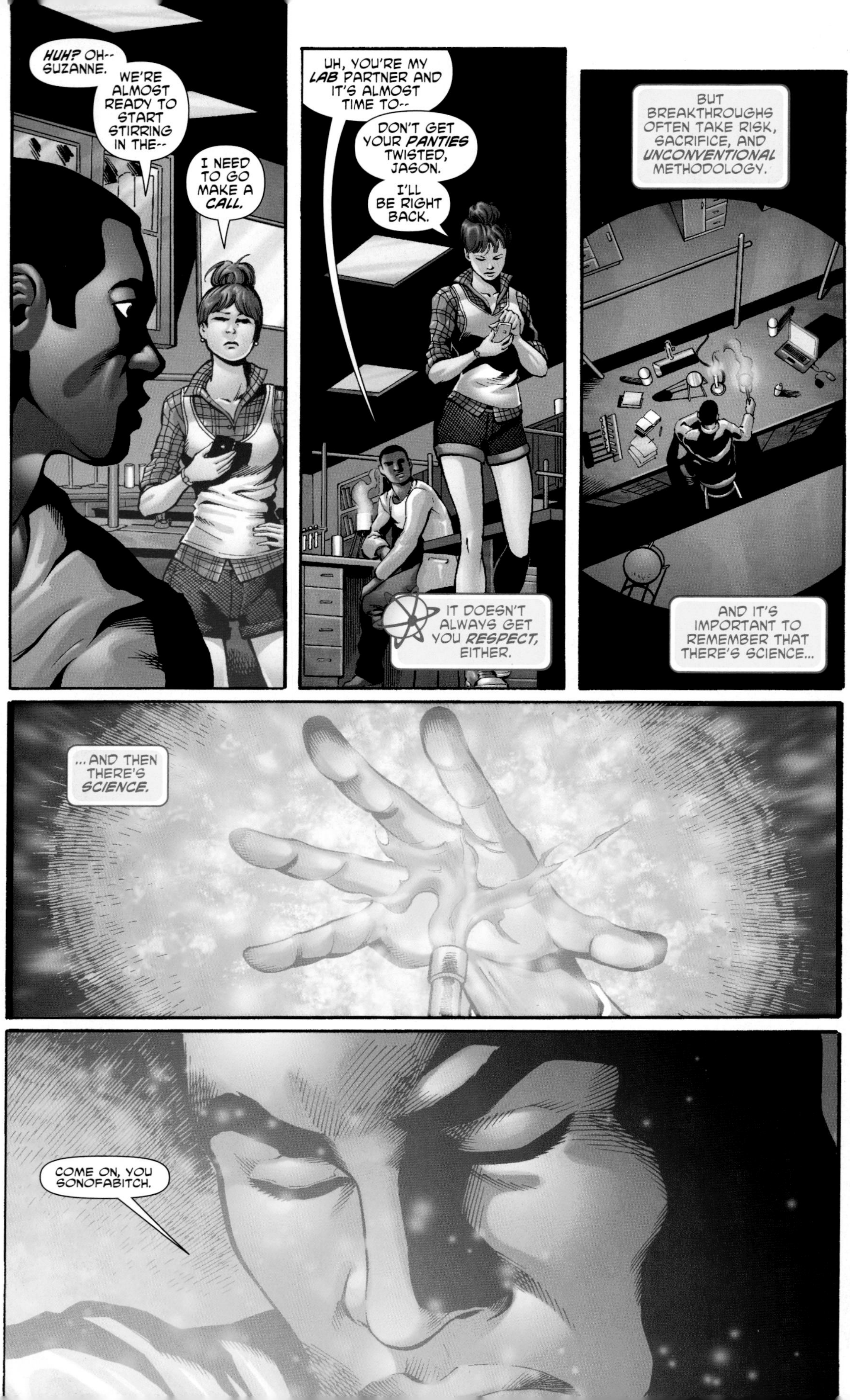
HUH? OH-- SUZANNE.
WE'RE ALMOST READY TO START STIRRING IN THE--
I NEED TO GO MAKE A CALL.
UH, YOU'RE MY LAB PARTNER AND IT'S ALMOST TIME TO--
DON'T GET YOUR PANTIES TWISTED, JASON.
I'LL BE RIGHT BACK.
IT DOESN'T ALWAYS GET YOU RESPECT, EITHER.
BUT BREAKTHROUGHS OFTEN TAKE RISK, SACRIFICE, AND UNCONVENTIONAL METHODOLOGY.
AND IT'S IMPORTANT TO REMEMBER THAT THERE'S SCIENCE...
...AND THEN THERE'S SCIENCE.
COME ON, YOU SONOFABITCH.

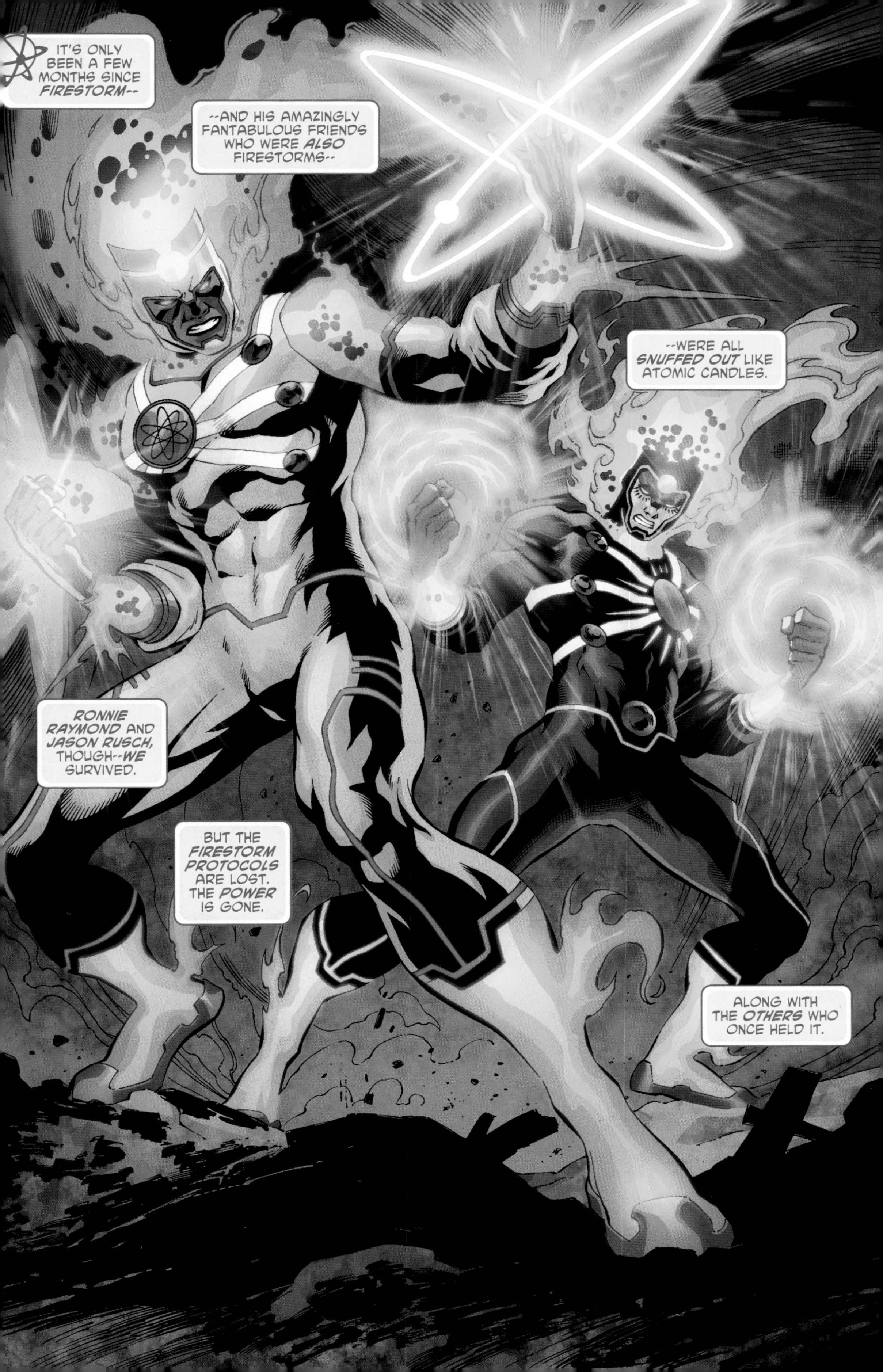
IT'S ONLY BEEN A FEW MONTHS SINCE FIRESTORM--
--AND HIS AMAZINGLY FANTABULOUS FRIENDS WHO WERE ALSO FIRESTORMS--
--WERE ALL SNUFFED OUT LIKE ATOMIC CANDLES.
RONNIE RAYMOND AND JASON RUSCH, THOUGH--WE SURVIVED.
BUT THE FIRESTORM PROTOCOLS ARE LOST. THE POWER IS GONE.
ALONG WITH THE OTHERS WHO ONCE HELD IT.

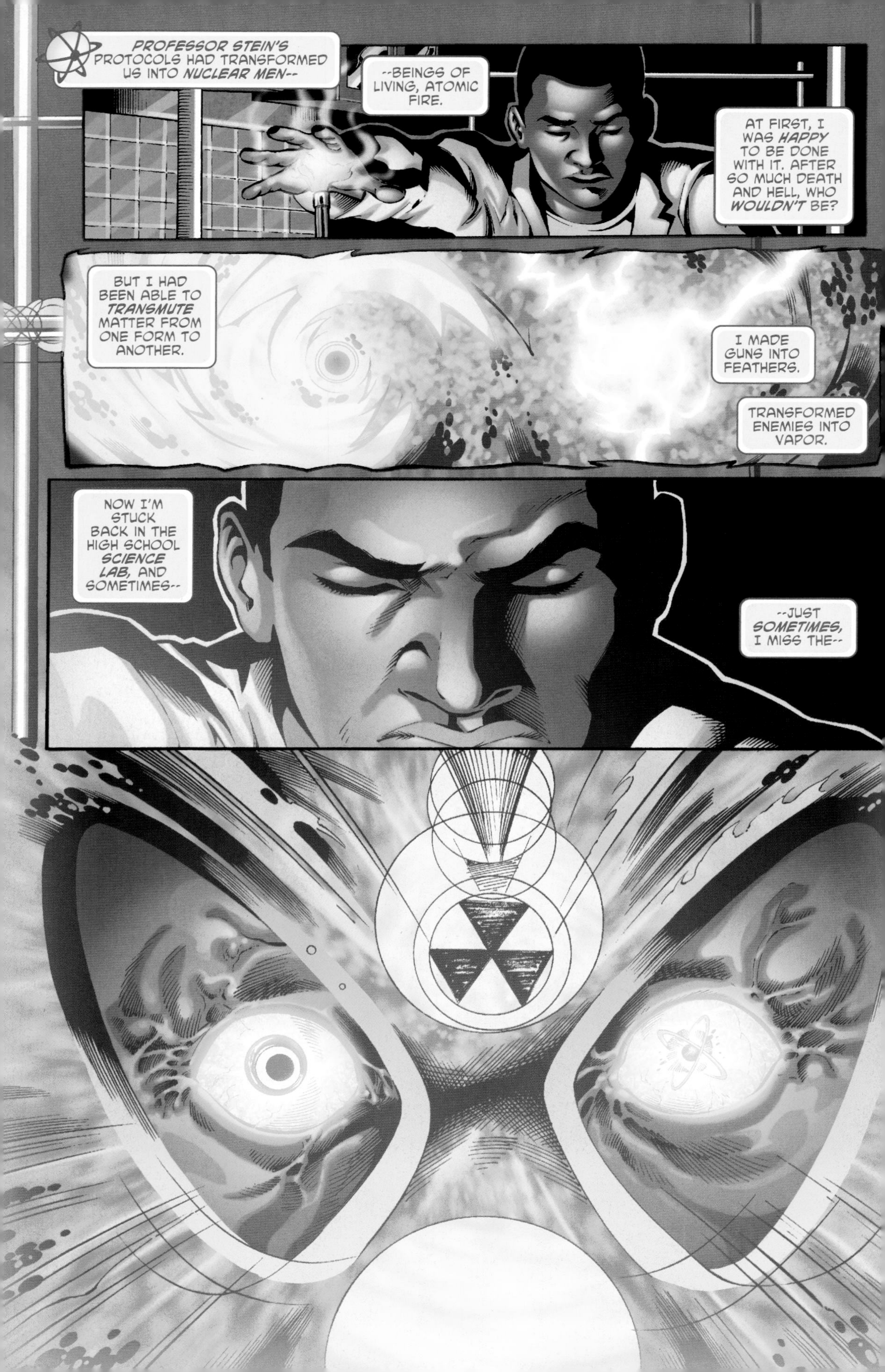

PROFESSOR STEIN'S PROTOCOLS HAD TRANSFORMED US INTO NUCLEAR MEN--
--BEINGS OF LIVING, ATOMIC FIRE.
AT FIRST, I WAS HAPPY TO BE DONE WITH IT. AFTER SO MUCH DEATH AND HELL, WHO WOULDN'T BE?
BUT I HAD BEEN ABLE TO TRANSMUTE MATTER FROM ONE FORM TO ANOTHER.
I MADE GUNS INTO FEATHERS.
TRANSFORMED ENEMIES INTO VAPOR.
NOW I'M STUCK BACK IN THE HIGH SCHOOL SCIENCE LAB, AND SOMETIMES--
--JUST SOMETIMES, I MISS THE--

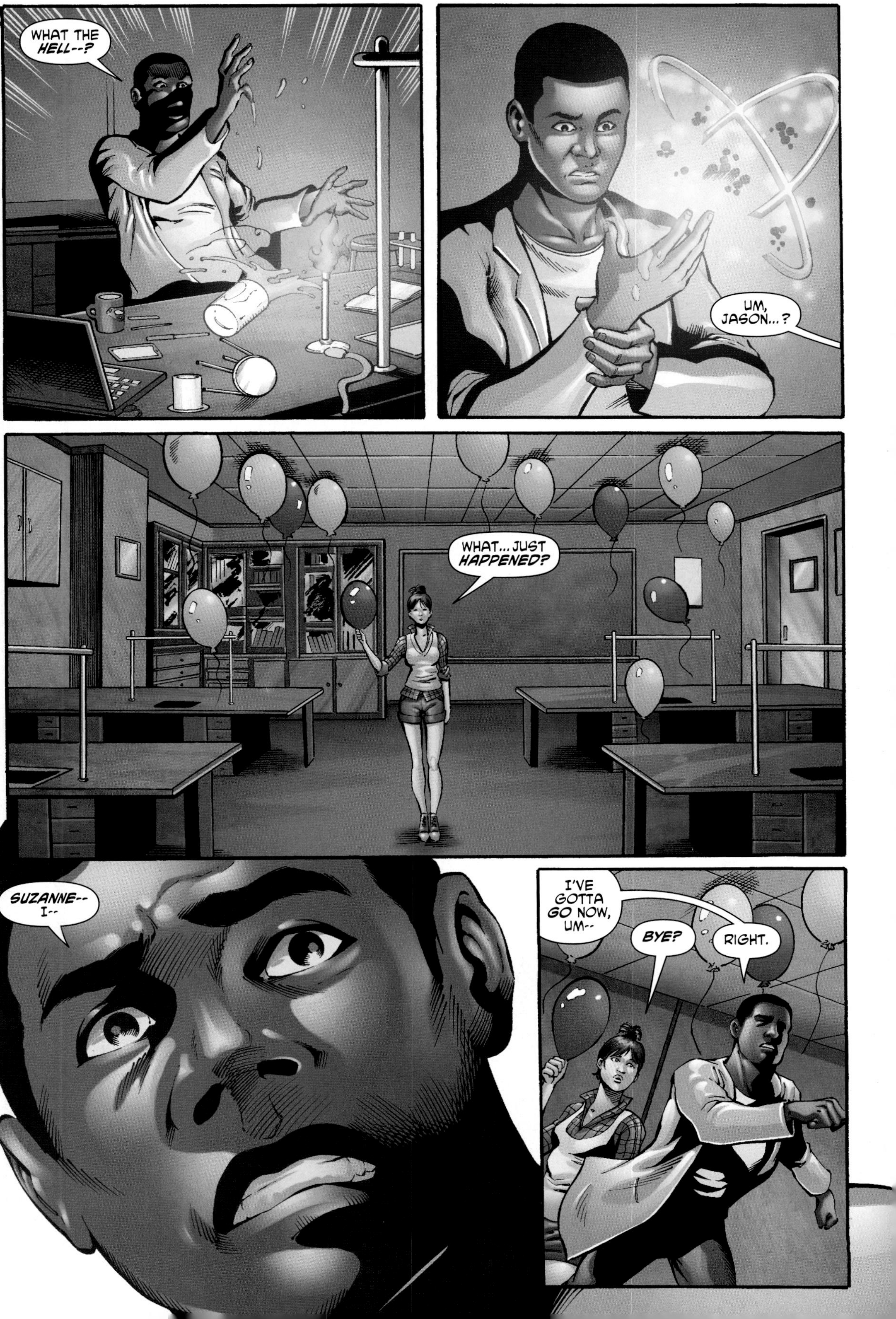
WHAT THE *HELL*--?
UM, JASON...?
WHAT... JUST *HAPPENED*?
SUZANNE-- I--
I'VE GOTTA GO NOW, UM--
BYE?
RIGHT.

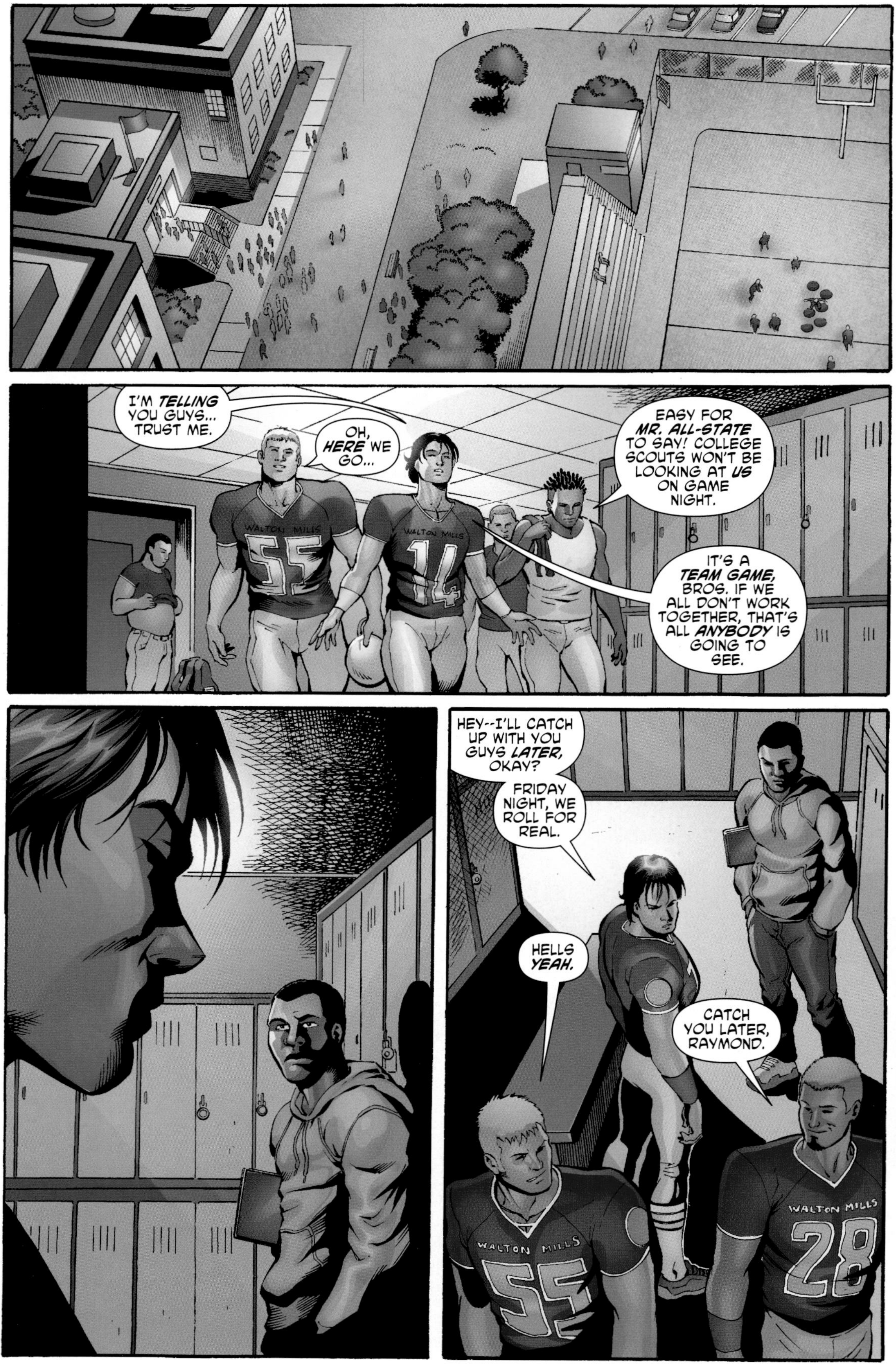
I'M *TELLING* YOU GUYS... TRUST ME.
OH, *HERE* WE GO...
EASY FOR *MR. ALL-STATE* TO SAY! COLLEGE SCOUTS WON'T BE LOOKING AT *US* ON GAME NIGHT.
IT'S A *TEAM GAME,* BROS. IF WE ALL DON'T WORK TOGETHER, THAT'S ALL *ANYBODY* IS GOING TO SEE.
WALTON MILLS
55
WALTON MILLS
14
HEY--I'LL CATCH UP WITH YOU GUYS *LATER,* OKAY?
FRIDAY NIGHT, WE ROLL FOR REAL.
HELLS *YEAH.*
CATCH YOU LATER, RAYMOND.
WALTON MILLS
55
WALTON MILLS
28

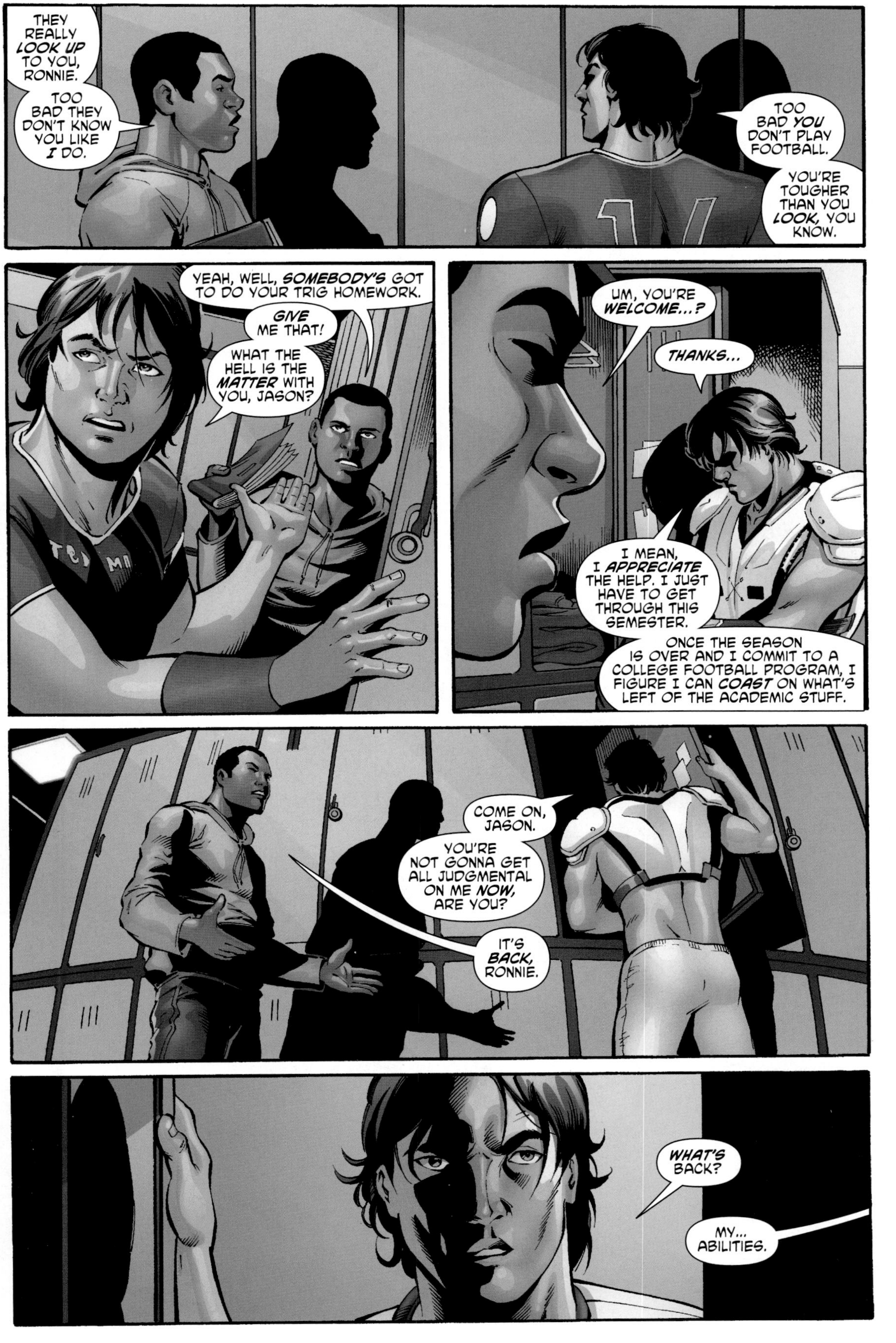
THEY REALLY LOOK UP TO YOU, RONNIE.
TOO BAD THEY DON'T KNOW YOU LIKE I DO.
TOO BAD YOU DON'T PLAY FOOTBALL.
YOU'RE TOUGHER THAN YOU LOOK, YOU KNOW.
YEAH, WELL, SOMEBODY'S GOT TO DO YOUR TRIG HOMEWORK.
GIVE ME THAT!
WHAT THE HELL IS THE MATTER WITH YOU, JASON?
UM, YOU'RE WELCOME...?
THANKS...
I MEAN, I APPRECIATE THE HELP. I JUST HAVE TO GET THROUGH THIS SEMESTER.
ONCE THE SEASON IS OVER AND I COMMIT TO A COLLEGE FOOTBALL PROGRAM, I FIGURE I CAN COAST ON WHAT'S LEFT OF THE ACADEMIC STUFF.
COME ON, JASON.
YOU'RE NOT GONNA GET ALL JUDGMENTAL ON ME NOW, ARE YOU?
IT'S BACK, RONNIE.
WHAT'S BACK?
MY... ABILITIES.

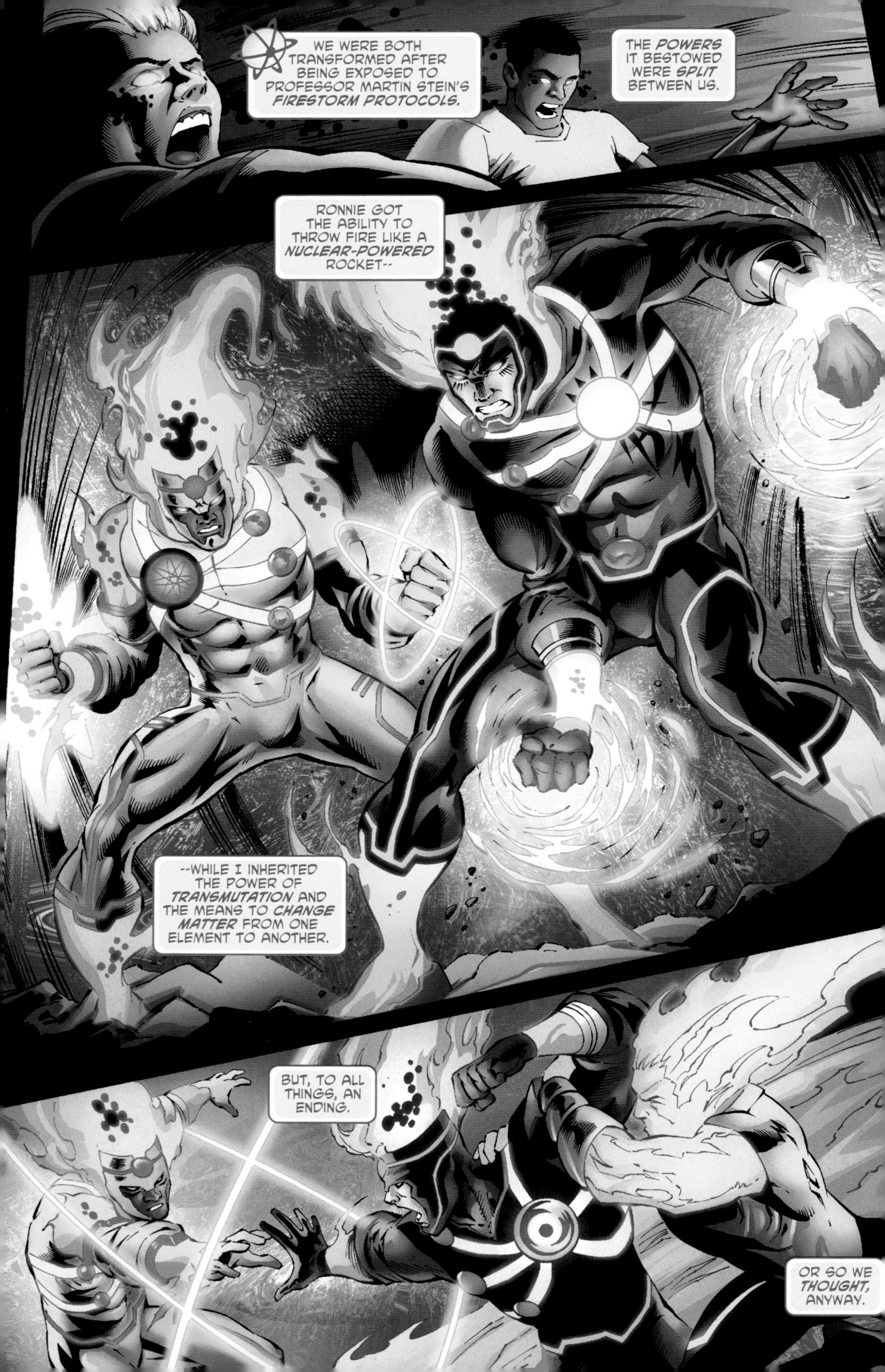
WE WERE BOTH TRANSFORMED AFTER BEING EXPOSED TO PROFESSOR MARTIN STEIN'S *FIRESTORM PROTOCOLS.*
THE *POWERS* IT BESTOWED WERE *SPLIT* BETWEEN US.
RONNIE GOT THE ABILITY TO THROW FIRE LIKE A *NUCLEAR-POWERED* ROCKET--
--WHILE I INHERITED THE POWER OF *TRANSMUTATION* AND THE MEANS TO *CHANGE MATTER* FROM ONE ELEMENT TO ANOTHER.
BUT, TO ALL THINGS, AN ENDING.
OR SO WE *THOUGHT,* ANYWAY.

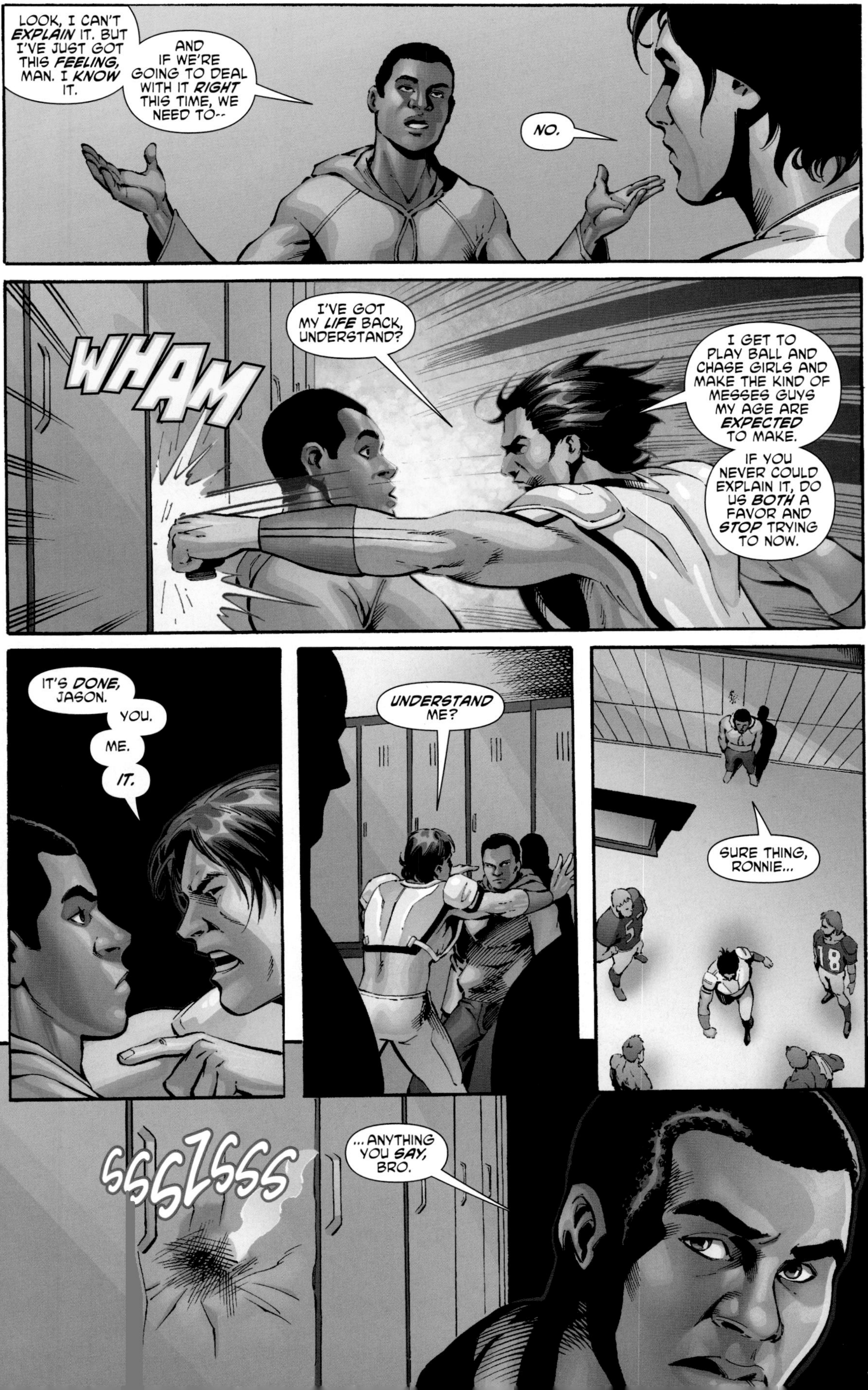
LOOK, I CAN'T EXPLAIN IT. BUT I'VE JUST GOT THIS FEELING, MAN. I KNOW IT.
AND IF WE'RE GOING TO DEAL WITH IT RIGHT THIS TIME, WE NEED TO--
NO.
WHAM
I'VE GOT MY LIFE BACK, UNDERSTAND?
I GET TO PLAY BALL AND CHASE GIRLS AND MAKE THE KIND OF MESSES GUYS MY AGE ARE EXPECTED TO MAKE.
IF YOU NEVER COULD EXPLAIN IT, DO US BOTH A FAVOR AND STOP TRYING TO NOW.
IT'S DONE, JASON.
YOU.
ME.
IT.
UNDERSTAND ME?
SURE THING, RONNIE...
SSSZSSS
...ANYTHING YOU SAY, BRO.

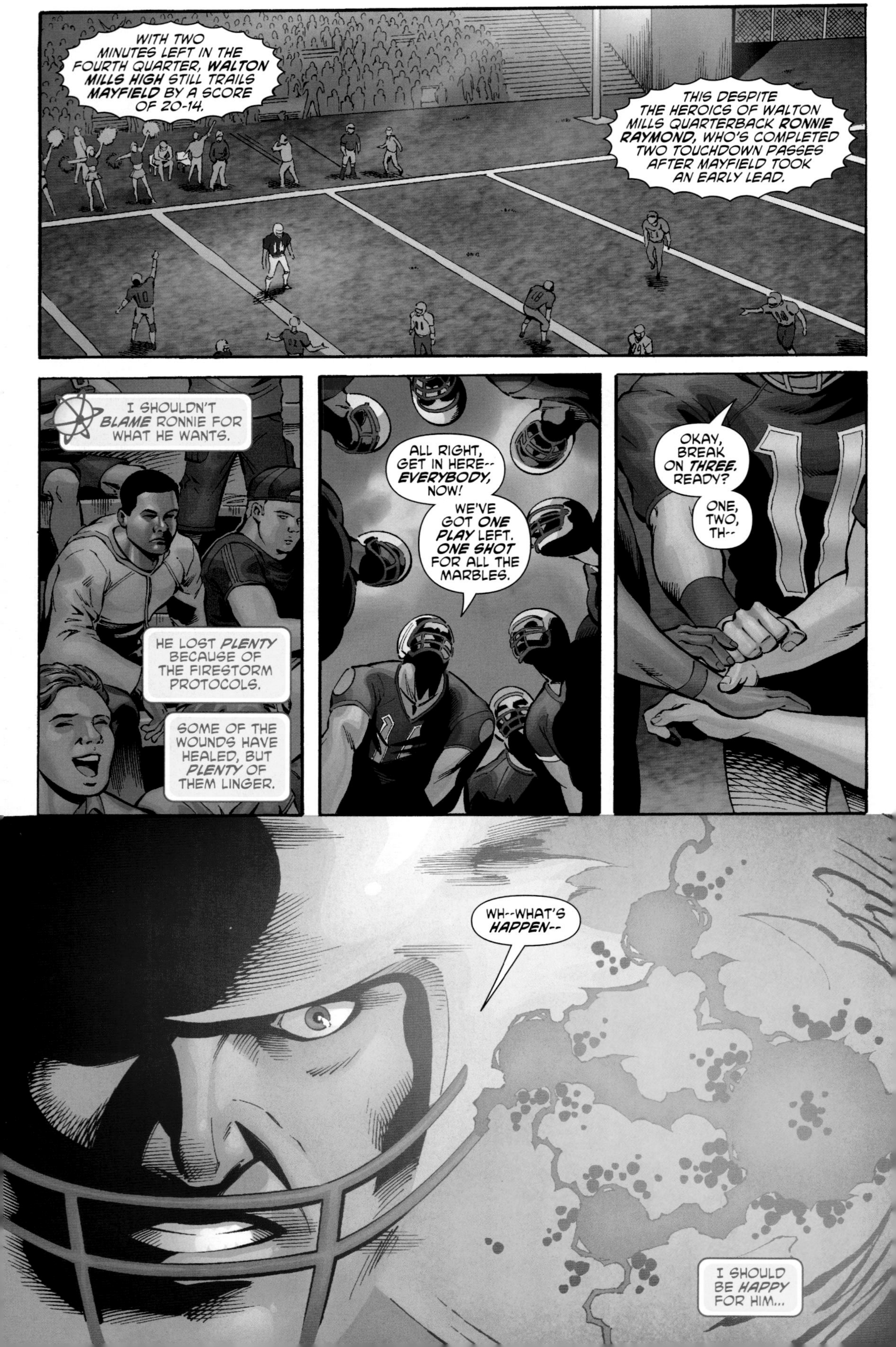
WITH TWO MINUTES LEFT IN THE FOURTH QUARTER, WALTON MILLS HIGH STILL TRAILS MAYFIELD BY A SCORE OF 20-14.
THIS DESPITE THE HEROICS OF WALTON MILLS QUARTERBACK RONNIE RAYMOND, WHO'S COMPLETED TWO TOUCHDOWN PASSES AFTER MAYFIELD TOOK AN EARLY LEAD.
I SHOULDN'T BLAME RONNIE FOR WHAT HE WANTS.
HE LOST PLENTY BECAUSE OF THE FIRESTORM PROTOCOLS.
SOME OF THE WOUNDS HAVE HEALED, BUT PLENTY OF THEM LINGER.
ALL RIGHT, GET IN HERE-- EVERYBODY, NOW!
WE'VE GOT ONE PLAY LEFT. ONE SHOT FOR ALL THE MARBLES.
OKAY, BREAK ON THREE. READY?
ONE, TWO, TH--
WH--WHAT'S HAPPEN--
I SHOULD BE HAPPY FOR HIM...

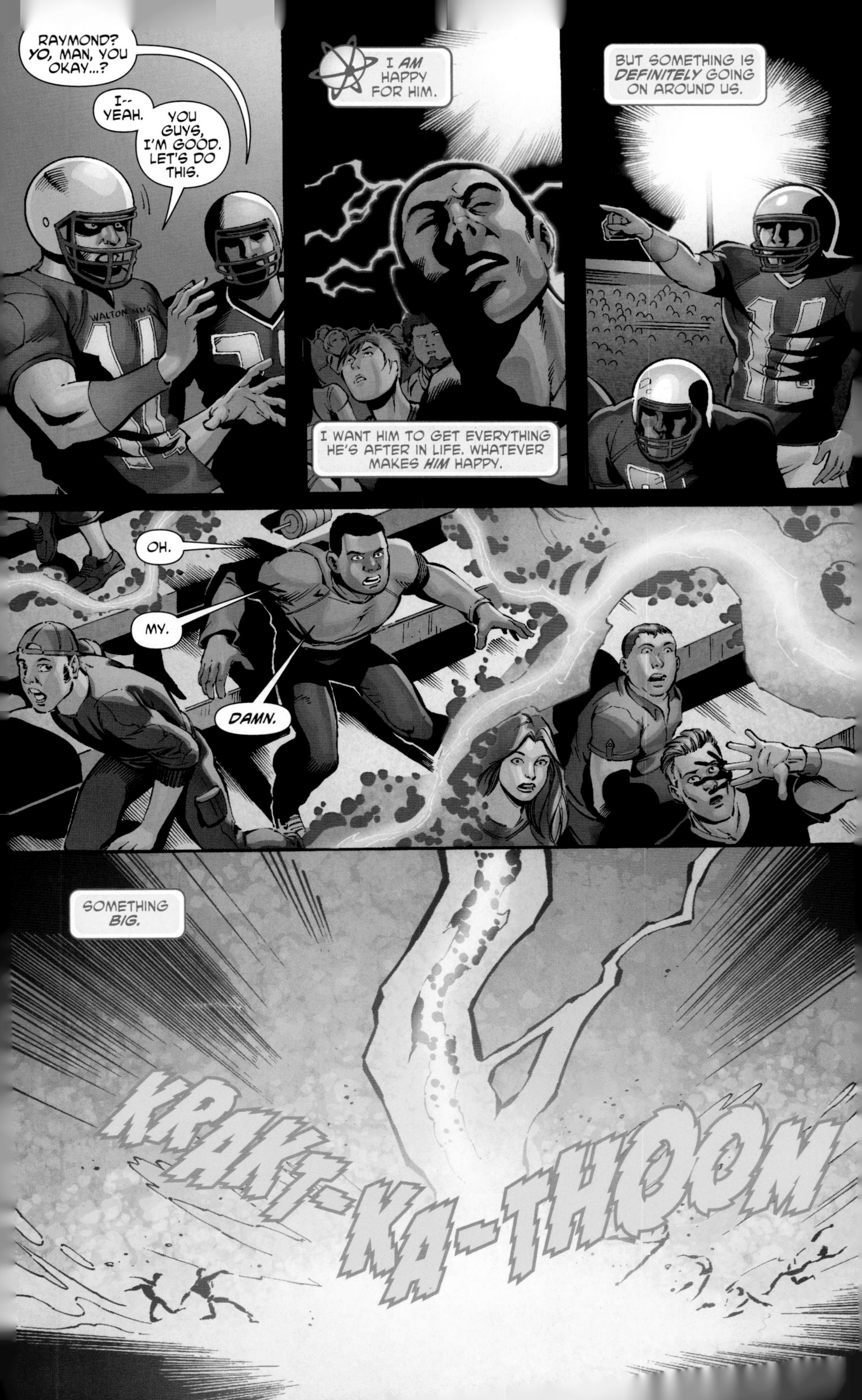
RAYMOND? YO, MAN, YOU OKAY...?
I-- YEAH.
YOU GUYS, I'M GOOD. LET'S DO THIS.
I AM HAPPY FOR HIM.
I WANT HIM TO GET EVERYTHING HE'S AFTER IN LIFE. WHATEVER MAKES HIM HAPPY.
BUT SOMETHING IS DEFINITELY GOING ON AROUND US.
OH.
MY.
DAMN.
SOMETHING BIG.
KRAKT-KA-THOOM

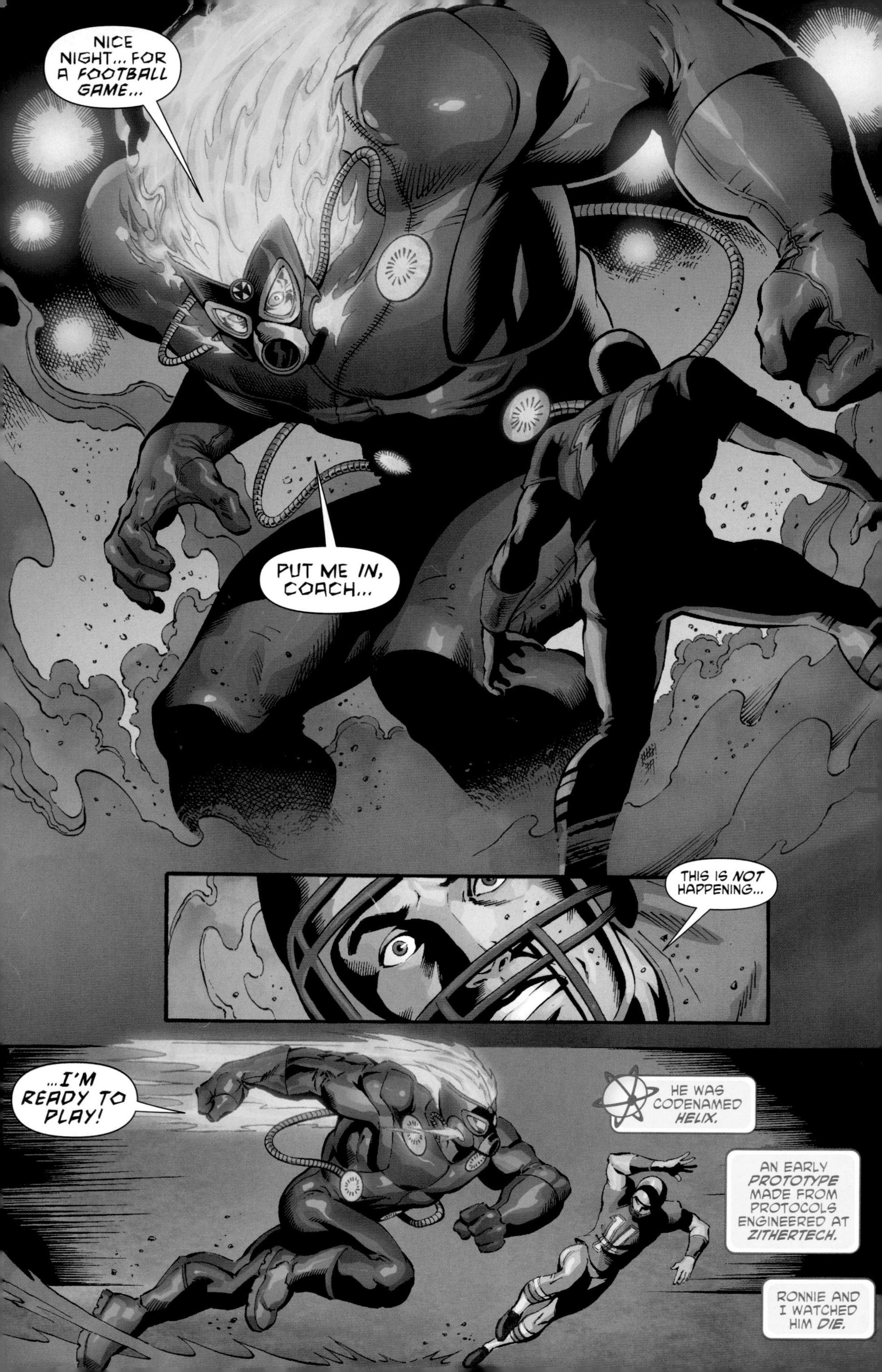
NICE NIGHT... FOR A FOOTBALL GAME...
PUT ME IN, COACH...
THIS IS NOT HAPPENING...
...I'M READY TO PLAY!
HE WAS CODENAMED HELIX.
AN EARLY PROTOTYPE MADE FROM PROTOCOLS ENGINEERED AT ZITHERTECH.
RONNIE AND I WATCHED HIM DIE.

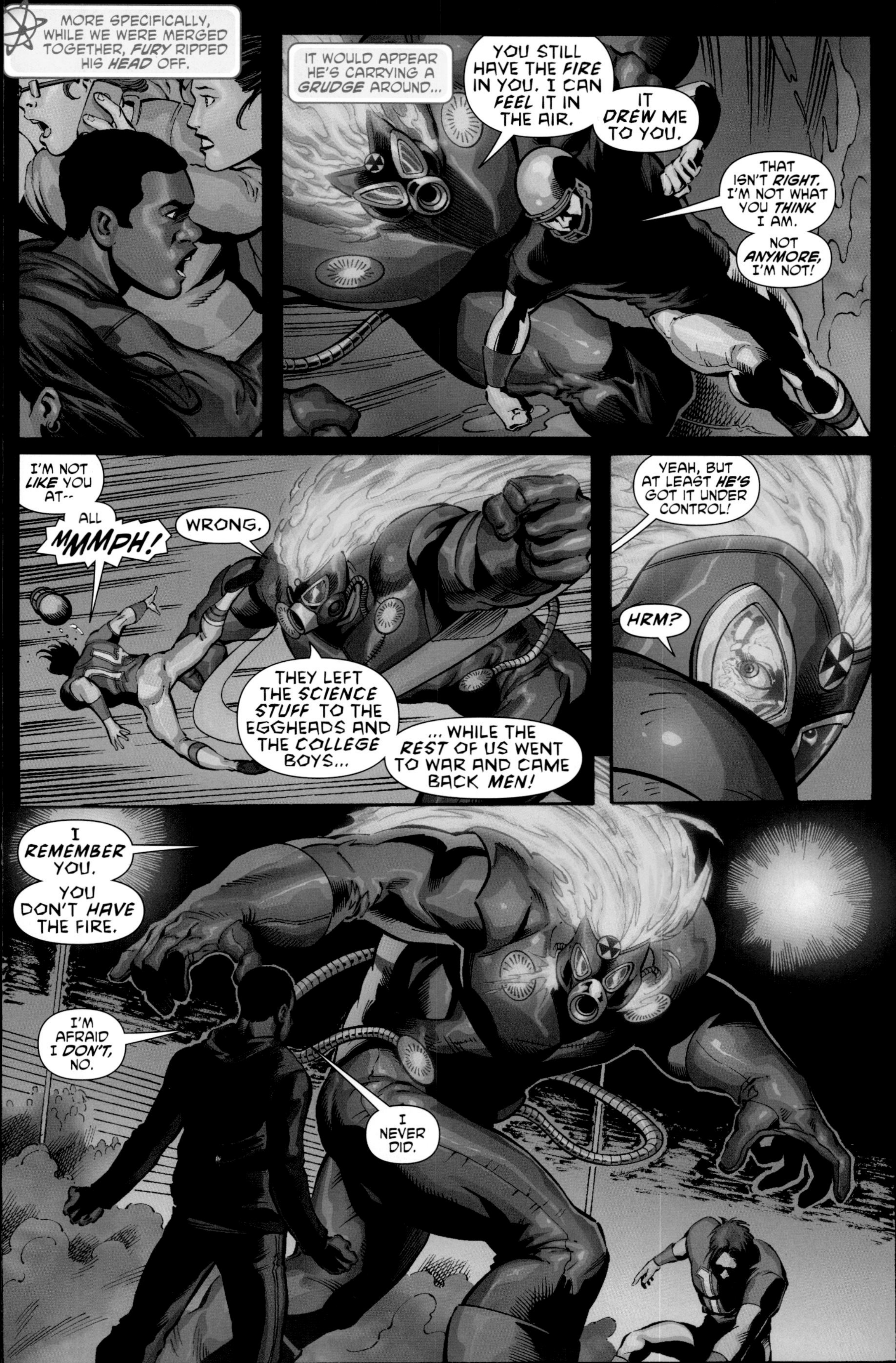
MORE SPECIFICALLY, WHILE WE WERE MERGED TOGETHER, FURY RIPPED HIS HEAD OFF.
IT WOULD APPEAR HE'S CARRYING A GRUDGE AROUND...
YOU STILL HAVE THE FIRE IN YOU. I CAN FEEL IT IN THE AIR.
IT DREW ME TO YOU.
THAT ISN'T RIGHT. I'M NOT WHAT YOU THINK I AM.
NOT ANYMORE, I'M NOT!
I'M NOT LIKE YOU AT--
ALL
MMMPH!
WRONG.
THEY LEFT THE SCIENCE STUFF TO THE EGGHEADS AND THE COLLEGE BOYS...
...WHILE THE REST OF US WENT TO WAR AND CAME BACK MEN!
YEAH, BUT AT LEAST HE'S GOT IT UNDER CONTROL!
HRM?
I REMEMBER YOU.
YOU DON'T HAVE THE FIRE.
I'M AFRAID I DON'T, NO.
I NEVER DID.

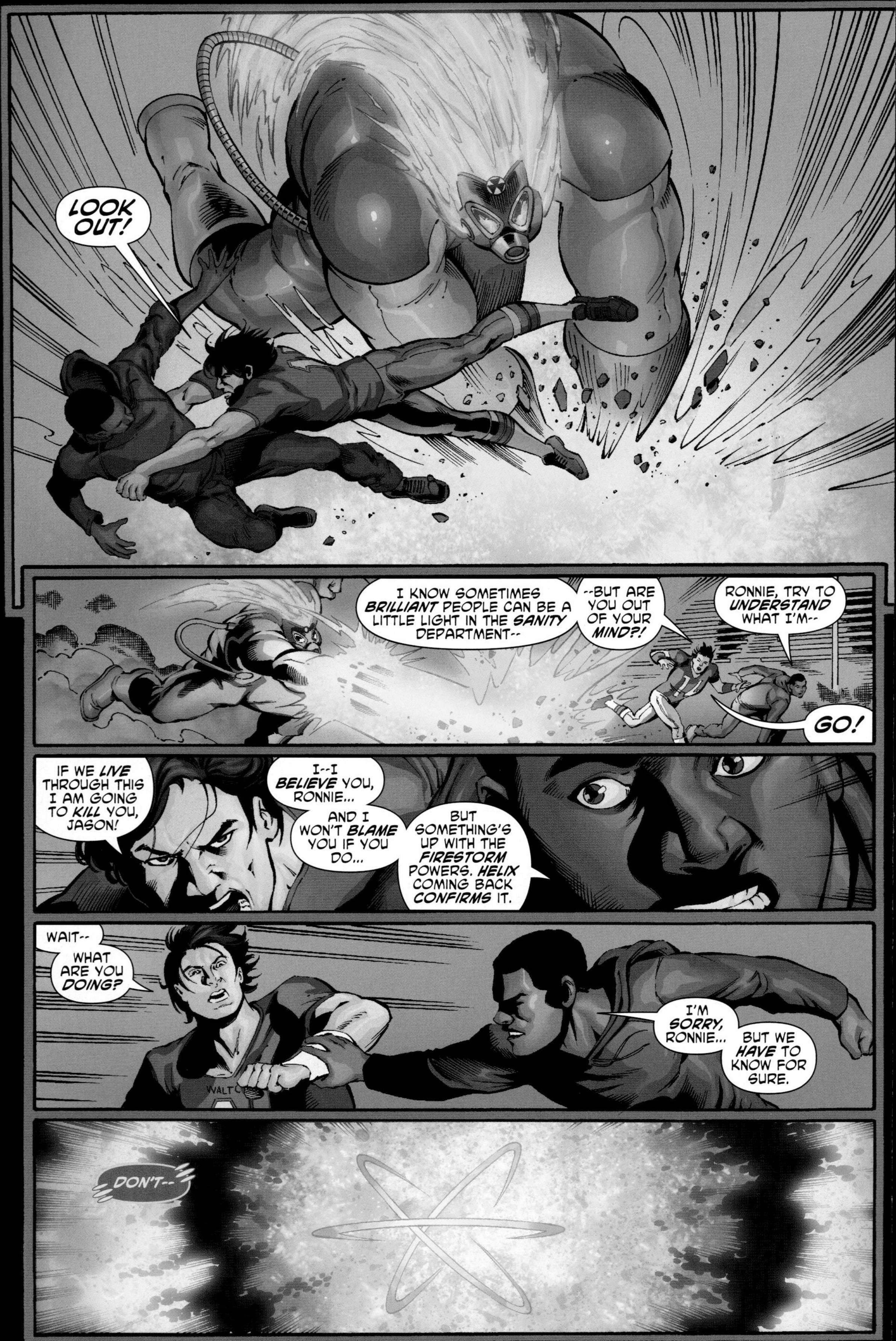
LOOK OUT!
I KNOW SOMETIMES BRILLIANT PEOPLE CAN BE A LITTLE LIGHT IN THE SANITY DEPARTMENT--
--BUT ARE YOU OUT OF YOUR MIND?!
RONNIE, TRY TO UNDERSTAND WHAT I'M--
GO!
IF WE LIVE THROUGH THIS I AM GOING TO KILL YOU, JASON!
I--I BELIEVE YOU, RONNIE...
AND I WON'T BLAME YOU IF YOU DO...
BUT SOMETHING'S UP WITH THE FIRESTORM POWERS. HELIX COMING BACK CONFIRMS IT.
WAIT--
WHAT ARE YOU DOING?
I'M SORRY, RONNIE...
BUT WE HAVE TO KNOW FOR SURE.
DON'T--

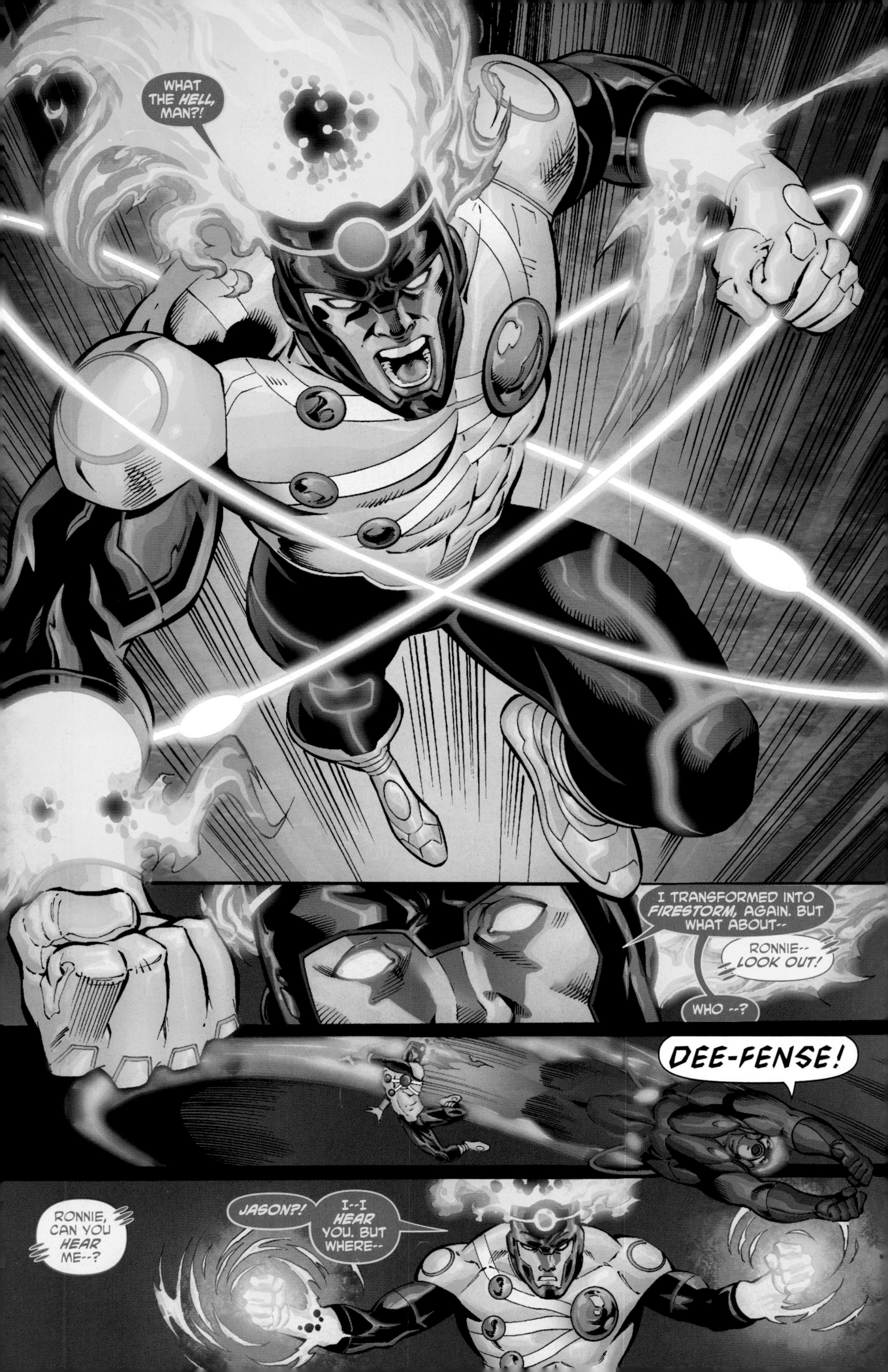
WHAT THE HELL, MAN?!
I TRANSFORMED INTO FIRESTORM, AGAIN. BUT WHAT ABOUT--
RONNIE-- LOOK OUT!
WHO --?
DEE-FENSE!
RONNIE, CAN YOU HEAR ME--?
JASON?!
I--I HEAR YOU. BUT WHERE--

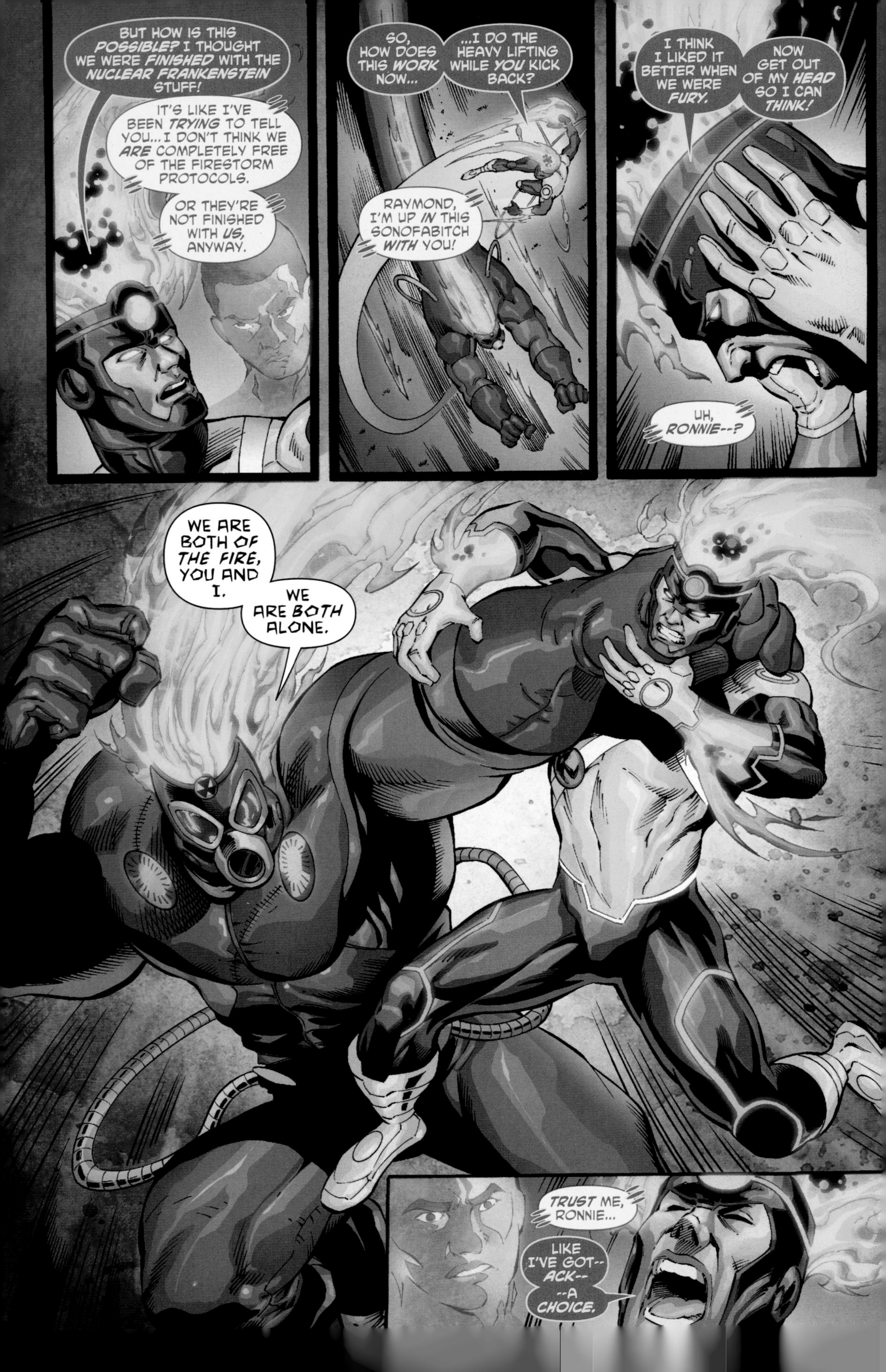
BUT HOW IS THIS POSSIBLE? I THOUGHT WE WERE FINISHED WITH THE NUCLEAR FRANKENSTEIN STUFF!
IT'S LIKE I'VE BEEN TRYING TO TELL YOU...I DON'T THINK WE ARE COMPLETELY FREE OF THE FIRESTORM PROTOCOLS.
OR THEY'RE NOT FINISHED WITH US, ANYWAY.
SO, HOW DOES THIS WORK NOW...
...I DO THE HEAVY LIFTING WHILE YOU KICK BACK?
RAYMOND, I'M UP IN THIS SONOFABITCH WITH YOU!
I THINK I LIKED IT BETTER WHEN WE WERE FURY.
NOW GET OUT OF MY HEAD SO I CAN THINK!
UH, RONNIE--?
WE ARE BOTH OF THE FIRE, YOU AND I.
WE ARE BOTH ALONE.
TRUST ME, RONNIE...
LIKE I'VE GOT--
ACK--
--A CHOICE.

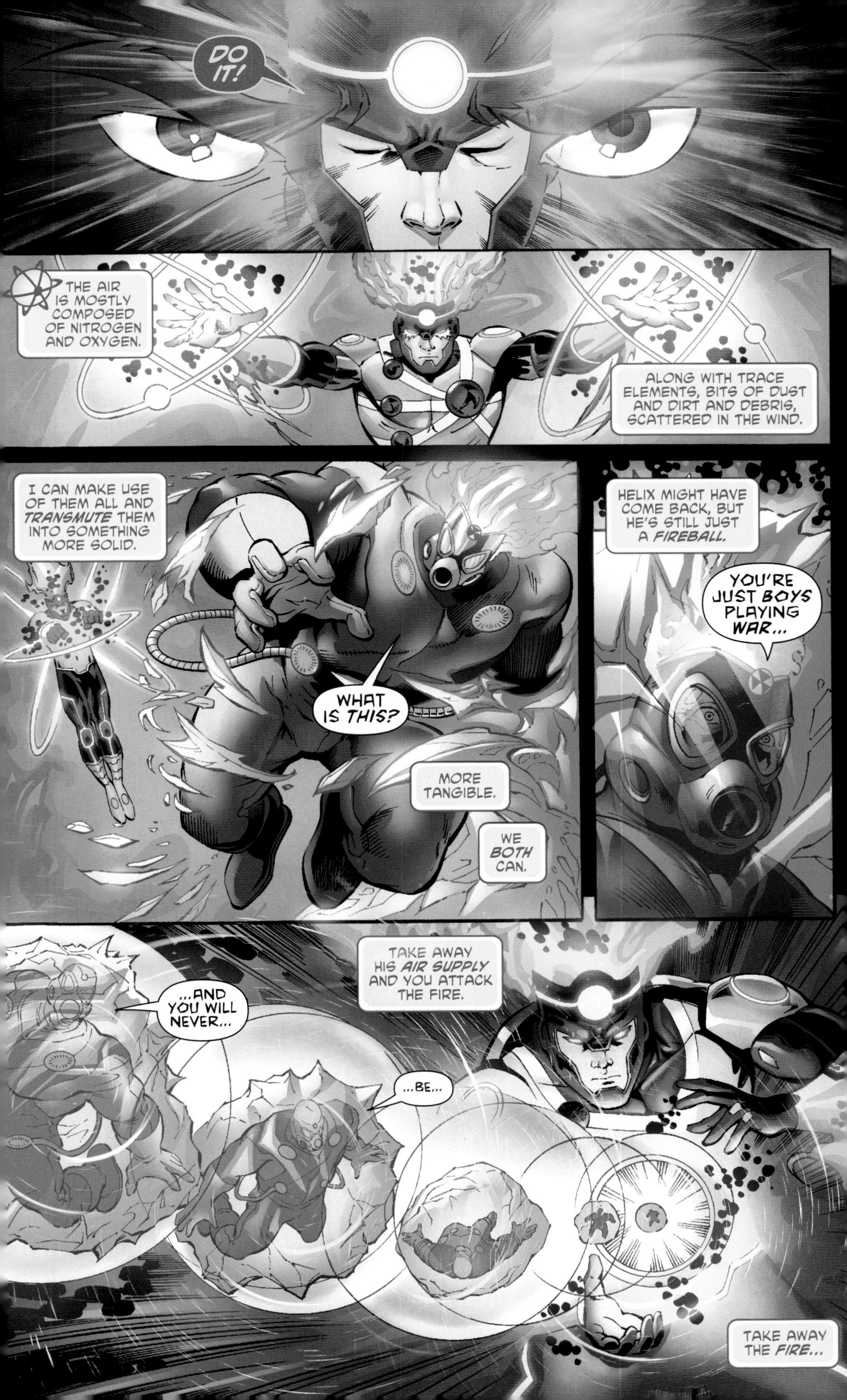
DO IT!
THE AIR IS MOSTLY COMPOSED OF NITROGEN AND OXYGEN.
ALONG WITH TRACE ELEMENTS, BITS OF DUST AND DIRT AND DEBRIS, SCATTERED IN THE WIND.
I CAN MAKE USE OF THEM ALL AND TRANSMUTE THEM INTO SOMETHING MORE SOLID.
WHAT IS THIS?
MORE TANGIBLE.
WE BOTH CAN.
HELIX MIGHT HAVE COME BACK, BUT HE'S STILL JUST A FIREBALL.
YOU'RE JUST BOYS PLAYING WAR...
TAKE AWAY HIS AIR SUPPLY AND YOU ATTACK THE FIRE.
...AND YOU WILL NEVER...
...BE...
TAKE AWAY THE FIRE...

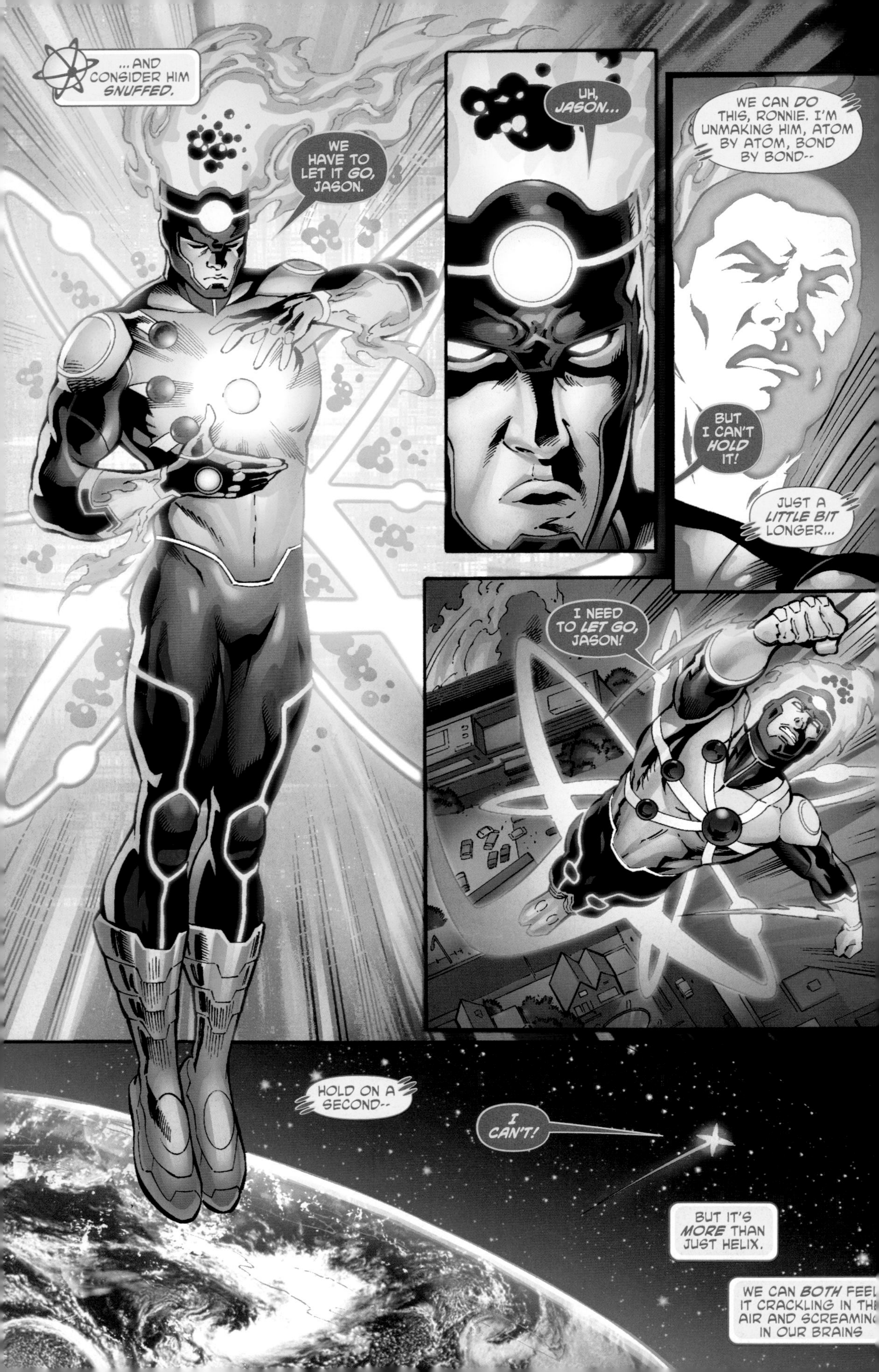
...AND CONSIDER HIM SNUFFED.
WE HAVE TO LET IT GO, JASON.
UH, JASON...
WE CAN DO THIS, RONNIE. I'M UNMAKING HIM, ATOM BY ATOM, BOND BY BOND--
BUT I CAN'T HOLD IT!
JUST A LITTLE BIT LONGER...
I NEED TO LET GO, JASON!
HOLD ON A SECOND--
I CAN'T!
BUT IT'S MORE THAN JUST HELIX.
WE CAN BOTH FEEL IT CRACKLING IN THE AIR AND SCREAMING IN OUR BRAINS

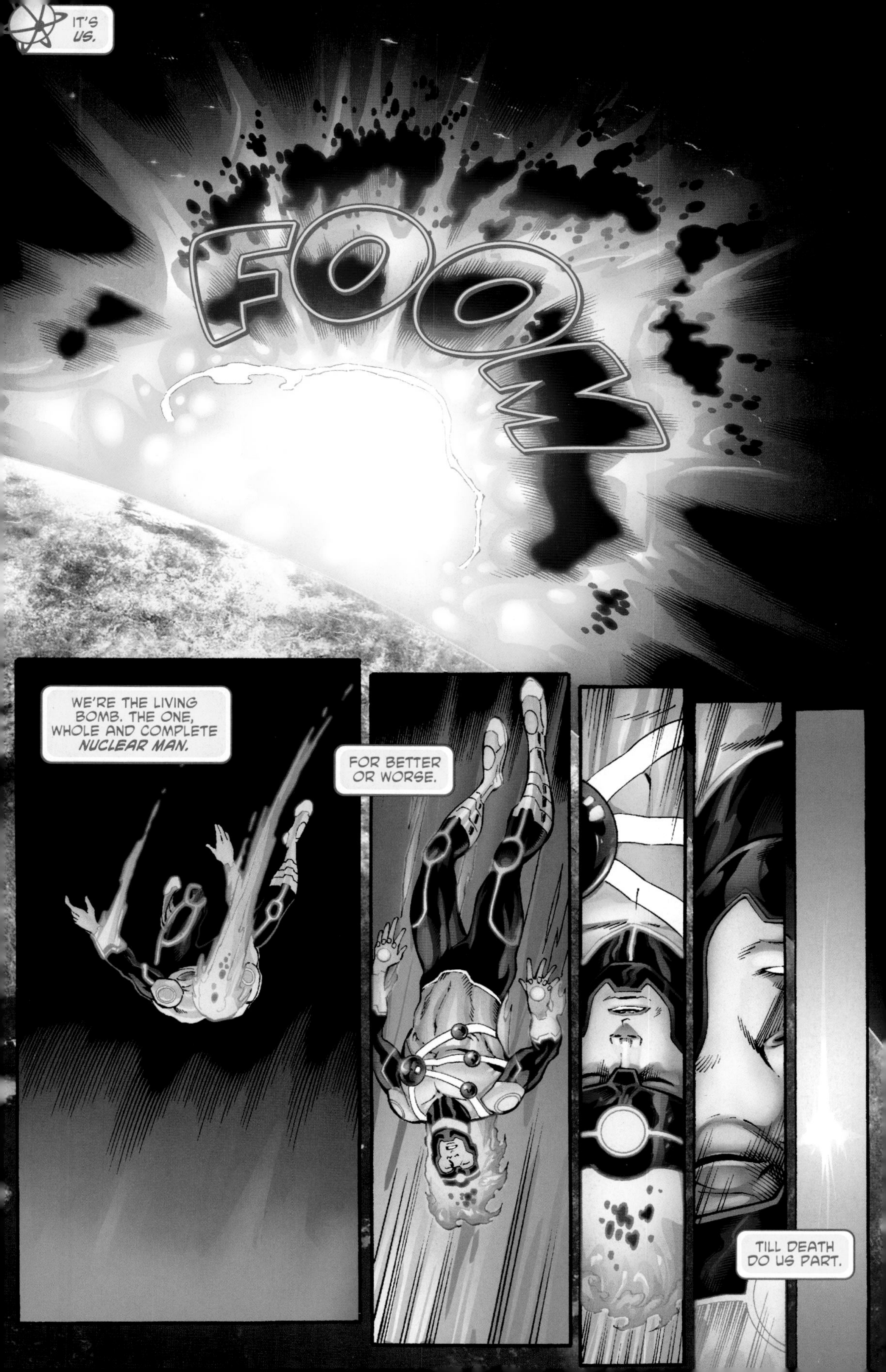
IT'S *US.*
FOOM
WE'RE THE LIVING BOMB. THE ONE, WHOLE AND COMPLETE *NUCLEAR MAN.*
FOR BETTER OR WORSE.
TILL DEATH DO US PART.

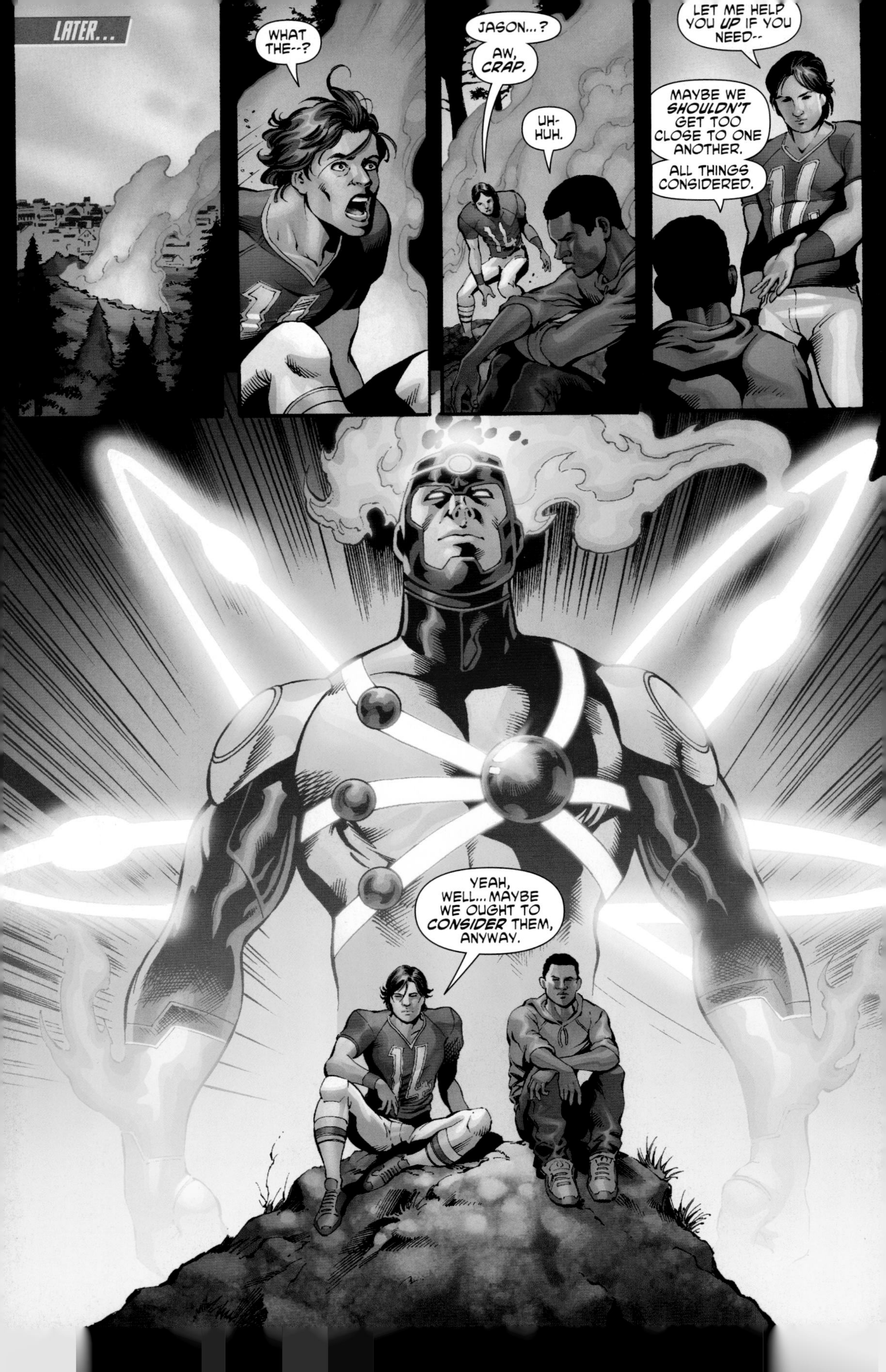
LATER...
WHAT THE--?
JASON...?
AW, CRAP.
UH-HUH.
LET ME HELP YOU UP IF YOU NEED--
MAYBE WE SHOULDN'T GET TOO CLOSE TO ONE ANOTHER.
ALL THINGS CONSIDERED.
YEAH, WELL... MAYBE WE OUGHT TO CONSIDER THEM, ANYWAY.

START AT THE BEGINNING!

JUSTICE LEAGUE
VOLUME 1: ORIGIN

AQUAMAN
VOLUME 1:
THE TRENCH

THE SAVAGE
HAWKMAN VOLUME 1:
DARKNESS RISING

GREEN ARROW
VOLUME 1:
THE MIDAS TOUCH

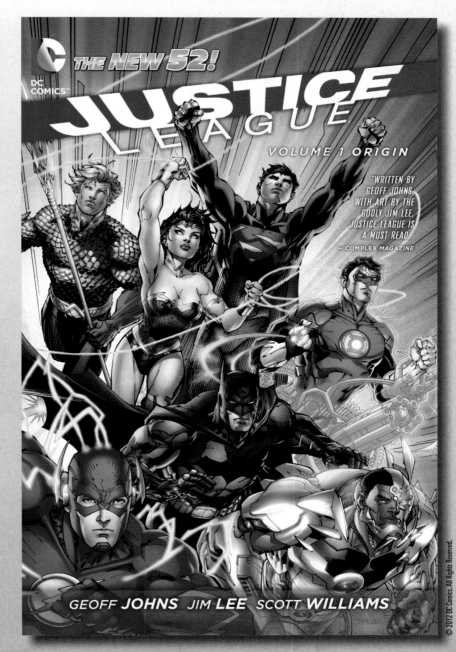

GEOFF **JOHNS**   JIM **LEE**   SCOTT **WILLIAMS**

START AT THE BEGINNING!

TEEN TITANS
VOLUME 1: IT'S
OUR RIGHT TO FIGHT

LEGION OF SUPER-
HEROES VOLUME 1:
HOSTILE WORLD

LEGION LOST
VOLUME 1: RUN FROM
TOMORROW

STATIC SHOCK
VOLUME 1:
SUPERCHARGED

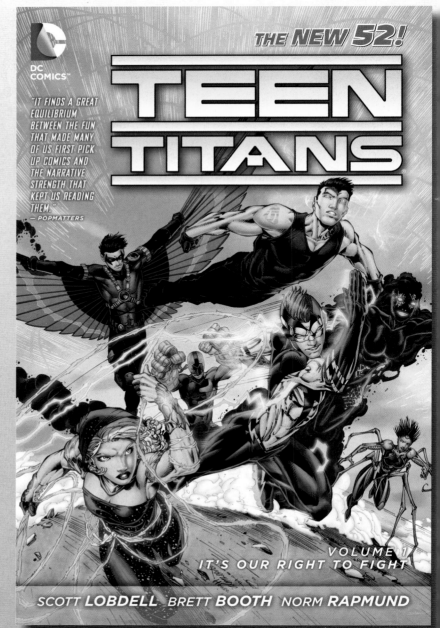

THE NEW 52!

"IT FINDS A GREAT EQUILIBRIUM BETWEEN THE FUN THAT MADE MANY OF US FIRST PICK UP COMICS AND THE NARRATIVE STRENGTH THAT KEPT US READING THEM."
— POPMATTERS

TEEN TITANS

VOLUME 1
IT'S OUR RIGHT TO FIGHT

SCOTT **LOBDELL** · BRETT **BOOTH** · NORM **RAPMUND**